Jerom Murch

Biographical Sketches of Bath Celebrities, Ancient and Modern

With Some Fragments of Local History

Jerom Murch

Biographical Sketches of Bath Celebrities, Ancient and Modern
With Some Fragments of Local History

ISBN/EAN: 9783337013486

Printed in Europe, USA, Canada, Australia, Japan

Cover: Foto ©ninafisch / pixelio.de

More available books at **www.hansebooks.com**

BIOGRAPHICAL SKETCHES

OF

BATH CELEBRITIES,

ANCIENT AND MODERN,

WITH SOME

FRAGMENTS OF LOCAL HISTORY.

By JEROM MURCH,

President of the Bath Royal Literary and Scientific Institution,
And Vice-President of the Somersetshire Archæological and Natural
History Society.

" For sluggard's brow the laurel never grows ;
Renown is not the child of indolent repose."
Thomson's Castle of Indolence.

LONDON : Isaac Pitman & Sons.
BATH : William Lewis & Son,
MDCCCXCIII.

TO

THE HALLOWED MEMORY

OF ONE WHO WAS

MY BELOVED COUNSELLOR

THROUGH SIXTY-TWO YEARS,

AND WHO AIDED ME IN REVISING THE

EARLIER PAGES OF THIS BOOK,

IT IS NOW

MOST GRATEFULLY INSCRIBED.

BATH CELEBRITIES.

CHAPTER.

  I. THE EARLY BRITISH PERIOD.
 II. THE ROMAN PERIOD.
III. THE SAXON PERIOD.
 IV. THE NORMAN PERIOD.
  V. THE EARLY MAYORS OF BATH.
 VI. SIR JOHN HARINGTON AND BISHOP MONTAGUE.
VII. WILLIAM PRYNNE.
VIII. DR. GUIDOTT AND HIS CONTEMPORARIES.
 IX. BEAU NASH.
  X. RALPH ALLEN.
 XI. JOHN PALMER. Part 1.
XII. THE SAME. Part 2.
XIII. PHYSICIANS OF THE TWO LAST CENTURIES. Part 1.
XIV. THE SAME. Part 2.
 XV. DR. HENRY HARINGTON.
XVI. SIR W. HERSCHEL AND CAROLINE HERSCHEL.
XVII. DR. W. SMITH AND CHARLES MOORE.
XVIII. THE TWO WOODS, GAINSBOROUGH AND HOARE.
XIX. THOMAS BARKER AND BENJAMIN BARKER.
 XX. FOUR DIVINES: HALES, CARTE, JAY AND KEMBLE.
XXI. BISHOP BAINES AND BISHOP CLIFFORD.
XXII. ARCHBISHOP MAGEE.
XXIII. ANSTEY, REV. R. WARNER AND REV. J. HUNTER.
XXIV. GENERAL SIR WILLIAM NAPIER.
XXV. WALTER SAVAGE LANDOR. Part 1.
XXVI. THE SAME. Part 2.
XXVII. WILLIAM BECKFORD. Part 1.
XXVIII. THE SAME. Part 2.
XXIX. MISS LINLEY.
XXX. MRS. SIDDONS.

PREFACE.

The following pages originated in a desire to bring together and put into popular form a few biographical facts of local interest. Bath has been long in high repute for its wonderful springs and remarkable beauty, but comparatively few know what a succession of eminent men have been connected with it. From time to time various writers have given valuable information, especial praise being due to a former and a present resident in the City ; the Rev. Joseph Hunter, F.S.A., who wrote on " The Connection of Bath with the Literature and Science of England," and Mr. R. E. M. Peach, the indefatigable author of " Historic Houses," " The Street Lore of Bath," and other instructive treatises.

But the aims of these and similar productions have been somewhat different from my own. With me the chief object has been a series of short biographies, following the stream of local history from the earliest times. And while taking a wider range of subjects I have also had in view a larger class of readers, those whose attachment to the City of Bath would make them usefully interested in the lives of its greatest ornaments. To Mr. Hunter's work, valuable as it is, little publicity was given ; only fifty copies of the original edition were printed, and when a second appeared, twenty-six years afterwards, its circulation was confined chiefly to the small body who wished for it, the Bath Literary Club.

My readers will scarcely expect to find, within the small compass of these pages, minute and complete narratives. Not only would many volumes have been necessary for such a task, but far more time and labour than an octogenarian could hope to give. Hence my desire has been to state briefly the more important facts, to arrange them as much as possible in chronological order, and to give information that would be acceptable to the people of a city which has long been dear to me. The "*Fragments of Local History*" were suggested by some of the memoirs as enabling me to deal more fully with matters in which the subjects of those memoirs were largely interested. To know something of the charitable institutions is to know more of the medical profession, and an account of other undertakings may help to show what the citizens generally have done.

I have only to add a few words of thankful acknowledgment. It would have been impossible to fulfil the task I undertook without the aid of libraries other than my own. The want has been abundantly met by the valuable "*Bath books*" of Mr. Peach, Mr. Frederick Shum and the Bath Literary and Scientific Institution. In only one instance did these collections fail me, and then the volume I wanted was kindly supplied by another friend, himself an authority on the subject which occupied my pen. Nor can I think lightly of the advantage of having had the sketches published weekly at first, as they have thus had a twofold revision. Errors, however, will probably be found ; Judgment and Memory are never infallible, and at an age approaching eighty-six are very liable to lead astray, but I have no fear that the verdict on this "*last fruit off an old tree*" will be too severe.

November, 1893.

BIOGRAPHICAL SKETCHES OF BATH CELEBRITIES,

ANCIENT AND MODERN.

CHAPTER I.

THE EARLY BRITISH PERIOD.

My plan in these sketches is to select from a long roll of remarkable men the chief of those who, while celebrated themselves, promoted the reputation and prosperity of Bath. In many cases their fame was not merely local; they filled offices and accomplished work of national importance, thus associating the city with the best interests of the country.

The order of the proposed sketches will be chronological. Scanty as the earlier materials are, I think they should not be unused. Some writer justly says, "We have a share in the past, and the past works in us." It is peculiarly so with regard to the City of the Springs, whose biography is chiefly valuable for its historical character. And although only short notices can be given of the early British, Roman and Saxon periods, they will be sufficient to show what a long chain time has produced, and how various are the links of which it is composed.

I shall not aim chiefly at giving new information. Much of what my narratives will contain may be found in various works by well-known authors. Some of it perchance has been gathered into my own papers, read from time to time before public bodies. My object now is to condense in historical sequence, incidents worthy of remembrance generally, but especially by those who are attached to Bath. Although local patriotism may be a lower quality than the earnest love of country, it is yet one to be cultivated, both for the pleasure it causes to its possessor and for the good it leads him to do. Although the charm of novelty may be wanting in sketches such as I now propose, they may yet be some stimulus to the same public spirit as that which animated men who did good work in the world—and is always needed for progress in small as well as large matters.

PRINCE BLADUD.

To not a few cities and nations, especially the older ones, the lot was given of having their early history marked by a mixture of fact and fable. The idea that Bath owes its origin to Bladud and the Swine is on a par with the idea that Rome is indebted for its existence to the nursing by a wolf of Romulus and Remus. Through many centuries both ideas were firmly fixed in the national mind, they were the subject of popular ballads, of tales by mothers to their children, of lays by poets and records by annalists. As to the Bladud story I find credit given to it by Geoffery of Monmouth in the twelfth century, by Leland, the learned antiquary, in the sixteenth, and by Wood, one of Bath's greatest architects, in the eighteenth. The hold that it gained in Bath is evident from the frequent use of the name of the British Prince. Not only were streets and inns and banks so designated in days gone by ; periodical publications of the present time, even the society journal of the city, announcing all the chief events of fashionable life, have assumed the historic appellation.

But in mentioning these reasons for beginning my sketches with one of Bladud, I would not have it supposed that there

is nothing to be said for the theory of an earlier origin of
Bath, or an earlier knowledge of the springs. Professor
Earle has shown in his valuable book, *Bath : Ancient and
Modern*, that there are good reasons for tracing the origin to an
anterior settlement on and around the adjoining hill of Solsbury, and, supposing such a settlement, it is hardly possible
that those who migrated hither from so short a distance would
know nothing of the springs. The termination " bury " means
a fort or stronghold, being to the inhabitants what mediæval
castles were to small isolated populations throughout Europe.
The prefix Sol, from whence Sul and Sulis, was the name of
the deity reverenced by successive generations in this part
of Somersetshire. It has been found inscribed on stones in
many parts of Bath at various periods. Similar considerations
led Professor Earle to opine that Solsbury was " more than
a hill fort, occupied on emergencies for purposes of protection, it was the venerable site of a populous British town."
This opinion appears to be justified by the well known origin
of various cities. Historians of Bristol state that a camp at
Clifton was the original settlement there, established on the
edge of the vast chasm in the banks of the Avon, and
fortified by an ancient British prince, to protect from Welsh
aggressions. The more easy access to the river for trading
purposes on the level bank of what became Bristol, would
operate at Caer Odor (the city of the chasm, as Clifton was
then called) in like manner to the attraction of the springs
at Solsbury ; there would be migration for good reasons in
both cases to the neighbouring localities. The analogy also
extends to the name of Bristol, one of the former names of
Clifton having been Caer Brito, which was first given to the
new settlement ; in the time of the Saxons it was Bristowe,
and afterwards Bristol.

Returning to Prince Bladud little more can be said than is told in the two legends which have successively gained credit. They agree in some important particulars such as the Prince being the son of Lud Hudibras, 800 years before Christ. The more incredible one also states that he was master of the Black Art, that by this means he created the first bath of the city, and that, conversing habitually with the Devil, he heard from him all he wanted to know. "Constantly devising some new wonder, he at length announced that he was about to fly in the air like a bird. He started for London on wings he had made, getting on well for some time, but finally meeting with contrary winds, his strength failed, the strings snapped, and he came down on the roof of Apollo's Temple in London, where he was dashed to pieces." Part of this myth is that a reign of 20 years being thus ended Bladud left a son called Leir, who reigned 60 years, that Leir had no son but three daughters, Germoyle, Regan, and Cordoyle. All this is recorded by Geoffery of Monmouth, translations of whose annals were well known and may yet be found in public libraries. Shakespeare was probably familiar with them. Malone says, " He had certainly read the account of Bladud as it occurs not far from that of Cymbeline." May not its mythical character have been a stimulus to his own imagination and had much to do with the production of the immortal play of King Lear ?

The other less marvellous legend I have given in an unpublished work containing photographs of medallions illustrating the connection of royalty with Bath on the Ecritoire presented to the Princess of Wales in 1870. Prefixed to the photographs are short notices of the people and events to which they refer. Bladud is represented by the artist as a forlorn lad, yet with a refined face, having a sheepskin over his head and shoulders, holding a spear and tending his pigs.*

The following is the version I gave of the more modern myth. " Prince Bladud, only son of Hudibras, King of Britain, 800 years before Christ, being afflicted with leprosy, was sent away from the Court of his father and wandered into Somersetshire. Arrived at Keynsham and in great distress,

---

* The Ecritoire is a beautiful specimen of the cabinet work for which Bath is remarkable. Being intended as a wedding present to the Princess of Wales on her marriage, it was adorned with seven china medallions illustrating the connection of royalty with the city. But various circumstances delayed the offering ; amongst them the elaborate character of the work, and the difficulty arising from the original limitation of the present to one class of inhabitants, the ladies, instead of including the citizens generally. At length the latter course was adopted ; a deputation, including the Mayor, were received at Marlborough House, by the Prince and Princess of Wales, and graciously informed that the Ecritoire would be highly valued for its beautiful workmanship, with the historical pictures, and sent to Sandringham for the use of the Princess. The subjects of the pictures were Prince Bladud and his Swine ; the Coronation of King Edgar in the Bath Abbey ; Canute of Denmark dictating to the Monks in the Bath Monastery ; the entrance of Edward III. into the ancient City ; Queen Elizabeth's visit to Bath ; Queen Anne and Prince George of Denmark received by the Corporation of Bath ; and the Duchess of Kent and Princess Victoria opening the Bath Park in 1832. The design for the Ecritoire was contributed by Major Davis, F.S.A., the drawings for the historical pictures by Mr. Arthur Murch, and the work carried out by Mr. Knight, of Milsom Street. A handsome volume with photographs of the medallions and printed accounts of the scenes to which they refer, accompanied the Ecritoire.

he obtained by some means charge of a herd of swine, which he drove across the Avon to the Valley, five miles distant, where, amidst tall weeds and brambles, he saw hot springs boiling up. Attracted by the heat the herd rushed in ; and the poor Prince, finding the shelter so sorely needed, took up his abode in the place, which is called to this day Swineswick or Swainswick. Day by day the animals wallowed in the mire till their skins showed a wonderful change for the better ; and their keeper, following their example, soon derived a similar benefit. In due time he re-appeared at Court, making himself known to the Queen, his mother, by means of a ring she had given him on leaving. Years passed before he succeeded to the throne ; but when he did so he revisited the scene of his wonderful cure, made cisterns around the springs and built houses for himself and his suite. Hence the city of Caer-brennen, afterwards called Akemannesceastre (the sick-man's city) then Bathan answering to the German Baden, subsequently Aquæ Solis (the name given by Antoninus in his Itinerary), and finally Bath."

Wood and other old writers amplify the story with no little confidence in modern credulity. They picture the recovered Prince distinguishing himself as the patron of all that was good. To him they attribute, as results of great travel and especially of his residence at Athens, the introduction into Britain not only of Greek philosophy, but of Greek religion. Some even give him the credit of building in Bath that magnificent temple of Minerva which is known to have existed there in the time of the Romans, the grand remains of which are still to be seen in the vestibule of the Royal Literary Institution. But here the credulous chroniclers were surely in error ; those remains—the noble friezes and cornices, the glorious pediment and sculptured symbolism, the owl and the helmet, point rather to the great people who for 400 years made Bath one of their chief British dwelling places, and whose votive altars and other monuments are so completely in harmony with the architecture of the temple.

One of the advantages of modern writers on subjects like these is that by careful consideration of historical materials, including recent archæological discoveries, they can come nearer to the truth than their predecessors. Thus can be ascertained how much of ancient legends is likely to be false and how much true, what tends to make a story worthy of general belief and what should be put aside as mere imaginative fringe. If the Solsbury origin of Bath be probable, if the springs were known before Bladud was sent from home, other things seemingly out of joint, become probable also. The British Queen is said to have given her poor son a ring when he went away. This is hardly compatible with her neglecting him so far as not to know what became of him, allowing him to wander no one knew where, and become a swineherd. But if a settlement at Bath already existed, if something, however little, was known of the springs, what more natural than that he should be sent there to be cured? The fond mother receives him again; his recovery becomes complete, and before succeeding to the throne he travels in search of knowledge and wisdom. Through all future years he never ceases to be grateful for his restoration by means of the springs. He constructs baths for the general use of them; he builds houses for his own occasional residence and that of his suite; he converts a small settlement into the beginning of a city. Much of all this being recorded by competent annalists, and the rest being highly probable, Prince Bladud may be fairly placed at the head of the roll of Ancient Bath Celebrities.

CHAPTER II.

THE ROMAN PERIOD.

The Bath Celebrities of the Roman Period consisted of
the foremost men of the Roman colony who occupied the
city four hundred years. Whatever Bladud may have done
or be supposed to have done on his return from Athens to
promote science and civilisation, there was now neither
ability nor enterprise to make Bath what it became after
Cæsar landed in Britain. Centuries had passed since
Bladud died; a succession of wars had devastated the country;
the mineral springs and their surroundings were forsaken.
Then at the beginning of the Christian Era came a new race
as conquerors but with high intents; they came to found a
colony of the great empire, whose works should be worthy of
its greatness. The springs would suit their luxurious tastes;
the scenery would remind them of what they had quitted;
there were quarries of stone for grand temples, beautiful
villas and spacious baths, all fit for citizens who came from
the Eternal City.

Such were the advantages enjoyed by the legion whom the
Emperor Claudius sent. That the chief officers were
cultivated men is evident from the numerous architectural
remains still existing. Nor was Italian refinement manifest
only in great public monuments like the Temple of Minerva,
whose remains are still with us. We have proofs of it also
in the lately uncovered baths, in Samian ware and other
pottery, lamps, cups, urns and vases which have been dug
up from time to time. Two works of art—a large bronze
medallion with the legend Pompeia on it, and a head
supposed to be a fragment of a statue of Apollo, now in the

Literary Institution, are, of themselves, sufficient to indicate the order of intellect that prevailed. In connection with all this, however, no name stands out with special prominence as that of a local celebrity ; a few emperors and generals share the chief honour of the public works because nothing could have been done without their initiation or sanction. All, therefore, that I can do in the way of biography is to mention the few to whom history has attributed certain undertakings.

The Emperor Claudius is believed to have visited Bath soon after the conquest of Britain. To him is given the credit of cleansing the neglected springs—a work to which his attention would be directed by his physician, Scribonius, who accompanied him. Warner says, "Extremely curious with respect to natural appearances were the bituminous cuticle covering the surface of the earth and the warm stagnant mass under the waters, appearances which would naturally attract notice. An immediate investigation of the causes of these phenomena would take place, and the mineral springs, which had wasted their medicinal virtues on the desert around, would be cleared and utilised." Scribonius is represented as being especially interested in the work, from his desire to make the waters available for the cure of painful disorders as well as for luxury and ordinary uses. By his advice Claudius was induced to forego the usual Roman practice of fixing the site of the camp on one of the adjoining hills, and to build the town in what Warner calls "the morassy hollow of a close vale." In modern times the sanitary objections to "the close vale" have been more clearly seen, with the effect of extending the city up the sides of the hills.

The plan of Claudius, formed during his short stay, was to

build a town 400 yards from east to west and 380 from north to south. It was to be surrounded by a wall 20 feet high, with angular towers at the corners, and four gates facing the four cardinal points. A small portion of a wall that succeeded the original one remains opposite the Mineral Water Hospital. Warner mentions that workmen, digging there in the middle of the last century, reached, at the depth of 11 feet, the foundations of the first rampart. The town ordered by the Emperor was to have the springs in the centre ; there were to be dwellings and stables for legionaries, consisting of 3,050 foot and 500 horse, and special directions were given for a residence for the commander in a suitable position. Roman architects and builders lost no time ; the town soon sprung up, adorned with baths and temples ; people flocked from the adjoining counties to join the new colony and share its advantages with distinguished Roman generals. Professor Earle supposes that " further knowledge would establish a considerable parallelism between the Aquæ Solis of this period and the Bath of the eighteenth century."

One of the chief benefactors was Julius Agricola, father-in-law of Tacitus, and general in the reigns of Vespasian, Titus and Domitian. It was by Vespasian that Agricola was appointed Governor of Britain, in which capacity he distinguished himself by reforming abuses that former governors had sanctioned, and by endeavouring to induce the Britons to conform to Roman customs. His policy was described by Tacitus in a well known passage quoted by Edmund Burke, in what Mr. P. B. Duncan, of New College, Oxford, writing on the subject in one of his essays, calls " his precious fragment of English history."* Agricola aimed to divert the

---

* It does not appear that these essays were published. The

Britons from warlike pursuits and rebellion against Roman
rule by softening their manners, promoting education of
various kinds, and doing all in his power to encourage

title page merely indicates that they were printed at Oxford by
Thomas Combe in 1840. If Mr. Philip Bury Duncan was not
one of the most celebrated of Bath men he was one of the most
useful. It will, therefore, not be inappropriate to borrow a note
from the pages of "Three Decades of the Bath Literary Club," a
paper read by myself in 1890. The lapse of three years has
made me slightly alter a date. "Here it would be almost ungrateful to omit a tribute to the memory of one who was long
pre-eminent in service to literature and science in Bath. Joined
in every good work by an excellent brother with whom he lived,
Mr. Philip Bury Duncan was one of the most prominent founders
of our Royal Literary and Scientific Institution. He had removed
to Bath from Oxford, where he was Resident Fellow of New
College and Curator of the Ashmolean Museum. His services to
the University were in later life suitably acknowledged by the
diploma of LL.D. The knowledge and experience gained there
proved of great value in the work of forming a high class library
at the Institution and beginning a local museum. To the
intellectual life then awakened in Bath he brought vigour by
lectures of no common interest at evening meetings at the
Institution. They are happily preserved in two small volumes
printed at Oxford, in 1840, entitled 'Essays and Miscellanea.'
The variety of subjects is as remarkable as the learning and
thoughtfulness with which they are treated. To mention only a
few : Painting, Sculpture, Botany, Zoology, Geology, Foreign
Travel, the Voice of Birds, Quackery, Conversation, Novels, the
Nature of Human Hair, and A Gentleman's Day in Antient Rome ;
no wonder that the pleasant lecture room was well filled. Mr.
Duncan was Chairman of the Institution when I joined it in 1834
—now fifty-nine years ago. We all admired his varied ability,

artistic taste. Young men of rank were persuaded to learn
the language and wear the patrician dress of Italy, although
these had hitherto been considered badges of slavery, while

his unceasing energy, his catholic disposition, and his quiet
munificence. When the Literary Club was formed he regretted
that age and infirmities prevented his becoming a member, but
we had his warmest sympathy, and an occasional literary contribution. He was succeeded, for a short time, in the chairmanship
of the Institution by Mr. Markland, and Mr. Markland by myself
in 1859. Thus the office has only been vacant twice in more
than sixty years." To this tribute may be added Mr. Duncan's
inscription in the essays to his brother, who was also an unwearied
benefactor of Bath.

TO

MY BELOVED BROTHER AND FRIEND,

JOHN SHUTE DUNCAN,

—" Qualem non candidiorem

" Terra tulit neque quo me sit devinctior alter ; "

WHO HAS ALWAYS EXHIBITED

THE TOTAL FORGETFULNESS OF SELF,

COMPARED TO WHICH,

THE VIRTUES OF HEROES SINK TO NOTHING.

IN MEMORIAL OF

A CONSTANT AND MUTUAL AFFECTION,

EXTENDED TO

THE SCRIPTURAL AGE OF MAN.

This being a note to a chapter on the Roman Period, it may be
further stated that the brothers Duncan were especially interested
in the preservation and arrangement of the grand Remains found
at various times in Bath, also that to commemorate this and
other services a brass plate was affixed in the vestibule of the
Institution, surmounted by two portraits in the same frame,
presented by the daughter of Mr. J. S. Duncan, Mrs. Fraser, late
of Manchester.

land-owners acquired agricultural knowledge as a means of improving their property. In the city of the springs, Agricola found ample scope for all this. Here were a people, able and willing to fall in with every scheme of refinement. Men and women who had come from lonely dwellings in the country to enjoy advantages hitherto unknown were delighted with the new life open to them. Thus would the city become, as Professor Earle suggests, " very much what Bath was in the eighteenth century." Who can doubt that the wise Governor of Britain was welcomed by all classes whenever he came to see how his orders, including the beautiful temple of Minerva, had been carried out?

I now come to action of a very different kind. A system of trade corporations had been highly developed throughout the Roman Empire. Professor Earle mentions that no less than forty-four guilds or societies of this kind were known to exist, and Warner gives a long account of a large company of Smiths at Bath. They were Armourers, connected with what was called the *fabrica*, a great military forge, a strong national institution, of which the Emperor Hadrian was the founder, by whose directions the branch at Bath is said to have been established. But on the last point the evidence is slight. Hadrian certainly came to Britain and probably to Bath. So much, moreover, was done by him in this country generally that on his return to Rome he was honoured with the title of Restorer of Britain. But whether he himself established the Bath branch of the Corporation of Armourers, or committed the work to one of his generals, is uncertain; indeed the fact that there was a great industry in the midst of the cultivated population of the city is the only one of importance. The object of these bodies in the various towns was to make arms for the use of the legions to which

they were attached, at public forges.   Officers were appointed
to receive and distribute the arms, which no person was
permitted to manufacture unless admitted as a member of
the company.   Besides the ordinary *fabricæ* for local legions,
there were the *fabricæ sacræ*, much larger establishments,
which supplied whole provinces, and even kingdoms.   There
are indications that Bath had one of these for the purpose of
furnishing arms to troops at a distance as well as to the
garrison of the neighbourhood.   The Rev. Joseph Hunter, in
his treatise on *The connection of Bath with the Literature
and Science of England*, says that this manufactory must
have caused the processes of metallurgy to be carried on to a
considerable extent, and that the furnaces thus used may
also have produced the beautiful bronzes I have mentioned,
with many other works of art.   Thus the city would become
one of bustle and business, the abode not only of people of
leisure, but of shrewd, skilful men.   Another respect, this, in
which Bath, of the second century, resembled Bath of
modern times ; for as Agricola's artists and Hadrian's
inventors gave it a name to live in the annals of industry in
their day, so did Ralph Allen and John Palmer, by their
wise enterprises, make it known in theirs.

 Although my object is biographical rather than historical,
I must not omit another matter in connection with the great
works of the time.   While artisans found abundant occupation
in Bath, unskilled labourers, probably slaves, were employed
by hundreds in constructing the wonderful roads to and from
the city.   Those marvellous highways were carried over hill
and dale, in lines as straight as possible, towards Durocorinium
(Cirencester), another to Verlucio (Westbury), a third to
Ischalis (Ilchester), a fourth to Abone (Bitton), on the way to
the Severn.   "The last place," says Warner, "was probably

made a station when Vespasian led his troops from Bath
immediately after taking possession of the country round it,
against the Silures, in the year 44 or 45." Two Roman
Celebrities have prominent places in the events of the period,
Plautius, a commander of the troops, who returned to Rome
in 49, receiving there an ovation for his meritorious services
in Britain, and Publius Ostorius Scapula, who succeeded him
at Bath. On the banks of the Severn is a village near where
the ancient Roman ferry crossed the river ; Ostorius erected
a fort there ; the place is called in Domesday book Oster-clive ;
its name is now Aust. Thus is the present connected with
the past.

It might have been supposed that some of the inscriptions
so beautifully cut on the votive altars and other monuments
still existing in the Bath Literary and Scientific Institution
would refer to men who might be designated Celebrities. But
it is hardly so ; they refer, interesting as they are, to people
of comparatively limited influence, such as an officer of the
army beloved by his troop, a freedman fulfilling a vow
connected with the health of his patron, and a priest of the
Goddess Sulis honoured in this way by his wife Calphurnia.
A few are important as bearing on historical facts like those
relating to the Government industry just mentioned. In the
vestibule of the Institution is an upright stone adorned by a
moulding and a triangular top with a device of fruit and
flowers. The inscription, which is wonderfully clear, is to the
memory of Julius Vitalis, who was smith or armourer to the
twentieth legion, and who is said to have been beloved by his
fraternity, they showing respect for his memory by placing
the stone over his remains. It was found in the year 1708
on the side of the London Road, Walcot ; interments of that
time, in Bath as at Rome, not being within the city but along

highways leading to it. Many of the inscriptions refer to the
divinity Sul. One suggests questions touching the early
progress of Christianity in Britain. I do not say more on the
subject because it has been ably dealt with by various
archæologists, and my object is chiefly biographical. All who
wish for ample information on the antiquities of Bath should
become acquainted with the descriptions in the *Aquæ Solis*
of the Rev. Prebendary Scarth, who conferred great obligations
on the city by a long course of learned and successful
research.

Is it too much to hope that any plan for protecting the
Roman Bath and connecting it with the proposed extension
of the Pump Room structure may include a spacious corridor
so as to bring all the important remains of the ancient city
into juxta position with the Bath? There are tesselated pave-
ments of villas in the neighbourhood as well as votive altars
and other monuments and ornaments that might be thus
shown to very instructive advantage, free access being allowed
at certain hours both to residents and visitors.

CHAPTER III.

THE SAXON PERIOD.

One hundred and sixty-seven years passed after the Roman troops were withdrawn from Britain and before the Saxon period commenced. The two most important events affecting Bath were the change of religion from Heathendom to Christianity and the great battle of Dyrham, A.D. 577, in which the three British Kings were defeated. The change of religion had begun in consequence of the Roman edict that all temples throughout the Empire should be henceforth used for Christian worship, but the people, exhausted by incessant struggles with northern invaders, could no longer resist the Saxon Chieftains. In vain had Arthur on former occasions fought and conquered again and again; in vain did the worn-out Britains revive the memories which Tennyson described :—

> "For many a petty king ere Arthur came
> Ruled in this isle, and ever waging war
> Each upon other, wasted all the land ;
> And still from time to time the Heathen host
> Swarmed over seas and harried what was left.
> And so there grew great tracts of wilderness,
> Wherein the beast was ever more and more,
> But man was less and less till Arthur came."

Terribly as the defeat was, aggravated by recollections like these, it was eventually overruled for good. The importance to Bath of Saxon rule, with all its far-reaching consequences, can scarcely be overrated. It gave not only new life but higher life ; slow in development it is true, but infinitely better than either the half savage state of British existence or

B

the military government of Rome, even with all its artistic alleviations. Both were inconsistent with genuine freedom, which could only be gained permanently, though perhaps slowly, by the influences of the Christian religion. Much as in these times, many of us, looking at the matter from our own stand point, may see that is objectionable in monastic institutions, yet who can doubt that it was by them chiefly the gradual improvement of the country was effected? Through them the rulers of the Saxon period worked ; the Kings Osric, Offa, Athelstan, and Ædgar, the ecclesiastics Dunstan and Ælphege, of whom I have now to write, would have been otherwise powerless. But before we can understand what they did, it is necessary to bear in mind the state of things with which they had to deal. For this purpose I will quote from the valuable historical essay by Professor Earle.

The habits of the Saxon conquerors, it appears, made them averse to city life. They loved the free and open country, and pitched their dwellings where a stream, a plain or a wood took their fancy. Even had it not been so they would have been repelled by the desolation everywhere visible. Bath, after being forsaken by the Romans, had been devastated by successive invaders ; streets, baths, temples, monuments were all in ruins ; what was there to tempt such a people to make it their home? In reference to this, Mr. Earle writes :—" There is at Exeter a book still lying where it was deposited about the year 1050 by Leofric, the tenth bishop of Crediton and first bishop of Exeter. It is a volume of English poetry, unmistakeably described in the extant catalogue of books given by him to his cathedral, and it is still in the keeping of the chapter. One of the oldest poems in the book is a testamentary piece descriptive of a city in ruins. There is massive masonry, the place was once handsomely built and decorated, and held by warriors, but now all tumbled about; works of art exposed to the sky, and forming a strange contrast to the desolation around; there is a wide pool of water hot with fire ; and there are the once frequented baths. This is no vague poetic dream, but the portrait of a definite spot. It suits the old Brito-Roman ruin of Akeman (as Bath was then called) after 577, and it suits no other place that I can think of in the habitable world."

How to restore this ruined city was the problem the rulers had to solve. The way that would naturally first occur to them was that of bringing people together by meeting their most obvious wants. The Christian religion, as I have intimated, had begun to interest many, and public worship would still have, as it had in heathen times, and will always have, a strong attractive power. Hence the earliest Saxon kings founded religious establishments. Historians differ as to whether Osric or Offa did most in this way ; they reigned over different provinces, but both had been converted to Christianity, and both were interested in the sick man's city. Osric led the way by founding a nunnery for patients near the springs about the year 676. From the beginning of Saxon rule the springs were a great means of effecting its object or restoring the city. The virtues so well known to the Romans were soon recognised by their practical successors, and quickened the process of reconstruction. But Osric was King of the Huiccü, the Jugantes of Tacitus, inhabitants, according to Bede, of Worcestershire, Warwickshire, and part of Gloucestershire, whereas Bath belonged to another kingdom, that of Wessex, the consent of whose sovereign it was neces- sary to obtain. It was given, and a woman named Bretana regularly appointed as a kind of abbess. The king enlarged the establishment by inducing one hundred families to join it. But, generous as the effort was, the times were against it, and the institution fell into decay.

Then came Offa, the renowned King of Mercia, who wrested Bath from the King of Wessex in the year 775, and established a college of secular canons, the germ of the celebrated Bath Monastery. Its progress was slow until the reign of Athelstan, which commenced in the early part of the tenth century. He had done much for Bath by establishing a mint, giving the city municipal privileges, and employing other means of raising it again to a high position. But his love of learning and literature would give him especial sympathies with the monastery; he, therefore, did much to amend its sinking fortunes. In addition to several large estates in the neighbourhood of the city he made valuable gifts to the library, taking a personal interest in selecting books, such as those on medical science, which would be practically useful. Thus the Abbey of Bath became, in the words of Mr. Earle, " a flourishing institution, beneficent, educational, and highly ornamental. It was imposing in every aspect; by its buildings, by its brother-hood, and by its political importance. Its church, the predecessor of that long Norman building of which we still see some of the pier-bases, was greatly admired. Of the religious reputation of the monastery we shall catch a glimpse presently. Of its library and literature some few specimens exist, especially one volume at Cambridge, which tells of the estates of the Abbey and of the benevolent agrarian policy of the abbots." Much might be said also of what they did in the manumission of slaves and other philanthropic move-ments in the West of England.

The "glimpse of the religious reputation " I have mentioned may be caught as we proceed to the close of the tenth century.

The church of the Abbey was then the scene of one of the most brilliant events in the history of Bath. King Ædgar was crowned with great pomp at the festival of Whitsuntide in the fourteenth year of his reign. It was an event that lit up the entire West of England, and gave to the city of the springs a radiance which it retained through many a year. From the Abbeys of Gloucestershire, Hampshire and Wiltshire, Dorset, Devon, and Cornwall dignitaries came to give grace to the ceremony. The old poets and annalists were especially jubilant on the subject. A book entitled *The Glory of Regality*, by Arthur Taylor, gives the original and translation of one of the poems. Reduced to prose it sets forth that Ædgar was crowned " with mickle pomp in the old borough of Achemannescestre, named by those who dwelt in it Bath, that there was mickle rejoicing on that happy day of Pentecost and that there were of priests a heap, of monks a vast crowd, of wise men a great gathering." How long the remembrance of the event lived in Bath is shown by Leland, who, writing 600 years afterwards, says it was still the custom there to elect a King at Whitsuntide and treat him with a banquet in commemoration of the pageant of 973. This continued as late as the time of Beau Nash.

The coronation of Ædgar at Bath may have been due to various causes. One, his own interest and that of his family in an important, historical city. Another, its central position as to some of the chief churches and monasteries. Another, the connection with it of the archbishop who officiated at the ceremony, Dunstan, and his great ally, Ælphege. Monastic life was rapidly becoming identified with the national life and monopolising the property of the country. Dunstan was especially interested in replacing the secular clergy with Benedictine monks, nowhere was this policy carried out more

vigorously than in Somersetshire and the adjoining counties.
Ædgar boasted of having founded forty-seven monasteries,
and intended to make the number fifty. All this may have
had much to do with the selection of Bath for the ceremony.
There was a curious question, of which even Professor
Freeman in his great work, *The Norman Conquest,* stated
he could find no adequate solution—why the coronation was
delayed so long? But it need not be discussed here, my
object being chiefly to show that Ædgar fairly ranks among
those who were honoured in the city.*

Dunstan was a celebrity of a different kind. Living in
early life at Glastonbury, first as an ascetic monk and afterwards as a powerful abbot, his influence in Bath would be

---

* *Why the coronation of Ædgar at Bath was delayed so long?*
Although the discussion of this question was not convenient
within the limits of the chapter as first issued a few considerations may be referred to here. I ventured to suggest
them in an inaugural address at a meeting of the Somersetshire
Archæological Society at Bath in 1876 and the address was
printed in the Journal of the Proceedings of the year. It
appeared to me, though with sincere deference to the judgment
of the Historian of the Norman Conquest, that the ceremony
which had been postponed through fourteen years may at length
have been fixed upon partly as a means of celebrating the
triumph and establishing the power of a new order of things.
Ædgar had very much at heart the identification of Monastic
Life with the National Life, thus binding the Church of England
and the People of England to Rome, and monopolising not only
the government but the property of the country. Ædgar took so
much pride in the Benedictine scheme that according to Sharon
Turner, he boasted, A.D. 964, of having founded forty-seven
monasteries and declared his intention to increase them to fifty.

considerable. His descent from a noble Wessex family
accounts for the secular accomplishments which distinguished
him as a young man and recommended him to the Court.
He played upon the harp, excelled in painting and
sculpture, advised the king on intricate State affairs, and at
times pretended to work miracles. But we are told by his
biographers that "he suffered much from the devil, who, being
especially offended by his miraculous pretensions, prompted
some envious courtiers to persuade Athelstan he was a
magician. The devil, so runs the legend, succeeded;
Dunstan was dismissed, forsook the world and became a
monk." Then began his connection with Somersetshire; he
built a small cell against the wall of the old church at
Glastonbury in order to give himself entirely to religious
exercises. Having thus recovered from the terrible imputa-
tion as to "the black art" he was again sought by Athelstan,
who, in choosing his chief advisers, fixed on those who
combined superior statesmanship with ecclesiastical zeal.
Dunstan was first made abbot of the rich monastery of
Glastonbury, and after other marks of royal favour—chequered,
however, by severe reverses—Archbishop of Canterbury.
This brought him again to Bath for the coronation. Much
had happened to him since the time of the tiny cell at
Glastonbury, but in the various chances and changes of life
he had always obeyed the call of duty. That was his
prominent characteristic. No dread of loss or exile prevented
his rebuking wickedness in high places. As statesman,
prelate, master, and friend, he was faithful to conscience and
his Christian work. His weaknesses were those of the age
in which he lived; his noble qualities deserve grateful
remembrance.

The remaining celebrity of the time and place is Ælphege,

in English, Ælfheah. His connection with Bath originated
with his friend Dunstan, whom he imitated by building a
small cell and living as an anchorite. He chose for his site
the village of Weston, where it is said he was born, though
his family who, like Dunstan's, were of noble rank, lived at a
distance. His rigid asceticism, which had grown into much
favour among those in his class of life, led many of them to
come to him for advice, some of whom became monks and
lived under his rule, while others gave him the means of
supporting the new brotherhood. This led to his appointment as abbot at the Bath monastery. Ædgar appears to
have had much confidence in him. "If it is true," says the
author of his life in the National Biography, "that the king
in 970 refounded the Church of Bath as a convent of regulars
the new society probably owed to Ælfheah a considerable
increase in its numbers."

In 984 he quitted Bath, where he had laboured so
successfully, to become Bishop of Winchester. There he
distinguished himself by his efforts to convert the northmen,
and especially by his influence with Olaf, the Norwegian king.
That he had the statesmanlike qualities as well as the
religious zeal of Dunstan was shown by the next mark of
royal confidence, his elevation to the Archbishopric of
Canterbury. Those qualities were prominent in his policy as
to the frequent Danish invasions which at that time so
troubled the Government, but although his conduct was
always humane and considerate, he at length fell a victim to
the savage barbarity of the invaders. They had assembled
in great force at Canterbury, besieged the city and burnt it.
The venerable prelate, with many of his people, was made
captive, half starved and otherwise ill-used. In the hope of
gaining a large ransom they were taken to the ships and kept

prisoners for seven months. At length came a day on which the ransom was to be paid, but Ælphege refused to save his life by sacrifices which his friends could ill afford to make. Then his enemies withdrew their offer ; in vain did one of their leaders, who had been much impressed by the Arch-bishop's teaching and example, offer gold and silver and all that he had to save him ; he was put to death with the most inconceivable aggravation of savage cruelty.

Although during the Saxon period Bath attracted fewer residents than in the Roman occupation, there must have been some in connection with the increase of trade. I have mentioned that Athelstan established a royal mint, coins from which may still be seen not only in the museums, of countries under English rule but in those of the North of Europe. No doubt the chief officers of the mint were men of ability and influence, trusted by the Government, and doing for commerce and industry what the armourers of the Roman period did for warlike purposes. Their names appear on the coins of several successive reigns, and the fact that those coins were issued for so long a period and in so few places (not even Bristol being one) shows the high position of Bath.

In concluding my account of the Roman period I mentioned Mr. Scarth's *Aquæ Solis* as very useful with regard to the antiquities of Bath. I would now suggest, as aids to a good understanding of the Saxon period, *The Saxon Chronicle*, Conybeare's *Illustrations of Anglo-Saxon Poetry*, and Sir Walter Scott's *Ivanhoe*.

CHAPTER IV.

THE NORMAN PERIOD.

JOHN DE VILLULA.

From the close of the Saxon period to the Norman Conquest the Danes were the ruling power, with the exception of three years marked by the restoration of Ethelred and the short reign of his son. History records that Sweyne, the father of Canute, made Bath his head-quarters in 1015, to receive the submission of the Western Thanes, also that the effigy of Canute appears on coins still existing from the Bath mint. Further, there is a legend that this sovereign often visited the Bath monastery to take counsel with the monks as to the laws he should frame for the kingdom, dictating what they should write. One of the medallions of the ecritoire presented to the Princess of Wales, and mentioned in a former sketch, represents the king thus engaged.

The connection of Sweyne with Bath makes the legend as to his son probable. It was a time when men knew no better way of relieving the pangs of conscience than by endowing and frequenting religious institutions. With Canute all high enjoyment was marred by the remembrance of the deeds of violence of which he had been guilty through a great part of his life. Sovereign at the same time of England, Denmark and Norway; possessing more power in each country than any of his predecessors, there was yet the "rooted sorrow," the "mind diseased," that made existence miserable. In vain did his courtiers remind him that his own valour and wisdom had won for him the proud eminence; he listened rather to the spiritual advisers of prayer, penance and self-denial; seeking relief chiefly in enriching chantries where masses might be said for the souls of those who had fallen in battle against him.

Canute's munificence in Bath would naturally cause his memory to be cherished. But not even the wealth and dignity of the Abbey could avert the fate that awaited the city after the Norman Conquest. In the war between the two sons of the Conqueror the entire country from Bristol to Worcester was devastated; Bristol was taken by Robert, the elder son; Bath he sacked and burnt. This occurred in 1087, and should be remembered with some other events in connection with the subsequent doings of the remarkable man who is the chief subject of the present sketch. The contest between the royal brothers had ended in the victory of Rufus, who received from his father a letter to Lanfranc, Archbishop of Canterbury, recommending that the rights of the elder should be cancelled and the younger called to succeed. The Domesday book contained particulars respecting Bath which facilitated the next great change in its fortunes. It was there shown to be a royal "ferme, held by the king," and was known to be disposable to any Norman rich enough to buy it. Rufus inherited the ferme and sold it to John de Villula for 500 marks.

The buyer was a physician of Tours, who came to England in the train of the Conqueror. After some time he came to Bath apparently with the view of practising in connection with the springs, but having acquired considerable wealth, being also both able and ambitious, he seized opportunities of personal advancement. Well known at the English court, and a favourite of Rufus, he had no difficulty in turning his position to advantage by buying not only the Royal ferme but also the bishopric of Somerset. All such offices were then saleable, the chief qualification being that the buyer should be a foreigner of some mark. As fast as the Saxons were dispossessed, as they generally were with ruthless cruelty, crowds of Norman, German, Belgian, and Italian aspirants were imported to take their places. De Villula became by means of his purchases a king-bishop; he had power, both temporal and spiritual, to do what he liked; his ability was equal to his ambition and, though Bath may have hated the foreign yoke, its people had some compensation. They saw the city gradually rebuilt; another great church erected on the site of the old one; visitors came again to the springs attracted by the medical reputation of the new owner and a spirit rekindled in the Abbey, making it the home of eminent men, such as the Roman city was in the times of Hadrian and Agricola.

De Villula lived but little at Wells although the seat of the bishopric of Somerset was there. He greatly preferred Bath as more interesting from its historical associations and giving wider scope for objects he had at heart. Thierry in his elaborate history of the Norman Conquest states that "the newly appointed bishops generally deserted the smaller towns in which episcopal seats had been fixed and built palaces in the larger towns." No doubt the existence of the monastery at Bath and the necessity of great attention to its interests would be one strong reason for transferring the seat, and another event occurred which strengthened the purpose of de Villula. Some time after he had obtained the bishopric, the Abbot of Bath, Ælsig, died, to whose office he succeeded, thus acquiring additional influence in the city. He employed it to reorganise the brotherhood and give the institution a higher character; at the same time exchanging the title of Bishop of Somerset for that of Bishop of Bath; the prior and monks of the Bath Abbey forming the chapter of the cathedral. As was to be expected this exaltation of Bath caused much mortification at Wells, which was increased by the rigorous treatment of the Canons there. They saw their revenues alienated, their beautiful refectory and dormitories pulled down, and themselves turned adrift from their peaceful homes to live amongst the laity. All this long rankled in their minds. We shall see presently how peace between the rival cities was at length restored. Meanwhile it is only just to de Villula to remember that if some parts of his policy were questionable others were eminently useful. At Wells he could not have done what he did at Bath in the way both of local and national progress, restoring a ruined historical city and gathering around him benefactors to the science and literature of the country.

Fifty years passed before the dissensions were healed. De Villula had died and been succeeded by Godfrey, a German promoted by the influence of the queen of Henry I. Godfrey, we are told, was "gentle and pious, sprung from a noble family, but could not get back the revenues for the Canons at Wells though he tried to do so." The next Bishop was Robert, "a monk of Lewes, who had been sent to Glastonbury to put the affairs of the Abbey in order;" "he also," says the historian I have just quoted, "was descended of illustrious parents, a religious man and expert in business." He became the peacemaker; to him was "resigned the land and rents of the impoverished Canons," and when he had completed some noble preparatory works he effected the union of Bath and Wells. I am now quoting chiefly from a very curious document written in Latin by one who is supposed to have been a Canon of Wells; it was discovered by the Rev. Joseph Hunter in a register of the priory of Bath, preserved in the library at Lincoln's Inn, and edited for the Camden

Society; the date of the document is probably that of the reign of Henry II.   The preparatory works to which I have alluded are thus mentioned:—"It is also to be added that the same bishop built, at great expense, the church of the blessed Peter the Apostle at Bath.   He built also a chapter house and cloister, dormitory, refectory and infirmary.   Nor ought it to be forgotten that the great church at Wells was built by his counsel and assistance."   Then the good monk proceeds to show how the great church was consecrated and dedicated by four bishops, how Robert appointed suitable cathedral officers to the satisfaction of both Bath and Wells, and how when all this was done he prepared "a charter of it for perpetual memory which the Pope confirmed." This ancient record is also valuable for the light it throws on the earlier history of the diocese, especially for its information respecting the Saxon bishops.   Returning to de Villula I have only to add a passage from Mr. Hunter's appendix to the Latin treatise, with reference to a criticism by the author of the document:—" But the testimony of William of Malmesbury will for ever vindicate the memory of one of the few promoters of exact knowledge and truth in England, and consequently of the best interests of the human race."   De Villula died in 1122, greatly respected.   Leland, who gives honour where honour is due, was affected by the sight of his tomb many years afterwards in one of his journeys, overgrown with weeds.   It was in "the middle of the presbytery of the fair church he had built, but which had become waste and unroofed."   Such was the state of the sepulchre of the physician from Tours who had reigned as Bishop at Bath thirty-four years.

Among the eminent men whom he gathered around him was one who received honourable mention from all the

historians of the period—Adelard Bathoniensis. He was
an Oriental scholar who, having acquired, says Mr. Hunter,
"what could be learned at home visited Spain, Egypt, and
Arabia. He brought from those countries treatises on natural
philosophy, and is in fact the main link by which western
science is connected with that of the east." To him Europe
owed the elements of Euclid not in the original Greek but
in an Arabic translation. He was also an inquirer into
nature, an original discoverer and altogether a profound
philosopher. Such a man must have given a character to
society at Bath and probably attracted hither multitudes of
inquirers eager to sit at his feet. Associated with Adelard in
the monastery was Hugolinus, called in Domesday book
"Interpres," a man of many languages. After them came
William of Bath, a divine; Henry of Bath, a lawyer; and
Reginald of Bath, a physician; all celebrities in their day,
adding to their ordinary avocations the advancement of
scientific and literary culture. Concerning Hugolinus there
is information in Domesday book. De Villula bought of
him for the Bath monastery some valuable properties. These
we learn were at "Eston," Batheaston, "Herlei," Warleigh,
and "Clafterton," Claverton. The purchase was made early
in the reign of Rufus.*

---

* It may not be inappropriate to add to the preceding sketch a
list of the Bishops of Bath and Wells as given in Mr. Earle's
History with the dates of their accession, remarking that John of
Tours and Godfrey though not titular bishops of both churches
were virtually so. The union took place under Bishop Robert.
It is interesting to observe that in this list is Reginald FitzJocelin,

CHAPTER V.

THE EARLY MAYORS OF BATH.

John de Villula died in the year 1122 in the reign of
Henry I. I have noticed other celebrities who brought us
down to the middle of the century. There is now a very long
interval unmarked by any distinguished life. But history is
not silent; the city made progress of various kinds, and
names identified with it appear from time to time. Although
little is said we may infer from the mere mention of some of
them in Domesday book that they were prominent men.
Others, like the first mayors and members of Parliament, find
their places in local history, and I am induced to keep up the
connection of my narratives by stating a few circumstances
relating to them.

the founder of S. John's Hospital in Bath, Thomas Wolsey, the
celebrated cardinal, James Montagu, who restored the Bath
Abbey Church, William Laud, of high ecclesiastical memory, and
Thomas Ken, the sainted author of the morning and evening
hymns. Bishop Ken, who spent much time at the beautiful seat
of Longleat, near Warminster, and whose study, commanding a
magnificent view, is still shown to visitors, bequeathed a large number of books, nearly 200 volumes, chiefly foreign, to the old Bath
Abbey Library where they remain with many others, alas, never
used. It is hoped that ere long they may, together with other
scattered collections, form part of a good public library worthy
of the city. The two last Bishops in the following list have been
much respected for their attention to this part of their diocese,
though living at the ancient palace at Wells. Lord Auckland
took a prominent part in opening the new wing of the Mineral

During the greater part of the nonbiographical interval the Bath monastery continued the home of learned men. Among them were the eminent physicians mentioned in my last sketch, who ministered to the bodily as well as spiritual wants of the people. John de Villula, it will be remembered, was a doctor of medicine before he was a bishop, "outrunning," his biographers say, "all his contemporaries in honour and profit." What Reginald of Bath did as a medical man we are not told; nor yet what were the services of one "Magister Johannes de Bathonia, Medicus" so the record runs, that he should have been granted "a suitable chamber with free

Water Hospital and preached a sermon on its behalf in London obtaining a good collection at a fashionable West End Church. Lord Arthur Hervey was one of the Company of Revisers of the authorised version of the Holy Scriptures.

BISHOPS OF BATH AND WELLS.

John of Tours 1088	John Clerk 1523
Godfrey 1123	William Knight 1541
Robert 1136	William Barlow 1549
Reginald FitzJocelin ... 1174	Gilbert Bourne 1554
Savaric 1192	Gilbert Berkeley 1560
Jocelin Troteman 1206	Thomas Godwin 1584
Roger 1244	John Still 1593
William Button 1248	James Montagu 1608
Walter Giffard 1265	Arthur Lake 1616
William Button 1267	William Laud 1626
Robert Burnell 1275	Leonard Mawe 1628
William de March 1293	Walter Curll 1629
Walter Hasleshaw 1302	William Piers 1632
John Drokensford 1309	Robert Creighton 1670
Ralph of Shrewsbury ... 1329	Peter Mews 1673
John Barnet 1363	Thomas Ken 1685
John Harewell 1366	Richard Kidder 1691
Walter Skirlaw 1386	George Hooper 1704
Ralph Erghum 1388	John Wynne 1727
Henry Bowett 1401	Edward Willes 1744
Nicholas Bubwith 1407	Charles Moss 1774
John Stafford 1425	Richard Beadon 1802
Thomas Beckington 1443	George Henry Law 1824
Robert Stillington 1466	Richard Bagot 1845
Rich Fox 1491	Robert Eden } 1854
Oliver King 1495	Lord Auckland }
Hadrian de Castello 1504	Arthur Hervey } 1870
Thomas Wolsey 1518	Lord A. Hervey }

C

ingress and egress for life," also ample allowances from the kitchen, each being duly named. But that such men were of some mark is evident and that King Athelstane, among the books he gave to the library of the monastery, made a point of including the best on medical science, indicates the estimation in which that science was held.

I may here advert to a trifling historical problem before quitting the Norman period. Following the usual authorities I have described Villula as coming "to England in the train of the Conqueror." A friendly critic has questioned the accuracy of this, and in favour of his view, he has urged some weighty considerations.

First, that in the absence of definite testimony the statement looks more like probable conjecture than matter of fact. Was the successful physician either a Norman or a subject of the Conqueror, but only what he was designated "John of Tours." ? It was there he "outran all his contemporaries in honor and profit" and laid the foundation of the rank and fortune which afterwards gave him such an important place in history. That he took orders at the beginning of his career was a fortunate incident inasmuch as it gave him the qualification for the Episcopal office. For all that he did before he came to England there would have been hardly time if he had come in the train of William. But by some means he was known to Rufus ; possibly his medical reputation caused a friendship, so that Rufus rather than William would be the attracting power. I have also been reminded that I have said nothing about the famous palace the aspiring churchman built in Bath. My reason for reticence was the extreme uncertainty as to where it stood, who occupied it and what became of it. Mr. Peach is of opinion that "it stood over the Roman baths and what remained of it was removed early in the seventeenth century and a bowling green laid out upon the site."

Now as to the earliest mayors. We have seen that Bath became a " burg " in the Saxon period. At the Norman Conquest such towns had long had coinage rights, market tolls, and various other local privileges. To these in the year 1194 was added first at Winchester, then at Bath, the power to try their own cases in their own courts and according to their own local laws. Then the increase of public business, required a presiding officer with more dignity and power than had been allowed previously; hence the appointment of a mayor. But prior to this privilege it was necessary to constitute the elective body. This caused the incorporation of certain citizens as freemen, who, in Bath, retained the title and exercised the rights until very recently. The admission to the freedom was obtained in later times, if not also in the early ones, by apprenticeship, a part of the Guild system which prevailed extensively in Europe. The importance of these bodies of freemen was recognised at the Reformation by the transfer to them of much monastic property. To those of Bath came the valuable Bath commons, the rent of which they continued to enjoy until the Corporation, empowered by Act of Parliament, and seeing the gradual extinction of the body, purchased for the benefit of the public, the interest of those who remained. I happened to be one of a few citizens who gave, before a committee of the House of Commons, the evidence which was required to legalise the transfer.

We pause here to consider the great significance of the Establishment of the Boroughs in England which has been ably treated by Professor Earle.

Warner states that the first Mayor of Bath was John Savage, appointed in the year 1412. He is placed at the head of a list of ten who filled the office before 1587, being all the names he had been able to collect. They appear at the head of the Roll in the Guildhall which is hung up in the Mayor's room. Professor Earle has given in his history the curious original English of the oath taken by the freemen in the mayoralty of John Savage, also the following translation :— " I engage to be attentive and obedient to the Mayor of Bath and all his successors ; and I will attach myself to no other authority to the prejudice of any burgess of Bath. Neither may I bring any suit against any burgess of Bath except in the Mayor's Court, if so be that the Mayor is willing to do me right and competent to do it. Saint Catherine's Day I engage to keep as a holy day yearly ; and to the best of my power I will help to maintain Saint Catherine's Chapel and the bridge. All other customs and liberties that belong to the aforesaid freedom I will well and truly keep and maintain. So help me God and holy angels."

The researches of Warner in the city archives as to the earliest mayors appear to have been less complete than those of another antiquary—Mr. H. Riley, who at the request of some learned body had access to them in later times. He discovered a Latin deed showing that the office of mayor existed as early as 1230, and as the deed throws curious light on the civic usages of the time I transcribe a copy of the translation by Mr. Riley :—

" Know present and to come, that I, Walter, son of Serle, in my lawful power have given to Juliana, daughter of William Springod, one seld to the south of the Stalls of Bath, which I bought of Robert Prither for 4 marks and half a mark of silver ; to hold and to have to himself and to whomsoever he shall wish to give or assign it; rendering for it yearly to the Lords of the fee at the Feast of S. Michael 7 pence and at Hock day 5 pence for Land gable (Land tax) for all service exaction and demand. And that this my gift may have the

strength of perpetual security, this present charter I have
corroborated with the impression of my seal—These being
witnesses, Caskill de Westone John Duport at that time Mayor
of Bath, Andrew the Clerk, Geoffry Wissi Hugh de Aystone,
Thomas Sweyn, Walter Cabbel and many others."

Mr. Riley traces the date to about 1230, and remarks:
"This is perhaps the very earliest mention of a Mayor of
Bath. The device of the seal has much the appearance of an
ancient gem."

More recently two Bath gentlemen have published a
valuable book showing that the Bath mayoralty had an
origin even earlier than that supposed by Mr. Riley. In
The Municipal Records of Bath, by Mr. Austin King and
Mr. B. H. Watts, we have a minute account, most clearly
stated, of all the Bath charters and their contents. Not only
this; we also learn what preceded them, what was the spirit
of the people who obtained them and how, step by step, the
citizens gained the right of self-government which is now more
prized. We are reminded that the *Saxon Chronicle* mentions
a Grieve of Bath named Alfred, who died in 907, that the
present Mayor is his official lineal descendant, that even the
changes of the Norman Conquest did not annihilate local
courts thus governed, that the Town Council of the present
day therefore represent the *Tun Moot* of Saxon times, and
that thus, through a thousand years, Bath has had a municipal
government. For these reasons it is a mistake to suppose
that the civic liberties of Bath date chiefly from the charter of
Elizabeth. Century after century charters were granted by
various sovereigns, from Richard Cœur de Lion to Henry
VIII., some granting privileges, others confirming them. The
charter of Elizabeth codified these, defined the constitution of
the governing body, stated the number of aldermen and

councillors to be appointed, and ordained such ceremonies as
carrying maces of gold or silver before the mayor ; but the
real power existed long before.   Who and what the
celebrities of the middle ages were we have very little
information.   Now and then the good deeds are mentioned of
some great benefactor like Reginald FitzJocelin, who, in the
twelfth century, rebuilt S. Michael's Church, and founded S.
John's Hospital.   We are also told of kings and queens who
held Bath as their property, and we might imagine Edward I.
and his high-spirited mother, Eleanor of Provence, showing
similar interest in the city to that displayed by the Roman and
Saxon sovereigns ; but after all this would be only imagining,
and it is better to deal with facts.

Unfortunately, facts are also scanty with regard to another
subject closely connected with that of the mayoralty—the
earliest members of Parliament for Bath.   We only know
when they were first returned, what were the names and
position of some of them, and how unwillingly, in many cases
they undertook the office.   The earliest known representatives
of Bath were Henry Bayton and Thomas Misleterre, returned
in 1297, the twenty-sixth year of the reign of Edward I.
Where they lived, or what was their position, we are not told,
but subsequent records show that the citizens chose men
from the neighbouring villages and the trading classes of
Bath.   Thus we have John de Suthstoke, John de Hampton,
Hugh de Wyke, Richard Wydicombe, William de Radestoke,
Roger le Tanner, John le Draper, Alexander le Teinturer
and William le Goldsmith.   These represented the city in
the thirteenth and fourteenth centuries ; their successors,
soon after the charter of Elizabeth, were generally men of
county position, bearing such names as Harington, Hungerford, Fitzharding, Horner, Langton, Popham and Blathwayt.

In the early period membership was deemed a burthen which men were anxious to avoid; in the later it was evidently an honour, though not then so eagerly sought as in modern times. When we reach the reign of Elizabeth, we hear of a few local celebrities, such as Sherstone, who was the first Mayor under her Majesty's charter, and his son-in-law, Prynne, who was twice elected member for the city and succeeded to the Recordership. Prior to this time, late in the fourteenth century, there was a celebrity of the other sex, though unfortunately, while we are told the names of mayors and members of Parliament, the only designation by which the good lady is known is that of " The Wyf of Bathe." She may be mentioned here, partly on her own account and partly because Chaucer could not have written of her as he did without knowing something of the city. At that time the woollen trade, which had long been carried on in Bath extensively, appears to have been very flourishing, "better cloth being sold than was produced by the looms of Ypres and Ghent." Whether the heroine or one of her five husbands was distinguished in this way the *Canterbury Tales* do not inform us, but the Father of English Song represents her as a learned lady who must have acquired some classical lore in Bath ; though it is stated by an annotator that what she quoted as from Ptolemy was not found in his works, and that she was in the habit of fathering on him wise sayings the real author of which she could not remember.

I have mentioned William Sherstone as the first Mayor under the charter of Elizabeth. He also was a clothier, a man of considerable substance, probably a landowner, at all events a large occupier. He lived in a house called the Barton, the name of the estate which he appears to have farmed, and

which was probably the Royal "Berton" of Saxon and
Norman times, originally purchased of the Crown by John
de Villula, and afterwards transferred, sometimes to kings
and queens and back again to courtiers or the city. The
house, much altered, now stands at the end of Barton street,
Queen square, and is part of the business premises of Messrs.
Jolly and Son. It is pleasant to think of it as the residence
of the first of Queen Elizabeth's mayors, with its then agreeable surroundings in open country, down to the Avon in one
direction, and across the commons to Weston in the other.
Pleasant also to think of him as the public spirited man who
probably first won his seat in the House of Commons, which
he retained through five Parliaments, as well as his three
successive mayoralties, by the earnestness and ability with
which he pressed the claim for incorporation on the Government. Tradition states that the Queen honoured Barton
house by sleeping there when she visited her godson, Sir
John Harington, at Kelstone, but of this there is no proof.
That a genuine Bath celebrity, however, William Prynne,
was a frequent visitor at the old mansion is highly probable,
as his father married Miss Marie Sherstone, the Mayor's
daughter, and he had much intercourse with the family for
many years.*

---

* As the last note contains a list of the Bishops of Bath and
Wells it may be interesting to note who the Mayors of Bath were
from the earliest recorded period. I have stated that Mr. Riley
discovered in the archives of the city that the earliest mention of
a Mayor, John Duport, is of the date 1230, in the reign of Henry
III., whereas Warner begins his list with John Savage, 1412.
The Bath historian gives a list of ten, the only names he had been
able to obtain from 1412 to 1587 inclusive, which are placed at

the head of the first roll now hung up in the Guildhall, this roll bringing the list down to 1799. The History of Bath being published soon afterwards could not include more; so the list now given contains the names from 1412 to the present time.

THE ROLL OF THE MAYORS OF BATH.

BEFORE THE MUNICIPAL REFORM ACT.

John Savage	1412	John Peewce 1658-9
Ralph Hunt	1414	John Bigges 1660
Richard Widecombe	1416	Jo. Ford 1661
John Savage	1425	Jo. Parker 1662
William Hayne	1471	Wm. Childe 1663
Richard Chapman	1503	Hen. Chapman 1664
Henry Covell	1533	Wa. Gibbes 1665
Edward Ludwell	1551	John Peewce 1666
Thomas Ash	1583	Tho. H. Gibbes 1667
John Court	1587	Rob. Chapman 1668
The Charter of Queen Elizabeth		Wm. Childe 1669
(32nd Elizabeth) 4th Sept. 1590.		Edward White 1670
William Sherstone	1590	Jo. Masters 1671
William Sherstone	1615	Hen. Chapman 1672
William Chapman	1616	Hen. Parker 1673
Walter Chapman	1617	Jo. Bush 1674-5
William Clift	1618	Wa. Gibbes 1676
Richard Gay	1619	Benja. Baber 1677
William Sherstone	1620	Robt. Chapman 1678
Thomas Moorford	1621	Jo. Masters 1679
Robert Frey	1622	William Bush 1680
William Chapman	1623	Edw. Buskett 1681
Matthew Rendall	1624	Robert Hayward 1682
Richard Gay	1625-30	Walter Hickes 1683
William Chapman	1630	Jo. Bush 1684
Richard Gay	1631	Jo. Gibbs 1685
Arthur Sherstone	1632	John Pococke 1686
Anthony Langston	1633	Benja. Baber 1687
Matthew Rendall	1634	Wa. Gibbes 1688
John Chapman	1635	Robt. Chapman 1689
John Biggs	1636	Jo. Masters 1690
Richard Chapman	1637	George Colliber 1691
Robert Fisher (1639 to 1644)	1638	William Bush 1692
John Parker	1644	Edw. Buskett 1693
John Chapman	1645	Robert Hayward 1694
John Biggs	1646	Walter Hickes... 1695
Jo. Muzood	1647	John Axford 1696
Walter Chapman	1648	Jo. Bush 1697
Richard Price	1649	Jo. Gibbes 1698
John Peewce	1650	Thomas Gibbes 1699
Walter Chapman	1651	Benja. Baber 1700
Jo. Parker	1652	Ric. Matters 1701
Jo. Muzood	1653	W. Chapman 1702
Jo. Parker	1654	Jo. Bush 1703
Walter Chapman	1655	William Bush 1704
Jo. Boys	1656	Waltr. Hickes 1705
Jo. Masters	1657	Edw. Woolmer 1706

Jo. Gibbs	1707	
Edwd. Bushell...	1708	
Charley Child	1709	
Walter Gibbes...	1710	
Thomas Gibbes	1711	
Richard Morgan	1712	
Richard Ford	1713	
Thos. Biggs	1714	
Wm. Long	1715	
Jno. Saunders	1716	
Ric. Matters	1717	
Thomas Henshell	1718	
Wm. Collibee	1719	
Edw. Woolmer	1720	
George Tryme	1721	
Wm. Bush	1722	
Jno. Hickes	1723	
Tho. Atwood	1724	
Rokwell Gibbs	1725	
Waltr. Chapman	1726	
Wm. Chapman	1727	
John Billing	1728	
Tran. Bave.	1729	
Richard Ford	1730	
William Horton	1731	
Milo Smith	1732	
Richard Morgan	1733	
Tho. Short	1734	
Tho. Atwood	1735	
Rd. Matravers...	1736	
James Atwood...	1737	
Jno. Saunders	1738	
Wm. Bush	1739	
Charles Stone	1740	
Hen. Atwood	1741	
A. Allen	1742	
Ambrose Bishop	1743	
John Chapman	1744	
John Cogswell	1745	
Tho. Atwood	1746	
Thursby Robinson ...	1747	
James Atwood...	1748	
Charles Stone	1749	
Hen. Atwood	1750	
Francis Hales	1751	
Tho. Atwood	1752-3	
John Chapman	1754	
Saml. Bush	1755	
Edward Bushell Collibee ...	1756	
Will. Chapman	1757	
Hen. Atwood	1758	
Frac. Hales	1759	
Thos. Atwood	1760	
John Champan	1761	
Francis Hales	1762	
Saml. Bush	1763	
John Horton	1764	
Edward Bushell Collibee ...	1765	
Hon. Wright	1766	
Will. Chapman	1767	

G. Biggs	1768	
Thos. Atwood	1769	
John Chapman	1770	
John Horton	1771	
Walter Wiltshire	1772	
Frans. Bennett	1773	
Phil. Ditcher	1774	
Edward Bushell Collibee ...	1775	
Hon. Wright	1776	
John Chapman	1777	
Simon Crook	1778	
John Chapman	1779	
Walter Wiltshire	1780	
Frans. Bennett	1781	
Leonard Coward	1782	
James Leake	1783	
Wm. Street	1784	
Edward Bushell Collibee ...	1785	
William Anderdon	1786	
Leonard Coward	1787	
Jac. Smith	1788	
Leonard Coward	1789	
John Horton	1790	
Walter Wiltshire	1791	
A. Moysey	1792	
H. Harington	1793	
Wm. Anderdon	1794	
J. Symons	1795	
J. Palmer	1796	
Chas. Phillott	1797	
Geo. Chapman	1798	
Jn. Horton	1799	
(Thus far Warner).		
H. Atwood	1800	
Wm. Watson	1801	
H. Parry	1802	
J. Symons	1803	
Wm. Anderdon	1804	
Chas. Phillott	1805	
Jno. Horton	1806	
H. Atwood	1807	
Henry Parry	1808	
J. Palmer	1809	
Ar. Moysey	1810	
J. Phillott	1811	
Chas. Crooke	1812	
Wm. Anderdon	1813	
Ch. T. Phillott	1814	
M. Nichols	1815	
Edmd. Anderdon	1816	
G. H. Tugwell	1817	
J. Kitson	1818	
Geo. Edwd. Allen	1819	
J. Wiltshire	1820	
Wm. Clarke	1821	
Chas. Crooke	1822	
Chas. Phillott	1823	
Emd. Anderdon	1824	
Geo. Edw. Allen	1825	
E. Pickwick	1826	

G. H. Tugwell	...	... 1827	Geo. Kitson ...	...	... 1831
W. Tudor ...	...	... 1828	William Clark	...	... 1832
J. H. Spry ...	...	... 1829	J. Philott ...	...	... 1833
J. F. Davis ...	...	... 1830	George Norman	...	...1834-5

AFTER THE ACT.

W. T. Blair (Jan. 1st)	... 1836	Thomas Barter	...	... 1862
W. T. Blair (Nov. 9th)	... 1836	Jerom Murch	...	1863-4
L. Barrow	... 1837	George Moger	...	1865
Henry Gordon ...	... 1838	W. J. Thompson	...	... 1866
Richard Strutth. Cruttwell	... 1839	Edw. W. Slack }		
William Hunt	... 1840	William Hunt }	...	... 1867
George Norman	... 1841	Thomas Jolly ...	...	... 1868
John Edridge	... 1842	Thomas Washbourne Gibbs...		1869
George Moger	... 1843	John Hulbert ...	...	1870-1
Henry Gordon ...	... 1844	R. S. Blaine ...	...	1872
S. Batchellor	... 1845	William Hunt	...	... 1873
Aug. Geo. Barrette ...	... 1846	J. A. Paynter ...	...	1874-5
William Hunt ...	... 1847	Jerom Murch ...	...	1876-7
William Sutcliffe ...	... 1848	James Chaffin ...		1878-9-80
Fred Dowding ...	1849-50	John S. Bartrum	...	... 1881
William Long ...	.. 1851	Handel Cossham	...	... 1882
F. T. Allen	... 1852	Thomas Wilton	...	... 1883
T. Gill	... 1853	Handel Cossham	...	... 1884
William Hunt... ...	... 1854	Anthony Hammond	...	... 1885
William Bush	... 1855	Jerom Murch ...	...	... 1886
R. Cook	... 1856	Anthony Hammond ...	...	... 1887
Randle Wilbraham Falconer.		H. W. Freeman	...	... 1888
M.D.	1857-8	John S. Bartrum	...	... 1889
Thos. Barrett, M.D. ...	... 1859	Jerom Murch ...	...	... 1890
Thomas Jolly	... 1860	John S. Turner	...	... 1891
Thomas Fuller... ...	... 1861	Jerom Murch ...	...	... 1892

CHAPTER VI.

SIR JOHN HARINGTON AND BISHOP MONTAGUE.

My sketch of William Sherston, first Mayor of Bath under the Charter of Elizabeth, introduced us to her Majesty's reign. It brought us to a period remarkable for the eminent men it produced: statesmen, warriors, divines, scholars, poets, dramatists, discoverers and philosophers. Although few were intimately connected with the Court, they all, in various ways, gave a splendour to the reign and struck a light that gradually pervaded the chief towns of England. Much need of that light was there in Bath; the dissolution of the monastery had sent its learned men adrift; the citizens saw their principal church roofless and desolate; and the few visitors who came for society or the springs found scanty attractions with abundant discomfort. Such was the state of things when Harington and Montague came on the scene; one was a country squire living at Kelston, the other the Bishop of the Diocese. The work in connection with which they are now introduced was the restoration of the Abbey Church, a work foremost among those for regaining the reputation of the city.

The Haringtons belonged to an ancient family in Cumberland. They derived their name from Haverington in that county, and suffered much in the wars of the Roses. One of them was the first Lord Harington, of Exton; another was grandfather of the author of *Oceana*. The father of the subject of this sketch was in the service of the Lord High Admiral Seymour, and restored the fortunes of his branch of the family by marrying Ethelreda, the natural daughter of Henry VIII. To this lady his Majesty granted, on the dissolution of monasteries, the forfeitures of several Somérset-shire manors, Kelston being one. Her husband had probably the literary tastes then growing among men of his station in life, which qualified him to be somewhat of a preceptor and companion to the Princess Elizabeth. A time came when he and his wife had to attend upon her in prison, for which and their general loyalty, she showed her gratitude after she ascended the throne by becoming godmother to their son, taking, afterwards, an interest in his education, and, though quick to rebuke him when he failed to please her, giving him, as long as she lived various proofs of regard.

On succeeding to the Kelston estate, Harington became interested in Bath. Among his friends was Dr. Montague, the Bishop of Bath and Wells, who is said to have been indebted to him for a previous preferment—the mastership of Sidney Sussex College, Cambridge. This appointment, or much interest with regard to it, was vested in Lady Sidney, an aunt of Harington. There is a story that the two friends, being caught in a shower near the Abbey, the layman advised the Bishop to take shelter in the church, and conducted him to the north aisle, which, being entirely roofless, afforded no protection. "Why, we are still in the rain," said the Bishop, "there is no roof to your church." "The more is the pity," answered his shrewd companion, "and the more need for your lordship's munificence" A quaint memorandum by Harington himself gives a more exact idea of what passed, while it indicates the practical, as well as poetical mind so obvious in his various works. I am indebted for the orthography to *Nugæ Antiquæ,* and for much information on the suhject to Britten's *History and Antiquities of the Abbey Church.* "Having long waitede for our goode Bishoppe to visit his poor sheepe and rotten folde, I rubbede my braines for suche rustic Latin as might remaine therein, and was bent to meete him at the place of visitation; and being well encouraged to speak roundelye of his service, to helpe us on to restoringe our churche to its olde state, or rather to a new state of bewtie. After all was ended and his benedictions given, I began with my own *Sis Nobiscum Domine*, and started up in the Churche isle with my Poetrie or rather Historie, for I sought not to give it the flower but looked for the goode fruit that might come of my spare sowing."

What the "goode fruit" was will be seen when we come to Bishop Montague. A few incidents in Harington's life may be here mentioned. He was educated at Cambridge, his tutor being Dr. John Still, afterwards Bishop of Bath and Wells, of whose influence on his mind he writes very gratefully. From Cambridge he went to study law at Lincoln's Inn, but soon found the atmosphere of the Court more to his taste. The Queen then lived much at Hatfield, where he enjoyed the companionship of her clever ladies, for whose amusement he translated the twenty-eighth book of Arisosto's *Orlando Furioso*—not the most seemly portion of that attractive book. Unluckily for Harington, his work fell into the Queen's hands, who blamed him for corrupting the morals of her women, and is said to have banished him to Kelston till he should have translated the whole folio. This was about the year 1590; the first edition of the work so completed was published in 1591. There is a copy of this edition in the Cambridge University library. It had been presented to the author's mother-in-law, Lady Rogers. At the end is a list, in his own handwriting, of all his poems on domestic occasions. He had then been married eight years. Lady Rogers lived at Cannington, in Somersetshire. Of the

Kelston household little is known except that the eldest son became a Cromwellite. The father's exuberant spirits found vent everywhere, at home and abroad, in a constant flow of epigrams, too seldom adapted to correct tastes. It was not until comparatively late in life that he cared for political employment, although even when he was at Cambridge the Queen sent him a copy of one of her speeches to Parliament, requesting him to " ponder well what she had said."

At the same period her great Minister, Lord Burleigh, with whom Harington's family were friendly, wrote a letter to him (given in *Nugæ Antiquæ*) which might have turned his thoughts to statesmanship. But being popular as an author, full of humour, and yet showing much practical sagacity, he preferred writing on his favourite subjects, and thus amusing both the public and himself. At length, after gravely offending the Queen by an inuendo in one of his books against the Earl of Leicester, and again receiving her forgiveness, he was sent with the Earl of Essex to Ireland on an ill-fated expedition as commander of horse. On this occasion he was knighted by Essex, another cause of offence to Elizabeth, who required that such honours should only be conferred by herself. Great disasters occurred in Ireland, compelling both Essex and Harington to return in haste and endeavour to make their peace with the Queen. But this time her anger was unappeasable. When her godson knelt before her she caught him by the girdle, swearing her usual oath that he and the fool Essex were too much for her, and bidding the unhappy knight "go quickly about his business." He therefore went back to Kelston, glad to be at home once more, resolved to "run no more risk of shipwreck on the Essex coast," and writing, " if I go into such troubles again I deserve the gallows for a meddling fool." Readers of Sir Walter

Scott's *Kenilworth* may remember that it contains frequent references to the Queen's "witty godson" as one who had experienced both the smiles and frowns which he describes. The novelist quotes a passage from *Nugæ Antiquæ* illustrative of his own account of the variable treatment of Leicester : " Her mind was oft time like the gentle air that cometh from the western point in a summer's morn—'twas sweet and refreshing for all around her ; her speech did so win all affections. And again she could put forth such alterations when obedience was lacking as left no doubt *whose* daughter she was. When she smiled it was a pure sunshine that every one did choose to bask in, if they could, but soon came a storm from a sudden gathering of clouds, and the thunder fell in a wondrous manner on all sides." Notwithstanding Harington's disgust with political life, a time came when office would have been a great boon to him. The Queen had died ; his means had been greatly reduced by extravagant habits and costly litigations. So he appealed to James I., who favoured him, but the application eventually failed. His mind had even turned again to Ireland, whose people he thought he understood, and of whose wants he was believed to have larger and more generous views than those of most of his contemporaries. But it was too late ; his health gave way and he died at Kelston, aged 51, leaving his wife and seven children.

That Sir John Harington was one of the most remarkable men of his time appears from the copious memoir of him in the *National Biography*. It includes an account of his numerous literary works, also references to books, such as Fuller's *Worthies of Somerset,* and Wood's *Athenæ Oxon,* treating of his life and character. Since I began this sketch I have been able to consult the Rev. J. J. Poynton's *Memoranda, Historical and Genealogical,* relating chiefly to members of the Harington family of later times, of whom, especially Dr. Henry Harington, I shall have to write later. Mr. Poynton's work, however, contains a copy of a curious deed in the Record Office showing the pugnacious side of Sir John's character, and giving "a fair example of how family quarrels were conducted in 1602." Lady Rogers, his wife's mother, had died in Bath; he, therefore, went immediately to Cannington to take possession of certain effects bequeathed to him; his brother-in-law disputed the claim, prohibited his entrance, and barricaded the house. On trying to force his way, "Sir John was seized by five or six men and locked in a dark room for nine hours." Then came Star Chamber proceedings against Mr. Rogers, one of those costly litigations from which Harington's fortune suffered so severely.

Before we proceed to Bishop Montague's claim to remembrance we may notice what others did in the matter of the Abbey Church. It was at the end of the fifteenth century that Dr. Oliver King, eminent both as statesman and divine, became Bishop of Bath and Wells, and being greatly distressed at the ruinous state of the old edifice, began to rebuild it. But he only lived a few years; the work proceeded slowly for want of funds notwithstanding his own munificence, and all he could do was to leave injunctions with the head of the Convent, Prior Birde, to carry out his design. Prior Birde also did what he could; he lessened the expenditure of the Convent in order that the money might be devoted to the church, and "he himself," says Wood, "expended so much of his own means that he died poor." Then followed another Prior equally zealous and generous; but the clouds were gathering for the great national tempest, the piety which had raised so many splendid ecclesiastical buildings was fading away, and State aid could no longer be obtained. To so low

D

an ebb had public feeling in the matter fallen that, though on the dissolution of the Bath Monastery the Commissioners offered to sell the church to the city for 500 marks, the offer was refused. Harington, of course, was ready with an epigram on the dignitaries in whose successive reigns the work languished : Bishop King, Cardinal Adrian, Cardinal Wolsey, Bishop Clark, and Bishop Knight :—

> "O Church ! I wail thy woful plight,
>   Whom King nor Card'nall, Clerke nor Knight,
>   Have yet restored to ancient right."

The poet, however, does justice to one good man—Thomas Bellott, steward, and afterwards executor, to Lord Burleigh, who contributed largely towards finishing a transept. After showing how the funds raised under the Queen's brief had been misappropriated, he writes, " And thus the church lies still, like the poore traveller spoiled and wounded by thieves. The Priest goes by, the Levites go by, but doe nothing : only a good Samaritan, honest Mr. Billet (worthy to be billetted in the New Jerusalem) hath pow'rd some oyle in the wounds and maintained it in life."

But then came the squire and the bishop. The latter responded to his friend's appeal by giving £1,000, and under-taking to do certain works. Warner gives the names of various benefactors, among whom were Sir Henry Montague, brother of the bishop, and then Lord Chief Justice, who was at the charge of the great west doors with their elaborate carving. The vestry was built by Sir Nicholas Slattern, of London ; additional donors being the Earls of Rutland, Suffolk, Hartford, Worcester, Northampton, and Shrewsbury ; Lady Hunsden, Lady Dorset, and Lady Boothe ; many trades-men, esquires, knights, and baronets, several of the Sherston family, *cum multis aliis.* Among the various friends to whom Harington wrote was Mr. Sutton, the wealthy founder of the Charter House School. The characteristic letter to him in *Nugœ Antiquœ* refers first to a report (for which the writer apologises) that Sutton intended to leave his money to Prince Charles, and then endeavours to persuade him to give some of it to the Abbey Church. "I would be glad to make you amends now by any endevor of mine. Only my old friend don't forget to be a benefactor to Bath Church in your life time, for alms in one's life is like light borne before one, whereas alms after death is like a candle carried behind one. You promised to see the church before this ; whensoever you come, my lodgings shall be at your commandmente ; the baths would strengthen your sinews, the alms would comfort your soul. The tower, the quire and two isles are all-ready finished by Mr. Billett, executor to the worthie Lord Treasurer Burleigh, and the walls are up ready for covering. The lead is promised by our bountifull Bishop, Dr. Montague, timber is promised by the Earl of Shrewsbury, the Earl of Hartford, the Lord Say, Mr. Hopton and others.

Of "the bountifull Bishop" Bath was naturally proud. The son of Sir E. Montague, he was born in 1568, his family being descended from the Montacutes, Earls of Salisbury. In 1593 he became master of Sidney Sussex College, Cambridge, as already mentioned, of which in the phraseology of Fuller, he was the Nursing-Father. In 1604 he was made Dean of Worcester by King James, "who," says the same author, did "*ken a man of merrit* as well as any Prince in Christendome." In 1608 he was advanced to the See of Bath and Wells, and in 1616 to that of Winchester. There he died at the end of two years. By his particular desire, he was buried in the Abbey Church at Bath, where a stately monument was erected by his four brothers, with a long Latin inscription. The monument was restored about twelve years ago at the expense of the late Mrs. Elliott, with the assistance of her friend, Mr. John Stone, Town Clerk of Bath. Bishop Montague was known in the literary world as the translator of the works of James I. into Latin. A copy, splendidly bound in velvet and gold, was given to the University of Cambridge by the King. In the reigns of Elizabeth and James, the diocese of Bath and Wells drew large revenues from the lead mines at Mendip. "Of this abundant crop," says Fuller, "Bishop Still is said to have had the harvest, Bishop Montague the gleanings and Bishop Lake the stubble; yet considerable was the profit to him and successors." In the history of Somersetshire few subjects are more interesting than that of the Mendip Lead Mines, and perhaps no work contains so much information respecting them as is scattered through the volumes of the Somersetshire Archæological Society. In vol. viii. there is a remarkably learned paper by Mr. James Yates on the "Mining Operations of the Romans in Britain," with an account of the ."Pigs" and their Roman inscriptions now in various English museums, lead being much used in those days, especially for coffins. The Rev. Prebendary Scarth, writing later of the Mendips, vol. xix., states, "In the time of Edward IV. these mines are said to have furnished employment to a great population of miners, the immense deposits of slags and slimes indicating the extent of the workings." Another antiquary, the Rev. W. A. Jones, of Taunton, shows, vol. xv., how the Bishop of the Diocese was appointed with others by the King, one of "The Four Lords Royal of Mendip," to adjudicate on a disputed question; how, on the summons of a special Commissioner, all the Commoners of the district to the number of 10,000, assembled before the "Lords Royal" "upon a place of Lord Bath's, called the Forge," and how the said judges after a full hearing of the case put their seals to a satisfactory settlement. And thus in due time do things apparently unconnected work together; the wonderful operations of Nature thousands of years ago produce the Mendip lead mines, and the revenues from the Mendip lead mines become in the sixteenth century a chief factor in the restoration of Bath Abbey Church.*

* Mr. Poynton informs me that the statement of various biographers, which I have adopted in page 45, that Lady Sidney was aunt to Sir John Harington is doubtful. The Sidney connection was with the Haringtons of Eston. The foundress of Sidney Sussex College was Lady Frances Sidney, Countess of Sussex, daughter of Sir W. Sidney, knighted at Flodden and aunt to Sir Philip Sidney. She left £5,000 to found the college.

From the same obliging writer I learn an incident illustrative of Sir John Harington's versatility, not mentioned, I believe, by his biographers, but referred to in a *Tract on the State of Ireland,* 1605, edited 1879 by the Rev. W. Macray, one of the Librarians of the Bodleian. It is that Sir John made overtures, when his fortune was low, to get appointed, *per saltum*, Archbishop of Dublin. The extravagant idea may have been prompted by a family tradition that an ancestor, Sir James Harington, a military knight in early life, had become successively Rector of Badsworth and Dean of York, preceding Cardinal Wolsey in that Deanery.

CHAPTER VII

WILLIAM PRYNNE.

Many years have passed since I collected materials for a paper on William Prynne. It was read before a meeting of the Bath Literary and Philosophical Association, and published at their request. In order to maintain the historical sequence of these sketches, I now reproduce the substance of it with some alterations and additions. Prynne was not only a Bath Celebrity; he was a very prominent figure in the national affairs of the period, and is even now regarded as a high constitutional authority.

He was able to trace his ancestry through four or five hundred years. The earliest progenitors on record lived in Shropshire somewhere near the Wenlock Ridge, which is broken by grassy hillocks, then called preens. There, in the twelfth century, dwelt a family who were owners of the surrounding country and hence acquired the name of their land, which became first Prin, afterwards Prynne. From Shropshire some of them migrated, early in the sixteenth century, to Bristol, two brothers gaining much repute as opulent merchants ; one served as sheriff in 1536, the other in 1549. Each was the father of sons still more distinguished, to whose descendants rank and fortune came in large measure ; the elder daughter of one of them, Sir Gilbert Prynne, married the great grandson of the Lord Protector Somerset, the younger Sir George Hastings, who was related to the Earl of Huntingdon.

A descendant of Sheriff Edward Prynne was an agriculturist living at Aust, near Bristol. He pastured his flocks on Clifton and Durdham Downs, long before the present streets, crescents, and terraces were built. His name was Erasmus; he was succeeded at Aust by his son Thomas, the father of the subject of the present sketch. Thomas, preferring a larger and better farm at Swainswick, removed thither, and was appointed general manager of the estate, of which his farm was a principal feature, belonging to Oriel College, Oxford. I gain much of the information in this sketch from a biographical *Fragment Relating to William Prynne*, edited by Mr. Bruce for the Camden Society. Many interesting particulars of the family and the parish associated with their name are also given in Mr. R. E. M. Peach's recent valuable work *The Annals of Swainswick*.

Thomas Prynne's settlement at Swainswick brought him into intimacy with the substantial Bath burgess, William Sherston, Mayor and member of Parliament, whose daughter Marie he married. Their first son and second child was born at Swainswick in 1600, and named William, after his grandfather, with whom in early life he spent much of his time; while at King Edward's School he was trained for the higher education of Oriel. All that we know of his parents suggests that to their opinions and character much of the work he did and the eminence he attained were due. The home of his childhood appears to have been suited to the development of an earnest, serious spirit. The son would naturally have his early sympathies ranged on the Puritan side by the national events discussed in the family circles at Swainswick and Bath. Among the earliest he could remember would be the Gunpowder plot, his grandfather having been in Parliament when it occurred and one of the intended victims, one also of the House who condemned the conspirators. Other events dwelt upon at the time would be the Spanish Armada, the new translation of the Scriptures and the death of Prince Henry, to whom the Puritans had fondly looked as their avowed protector. All these would be topics of conversation in the Prynne and Sherston households ; they would be warmly discussed by the Mayor's constituents, and influence the formation of his grandson's mind.

Prynne went to Oxford in 1616. The connection of his father with Oriel College probably caused his aptitude for scholarship to be encouraged. At that time Oxford was chiefly Puritan ; the contest between the two parties in the Church had, however, commenced. Laud had become a favourite of James I., and obtained, as one of his first steps on the State ladder, an appointment for the better government of the University. This signified that the study of the Fathers, Council and Schoolmen was to be substituted for systems of Theology founded upon the Scriptures. Although Prynne was one of the students who came under the operation of the new mandate, it may be doubted whether in his time it was fully carried out. The Vice-Chancellor, who was also Dean of Christchurch, and the two Professors of Divinity were against it, yielding a mere perfunctory obedience to the royal will. Encouraged by them, Prynne's course of study resulted in deeper attachment to the religious teachings of his home, and a clearer insight into the objects of Laud. There was much in the circumstances of time and place to make the aspiring churchman an object of his adverse criticism, though it was after his residence at Oxford that Laud became Bishop of Bath and Wells, and while filling that office was selected to crown Charles I. But the subsequent translations to London and Canterbury, the iniquitous proceedings of the Star Chamber, and the general course of ecclesiastical events gave the names and doings of the two men connected prominence, till in the changes of political life Laud caused Prynne to be brought before one tribunal and cruelly punished, and Prynne was the chief manager of the trial of Laud, a trial which ended in a terrible death at another.

Prynne lost his father in 1620, four years after he first went to Oxford. He then took his Bachelor's degree and quitted the University with some idea of succeeding to the management of the Oriel College estate, as his father had left him a share of the lease of the farm and property connected with it. His decision, however, was for the Bar, to which he was called at Lincoln's Inn, where, though the legal training which led to so much eminence in after life must have been good, we chiefly hear of his theological sympathies. His Inn of Court was that of Sir Thomas More and Lord Ellesmere ; it had had its own preacher since 1581, and could boast of a succession of Puritan divines of great reputation, men of larger and more liberal minds than those of their brethren generally. Donne the poet held the office at the time of Prynne's admission. Some of his most eloquent sermons were preached in the new chapel, one especially at the opening. It was Donne who laid the first stone of the new building, and urged his friends to spare no cost in adorning it. Accordingly, while a few of the more wealthy and distinguished gave entire windows of stained glass, seventy-five of the fellows, among whom was Prynne, contributed emblazonments of their coats of arms. On the removal of Donne to the Deanery of St. Paul's he was succeeded by Dr. Preston, afterwards master of Emanuel College, another eminent Puritan, and, like Donne, an intimate friend of Prynne. But fond as the Swainswick student was of controversial divinity, such was his repute for legal learning that he was chosen at an unusually early age first reader and then bencher of his Inn. Among those who pursued their studies at the same time and place were Noy, Glyn, Sherfield, Hakewill, Lenthal, St. John, and Wilbraham, men who, with widely different opinions, had much interest in the troubles of the succeeding reigns. While on the one hand party ties would be strengthened by congenial professional companionships, on the other the friendship of Donne and Preston, and the examples of Milton and Andrew Marvell, would encourage higher and larger tastes. Still, it must have been at Lincoln's Inn that the foundation was laid of that marvellous constitutional knowledge which is manifest in Prynne's later works, giving him a reputation more solid and lasting than any he acquired in other ways.

At the time at which we are now arrived Prynne was 25 years of age. He was in practice as a barrister with good prospects, but his chief vocation even now was authorship. Mr. Bruce, in *The Fragment*, from which I have quoted, gives a list of 196 books written by him. It extends over three momentous periods of English history, from 1627 to 1670, another book appearing 20 years after his death. The first was *The Perpetuitie of a Regenerate Man's Estate ;* the next *The Unloveliness of Love Lockes,* proving the wearing or nourishing of a Love Locke to be altogether unseemly and unlawful unto Christians. Imagine a young barrister gravely writing a quarto volume against such a fashion! It suggests the question—were the wives and daughters of the Cavaliers the only ladies he lectured, or were delinquents among the fair Puritans, and, if so, did they follow his advice ? Then came, successively, treatises against *Pledging of Healths*, against *Arminianism in the Church of England*, against *The Popish Bowing at the name of Jesus*. All these books abound in strong reflections on the Government, and especially on the ecclesiastical party of which Laud was the head. But the author was not prosecuted until he published, in 1633, his *Histrio Mastrix : The Player's Scourge or Actor's Tragedie*, an enormous quarto of a thousand pages, decrying not only plays, music and dancing, but maypoles, bonfires, hunting, and public festivals of all kinds. His language, even for those times, was extremely coarse and bitter. Play houses he calls "Satan's chapels," playgoers "little better than incarnate devils," play actors the vilest names in the Billinsgate vocabulary. Any facts he mentions lose their force in consequence of the personal vituperation with which they were connected. Much of it being applied to kings and queens, was supposed to refer to the Royal Family of England. Henrietta, wife of Charles I., had a strong liking for the drama, and sometimes acted on a private stage. This was alleged to be in the author's mind when he denounced Nero as worthy of death for enjoying the same amusement. Such language was eagerly caught hold of by Laud, who had long wanted some tangible ground for prosecution, who had the ear of the king in any matter requiring Royal authority, and who was able to carry out his purpose relentlessly in the Star Chamber, the most terrible court ever known in England.

Prynne's prolific authorship formed a pleasant link of his connection with Bath. Even so long ago as his time there was a library in the Abbey Church to which presents of his books were sent, some by himself alone, others jointly with his London publisher, Mr. Michael Sparke. There they are now in good condition, after the lapse of two hundred years. A record of these and other interesting benefactions may be seen in a vellum catalogue in the library. It contains the titles of about thirty volumes of Prynne's works, a few consisting of several smaller ones bound together. The first he gave was the first he published, *The Perpetuitie of a*

Regenerate Man's Estate, a quarto of the date of 1627. There is also the celebrated *Canterburies Doome*, a history of the trial of Archbishop Laud, which he was requested to write by the House of Commons. Most valuable of all are three folio volumes of his edition of *Sir Robert Cotton's Records*, a work which not many years ago was sold at an auction in London for the large sum of £164. It is hard to believe that the man who thus added to the permanent literature of England, also plunged into such fierce polemical contests and thereby brought upon himself sufferings so terrible. What a contrast is the earnest student of constitutional history, working days and nights in the solitude of his study, to the mutilated convict returning from the pillory amid shouting multitudes, and composing those memorable lines :—

"My face for ever scarred with burning brands by Laud,
Exulting I return glad sacrifice to God."

These lines referred to the conclusion of his second great trial. There was one previously in which he was charged with having published a libel on Queen Henrietta, in his book *Histrio Mastrix, the Player's Scourge or Actor's Tragedie*. No one expected, even then, that the Star Chamber would deal leniently with him, his twenty-three judges with Archbishop Laud and the Lord Treasurer at their head were too well known. Their sentence for this offence was that Prynne be fined £3,000, degraded from the Bar, expelled from Oxford and Lincoln's Inn, stand in the pillory both at Westminster and Cheapside, have an ear cut off at each place, and see his book burnt by the common hangman.

If there were no hope for him at the time of the first trial, what must have been the eneral feeling when the second took place? During the three following years he employed himself incessantly in writing and publishing bitter attacks on the Government, especially on Laud. At first milder treatment was tried by his judges ; for a letter to the Archbishop written in the Fleet and exposing the horrors of the Star Chamber, he was simply reprimanded and ordered back to prison. But Prynne was not now in a mood to be affected by leniency, though with strange inconsistency he had in his confinement presented a petition asking for it ; even professing " unfeigned sorrow for passages which had fallen inconsiderately from his pen." But his *cacoethes scribendi* impelled him to fresh attacks. Special offence was given by his *News from Ipswich ;* for this the Star Chamber inflicted another fine, this time £5,000, and sentenced him to lose the remainder of his ears in the pillory, to be branded on both cheeks with the letters S.L. (Schismatic libeller), and to be perpetually imprisoned in Carnarvon Castle. It was on his return to the Tower after the execution of the sentence, that he wrote in Latin the exulting lines, a translation of which has been quoted.

In the historical fragment edited by Mr. Bruce, there is a touching account of the scene at the scaffold. It shows how two other offenders, Bastwicke and Burton, stood on the pillory with Prynne, and how as they walked to it the people strewed herbs and flowers before them. "The hangman," says the writer, " burnt Prin in both the cheekes, and because hee burnt one cheeke with a letter the wrong waye hee burnt that again, a surgeon clapping on a plaister to take out the fire." From the Tower Prynne was taken to Carnarvon Castle, but did not remain there long in consequence chiefly of the number of visitors admitted to see him. Removal was then ordered to Mount Orgueil Castle in the island of Jersey, of which Sir Philip Carteret, a devoted Royalist, was Governor, but he also was too indulgent to satisfy the Government. Although obeying orders so far as to exclude visitors, both he and the ladies of his family did all in their power to soften the rigours of confinement. Seeing that their prisoner was a scholar and a gentleman they cheered him with their society and allowed him other relaxations suited to his case. The stern Puritan who had declaimed on the "unloveliness of love-locks," preferred nevertheless, to spend the evenings of three long years in the drawing-room of the castle, rather than hear the waves dash against the walls of his solitary cell. Nor was the kindness lost upon him ; a time came when Sir Philip Carteret was bitterly attacked by a portion of the Puritan party, then in power, and Prynne, at the risk of forfeiting his popularity, successfully defended him. "I should have shown myself," he said, "a monster of ingratitude if I had not contributed my best assistance to support him against the aspersions of his inveterate, backbiting enemies, who endeavoured to oust him from his offices only that they might step into them."

Although Prynne had been a prisoner so long, he was not released from Jersey Castle by the expiration of his term. During his confinement political events of great magnitude had followed in rapid succession, and at length culminated in others entirely altering the complexion of public affairs. England having been twelve years without a Parliament, the king could no longer forego calling one, but as soon as it met, the conduct of Charles and his Ministers was attacked with a vehemence which caused its speedy dissolution. Another was elected, the Long Parliament, which proved still more intractable. "The meeting of this," says Macaulay, "was one of the great eras in the history of the civilised world. Whatever of political freedom exists either in Europe or America has sprung directly or indirectly from those institutions which it either secured or reformed." One of its first acts was to release from prison the victims of the Star Chamber. The sentences were declared illegal and the judges ordered to make reparation. Especial interest was shown by the multitude in the deliverance of Prynne, Bastwicke, and Burton. When they landed in England they were received with the strongest demonstrations of joy. On their approach to any town large masses of people crowded to welcome them, bringing liberal presents to defray all their charges. As they drew near London the excitement increased. Flowers were strewed in their paths; trees were planted by the roadside; and the shouts which rent the air were mingled with invectives against their persecutors. The restored captives soon proved that they had neither forgotten nor forgiven the wrongs they had endured. Prynne was elected member for Newport in Cornwall, and became as prominent by his speeches in Parliament as by his books. While others pushed forward the impeachment of Stafford, he was chief manager of the trial of Laud. Human nature, however, was not then exalted by what he did. That retribution should at length come to Laud was to be expected. That one who had been so arbitrary, cruel, and unjust should be severely punished was not surprising. Nor the fine of £20,000 for obtaining canons from Convocation, stretching the King's Prerogative, and even the execrations of the multitude who followed him to the Tower. Still it was sad to see his old enemy foremost in every petty act of annoyance; searching the wardrobes of Lambeth Palace, emptying the primate's pockets for proofs against him, carrying away his diary, his little book of private devotion, and the bundles of papers he had prepared for his defence. For though the temper of the times as well as Laud's political offences may be urged in extenuation of Prynne's animosity, though he had various qualities which command our admiration, it is evident that now, as at other times, true greatness was not one of them; he forgot all the Christian precepts he urged in his own letter to Laud when he himself wanted forbearance; he lost the high place in history which would otherwise have been undoubtedly accorded to him.

Terrible indeed were the reverses of the Archbishop. First the overthrow of all his hopes of ecclesiastical ascendency. News came from Scotland that the Liturgy was rejected, and that the Covenanters were triumphant. Archy Armstrong, the King's fool, meeting Laud and relying on the privilege of his office, asked, "Whea's fule now?" In happier times the taunt would only have been laughed at; now, the poor jester's motley coat was pulled over his ears, and himself banished from the Court. Then came the Oxford retribution; he who caused the expulsion of Prynne from the University, who had feasted a royal party at Christ Church, and who had even ordered comedies for their amusement, had to resign the Chancellorship. He was even sent to the Tower, and was denied, with unjustifiable severity, even coals and wood in the depth of winter. Each of the three weary years of his confinement saw the quarrel between the king and the Parliament become fiercer and more desperate. Finally, he was brought to trial, Prynne acting as solicitor to the House of Commons, and, after much delay by the Peers before whom he was tried, condemned to death. It was now his turn to implore for mercy, but all he could obtain was an alteration of the sentence from hanging to beheading.

And what was Prynne's own fate in the immediate future? Not to find his path strewn with roses and leading to power in high places. No doubt his sufferings and his ability caused what he still wrote in his books to be read eagerly, and what he often said in Parliament to have some weight. But the leaders of his party dreaded his imprudence too much to give him high office, and contended themselves with appointing him a visitor of the University of Oxford, one of a body of fourteen lawyers and ten divines to rectify alleged evils. This employment was probably intended to divert his mind from the great struggle then impending between the Presbyterian and Independent sections of the Puritan party, the former being willing to make terms with the king; the latter intent on carrying out a "root and branch policy." Prynne had lately become in favour of a compromise. He made a violent speech in Parliament supporting it, but so powerful were his opponents that he was forbidden, two days afterwards, to enter the House. Again, however, he resumed his pen, and sent forth his defiance in pamphlet after pamphlet, each more vituperative than the last. In one, his attacks on the great leader of the Independents, Oliver Cromwell, were so fierce that he was a third time committed to prison, the one now allotted to him being Dunster Castle. Here he was kept between two and three years, as we learn from his book addressed *to Mr. John Bradshaw and his associates at Whitehall, stiling themselves the Council of State.* Cromwell, though now rarely yielding to any argument from books, appears to have been impressed with the remonstrance of Prynne on the violation of Magna Charta in his case, and ordered him to be set free.

The joy with which he regained his liberty can be easily imagined. It is pleasant to think of him on his way back to London stopping at sunny Swainswick, and receiving the greetings of his friends at Bath. But there was no "second spring" for him on his return to the battle-field of London

E

politics; the autumn of his life had come and, with it, changes, which to most men have been more sad than any in nature. He was an instance of the transition, not uncommon in violent and impulsive men, from one set of political opinions in early life to another, the very opposite, in declining age. No doubt he would have pleaded, he did plead in answer to charges of apostasy, that times had changed and he was justified in changing with them. This was his defence in answer to the pamphlet of an opponent, *Prynne against Prynne*. Other books which he published at this time indicate the course his mind was taking. Therefore, when in 1639 he resumed his place in the House of Commons no one wondered that he was intent on restoring Charles II. Yet it was strange to see the grandson of William Sherston soliciting the electors of Bath to support him in his altered character. It should be remembered, however, what a small body they were—the old close Corporation, and how they had veered backward and forward many a year. They sent him to what was called the healing Parliament, and on the Restoration his services to the Royalists were rewarded by his appointment as Chief Keeper of the Public Records, an office for which he was no doubt eminently fitted, with a salary of £500. In 1661 he was again elected for Bath, and showed his gratitude to his constituents by vehemently opposing a bill for reforming Corporations. So offensive was his opposition that, two days after his speech, he was compelled to ask pardon of the House in order to avoid another imprisonment.

It was towards the close of life that Prynne resumed most closely his connexion with Bath. I have not mentioned his first Recordership to which he was appointed in 1647, as successor to Serjeant Hyde. He then received eighteen votes of the Corporation against four given to Mr. John Harington, of Kelston, but was compelled to vacate the office on his imprisonment. His second appointment was while he sat as member for the city. The records at the Guildhall contain many proofs of his interest in civic proceedings. On one occasion two members of the Corporation went to London to see him in order to obtain the summer assize at Bath. On another he was the medium of one of those presents to the king which some towns were induced to offer—in this instance £100. On another his abilities and influence were employed to promote a scheme for making the Bath river navigable to Bristol.

His local ties and sympathies are nowhere more manifest than in his will made in 1669. It brings us back to the associations of early years and the claims of kindred. I have mentioned his presents of books to the Abbey Library ; others went to Oriel College ; the MSS. to Lincoln's Inn. His interest in the lease at Swainswick he gave to his brother and sister. The poor boys and girls of his native parish were remembered by a legacy of £10 for binding them apprentices. Thus in small as in great matters his heart was right, and if the shadows of human imperfection were deep his memory will yet be cherished for his marvellous energy, his constitutional learning and his strict integrity.

CHAPTER VIII.

DR. GUIDOTT AND HIS CONTEMPORARIES.

Dr. Guidott was celebrated as an eminent physician and a voluminous writer of the seventeenth century. One of his books, entitled *A Discourse of Bath and the Hot Waters there*, contains memoirs of eighteen contemporaries. In this sketch I propose to introduce a few of the more renowned of these, glancing first at the local medical literature anterior to their time. In a future sketch my readers will be made acquainted with the more celebrated of their successors practising in Bath in the eighteenth and the earlier part of the nineteenth centuries.

DR. WILLIAM TURNER.

The oldest book on medical practise in Bath, of which there is any knowledge, was written by Dr. William Turner. It is a thin, black-letter folio of great rarity and interest, printed in Germany in 1552, and entitled, *A Booke of the Natures and Properties as well of the Bathes in England as of other Bathes in Germany and Italy*. The author was some years abroad in the service of the Duke of Somerset, to whose son, the Earl of Hereford, he dedicates the book, and by whose influence he obtained Church preferment ; for although in the title-page he only styles himself doctor of physic, he was really also Dean of Wells. An extract from his pages will give an opinion of the quality of the Bath springs three hundred and forty years ago : "Hearing after my return to England that their was a natural bathe within your father's Dukedom, I ceased not till I got license to go to the same bathe, which done I carried certain diseased persons with me, with whom I tarried as long as I could. And afterwards, being Dean of Wells, which place is not far from Bathe, and having liberty to tarry there as long as I list, I tried the same bathes a little further, and found by experience that they were a very excellent tresure, a most precious gift of God."

DR. JOHN JONES.

There is another curious old book of the sixteenth century by Dr. John Jones, a worthy Welshman, with the title, *The Bathes of Bathes Ayde, wonderful and most excellent agaynst very many Sicknesses.* The date is 1572, just twenty years after Dr. Turner's, like which it is in good clear black letter. The author obtained celebrity by practising at stated times in some of the chief cities in England, coming to Bath for what was then, even in Queen Elizabeth's reign, "the season." That he practised in various places would tend to make the waters known, while still further publicity would be given to them by his book, which connected their application with what were then known as the general principles of medical and surgical science. Among the amusing part of the contents is a genealogical table, prefaced by the statement that, according to the chronology of Scripture, Bladud discovered the springs "about the year 3080 of the age of the world, and 890 before the incarnation of Christ, Elisha being then prophet in Israel." Here follow 29 circles representing 29 generations between Adam and Eve and Elisha, all which I mention to give some idea of the fanciful British medical literature of the sixteenth century. In order to make known the true nature of the Bath waters, and to secure good advice to patients needing them in various parts of the country, Dr. Jones shrewdly recommends that church preferment should be given to medical men of the principal towns for the express purpose, naming Salisbury, Worcester, Hereford, Gloucester, Bristol, Exeter, and Wells, the farthest not to be more than a day's journey from the springs. What a joy it would be to the good man if he could arise and see his idea more fully carried out in the Bath Mineral Water Hospital, with its comfortable wards, its admirable management, and its hundred and fifty grateful patients from all parts of the country.

DR. GUIDOTT.

Dr. Turner and Dr. Jones in the sixteenth century prepared the way for Dr. Guidott and his contemporaries in the seventeenth. The Springs were now beginning to regain their ancient Roman fame ; distinguished people once more came to them, and men of fair education competed for practise. Dr. Guidott's book, from which I quote, includes a period of seventy years, treats many subjects connected with the composition and administration of the waters, and is prefaced by an " Epistle Dedicatory " to his " Right Worshipfull and much honoured Friend, Sir Edward Greaves, Baronet," who was also an eminent physician. The author was born in 1638, at Lymington, the eldest son of Francis Guidott, and a great grandson of Signor Antonio Guidotti, a native of Florence, who came to England in the reign of Edward VI., by whom he was knighted. This descendant was sent to school at Dorchester, and in 1656 became a Commoner of Wadham College, Oxford, where he studied anatomy and medicine, and after being admitted M.B. in July, 1666, began to practise " about Oxford." In the following year he removed to Bath, " encouraged," he says, " by Dr. John Maplet, a noted physician of that place, who helped him to attain extensive practise, most of which," says the author of a memoir in the

National Biography "he had lost in 1679 by his impudence, lampooning and libelling." Another writer states that "although his ability brought him considerable practise, his temper and his crusade against quackery brought him many enemies." In a preface to Dr. Jorden's *Discourse of Natural Bathes*, he writes, "Empiricks and juggling Medicasters do so much abound, that 'tis almost as hard a matter now to meet with a regular and accomplished physician as it was in former times for Diogenes to meet with an honest man." That he himself was competent appears in his various books, of which a very long list is given in the *National Biography*, and his skill may be inferred from the fact that for some years he practised in London as well as in Bath, also that he was offered professional chairs at Venice and Leyden, but declined both. The time and place of his death are not mentioned. He was living in Bath as late as 1698.

Dr. Edward Jorden.

One of the chief physicians in Dr. Guidott's list is Dr. Edward Jorden. He was a man of good family, took his degree at Padua, travelled much on the continent, practised some time in London, and eventually settled in Bath. Greatly devoted to chemistry "he was at considerable charges." says his biographer, "about the ordering of Alom, which not succeeding as he expected, he was thereby much prejudiced in his estate. But his life was so answerable to the Port and Dignity of the Faculty he professed that he had the applause of the Learned, the respect of the Rich, the prayers of the Poor, and the Love of all." While living in London he became Licentiate of the College of Physicians, and enjoyed the confidence of James I. One of his intimate friends was the medical baronet already mentioned, Sir Edward Greaves, of All Soul's College, Oxford, Physician in Ordinary to the King, often practising in Bath, and taking the lead among his brethren not more by his rank and wealth than by his professional skill. In wealth he seems to have been surpassed by Dr. Samuel Baue, a native of Cologne, famed for two things besides medical proficiency, his knowledge of languages and his fashionable costume, his patients having the pleasure of seeing him "day by day in purple velvet, and the finest linen much bedecked with lace." His family acquired a good position in Somersetshire, intermarrying with various residents; a Miss Baue became the wife of Dr. Edward Harington.

Dr. John Maplet.

Of higher professional mark was Dr. John Maplet, who we have seen was instrumental in bringing Dr. Guidott to Bath, and whose position, acquirements and character were all remarkable. Educated at Christchurch, Oxford, first Proctor of the University and then Principal of a College, his antecedents favoured his success in the city of the Springs. Previously, however, he accepted invitations to travel on the Continent with two Lord Falklands successively, the elder brother for two years, and then on his death the younger. Returning to England he practised at Bristol in the summer and at Bath in the winter, employing the intervals of his professional work in elegant authorship, notably Latin epistles to distinguished friends. The medical literature of the time owed something to another of Guidott's contemporaries, Dr. Venner. A huge Monument in the Abbey Church sets forth how learned and charitable he was, especially that he wrote a book with the title, *Via Recta ad Vitam Longam.* If he followed his own rules as to diet and regimen he was a good example of their efficacy, for he lived to the age of eighty-five.

VISIT OF PEPYS.

There is a pleasant notice of the Venner and other Monuments in the well-known Diary of Pepys. The gossiping chronicler came for the waters in 1668 and amused himself with jotting down what he saw and heard on a certain Sunday. "Up and walked about the town. Saw a pretty good market-place and many good streets and very fair stone houses. And so to the great church and saw Bishop Montague's tomb. Many brave people came, among others, two men were brought in on litters and set down in the chancel, but I did not know a face. Here a good organ ; but a vain pragmatical fellow preached a ridiculous affected sermon and made me angry, likewise some gentlemen who sat next me and sang well. So home, walking round the walls of the city, which are good and the battlements all whole. After dinner comes Mr. Butt again to see me, so he and I to church where the same idle fellow preached, so I slept most of the sermon. Next day to this church again to see it and look over the monuments, among others Dr. Venner's and Pilling's, also a lady of Sir W. Waller's, he lying with his face broken." Pilling was rector of Bath 35 years ; Lady Waller was daughter of Sir Richard Reynell, and wife of the Parliamentary General. The "good market-place, many good streets and fair stone houses" which attracted the attention of Pepys indicate a continuance of the enlargements and improvements begun in the previous century, and show that Bath was beginning to lose the wretched aspect described by Macaulay on the authority of Wood. There would not have been so many accomplished medical men, some of them making handsome fortunes, if there had not been a corresponding number of well-to-do patients. The awakened city evidently grew in proportion to the steady increase of both.

Doctors Somerschall, Mayhow and Peirce.

Dr. Guidott's abhorrence of quackery has been mentioned. His last memoir is of one Dr. Somerschall, or Seneschall, who figured as an alchemist.   One of his modes of gaining notoriety was that of wearing a fur coat in summer, which does not appear to have answered so well as Dr. Baue's purple velvet and beautiful lace.   Two other men of considerable eminence the biographer omits, Dr. Mayhow and Dr. Peirce, probably rivals, and, on some disputed matters, antagonists. Mayhow, who published his opinion of the Bath waters, differed from his brethren as to the theory that nitre and sulphur were components, and he gave some sound chemical reasons for his view.   Peirce was a considerable author and ranked high in his profession.   He was a Commoner of Lincoln's Inn, Oxford, and was created M.D. by his University. In longevity he excelled Venner, living to be nearly a hundred years of age.   When and why he disagreed with Guidott it is not difficult to learn ; there are passages in the writings of both which show that the green-eyed monster had much to do with it.   Both published lists of cases closely resembling those now treated in the Bath Mineral Water Hospital   In Peirce's experience there is also this similarity ; he lodged a large number of patients in his own house, attending constantly to the cases.   It was what was called the Old Abbey House, than which, with regard to size and situation, nothing could be more convenient.   It was just between the church and the bath; the church was reached by crossing a small garden, the bath from a gallery overlooking it.   The need of such facilities in later times, especially of immediate contiguity with bathing appliances had much to do with the erection of the present Grand Pump

Room Hotel, where patients may bathe without going out of doors. The Abbey House, Mr. Peach states in one of his valuable works of local history, was built on the site of the palace of John de Villula, occupied by Dr. Peirce in 1653, and demolished for improvements in 1755.

DR. JOHNSON.

There was another eminent physician of the seventeenth century not mentioned by Dr. Guidott : Dr. Johnson, famed as the editor of the *Herbal of Gerarde*, then one of the best botanical works in England. He also published a translation of Ambrose Pary's medical and surgical works, and others relating to botany, of which *Iter in Agrum Cantianum*, 1620, and *Ericetum Hamstedianum*, 1632, were the first local catalogues of plants published in England. He died in 1644. This glance at the Bath Medical Celebrities of the seventeenth century has also included the chief causes of the progress of the city in the same period. The latter are remarkable when it is considered what an eventful era the century was throughout the country, its civic changes and national commotions affecting Bath considerably. We have seen how the growing importance of the city was recognised by the charter of Elizabeth, and every reader of history remembers the fierce political warfare waged on the surrounding hills and even in the streets. It was the time of the conflicts between the Royalists and Republicans, one holding the city a certain number of years till it was regained by the other ; the time being marked by the memorable battle on Lansdown, described in Clarendon's history of the Great Rebellion. Still through all the din of war and the strife of faction, through alarms from foes and treachery by friends, there were two predominating influences to keep up steadily

the progress of the city—the springs and the medical
profession. Of this there is ample proof if the influx of
distinguished visitors be any evidence. Never within so short
a period as that from the middle of the seventeenth to the
middle of the eighteenth century have there been so many
visits from royal personages for the benefit of the waters.
Charles II. came attended by his chief physician, Sir
Alexander Fraser in 1640, again with his queen Henrietta
Maria in 1644; in 1663, Charles II. brought his wife; the
Princess Anne and her husband came in 1692, Anne
returning when she was queen in 1702. Through the next
fifty years the bells rang in at intervals the Princess Amelia,
William, Prince of Orange, James II. and his Queen, Mary
of Modena, Frederick, Prince of Wales, and his Consort, and
the Princess Mary, daughter of George II., with her niece the
Princess Caroline.

Dr. THOMAS LINACRE.

The visits of all these royalties for the waters naturally
attracted a great number of people of rank and fashion.
But would any of them have come if Bath had not been
noted for its medical men, for the skill with which its
waters were administered, and the generally high character
of the profession? At the beginning of this sketch I
noticed the dawnings of improvement in this respect as
evidenced by the physicians who appeared on the scene in
the early part of the century, but I omitted to mention one
to whom the country at large owed a vast debt of gratitude.
This was Linacre, one of the greatest benefactors of the age,
who, living in the sixteenth century, grieved sorely at the
abundances of incompetent practitioners and the absence of
all legal restraint. Himself a man of high character and rare

attainments, taught by Vitelli at Oxford and Demetrius at Florence, physician successively to Lorenzo de Medici, Henry VII., and Henry VIII., friend of Tonstall, Latimer, Melancthon, Sir Thomas More and Cardinal Wolsey, who more likely to command attention to a great scheme of reform? His was one of numerous instances of the combination at that time of medical and ecclesiastical duties. Ten years prior to his appearance as a medical reformer, he became a priest, officiating first as Rector of a small parish in Kent, and afterwards as Prebendary of Easton-in-Gordano, at Wells. While filling these offices he devised a remedy for the evils of the medical profession by originating the Royal College of Physicians, in which he had the powerful aid of the King, Henry VIII., and his minister, Wolsey. The biographies of the period contain many proofs of the great value of the College, and of the intellectual influence of Linacre on the coming race of medical students. Sir Thomas Elyot, styled "Knight, Diplomatist, and Scholar," wrote about 1530 a remarkable book on education, *The Governour*, which passed through eight editions. A new one was printed as late as 1881, and the *Times* in reviewing it spoke of the author as owing his training to "the group of learned men who clustered round Sir Thomas More, notably to Linacre the Head of the College of Physicans, and one of the chief representatives of the new learning in England." That Bath profited by the new institution there can be no doubt. To such a place, then so full of idle and ignorant people who had much money to spend, its requirements, dealing destruction to empirics, must have been invaluable. How these men played off their tricks, what fruitful subjects of satire they afforded, we learn from the pages of Anstey, Smollett and Fielding. By whose wise exertions the next generation and

all succeeding generations of medical men were trained to
supersede them is taught by a study of the noble life of
Linacre. One of the best memoirs in the National Biography
is that of this remarkable man.*

* A correspondent of the *Bath Herald*, well-known as an earnest
antiquary, communicated to that journal some interesting
additional particulars respecting Dr. Turner, Dean of Wells. I
did not state them in my sketch because I was compelled to
study compression, and the Dean, though a useful visitor in Bath,
does not rank as one of its own celebrities. But having now
more space I gladly introduce Mr. Frederick Shum's letter with
my grateful acknowledgment.

To the EDITOR *of* THE BATH HERALD.

SIR,—Your readers are greatly indebted to Mr. Murch for his interesting
papers on Bath Worthies. It is with a view of drawing attention to the series
of papers still appearing in the *Bath Herald* that I send you additional
particulars of that distinguished Somersetshire theologian, Dr. William Turner,
Dean of Wells, who was only briefly referred to by Mr. Murch as being the
author of the first printed book on the Thermal Waters of Bath. Apart from
his slight connection with Bath he attained great celebrity, both in England
and on the Continent, and was a man of great mark among the pioneers of the
Reformation.

Not only was he one of the earliest writers on the Bath Waters, but he was
also the author of "the first true botanical work in this country," and has been
rightly named the father of English botany, as another Bath celebrity, Mr.
William Smith, is known as the father of English geology. This rare volume,
which with his first edition of the Bath Waters is in the "Collection of Bath
Books," contains the first record locally of our native plants ; it was published
in 1538, and entitled "Libellus de re Herbaria Novus."

Dr. William Turner in learning, science and religion was far in advance of
the times in which he lived. Born at Morpeth, in Northumberland, he entered
Pembroke College, Cambridge, and shortly after taking his B.A. degree in 1529
was elected Fellow and treasurer of his college. He applied himself with great
ardour to the study of physic and theology, and was highly esteemed by
members of the University. While an under-graduate he became a disciple of
Latimer, and an intimate friend of Ridley, the Bishop Martyr.

During his residence at Cambridge public disputations were held there on the tenets of the Reformers, and the University decided in favour of the King against the Pope. Turner had the courage of his convictions, and as a young man fearlessly and zealously preached the doctrines of the Reformation, travelling like John Wesley 200 years later, through the villages, towns, and cities of England to make known the truth to the common people. He was imprisoned, but, nevertheless, received sympathy and assistance from Pembroke College, who voted him a sum of money in 1542. After his release from prison he travelled to Italy, where he continued his studies, and at Ferrara was created Doctor of Medicine. He then proceeded to Germany and Holland in pursuit of botanical specimens, residing for a considerable time in Barle and Cologne. It was at this period he wrote his brief but telling religious pieces, printing them at these two centres and circulating them in England, where they were eagerly read by his countrymen, but were eventually prohibited by King Henry VIII. in the last year of his reign.

On the accession of Edward VI., in 1547, he returned to England, was appointed physician to the Duke of Somerset, and received from the Archbishop of York a living in that city. In 1550 he was preferred to the City of Wells, and created a Doctor of Medicine in Oxford. His energy and learning, his wit and varied accomplishments, rendered him as popular at home as he had been on the Continent. When Queen Mary succeeded, he was deprived of his appointments, and compelled to take refuge in Germany, where he prosecuted his botanical studies and scientific researches, cultivated the gardens in which he had planted his specimens, and from time to time issued his tracts. His works were a second time prohibited by the Crown, and the Wardens of the various London Companies were ordered to give up all copies when discovered. Hence the rarity of Turner's books. In 1558, on the accession of Queen Elizabeth, he came to England, and preached at S. Paul's on the 10th of September, before a vast assemblage of people, and shortly afterwards was reinstated in his deanery, with the addition of several rectories in Somerset. He died 7th July, 1568, and was buried in the Church of St. Olave, where may now be seen a tablet, written in Latin, to his memory. '

The indomitable character of the man may be seen in his works to-day, as it was equally patent to his contemporaries, who were witnesses of his self-denying labours 350 years ago.

Yours faithfully,

Bath ; Jan. 21st, 1893.   F. S.

CHAPTER IX.

BEAU NASH.

It may seem incongruous to connect the name of the great Roman historian with that of a Bath master of the ceremonies, and yet there is a remark of Tacitus applicable to Richard Nash : *Non semper errat fama aliquando eligit.* We remember, however, that if " Fame is not always mistaken but sometimes chooses right," it is partly because she deals with circumstances as they exist at certain times and gives her laurel crown accordingly. Nash was the man for the hour, the place and the people ; he appeared when just such a man was needed as a controlling power in a disorganised community ; and whatever his faults may have been or those of the subjects over whom he ruled (in both cases sufficiently obvious), the difficult work was accomplished and hence his renown.

At the beginning of the eighteenth century Bath was one of the most remarkable places in the kingdom. It may be said that in some respects pertaining to time and place it was unique. First there were the springs rapidly regaining the reputation they possessed during the Roman settlement, fifteen hundred years before. Then the advent of a higher class of medical men with a sounder knowledge of the laws of health and superior social qualifications. It was also the time when the general revival after the middle ages, which was felt throughout Europe, operated in making the class of well-to-do English people who lived in lone country houses dissatisfied therewith. To all such people Bath had many attractions ; they found, besides health-giving springs and skilful physicians, convenient houses, society of all kinds,

fashionable amusements, and a beautiful neighbourhood.
What city then could be compared with it? How natural
that country squires and their families, men and women with
mere rustic antecedents and even men and women of
questionable character should congregate there. And how
necessary that some master spirit should appear invested
with authority by the inexperienced crowd themselves to lay
down laws for their guidance and bring order out of
confusion.

Richard Nash was born at Swansea in 1674. His father
was a gentleman whose principal income was derived from a
partnership in a glass manufactory. His mother was niece
to Colonel Poyer, who suffered death for defending Pembroke
Castle against the troops of the Commonwealth. The father
strained his resources to give his son a good education, sending him first to Carmarthen School and then to Jesus
College, Oxford, to prepare him for the study of the law.
Young Nash soon showed, however, that though much might
be expected from his genius nothing could be hoped from
his industry, his distinction being chiefly for proficiency in
the youthful follies of the time. Before he was seventeen he
went through all the mazes of a college intrigue. He tried
to extricate himself by an offer of marriage which was
accepted, but which his tutors and other friends contrived to
get cancelled. Then he determined to enter the army, bought a
pair of colours and "dressed to the very edge of his finances,"
but soon becoming disgusted with the life of a soldier he
resumed his inclination for the bar. Thus in the reign of
William III. Nash was a member of the Middle Temple. It
had been long customary for the Inns of Court to give a
revel or pageant on the accession of a monarch. For many
years poets were the conductors because plays were exhibited

F

and complimentary verses recited.   By degrees the literary
feature was eliminated, the last poet honoured with the
commission being Sir John Davis.   Nash was now the man
to meet the altered taste, and his connection with the Temple
made the choice appropriate.   The King was so struck with
his ability on the occasion that he made him an offer of
knighthood.   This, however, the *Arbiter Elegantiarum*
thought it prudent to decline.   " Please your Majesty," he
replied, "if you propose to make me a knight, may it be one
of the poor knights of Windsor for then I should have a
fortune at least sufficient to support the title."   Another
story, not improbable, is that when Queen Anne visited Bath
she asked him why he refused the honour, and he answered,
" Because Sir William Reed, the mountebank, should not
call me brother."   The hint given to King William about the
poor knights was not taken, but though Nash failed to
improve his circumstances immediately, he yet gained many
friends and had his path smoothed for the office he soon
after filled at Bath.

It was early in the first decade of the century that he came.
There was already a master of the ceremonies, Captain
Webster, when the amusements were only in an embryo state.
The company assembled on a bowling green where they
enjoyed country dances to the music of a violin and hautboy.
At other times they sauntered in the Orange Grove, so-called,
not because the pretty square had orange trees ; the saunter-
ing was between three rows of sycamores.   The name is said
to have originated in the fact that in 1734 a column was
erected in the centre to commemorate the cure of the Prince
of Orange.   Webster succeeded sufficiently to cause a migration of the dancers from the bowling-green to the Townhall,
each gentleman paying half-a-guinea for admission.   But

progress was slow, and Nash, it is said, though at first only a visitor, availed himself of a curious incident to rival the original M.C. Some eminent London physician, disliking the reputation Bath had acquired, published a pamphlet threatening to put a toad into the springs. Nash, hearing this, assured the good people who were somewhat alarmed at the idea, that if they would give him leave he would charm away the poison of the doctor's toad. "But how?" they asked. "Why," he said, "as the venom of the tarantula is charmed, by music." They consented; he established a band of such merit that numbers flocked to hear it, and the fame of the city rapidly increased.

It is true that there have been doubts as to the truth of this story with reference to Bath and to Dr. Radcliffe, who was supposed to have been the physician. A modern writer states that the spring was really in Northamptonshire and the antagonist Dr. Willis. Possibly Nash caught at the idea to turn it to his purpose. At all events he charmed the people if not the toad, and they showed their gratitude in no stinted measure. Webster had proved himself a low-minded, disreputable gambler, and was killed in a duel. The city then gave Nash full power to make any laws and levy any taxes he wanted for his purpose, installing him master of the ceremonies and King of Bath. Never was local sovereignty more complete. He strengthened it by exactly the kind of measures the city needed. His first care was to put his band on a higher and more permanent footing. Then he promoted the completion of the Pump Room, which was begun by Webster in 1704, and opened under his successor's auspices in 1706. It was first enlarged in 1751, afterwards still further many years later, and eventually it gave way to the present building, erected from designs by Baldwin in 1781. Nash, com-

mencing his reign in 1704, directed that the balls should begin
punctually at six and end at eleven ; the closing rule being
especially strict lest the good effect of the waters should be
counteracted.   Not even the Princess Amelia could get it
relaxed in her favour.   In matters of dress at the balls, Nash
was a thorough and much-needed autocrat.   The Duchess of
Queensbury appeared at one of the Dress Balls in an apron
of point lace, said to be worth five hundred guineas.   " Be
so good as to take it off, Madam" was the mandate.   Her
Grace obeyed.   Nash took it and threw it to her attendants.
Gentlemen were required to abstain from oaths, swords, and
top-boots.   Strict laws were issued against duelling, and
various facilities were given for the termination of quarrels.
No one could settle questions of precedence better.   He is
said to have been acquainted with the rank and quality of
almost every important family in the kingdom.   If he found
scandal causing divisions and animosities he discovered who
were the authors and withheld his favour until the offence
ceased.

No doubt much of Nash's power was caused by his deference to human weaknesses.   Thus he even acquired the
homage of the constituted authorities, a strange instance of
civic submission.   Who would now believe that the magistrates of the Old Roman city paid the same respect to the
fictitious royalty of Nash as was given to genuine kings and
queens ?   Can it be imagined that, although under the circumstances a certain deference might have been expedient,
they would be dazzled or rather dazed by his tawdry chariot,
his six grey horses, his footmen, outsiders, and French horns ?
For thus was it he travelled to keep in order his other subjects at Tunbridge Wells.   The reason he gave for always
wearing a white hat was that it might not be stolen, as if its

shape and quality were not sufficiently distinctive. The connivance of the magistrates and corporation in all these follies is still less to their credit when it is remembered how the mock state was kept up. The fees of office were, of course, utterly inadequate; so that the chief part of the burthen was borne by the gaming-table. Bath then swarmed not only with people of distinction, but with needy adventurers to whom gambling was the great financial resource. Nash was known for his proficiency in it from early manhood; he maintained himself by it while professing to study law in the temple; but, so low was the scale of morality everywhere, that no disgrace accompanied it, and his success in filling Bath with visitors blinded the world to the means by which he supported the grandeur.

Some writer has pleaded that while Nash shared the passion of the age in this respect he was better than other adventurers, inasmuch as he never cheated. To this may possibly be added the fact that, though for many years he won enough to defray current expenses, he did not save enough to avoid at the close of life the most distressing poverty. Always both impulsive and generous, one quality made him the victim of chance rather than skill and judgment at the gaming table, the other led him to give and forgive with the freedom of a really rich man. A gentleman of broken fortune, once standing behind his chair as he played a game of picquet for two hundred pounds, and observing with what indifference he won the money, observed to a friend, " Heavens, how happy would all that money make me." Nash heard it, put the money into his hand, and said, " For once I have done some good, go and be happy." Nor was his kind-heartedness merely occasional; the records of his life contain many similar instances. In the meridian of

his fortune his gifts to the needy are said to have been equal
to his other expenses.   During the exceptionally severe
winter of 1739, his personal exertions to relieve distress were
unremitting ; he went among the poor in their own houses,
and gave his best attention to the most deserving and
industrious.

Neither was charity with him confined to objects of the day
and hour.   He established a long claim to gratitude in connection with a scheme for making the springs available to the
poor from distant places by means of a Mineral Water
Hospital. He was certainly one of its most active and
successful promoters ; he induced some of the best men of
the city to frame the constitution and procure the Act of
Parliament by which it is governed to this day ; he had the
assistance of Wood, the eminent architect, as to the designs,
and of Ralph Allen, Dr. Oliver, the Rector of Bath, and Dr.
Stevenson, the Nonconformist Minister, in obtaining funds.
The fact that he was one of the treasurers from the opening
in 1742 till his death in 1761, shows the confidence he
enjoyed.   An appropriate compliment was paid to his memory
by a marble statue in the Pump Room, the work of Prince
Hoare ; with an outline of the plan of the hospital in his
hand. Through a hundred and fifty years has this noble
institution conferred incalculable and ever increasing benefits ;
not confined only to those who in the city need the waters,
but to sufferers from rheumatism, sciatica, paralysis, and other
disorders in any part of the kingdom.   It is pleasant to know
that succeeding generations of the worthies of Bath have
kept pace with time by increasing the facilities and advantages of the hospital. First, space was gained by an additional
story ; then the patients, instead of being taken to the springs
in Sedan chairs, had the water conveyed through pipes to the

building; subsequently a new wing for day-rooms, an exercise ground on the premises, and other additions and improvements have testified to the laudable desire to insure to as large a number as possible the full benefit of the institution.

The ultimate disastrous change in the fortunes of Nash was due to wise legislation for repressing gambling. Early in the reign of George III. the most prevalent games, those which were chiefly played in Bath, were declared fraudulent and unlawful. There had been, however, an extremely profitable game set up at Tunbridge, called E.O., the promoters of which managed to evade the law, and with them Nash as a last resource confederated at Bath. But Parliament was not to be baulked; the offenders were discovered, and a more stringent Act was passed, destroying all the hopes of the once powerful autocrat, and leaving him a dreary prospect for the remainder of his life. Happily this was not prolonged; he had nearly reached the end when grim poverty began to darken his dwelling, the home in S. John's court where his kindness had gained the hearts of all who served him. A weekly pension was allowed him by the Corporation just sufficient for his maintenance until death came. This was in 1761, at the age of 88; he was honoured with a public funeral and a handsome monument in the Abbey, in addition to the marble statue elsewhere, already mentioned.

In the early part of this sketch it may be thought that I have attached undue importance to Nash's share in the revival of Bath. Some writer has said that such a city could not have "danced or gambled into existence," and that the chief agencies in its prosperity have been its great natural advantages. There can be no doubt of this; nor can we fail to remember thankfully how, while lower influences have, in each succeeding decade, passed away more and more, the

higher ones have gained ever increasing power. If the follies
and vices which threw their dark shadow over English social
life in the eighteenth century affected deeply for a time the
national character, there is surely much in the higher public
spirit and greater private excellence of recent times to inspire
hope for the future. With regard to the moral responsibilities
of individual men and women who have been leaders of an
era, Justice as well as Charity requires that the circumstances
under which their minds and lives were formed should be
always considered. In many cases the wonder is, not that
they failed to do more good, but that they succeeded in doing
so much. The great point is to judge fairly if possible.
There are two scraps of poetry on Nash's character. One,
the lines on his monument in Bath Abbey, which appear to
perpetuate exaggerated eulogy ; the other, the epigram
ascribed by Goldsmith to Lord Chesterfield, surely much
nearer reality; the epigram having been caused by the
position of Nash's portrait in a public ballroom between the
busts of Newton and Pope.

> " Immortal Newton never spoke
>   More truth than here you'll find,
> Nor Pope himself e'er pen'd a joke
>   Severer on mankind.
>
> Nash represents man in the mass
>   Made up of wrong and right,
>   Sometimes a knave, sometimes an ass,
>   Now blunt and now polite.
>
> This Picture placed these busts between
>   Gives Satire its full strength,
> Wisdom and Wit are little seen
>   But Folly at full length."

Chapter X.

RALPH ALLEN.

The shade of Ralph Allen might well complain if he were omitted in an account of Bath Celebrities. No name during his useful life was better known in the city that he loved and through a large part of the West of England. Few local worthies since his death, a hundred and fifty years ago, have been held in higher repute for solid service to the country and effectual quickening of the national life. Well may proofs of general gratitude be still seen in appropriate places : marble busts in the Guildhall and Mineral Water Hospital ; portraits, painted and engraved, in many a private dwelling. Often are philanthropists of the present day reminded of his modest benevolence by Pope's well-known couplet, and of his social attractiveness by Fielding's description of Squire Allworthy. But to many Bath citizens of these modern times the tale of his remarkable life and its memorable work is probably still unknown ; here, at all events, it must not be untold.

Ralph Allen was born in 1693 or 1694. He was the son of worthy parents who kept an inn at St. Blaise, near St. Austell, in Cornwall. Their vocation led Pope in the couplet just mentioned to designate him as "low-born," an epithet changed, after remonstrance by Bishop Warburton, to "humble." The paltry attempt at disparagement may be almost pardoned for the prominence given to a rare quality in the lines as they stand :—

> "Let humble Allen, with an awkward shame,
> Do good by stealth and blush to find it fame."

But no one who has known successive generations of the Allen family could fail to see that, whatever the outward circum-

stances of earlier ancestors may have been, there has been no
lack of the innate dignity characteristic of nature's gentlemen.
I remember, when travelling in Italy many years ago, stopping
at a small inn kept by a man apparently very "humble," and
yet it came out that he was of noble extraction ; while
singularly attentive and obliging, he always avoided undig-
nified positions.

Here my readers will allow me to repeat a few facts stated
in a paper I once read at a literary meeting.   In another
Cornish village, St. Columb, there was a good old grandmother
who kept a post office.   To her Ralph was sent when a boy in
order that he might help her in sorting and carrying out the
letters.   Cornwall, it should be remembered, was then a more
important county than many others in consequence of its great
mining business and its large share of Parliamentary
representation.   In that little village office the lad of St.
Blaise, by turning his opportunities to good account, laid the
foundation of his future fortune. The Inspector of the district
noted his ability and steadiness, and a neighbouring
magistrate, Sir John Trevelyan, who was accustomed to visit
Bath, aided in obtaining employment for him here.

At the age of eighteen Allen became a clerk in the Bath
post office.   Continuing to commend himself to influential
persons, he soon received the appointment of postmaster.
Some writers represent that the more immediate cause of his
promotion was the zeal he showed in opening letters of
suspected persons and thus discovering a conspiracy against
the Government.   Undoubtedly the friends of the Pretender
were active in the West of England, and Allen may have
obeyed instructions which the Government thought itself
justified in giving.   At all events, important intelligence was
given to General Wade, who was then quartered with troops

at Bath, and who became another powerful friend of the Cornish youth. Ere long Allen married Wade's natural daughter, one of the happiest events of his prosperous life. That in addition to the lady's good qualities she had some fortune may be inferred from the fact that her husband soon engaged in his great undertaking of the Combe Down stone quarries. Another step of the ladder he ascended so rapidly within a few years was the Bath Corporation, then possessing the privilege of electing the members of Parliament for the city. He joined this body in 1722, was eventually chosen Mayor of Bath, and for many years took the lead in Municipal affairs, exercising special influence in all that related to Mr. Pitt's representation of the city.

Thus we are introduced to the new system of the cross posts. In no place could the experiment have originated more favourably. The geographical position of Bath combined with its waters, scenery and society to make it a place of great resort for influential people. Ralph Allen, brought by his office into frequent intercourse, was able to confer with them as to the plans he had in view. Mr. Pitt, afterwards Earl of Chatham, had built a house in the Circus, lived there during the season, and was a medium with the Government as one of the members for the city, but all this was long after the first contract for the cross posts. It is due to Allen to remember that with himself, with his own power of calculation and management, the plans had their origin, and by his energy and perseverance in the employment of suitable means they were carried out. Nor should the difficulties be forgotten — difficulties arising from the want of communication which he endeavoured to lessen. With roads so few and bad, with conveyances so poor and slow, with people for obeying his instructions so dull and ignorant, no common skill was needed to organise a system covering a large extent of country.   Any one who has read Arthur Young's *Tour in the North of England*, or the novels of Fielding, Smollett, and Richardson, with their vivid description of the state of England at the period, can imagine the obstacles which a post office reformer would have to overcome.

Up to this time legislation had not done much to improve postal communication.   The two most important Acts were one of the Commonwealth (1657), among the latest of the Long Parliament, and another of the reign of Queen Anne. The former begins by reciting the various advantages, social, commercial, and political of a General Post Office, and gives it a more permanent form by placing it under the control of a Postmaster-General.   To him was committed the duty not only of arranging the tariff and transmitting letters, but of providing horses for travellers riding post.   The Act of Queen Anne (1710) gave increased facilities, but prior to Ralph Allen's time it was almost a dead letter for want of the requisite spirit and intelligence.   He, therefore, proposed to establish cross posts from Exeter to Chester by way of Bath, Bristol, Gloucester, and Worcester, thus connecting the West of England with Lancashire districts and the mail route to Ireland.   Previously letters between neighbouring towns had been conveyed by circuitous routes, often going to London and coming back by different roads.   Allen persuaded the Government to allow him to construct his system, and to have successive leases at rents regulated by the results. In addition to all the costs of the new service he paid £2,000 a year for the first contract, £4,000 for the second, £6,000 for the third, and £8,000 for the fourth, the last being for the remainder of his life.   General Wade was his bondsman to the Treasury.   It was difficult to ascertain—indeed no one but himself and his clerks could discover what his profits really were, the receipts from the cross posts being collected, not by the Government but by themselves. By an account which was found among Allen's papers after his death, it appeared that he calculated his net profits at £10,000 a year or half a million sterling altogether. But there is another statement from which I obtain much of the information I am now giving. Allen employed an intelligent man called Jones as clerk of the works from 1731 till his death in 1764. Jones kept a diary, which still exists, and states that twenty-six years before Allen's death he saw an account showing a clear gain of £16,000 a year. This, however, may have been only for a time, though his great outlay for many years in buying large estates, planting innumerable acres, and erecting costly buildings proves that his income from various sources must have been very considerable.

If we inquire how the country was served by these contracts the answer is satisfactory. On each renewal additional work was required, and, so far as we are able to judge, faithfully done. At Allen's death, when the system had been in operation 44 years, cross posts had extended to all parts of the kingdom. Then such large dimensions had been attained as to be nearly unmanageable in private hands, and the authorities were not sorry to see the responsibility lapse to the Crown. A new office called the " bye letter office " was then established in London under the charge of a manager at a salary of £300. At the end of the first year profits to the amount of £20,000 were added to his Majesty's income. In 1799, when the management was transferred to the general office, they had reached the yearly sum of £200,000. Notwithstanding this there was no reduction of postage; on the contrary it was increased from time to time to meet war expenses and for other purposes. According to the terms of Queen Anne's Act large pensions were to be paid out of the surplus revenues of the post office and the remainder retained by the Queen "for the better support of her Majesty's household and for the honour and dignity of the Crown of Great Britain." On the accession of the three first Georges successively Bills were passed in accordance, though at a later period, while £7,000 a year was fixed as the sum for the civil list the entire net revenue was directed to be carried to the consolidated fund.

In considering the history of the post office up to the time of Allen's death we have passed over much that is interesting in his personal history. The wealth and position he acquired gave him an influence which he employed in ways not less honourable to himself than beneficial to the neighbourhood. His wealth was by no means entirely due to his Government contracts ; he continued the business to which I have referred, of quarrymaster on Combe Down, where the cottages he built for his workmen originated the present village. Prior Park is said to have been erected in order that he might exhibit the qualities of the Bath stone, which also became manifest in other large buildings of the period, notably the Exchange at Bristol, the General Hospital at Bath, and St. Bartholomew's in London. The rapid growth of Bath in the last century conduced largely to the success of the quarries. Their owner sold the stone for the houses in Queen Square, Wood Street, the Orange Grove, and the North and South Parades. But who would grudge him his prosperity ? Who that knew how large-hearted he was, how generous and hospitable in private life, how ready to forward every good public object ? To set apart £1,000 annually for quiet acts of kindness was one of his earliest objects. To send Fielding two hundred guineas

from this fund, even before he knew him, as soon as he heard
he was in distress, was a mode of doing good habitual to him.
Equally characteristic were his legacies of various kinds,
including a handsome annuity for educating Fielding's
children, when fatherless, and £1,000 to Mr. Pitt, because he
was poor. Ralph Allen was the chief supporter of Beau
Nash's noble object—a hospital for the poor from all parts of
the kingdom whose cases needed the Bath Waters. At once
he gave £1,000 to it, and promised all the stone for the
building ready cut and delivered. He gave £500 towards
re-building the Guildhall in 1763. He clothed and equipped
a hundred Volunteers on the breaking out of the Rebellion.
He built a bridge at Newton St. Loe at a cost of £4,000. As
he acquired successively on the other side of Bath the estates
of Combe Down, Claverton, and Hampton Manor, he covered
the hills with plantations, which now at a distance of a
hundred and fifty years give beauty and glory to the landscape. Let every lover of fine old trees, everyone who enjoys
the walks and drives of the neighbourhood, bless the mind
that conceived this great source of delight to future generations. Allen's splendid notions as to Prior Park are said to
have utterly confounded his friend and architect, John Wood,
but he carried them out. It is generally known that he
built "Sham Castle" as a prominent object from many parts
of Bath. In later life he spent three months annually at
Weymouth. He had also a residence at Bathampton, to which
he occasionally retired for repose.

In social life the Allworthy of *Tom Jones* was as genial as
in giving aid to the needy. Fielding dined at his table daily
when he lived near. Pope, Mason, Hartley, Richardson,
Graves of Claverton, Hoare, the painter, Gainsborough,
Bishops Hurd, Sherlock, and Warburton, Lord Chatham, and

the younger Pitt—all enjoyed his hospitality; and members of the Royal family visiting Bath accepted his invitations. Prior Park was then on a small scale to Bath what Holland House was in later days on a larger to London, the house where the most celebrated men of the day met and where the spirit of kindness flowing from the host and hostess gave brightness to the wit and flavour to the wisdom of the various guests. Honour therefore to the memory of the first post office reformer. If he earned a splendid fortune he gave a bright example of the best way of spending money. The beautiful house which he built, the magnificent trees which he planted, the landscape full of Italian loveliness which he adorned, are all memorials of a taste worthy one of nature's nobles. And when he was carried to his grave in the sweet God's Acre at Claverton, realising the exquisite wish of Goldsmith to be laid amid the bowers he loved, who would not hope he might long rank high with men immortalised by an older poet, men

> " Who by new arts life's uses have improved,
> And for good deeds are honoured and beloved ? "

He died in 1764, at the age of 71. The inscription on the tomb records his "full hopes of everlasting happiness in another state."

"Ralph Allen" says the author of the memoir in the *National Biography*, " was rather above the middle height, of stout build, very grave and well-looking, extremely plain in his costume, and remarkably courteous in his behaviour. His character has been drawn in the most glowing terms by Pitt, Bishop Hurd, Bishop Warburton, Mrs. Delany, and others, all bearing testimony to his simplicity, benevolence, splendid hospitality, strong natural abilities, and domestic virtues. His nephew, Thomas Daniell, became a wealthy merchant of Truro, whose son, Ralph Allen Daniell, was M.P. for West Looe." The second Mrs. Allen was sister to Captain Tucker, whose daughter, after living at Prior Park some years, married the Rev. William Warburton, afterwards Bishop of Gloucester, and on Allen's death he entered into possession of Prior Park. This little family history illustrates the truth that important destinies often follow trifling incidents. Pope was a friend and often a guest, ultimately an ungrateful one, of Allen. Warburton, being a friend of Pope, once wrote a letter proposing to visit him at Twickenham. Pope happened to be at Prior Park when the letter arrived and caused him, on receiving it at dinner, to look perplexed. "What is the matter?" said Allen. "Oh, a Lincolnshire parson wants to visit me and I can't have him." "If that be all let him come here." He came, repeated his visits, and married Miss Tucker. For some time after his marriage Warburton lived at Prior Park and in future years was often there. His social powers, his learned books, and his good connections, advanced him step by step until, through Allen's influence with William Pitt, he reached the See of Gloucester. Prior Park then saw him but seldom, and after his death, in 1779, his widow, having married his chaplain, the Rev. Stafford Smith, lived chiefly in Queen Square, Bath. By arrangement or inheritance, the next possessor of the Postmaster's mansion was Viscount Hawarden, who married a daughter of Philip Allen, Ralph's brother. He lived there 24 years, and was succeeded by his son, the second Viscount, who died in 1807 without issue, when all direct connection of Prior Park with the Allen family ceased. There is much that is interesting in the subsequent ownership of the estate, and much that awakens pleasant

G

recollections, but here the present sketch must end. In 1816 the Claverton property was purchased by Mr. Vivian, solicitor to the Excise, who pulled down the old Hungerford house, and built another on the crest of the hill, now occupied by its present owner, Mr. H. D. Skrine. The Bathampton Estate has been inherited successively by Mr. George Edward Allen, great nephew of Ralph, Major Ralph Shuttleworth Allen, M.P., *his* nephew, and Colonel F. Allen, son of the last mentioned.*

---

* In my original sketch of Ralph Allen, in the *Bath Herald*, I fell into an error on the authority of the National Biography, where it is stated that "By his second wife he had an only child, Ralph, who became comptroller of the bye letter office, but of whom little further is known." I was surprised that no previous writer had mentioned this son ; it seemed possible, however, that there should be some reason for reticence, and I relied (unwisely it seems) on the general accuracy of the great biographical work. Moreover seven years had passed since the publication of the volume, and no correction, so far as I knew, of this statement had appeared. The author appears to have founded it on confused ideas of a few facts. There was a Ralph Allen Warburton, only child of Bishop Warburton, who died in early youth, and there was a postmaster (not comptroller), Philip Allen, who succeeded his brother Ralph in that capacity, but that brother, I am now reassured, with certainty, never had a son.

Those who wish for further information on the subject of this sketch would find it in a volume of *Remains in Prose and Verse* of the Rev. Francis Kilvert. It contains an *Essay on Ralph Allen and Prior Park* read before the Bath Literary Club in 1857 and, some years afterwards, was pronounced by the Rev. Joseph Hunter in a letter to the author " by far the best memoir of Allen that had yet

appeared." The essay is chiefly valuable for the light it throws on
the friendships between Allen and his eminent visitors, Pope,
Fielding, Warburton and other celebrities, as also on the acquisition
and expenditure of the Postmaster's handsome fortune. But the
volume altogether is more than usually interesting inasmuch as it
perpetuates the memory of Mr. Kilvert, who, if not a celebrity of
Bath was undoubtedly one of its greatest worthies. Without the
slightest appearance of self-importance, he was remarkable
amongst his fellow citizens for a combination of qualities which
gave him no common social influence. While there was an air of
dignified simplicity about him which could not fail to strike a
stranger, his friends felt that to be favoured with his companionship was to be in the way of growing better as plants improve
under the sun and air they love. If " Simon, the son of Onias,
made the garment of holiness honorable," Francis Kilvert made it
. so natural, so gently and genially attractive that one wondered
it was not universally worn, except that in his case it seemed
a part of his very nature. As a clergyman though by his
preaching and his published sermons he gained the reputation
of an able and zealous churchman, yet by his courtesy, charity
and large mindedness he won the affectionate regard of many
who did not worship at the same altar. As a teacher of youth
parents deemed it a privilege to have sons under his care, and
many were the proofs that with all his high classical attainments,
with all his success in producing good sound scholarship, his
constant aim was pure and elevated character. As a literary man
how charming was his society, how substantial were his services;
whether one thinks of such works as the *Remains of Bishop
Warburton* and the *Life of Bishop Hurd* his distinguished relative,
or of the essay on the author of *The Spiritual Quixote*, the poems
he wrote from time to time and the monthly symposia of the
Literary Club which he enjoyed, it is the same. He was also
just the man to appreciate Allen; he never had a more genial
task than that of writing his life; to know that the great and

good Post Office Reformer often came with Warburton to the
humble parsonage at Claverton which he occupied at the
beginning of his ministry, to remember that Shenstone enjoyed
its beautiful garden and that the Venerable Richard Graves spent
fifty years on the spot, endeared it unspeakably to Mr. Kilvert.
I find in the collection of the fragments which pious hands
brought together in the *Remains* that a foremost place was
justly given to lines entitled, *An Israelite Indeed*, and, as they
appear to have been an unconscious portrait of the author himself I conclude my tribute by transcribing them.

> "Whene'er I see a calm consistent walk,
> Deep piety that finds not vent in talk,
> Faith that can realise a world on high,
> Hope's anchor—hold, the glow of Charity,
> The liberal hand that grasps no hoarded pelf,
> Humility that last and least counts self,
> Candour that thinks no ill, imputes no guile,
> Courage that spurns at Fortune's frown or smile,
> Whatever that real Christian's name or creed,
> In him I hail an Israelite indeed,
> To him the hand of fellowship I give,
> Content with him to die, with him to live."

Chapter XI.

JOHN PALMER.

Part I.

Those who imagine that the history of Bath is the history of a mere pleasure-seeking city should think of some of the Celebrities in these sketches. Nor have a few of the more eminent yet appeared ; we have still to glance at the Literati of the later period and at Contemporaries in various professions who distinguished both themselves and the city. But if there had been only the two men who did so much in postal matters, Ralph Allen and John Palmer, who worked for similar objects, in the same city and during the same century, the mistake would be rectified. In order to connect the historical parts of my narrative as closely as possible I proceed at once to Palmer's share in the great improvements.

We have seen how Allen increased the cross posts but not yet how the letters were carried. We know that the bags made up were called mails, but we have still to ask who and what conveyed the bags ? Let no one imagine the mail coach of modern days running through all parts of the kingdom, or indeed anywhere in those days. That, however, was a sight which those of us who have seen it do not wish to forget—the dashing coachman with his four mettlesome steeds, the redcoated guard blowing cheerily on his horn as they drove through the quiet villages. There was an annual custom—a procession of thirty or forty beautiful mail coaches which I saw in London on a king's birthday sixty-five years ago, the horses with new harness, the coachmen and guards

with new liveries, delighting hundreds of spectators who lined
Piccadilly. Very different all this from the wretched boys
on worn-out hacks in the times we are reviewing.

No other mode existed before the close of the sixteenth
century, carriages of every kind being unknown even to
people of fortune and great officers of State. And if judges
had to go circuit in jack-boots, if ladies could only travel to
town from their country seats on a pillion behind some
relative or serving man, if even Queen Elizabeth was bound to
place herself at the rear of her Lord Chancellor when she
went from Greenwich to the city, what better conveyance
could be expected for letters ? Only of neither the men nor
the steeds let too favourable an idea be formed. Few post
boys in the provinces were required to go at a greater rate
than three or four miles an hour, and the want of discipline
among them was grievous. They drank, they loitered, they
played games on the road, they cheated the Government by
carrying letters for their own profit at lower rates, they were
an easy prey to any robber or ill-disposed person who chose
to interfere with them. An amusing anecdote in Campbell's
Tales of the Highlands illustrates the way in which
expresses were forwarded :—"Near Inverary we regained a
spot of comparative civilisation, and came up with the post
boy whose horse was quietly grazing at some distance while
Red Jacket himself was immersed in play with other lads.
'You rascal,' I said to him, 'are you the post boy and thus
spending your time ?' 'Nae, nae, sir,' he answered, ' I'm no
the post, I'm only an express.' "

The first carriage of any kind for the use of the public was
a rude wagon without springs, the body resting solidly on the
axle. About the year 1608 this came to be used for carrying
letters on the principal roads in connection with passengers

and goods. Fifty years afterwards stage wagons travelled regularly between London and Liverpool, starting from an inn in Aldermanbury every Monday and Thursday, occupying ten days in the summer and eleven or twelve in the winter. Then came stage coaches, a great improvement, though for a long time the speed was only two or three miles an hour even on the better roads around London. It was considered a great effort when in 1690 a stage coach undertook to convey passengers all the way to York in seven days, except while the Midland Counties were impassable from floods. Even when Allen was intent on facilitating communication as much as possible, the Fly Coach, as it was called, from London to Exeter, occupied five days, one of the incidents being that a halt was made at Axminster in the early morning long enough to allow a woman-barber *to shave the coach*. Thoresby, the antiquary and naturalist, relates that in his expeditions to the North by those conveyances, he was in the habit of stopping occasionally to go in search of fossil shells in the fields or on the road-side. At the beginning of a long journey it was the custom of the travellers to choose a chairman who regulated all such discussions as those relating to the inns where the party should dine or sleep. But there were times when the coachman chose to have his own way, and in 1760 an action was tried in the Court of King's Bench to recover damages from a driver who had wanted to compel the passengers to dine at some low inn in which he had an interest. The passengers had rebelled, had walked on to a respectable place at some distance and had eaten their dinner, with the mortification, however, of then seeing the coach go past at full speed and leave them to get to London as best they could. The jury gave them such comfort as was possible in damages to the amount of twenty pounds. John Palmer's mail coaches appear to have been suggested originally by cases of practical inconvenience to himself. He was manager of the Bath Theatre, and in that capacity had to take long journeys to engage performers for his company. Not only was he often delayed in going from Bath to London, which occupied three days, and from Bath to other places on still worse roads, but when he had promised some bright particular star for a certain night the audience was disappointed because the miserable coach had not arrived. Before, however, we enter on his scheme, it may be well to notice some of the incidents of his life, which, as in Allen's case, largely affected the history of the English post office and gave our city a prominence both honourable and beneficial.

John Palmer was born in the year 1742. His father was a respectable brewer, and his mother belonged to an old and good family. His early education was for the Church, to which, however, he objected, preferring the army. To the army his father objected, and at length his lot was fixed in the brewery, where he found time for pursuits more congenial with his tastes. He followed a pack of hounds belonging to a clerical relative in the neighbourhood, and he cultivated a love of the drama then highly popular, the latter under great disadvantage, for while his kinsman mounted him well the only building available for a theatre was an old, ruinous barn. Long and loud had been the complaints about this building ; not only did the people of rank and fashion who now came to Bath in great numbers denounce it, but even the performers were ashamed of it. To erect a building worthy of the city which had become more attractive than any in the kingdom was an object in harmony with John Palmer's enterprising character. His father's public spirit led him to unite with nine of the principal inhabitants in building a theatre in Orchard Street, afterwards used as a Catholic Chapel. The appeal for aid for this building was prefaced by the lines :—

> " Plays are like mirrors made for men to see
> How bad they are how good they ought to be."

Whether the instruction was equal to the amusement we are not informed, but in another half-century a still larger and more commodious theatre was wanted and rose in Beauford Square. This met the fate of so many in modern times— the interior was destroyed by fire on Good Friday, 1862. The shell being preserved it was immediately rebuilt at a cost of £12,000, and is now in use. Many who were present at the opening performance, *The Midsummer Night's Dream*, March 4th, 1863, have still a vivid recollection of the interest displayed by the old city when the love of the drama, so true and strong in former days, was once more revived. In the excellent company Mr. Chute, the manager, brought together was Miss Ellen Terry, her first appearance in Bath. A copy of the hand-bill is given in Mr. Belville S. Penley's *History of the Bath Stage* lately published. Returning to Palmer's theatre we learn that to insure its success the father bought up the shares of the old company and the son now devoted himself entirely to the business. After spending some time in London, where he was rewarded with an Act of Parliament protecting the property and a royal patent giving it an envied distinction, he returned to grapple with the obstacles occasioned by the unpopularity of the manager. There was in fact for some reason a strike among the staff ; all declared that they would perform no longer. John Palmer saw that only one course was open to him ; he mounted his horse and proceeded on a tour of several

hundred miles in search of a new company. At the end of
a fortnight he came back again successful, having been
joined by recruits of considerable reputation at various towns,
which led him to adopt the plan of an annual journey to
visit all the best theatres and maintain the efficiency of his
staff. Soon after he had arranged these matters to the
satisfaction of Bath he undertook similar responsibilities at
Bristol, having also acquired an interest in its theatre, for
which he likewise obtained a patent, and by working the
two together he was able to promote the prosperity of both.

It was amid these labours that Palmer conceived his
projects of mail coaches. His spirit chafed against the waste
of time and temper to himself and others by the existing
locomotion. At Bath he heard continually of the annoyances
to distinguished visitors by the state of the roads and the slow-
ness of carriages. At Bristol he learned from the merchants
what a blessing it would be if they could travel to London or
obtain their letters in fourteen or fifteen hours instead of
three days. He had only to look at Prior Park and remember its venerable owner in former years to see what great
difficulties could be conquered and what ample rewards might
follow. But John Palmer had a much more arduous task
than Ralph Allen even in obtaining attention to his proposal;
partly for this reason, that while one did the work himself
the other could only show how it was to be done. This, however, Palmer showed most clearly in a report addressed to the
younger Pitt, who was then Prime Minister, stating the chief
causes of complaint and the plans he proposed. "The Post,"
he says in this able document, "instead of being the quickest
conveyance in the country is almost the slowest. The roads
have been greatly improved; other carriers mend their speed,
but letters are as tardy as ever. Carried generally by idle

boys on worn-out hacks, they are often stolen on the road, so that in many cases other modes are employed and the Government loses the profit. If tradesmen for greater security send by the stage coach why should not the stage coach carry the mail bags with the additional protection of armed guards? Let there be a complete system of such coaches; let them run on all the principal roads of the kingdom; let them leave London daily at the same time and arrive at the various towns at fixed hours; let there be regular communication through the cross post with places out of the direct lines; and let the roads be extended and improved wherever the wants of the public are sufficient to justify the outlay."

Such were the leading features of Palmer's scheme. We are now come, it should be remembered, to the year 1784. Trade had increased considerably and the country required to be more opened out. Civil engineering, a profession which had lately acquired dignity and importance, became available for the purpose. Watts and Boulton, Rennie and Telford, Brindley and Smeaton made roads, bridges, and canals, even in remote districts hitherto little known. But notwithstanding all this Palmer for a long time argued in vain. The post office authorities whom Mr. Pitt consulted were against him to a man. Who was Palmer that his plans should be listened to in opposition to those who had had the subject before them so many years? What should a brewer, a theatre manager, a crazy enthusiast living down at Bath, know about the working arrangements which had been long cared for by men of great experience? If you do what he recommends you will only endanger the revenue at present produced by the post office, but you will fling the commercial correspondence of the country into the utmost confusion and raise a clamour which it will be impossible to appease. This was actually the language of the gentlemen consulted by the Prime Minister. " Mr. Palmer," continues a Mr. Hodgson, " says that the post is slow and ought to outstrip all other conveyances, I cannot see it." "He proposes," adds another official, "that there should be mail guards; of what use would they be ? The man would have to be waited for at every ale-house the coach passed." " If desperate fellows were determined on robbery, would firearms be of any avail ? or would not the crime of murder lie at some one's door ?" "And after every effort what is proposed could not be done ; to bring the Bath mail to London in sixteen or eighteen hours would be impossible."

Mr. Pitt heard or read all this but quietly judged for him-self. Like his father, the Earl of Chatham, as we are reminded by Mr. Commissioner Hill, in a paper on the subject, he did not believe in impossibilities. With the clear vision for which he was so famed he saw that the scheme would be both practicable and possible and resolved that it should be tried. Some impulse may have been given to him by his intercourse with the city of Bath, for the representation of which he had been proposed as a candidate in the same year, though unsuccessfully.

In Lord Rosebery's nobly impartial *Life of Pitt*, there is the remark (p. 99) with reference to this period " It is doing Pitt no injustice to say that in the earlier years of his adminis-tration his mind was given rather to domestic questions than to foreign affairs." We have proofs of it in what he did to abolish corruption in high places, to reform the national finances, and to amend the representation of the people. And remembering this it is easy to imagine he would lend a willing car to John Palmer's scheme for saving time in the transit of letters. Of the figureheads by whom it was opposed it was well said they were possibly honest but certainly wooden. The nation was becoming weary of them with regard to many matters. " In their despair," said Lord Rosebery, " men looked round for one who should cast the money changers out of the temple of Government. At this moment there appeared a young University student, rich with lofty eloquence, and heir to an immortal name, untainted in character, spotless in life, showing the first day he met Parliament as Minister a supreme disdain for the material prizes of political life." . . . " In a few months the elder Pitt had raised England from the ground and placed her at the head of Europe. Might not something be hoped of the son ? " In the concluding part of this sketch it will be seen how the son dealt with the mail coach problem.

Chapter XII.

JOHN PALMER.

Part II.

Mr. Pitt's influence prevailed ultimately in causing a trial
of John Palmer's plan of mail coaches. It was not necessary
to wait for long discussions in Parliament; the power to give
the order belonged to the Postmaster-General. But before he
could act it was considered necessary to settle the amount of
Palmer's remuneration; and here even Mr. Pitt's financial
ability failed for some time. He left the matter to be dealt
with by his private secretary, Pretyman, afterwards Bishop of
Lincoln, who corresponded with the Lords of the Treasury on
one side and Palmer on the other. Unfortunately no written
agreement had been entered into, only a verbal understanding
that two and a half per cent. on the increased revenue of the
Post Office should be paid for life if the plan succeeded, and
nothing if it failed. But Mr. Pitt refused to allow longer
delay, and required that a beginning should be made at once,
whch led to the following announcement issued on the 24th
of July, 1784 :—"His Majesty's Postmaster-General being
inclined to make an experiment for the more expeditious
conveyance of mails of letters by stage coaches, machines,
&c., has been pleased to order that a trial shall be made upon
the road between London and Bristol, to commence at each
place on Monday, the 2nd August next." Then follows a list
of places, letters for which could be sent by these mail
coaches, and the announcement concludes : "All persons are
therefore to take notice that the letters put into any receiving
house before six in the evening or into this chief office before
seven will be forwarded by the new conveyance; all others

for the said post towns and their districts put in afterwards or given to the bellmen must remain until the following post at the same hours."

Soon all the gloomy predictions of the officials were scattered to the winds. A proud day for John Palmer was that on which his plan was tested within three weeks of the Treasury announcement. The distance between London and Bath was accomplished in fourteen hours, between eight in the morning and eleven at night. Going back one hundred and nine years we can imagine the joy of the Bath people when a mail worthy to be called "his Majesty's" arrived for the first time. Their indefatigable townsman, the projector, had removed to London some time previously in order that he might superintend the arrangements and see that they were not thwarted by interested opponents. On the first day of the change he was installed at the Post Office with the title of Surveyor and Controller-General and a salary of £1,500 a year, together with the commission of two and a half per cent. upon any excess of net revenue over £240,000, the amount at which the profit to the Government stood at the date of his appointment. The *Bath Chronicle* of February 24, 1785, contains an account of a meeting of the Bath Corporation, at which resolutions were passed thanking Mr. Palmer for the great benefit derived from his plan and praying Mr. Pitt not to allow it to be delayed or thwarted. In the memorial to Mr. Pitt are these words : " We cannot but avow both pride and pleasure in the reflection that the only substantial reforms in a department of such great importance to this commercial country have been contrived and executed, the first by a member of this Corporation and the present by a native of this city as well as one of our Council." The same paper also contains a memorial to Mr. Pitt from the merchants of

Bristol and a resolution of thanks to Mr. Palmer. Tokens struck in Bath in commemoration of the establishment of mail coaches by a townsman may be seen in the Bath Museum. One has the motto: "To Trade Expedition, to Property Protection." Another: ".Gratitude to J. Palmer, esq., for benefits received from mail coaches."

The rates of postage were slightly raised in consideration of the greater advantages to the public, but cheerfully paid, and the number of letters soon increased. Coaches were at once applied for by the municipalities of the largest towns, Liverpool being the first to aim at equality with Bristol, and York claiming what was due to the great highway to the North. "At first," says Mr. Baines in his *History of Liverpool*, "these coaches were small vehicles drawn by two horses which were changed every six miles; they carried four passengers besides the coachman and guard, the latter being armed to the teeth as a security against highwaymen." The speed in Lancashire and some other districts began at only six miles an hour. On the Bath Road it must have been greater, probably seven or eight, and ere long nine. That it was increased cautiously was owing not only to the state of the roads but to the official habit of magnifying difficulties. From end to end of the kingdom the public were frightened by assurances that if the speed got up to ten miles an hour it would be a clear tempting of Providence; the brain would be injured; dreadful accidents would certainly happen; all who travelled must first make their wills. Lord Chancellor Campbell relates that when a young man he was frequently warned against the mail coaches improved by Palmer on account of the fearful rate at which they flew, and instances were offered to him of passengers who had died suddenly of apoplexy from the rapidity of the motion.

If the day on which the first mail coach ran to Bath was a day of triumph to Palmer how great must his satisfaction have been the next few months. Contracts for the mails were made at £20,000 a year below the original estimates; the discontinuance of postboys was followed by a diminution of robberies, and improved supervision prevented defalcation in country offices. While all classes, especially those in trade, welcomed the change with thankfulness, the revenue, which had been stagnant forty years, quickly showed signs of improvement, and when the plan was fairly in operation justified every hope that had been formed. Notwithstanding all this, Palmer found himself hampered continually, wearied with technical objections and unable to carry out much that he wished. The Postmasters-General (for there were then two, Lord Walsingham and the Earl of Chesterfield,) gave heed to every objection raised by inferior officers and took part in the various controversies which arose. Who can wonder that Palmer, thus annoyed, sometimes failed in judgment and temper, falling into snares which artful men had laid for him, and trying to carry his measures by questionable means? He was unfortunate in his deputy, a gentleman named Bonner, to whom he wrote freely on the conduct of which he complained, and who on being suspended after a violent dispute made known Palmer's letters, some of which were certainly imprudent. Bonner appealed to the Postmaster-General, who ordered him to be restored, but Palmer refused to receive him and was therefore suspended in his turn. To his own appeal there was no response; the Government considered, rightly or wrongly, that he could not work with the other authorities, and in spite of all his claims he was dismissed. This occurred in 1792, after about eight years' service. The remuneration which had been

H

agreed upon was altered to a fixed annual sum of £3,000.
It was in vain that, acting on counsel's opinion, Palmer
contended for a larger pension ; the Lords of the Treasury
firmly refused, and he was compelled to submit.

But it was only for a time. Such a man with so good a
cause and so many friends could not fail to renew his efforts.
He was now in his fiftieth year and might fairly expect long
life. No more work was given to him by the Government,
nor does he appear to have again engaged in business of any
kind. It was natural therefore that he should employ himself, though for the long period of sixteen years, in showing
the justice of his claim. At length he formally petitioned
the House of Commons, and a committee was appointed to
report on his case. Mr. Pierrepoint, connected with Bath as
one of the Manvers family, moving for the committee, laid
great stress on the fact that in case of failure he was to receive
nothing. The report stated that though he had experienced
constant opposition from the oldest and ablest officers in the
service he had surpassed the expectations he had held out
both as to despatch and expense, the revenue having increased
since 1783 to the amount of nearly half-a-million. Sheridan,
also well known in Bath, supported his claim in a brilliant
speech. " None but an enthusiast " (he said) " could have
formed such a plan, none but an enthusiast could have made
such an agreement ; none but an enthusiast could have
carried it into execution ; and I am confident that no man in
this country or any other could have done it but that very
individual John Palmer."

Still all was in vain. The report was not adopted. The
House refused to alter the compensation. Palmer withdrew,
weary but not despairing. Public opinion cheered him by
frequent manifestations of gratitude. Eighteen towns and

cities, including York, Chester, Glasgow, Aberdeen, Liverpool
and Edinburgh, presented him with their freedom. From
Glasgow he also received a handsome silver cup which,
having descended to his grand-daughter, Miss Palmer, was
given by that lady in 1875 to the Bath Corporation. An
alderman of Bath, he was twice elected Mayor and four times
member of Parliament; to the Mayoralty in 1796 and 1809;
to the Parliamentary representation in 1801, 1802, 1806, and
1807. Thus encouraged he renewed from time to time his
efforts to obtain justice, placing in the hands of every member
of Parliament particulars of his case, and spending altogether
no less a sum than £13,000. At length his son, then Major
Palmer, having succeeded him in the representation of Bath
succeeded also to this arduous task. In 1808 he moved a
resolution which, although opposed by the Government, was
agreed to by some of their supporters and strongly advocated
by leading members of the other party, Lord Henry Petty, Sir
Francis Burdett, Mr. Windham, and others. The resolution
was to the effect that he was entitled to the sum he claimed, the
percentage for fifteen years, and henceforward during his life.
It was carried by a majority of eighty-six against the
Ministers, and £54,700 was at once paid to him. This, and
the continuance of the percentage as long as he lived,
eleven years, during which the revenue steadily increased,
made the close of his life enjoyable. He had also the
happiness of seeing two of his sons distinguish themselves in
their professions. The elder, who became Major-General
Palmer, represented Bath with Mr. Roebuck as late as 1837.
Another, the third son, Edmund, was a gallant naval officer,
who in 1814 captured a frigate in the French war. He
married a niece of Admiral Earl St. Vincent, who after his
death lived some time in Bath. Mr. Palmer, the Bath

worthy, died at Brighton in 1818.   His remains were brought
to Bath and interred in the Abbey Church.   Unfortunately
no inscription marks his resting place.   It was delayed
because a public movement for a monument was expected
but the exact spot is known to his family, one of whom
possesses a fine portrait of him by Gainsborough.

The English are unlike other nations with regard to their
eminent men.   If any town in France, Belgium, Switzerland,
Germany, or Italy, had produced a Ralph Allen or a John
Palmer it would have had some worthy memorial.   We
content ourselves with now and then talking about local
celebrities and then allowing them to be forgotten, regardless
of the inspiration which the young especially never fail to
gain in such cases.   In this respect the third great postal
reformer was honoured ultimately as he deserved.   True,
Rowland Hill was not without sore trials and anxieties, even
to sharing the fate of Palmer in being dismissed from the
service.   But in his case, as in that of his predecessor, the
country appreciated what the Government could not understand ; the people had no doubt of either the advantage or
the practicability of Penny Postage.   On Rowland Hill's
dismissal by a new Government, a national testimonial was
raised, to which Bath contributed its share, consisting chiefly
of small subscriptions by the middle and working classes,
and resulting in a cheque to the great benefactor of £13,000.
After some time he was reinstated ; it was found that the
work could not advance without him ; he was allowed a
greatly improved staff, including his brother as a chief officer ;
and aided by a good succession of Postmaster-Generals he
established important principles and secured good practical
results.   The Queen joined in welcoming his return to office
by making him a K.C.B.   But at length another trouble

arose ; a new Postmaster-General, Lord Stanley of Alderley, could not see with him on the vital point. He had laboured to establish a system of service on the principle that merit should have the chief weight, patronage comparatively little, and Lord Stanley cancelled the rule. This affected Hill's position seriously, because men were appointed who disliked his plans and disregarded his orders. He appealed to the Treasury but in vain, and finding his strength as an old man unequal to perpetual conflicts, he resigned. On all sides, however, he now received abundant acknowledgments. The Queen sent a message to Parliament, recommending a grant of £20,000. The Prime Minister (Lord Palmerston) moved it and the House carried it without a division. He was also to receive for life his full salary of £2,000 a year. Other proofs of appreciation were not wanting. The Corporation of London gave him the Freedom of the City ; the Royal Society made him a Fellow ; the University of Oxford a D.C.L. As age increased he had more and more of the accompaniments due to it after a life like his :

" Love, obedience, honour, troops of friends."

And, finally, when fourscore and four years had yielded their full fruit, he was laid where such men ought to lie, where the worlds true nobility ought to rest, in Westminster Abbey.

In thus concluding the present sketch I have gone beyond the lines of local biography in order to complete to a certain point the narrative of postal reform. May I not also repeat what I ventured to say many years ago, while addressing an audience on the same subject, that in the history of the English Post Office two lessons are remarkably prominent : That a good step in advance often leads to others far better, and that from all stations of life power for large, good move-

ments comes out.   The son of a Cornish publican, the
manager of a Bath brewery, the assistant to a Birmingham
schoolmaster become great public benefactors, simply by
applying with all their might their various gifts to the work
which their hands found them to do.

CHAPTER XIII.

PHYSICIANS OF THE EIGHTEENTH AND NINETEENTH CENTURIES.

PART I.

The sketch of Dr. Guidott and his contemporaries in a former chapter, brought us to the close of the seventeenth century. There are still to be noticed the more eminent Bath physicians of the eighteenth and those who have passed away of the nineteenth Comparatively small as the number is, the space here allotted to each must be limited, the order of treatment being still to a great extent chronological. Of one of the remaining list, Dr. Henry Harington, his family history begun in my earlier series, and his varied accomplishments which were more than usually remarkable, will require a distinct sketch.

DR. HARTLEY.

It has been already shown in these pages how the intellectual character of the medical profession rose from the time of Linacre. Very striking was the increase in the range of knowledge combined with greater thoroughness and practical power. Of this there was an admirable example in Dr. Hartley, who was born at the beginning of the nineteenth century and adorned its fourth and fifth decades. The son of a Yorkshire clergyman, he was sent to Cambridge with a view to orders in the Church of England, but having doubts about the Articles and being extremely conscientious, he preferred the study of medicine. After practising for a time in Newark, Bury St. Edmunds and London, he eventually

settled in Bath, where, though regarded with much confidence
as a skilful physician, his easy circumstances induced him to
give his chief time to philosophical investigations. They formed
his favourite employment and were the real foundation of his
celebrity. He had studied logic and mathematics under
Professor Saunderson, Sir Isaac Newton was his guide on
some important scientific points, and John Locke on moral
and metaphysical questions. The result of his studies was his
great work, *Observations on Man, his Frame, his Duty, and
his Expectations*, in two thick octavo volumes, printed in
1749, by Richard Cruttwell, of Bath. He did not expect it
would be welcomed immediately by the philosophical world ;
nor in this did he misread the signs of the times, as the
subject received little attention until Dr. Priestley, in 1775,
combated his leading theory. It was said, however, that all
the Birmingham philosopher did was to convince the world of
his own materialism and of his desire to show that Hartley's
doctrine as to the properties of the brain and nerves led to a
similar conclusion. This did not trouble the author or his
friends because his great reputation rested also on other
grounds, notably his profound scholarship and his practical
benevolence. In the fifth edition of the book now before me,
also printed by Cruttwell, and published in 1810, there is an
engraved portrait indicating the beautiful characteristics by
which he gained the love and respect of all who knew him.
No one can look at that portrait and wonder that Hartley was
admired and beloved by a large circle. The friend of Ralph
Allen and the best of the visitors at Prior Park, he
corresponded with some of the most eminent men of the time.
Among them were Hooke the Roman historian ; Dr. Jortin
the authority in ecclesiastical history, Dr. Hales and other
prominent members of the Royal Society, Butler, Hoadley,

and Warburton, distinguished prelates of the Church of England. With Pope also he was intimate, though not insensible to what he thought the poet's shortcomings. He regarded the *Essay on Man* as written under the influence of Lord Bolingbroke, and advocating the sufficiency of human philosophy to the exclusion of divine revelation. Through life, however, he retained a strong opinion that religion should unite mankind by practical rather than dogmatic bonds, and, while continuing in communion with the Church of his fathers, he acted invariably on the most comprehensive lines. His professional skill was perhaps better known to the poor than to the rich; he often visited the humblest dwellings and was welcomed in cases both of mental and bodily distress. His chief medical works were written to alleviate the malady of the stone, which he himself suffered from and which appears to have hastened his end. He died in Bath in 1757 in his fifty-second year leaving issue by two marriages. His son, who succeeded him in his house in Belvedere, became member of Parliament for Hull, and distinguished himself by his strenuous opposition to the American war, also as one of the earliest advocates of the abolition of the slave trade.

The next celebrity is

DR. CHEYNE,

a friend of Dr. Hartley, like him an author, a pleasant companion, and a skilful physician, but a very different man. He also was originally destined for the Church, partly, perhaps, because he was related to Bishop Burnet, but by the advice of his tutor, Dr. Pitcairn, he resolved to study medicine. One point of difference in Hartley and Cheyne appears at the beginning of their respective careers; Hartley abstemious and more intent on attainments in science than professional success, Cheyne becoming a *bon vivant* in order to obtain patients. When about thirty years of age, he migrated from his home in Scotland to begin practise in London, where a strange experience awaited him; he found that to be a bottle companion to the younger gentry who were free livers would do more for him than if he were laden with University honours. In a letter to a friend he avows that he adopted the method because he had observed it to succeed with others. Year after year he continued it until his convivial irregularities caused a state of health which rendered advancement in his profession at that time impossible. He grew excessively fat, short-breathed, lethargic and listless, swollen to such an enormous size as to exceed thirty-two stone in weight. He also laboured under a nervous and scorbutic disorder to the most violent degree, so that his life became an intolerable burthen. Having tried in vain all the usual medicines he resolved to go into the country and adopt a milk and vegetable diet, which graudally removed his complaints. After some time he was advised to try the Bath waters to complete his restoration, and he succeeded so well that it caused his settlement in Bath. We have seen that several physicians of note divided their time between Bath and London; this also Dr. Cheyne did, and, being at length presentable as to appearance, regained some of his patients in the Metropolis. His facile pen greatly promoted his popularity, but here again he was unlike Hartley, who wrote slowly and for future times rather than for the present, whereas Cheyne threw off treatise after treatise on Health, on Nervous Diseases, on Vegetable Diet, and on the Bath Waters, rapidly, for immediate effect. The fact that his own experience confirmed his theories and dictated his advice promoted the sale of his books, while a certain scientific character was given to them. At a period when special theories were in fashion he ranked with the physicians (to use the jargon of the time) " who accounted for the operations of medicines and the morbid alterations in the human body on mechanical principles." Even in the present day, however, his *Essay on the Gout and the Bath Waters*, which passed through seven editions, might be read with advantage. Although retaining his abstemious habits through all the temptations of Bath society his social powers were valued by a large circle. He was intimate with Allen, the physician of Nash, on pleasant terms generally with his brethren, and bore with good humour their constant banter on his milk and vegetable diet. Nor should it be forgotten that in later life, when scoffing on serious subjects was so general, he did what he could to discourage it and to maintain habitual reverence for religion. Dr. Hartley visited him in his last illness. He died in 1752 at the age of seventy-two, and was buried at Weston, near Bath, where also his wife and brother, who was vicar of the parish thirty years, were afterwards interred.

Dr. William Oliver.

Who has not heard of Oliver biscuits? And who that knows what they are does not appreciate them? They are included in the list of Local Delicacies given in Mr. Peach's recent interesting book, *The Street Lore of Bath*, where we learn when they were first made for sale, and how they have maintained their prestige. Other things have also caused this good Doctor to be remembered in Bath. He was one of the founders and first physicians of the Bath Mineral Water Hospital. In a large picture in the Board Room, there is a portrait of him sitting opposite two patients on whose cases he is deciding. And he is mentioned in various books of the period as one of those who, by their skill, energy, good judgment and high character did much for the rising prosperity of Bath.

Of his family and early history little is known. There were two physicians of the name at intervals in the early part of the nineteenth century. Short memoirs of both appear in the appendix to *Britton's History of Bath Abbey*, but the author fails to establish a relationship. The first of them, who preceded the subject of this sketch, was descended from an old Cornish family, and while studying at a Dutch University joined the expedition to England under the Prince of Orange. Like his namesake he was a Fellow of the Royal Society, to which he communicated learned papers after his settlement in Bath. The family of the second Dr. Oliver, the inventor of the biscuit, though not known here previously, became established in the neighbourhood after his death, holding property and occupying a handsome house at Weston.

Different in one respect from other physicians of the time his fame was entirely local. Probably he found his Bath patients become so numerous that he did not need the fashionable custom of giving part of his time to London. People of distinction were now flocking here more and more, attracted by the gaieties over which Nash presided as much as by the increasing reputation of the springs. Yet there are proofs that regard and confidence were not confined to the wealthy; Dr. Oliver's good work at the hospital would have been sufficient to commend him to the middle and poorer classes, among whom he was deservedly popular. One of his patients, Miss Mary Chandler, a worthy milliner much respected, whom he attended in a dangerous illness, published a volume of poems which ran through four editions and was the medium of her gratitude to her doctor :—

"Pure goodness winged your feet, inspired your tongue ;
Soft were your accents but your reasoning strong.
Heaven bade me live and you prescribed the way ;
To you, next Heaven, my grateful thanks I pay.
And now I breathe and live and sing anew,
And owe my breath and life and song to you."

Dr. Oliver died in 1764, and was buried like his contemporary, Dr. Cheyne, in Weston Church, where, as well as in the Bath Abbey, his friends placed a monument with a eulogistic inscription. The following medical men of Bath were also interred at Weston :—George Cheyne, M.D., 1740 ; John Clarke Scott, M.D., 1805 ; William Falconer, M.D., 1824 ; Edward Percival, M.D., 1831 ; Thomas Falconer Clerk, M.D., 1839 ; George Kitson, Surgeon, 1859 ; Charles Parry, M.D., 1860.

THREE DOCTOR FALCONERS.

It is remarkable that father, son, and grandson, succeeded each other at Bath in the medical profession. Much might be said of their ancestors as well as of themselves, distinguished as they were in Scottish history and in science and literature. The family were of Caledonian origin ; its genealogical head was Sir Alexander Falconer, a Lord of Session in 1639, and among subsequent family connections were Hume the historian, Drummond of Hawthornden the poet, and Pennant the antiquary and naturalist.

The first Dr. Falconer was son of the Recorder of Chester, where he was born in 1744. It appears that the recorder became a freeman of Chester in 1733, and that all the male

representatives of the family have been successively admitted
to the privilege. The last was Mr. Thomas Wentworth
Falconer of the Sarawak Civil Service, son of Dr. Randle
Wilbraham Falconer, of Bath, and very recently received by
the Mayor of Chester into the civic brotherhood. The son of
the recorder settled at Bath in 1770, was admitted a Fellow of
the Royal Society in 1773, became physician to the Mineral
Water Hospital in 1784, and died at his house in the Circus,
No. 29, in 1824. Probably no Bath physician has equalled
him in authorship, if we may judge from a list of forty-seven
books written by him. Many are on medical subjects, some
on classical and theological, some on botany and natural
history, the latter including papers for two societies in which
he took great interest—the Bath and West of England, and
the Manchester Literary and Philosophical.

His books on the Bath waters were long in high repute.
To an *Essay on the Influence of the Passions on the
Disorders of the Body*, the third edition of which was published in 1796, was adjudged the first Fothergilian Gold
Medal. To another on *The Diseases of the Hip Joint, and
on the Use of the Bath Waters as a Remedy*, published in
1805, the Medical Society of London adjudged its silver
medal. The list containing these particulars is appended by
his grandson, Mr. Thomas Falconer, County Court Judge, to
the third edition of a book of great research and ability—*A
Dissertation on St. Paul's Voyage from Cæsarea to Puteoli*.
Referring to *Observations relating to Natural History
selected from the Principal Writers of Antiquity*, Dr. Parr
says:—"I have lately been instrumental in procuring from the
Cambridge Press the publication of a work on botanical
subjects by my friend, Dr. Falconer, whose knowledge is
various and profound, and whose discrimination on all topics

of literature are ready, vigorous and comprehensive." The high opinion entertained of him by his brethren in the Metropolis led to his being consulted by a large number of distinguished people who came to Bath, among them Mr. Pitt, whom he attended here in his last illness in 1805. With reference to his position in local society, about that time in its most brilliant phase, Mrs. Piozzi relates that when any doubt existed among the *literati*, either on a point of scholarship or an historical fact, the common remark was, " We must go to Falconer."

His son, Dr. Thomas Falconer, also lived at No. 29, in the Bath Circus. After graduating at Oxford in 1810 as a student for the Church, he filled the post of Bampton lecturer. He was distinguished by a wide field of knowledge, manifest in the authorship of twenty-three works, classical, medical and theological. Dalzell, Greek professor at Edinburgh, was much struck with his acquirements as a scholar, and Nares, so renowned for his erudition, calls himself a " humble admirer of his great talents." That he was chosen by his University (Oxford) to edit the *Geography of Strabo* is a sufficient indication of his learning. As a clergyman he often assisted his friend, the Bath historian, the Rev. Richard Warner, in his clerical work in St. James's parish, and after receiving the degree of M.D., gave much medical advice to the poor. He has been justly described as " a man of singular independence of character, a fine scholar and a notable citizen." He had five sons and two daughters. His eldest son, Rector of Bushey, translated his edition of the *Geography of Strabo* for Bohn's Library; another son was many years judge of a County Court in South Wales; and the youngest, Dr. Randle Wilbraham Falconer, was the third physician of the family.

One of the daughters married the Right Hon. J. A. Roebuck, M.P. This second Dr. Falconer died in 1839, and was buried near his father in Weston Churchyard.

To the memory of Dr. Randle Wilbraham Falconer an appropriate tribute was paid in a memoir by Mr. Peach soon after his death, which, to the sorrow of a large circle of friends, occurred in 1881. What he did for the city as a twice-elected mayor, as a humane and judicious magistrate, as a physician advancing the best interests of the profession both by his pen and practise, and as a supporter of numerous useful institutions, all this is held in grateful remembrance. Who that was privileged to work with him would forget his efforts to establish the Bath City Lectures, which were successful, or those for a Public Abattoir and a Public Library, which were unsuccessful? Forty years have passed since those efforts were made. So much has been done in the interval for the benefit of the city that it may be hoped the spirit of 1853 has gained fresh strength, and the objects then advocated may yet be accomplished. More and more obvious is the need of a Public Library since the Schools for Technical Education have been founded, the provision for which can hardly be deemed complete without such an institution in immediate connection with them and the benefit of which might be shared by every class in the city. Like his brother, the County Court Judge, who by his benevolence and public spirit in South Wales gained so much distinction, Dr. Randle Wilbraham Falconer threw bread upon the waters which was sure to be found after many days. Both helped to make the world better than they found it, and neither will soon be forgotten in the city which they loved.

CHAPTER XIV.

PHYSICIANS OF THE EIGHTEENTH AND NINETEENTH CENTURIES.

PART II.

If it be thought that members of the medical profession occupy too large a space in these pages, it should be remembered that for several centuries no other profession has been so prominent in Bath. Next to the springs they have been the chief attraction to visitors; what they could do to restore health or alleviate maladies has been the chief consideration; many celebrated men of other kinds might come and go; celebrated physicians were always here. Those of whom I have now to write are Dr. Sibthorpe, Dr. Cogan, Sir George Gibbes, Dr. Parry and Dr. Barlow.

DR. SIBTHORPE.

It has been said that Dr. Sibthorpe must have been an eminent man to have had such a beautiful monument in Bath Abbey. Certainly the skill of Flaxman was rarely employed with greater success, and the effect is more striking in consequence of the generally poor character of the sculpture around. Excepting another work by Flaxman, two by Chantry, and a few by Hoare, Nollekens, Westmacott and the Bacons, the hundreds of tombs, tablets, emblems and medallions in the Abbey have scarcely any artistic feature to recommend them. Not that the families who ordered the memorials can be blamed; men like the brothers of Bishop

J

Montague and the friends of Waller, the Parliamentary General, did the best they could in the then state of English Art.

That Dr. Sibthorpe *was* eminent there can be no doubt. Few among the concourse among whom he lies better deserved a handsome monument. He spent his short life in advancing the science of botany, travelling over the world to increase a knowledge of Nature's most beautiful works. He first visited France and Italy after completing his University studies ; then on his return was appointed Professor of Botany at Oxford in succession to his father. Twice in subsequent years he sailed to Greece, travelled in parts of the country usually unexplored, accumulated specimens of rare plants and returned to embody the scientific results in a splendid work which unfortunately could not be published until after his death. The last journey in 1749 was undertaken at a time when his delicate health made it hazardous. Not recovering he settled at Bath for a better climate and congenial society, continuing the preparation of his work until his pen was laid aside for ever. His *Flora Oxoniensis* he had published at Bath about 1794 ; for his *Flora Græca* he left an estate to the University of Oxford, requiring that any surplus should be devoted to founding a Professorship of Rural Economy. He died at Bath in 1800 at the age of thirty-eight.

DR. COGAN.

This gentleman was a striking instance of the versatility of some physicians of the period. Probably his varied training may account in some measure for his divers tastes and pursuits. Beginning his education at a good school at Kibworth under Dr. Aikin, the father of Mrs. Barbauld, he continued it for the Nonconformist ministry at Mile-end and Homerton. His earliest settlement was as pastor of a congregation at the Hague, from whence he came back again to England for another at Southampton, but here as in the Dutch city his stay was short. There were two causes for the next step : he announced to his flock that he had become a Unitarian, of which they disapproved, and he had gained in Holland the affections of a young lady whom he wished to marry. So he returned to Holland, studied medicine at Leyden, wrote in 1767 a learned thesis, took his degree, married the lady, and practised successively at Leyden, Amsterdam, and Rotterdam. After a few years thus spent he returned to London and devoted himself to the obstetrical branch of his profession. It may be supposed that he was also devoted to books from his settlement at Paternoster Row ; there, however, he soon became in request, chiefly with the city ladies, and by their means established a prosperous reputation. I learn this from a little work by Dr. Julian Hunter entitled *Old Age in Bath.* The subjects are Dr. Sherwen and Dr. Cogan, two physicians well known to his father, the Rev. Joseph Hunter. Dr. Sherwen's fame was literary rather than medical, being gained chiefly by the prominent part he took in the Chatterton controversy.

Respecting Dr. Cogan's devotion to midwifery, Dr. Hunter remarks that the practise of it was at that time with men both a speciality and a novelty. The other sex had been accustomed to officiate in such cases, a woman having presided over the births of all the sons of Queen Charlotte. It may be easily imagined that Mrs. Gamps abounded in those days and that a demand had arisen for well-qualified men as accoucheurs. If Dr. Cogan had been living now he would probably have been one of the first to see that women of the requisite mental and moral power might be advan-

tageously trained for a kind of practise so peculiarly suited
to them. But he had to deal with the case as it stood;
public opinion was against the Mrs. Gamps and in favour of
educated men; he was known to be one of much skill and
judgment and easily gained a large practise. Often sent for
at a late hour of the day he and his kind of work were so well
known that people who met him on his nocturnal expeditions
would say, "there goes Dr. Cogan to a lying-in." Even the
footpads, so common at the time, were said to have spared
him, and the police gave more than the usual protection. It
is related that on one occasion he was taken blind-folded to a
certain large house, carried to a lady's room, paid a fifty
pound note and conducted back without knowing his
employer. Another lady who needed no concealment once
remonstrated with him on his dress, which was not in the
usual professional style: "Pray, sir, can you be a doctor;
you dress like a gentleman." He answered, "Really, madam,
if it will increase your confidence or contribute to your ease
I will send for my cane and my very best wig."

Dr. Cogan's London reputation also grew in other ways.
While living at Amsterdam he had been interested in a
society for recovering the drowned. In 1773 he translated
the memoirs of this society for publication in London, and in
1774 he and his friend, Dr. Hawes, founded the Royal
Humane Society of London. To his pen were due its first
six annual reports, by the circulation of which and his own
personal efforts an impulse was given to the establishment of
similar institutions in many parts of the world. Having no
children and not being eager for wealth, Dr. Cogan disposed
of his practise to Dr. Sims who became the first accoucheur
in London. Then he returned for a short time to Holland
to pursue the study of moral philosophy for which he had

already gained repute. There, to gratify at the same time his Dutch wife and his own agricultural taste, he hired a fine family estate called Zulenstein. But it was a time when revolution was in the air all over the continent. He was driven back to England and settled at Bath, living here about twenty years. His time was much devoted to the publication of his various philosophical works, notably his *Treatise on the Passions*, which passed through several editions. He had been known as an author in London by a *Life of John Buncle, junior, Gentleman*, intended as a sequel to Mr. Amory's popular novel with a similar title. Other works of more or less merit and on a great variety of subjects owed their authorship to him.

The activity of Dr. Cogan's mind was certainly not diminished by the climate of Bath. He had always a passion for farming, to indulge which he took land at South Wraxall and was well known both as a practical and theoretical agriculturist. He took a prominent part with Sir Benjamin Hobhouse, Dr. Falconer and Dr. Parry on the Council of the Bath and West of England Society in its early days, often winning prizes at the annual exhibitions. He founded a Bath Humane Society which still exists after the lapse of four-score and ten years, and he always kept up his connection with the parent society in London, watching over its interests and attending its annual meetings. At one of these he received the beautiful gold medal of which only five were minted, one each for George III., the Duke of Kent, the Duke of Sussex, Dr. Hawes and himself. At another meeting there was a curious scene: a Royal Highness in the chair, Dr. Lettsom the eminent Quaker physician the chief speaker, Dr. Cogan singing songs of his own composition, and a solemn procession of persons who had been rescued from drowning walking round the room while the company joined in the choruses. His steadfast attachment to the institution was shown by a bequest of £100 in his will.

Dr. Cogan's ready wit and habitual cheerfulness made him a welcome guest in the circles he joined. It happened that in Bath some of these were followers of Mr. Jay, others those of the Unitarian minister, Mr. Hunter; with the former he became intimate, because Mrs. Cogan, being a Dutch Calvinist, attended his chapel, and his connection with the latter may be inferred from the fact that he was one of those who invited Mr. Hunter to settle in Bath. His religion had no trace of sectarianism in it; the theological works he published were remarkable for their catholic spirit; he is represented by an American biographer as "steadying the trembling hand of eighty-two to show that the chief object of the Great Creator is the happiness of all his creatures, and that man has no higher mission than to aid by every possible means in its fulfilment." Dr. Cogan having removed to London on the death of his wife died there in 1818. He followed soon afterwards and was buried at Hackney. He requested that the inscription on his grave-stone should be "Jesus said: I am the Resurrection and the Life." Mrs. Cogan's resting place was at Widcombe.

Dr. Cogan had a half-brother of much repute as a Greek scholar and schoolmaster—the Rev. Eliezer Cogan. In early life he also became a Unitarian, and for many years ministered to a church of that body at Walthamstow. On being introduced to Porson with the remark that he was intensely devoted to Greek, the Professor answered, "If so you must be content with bread and cheese for the rest of your life." But he could not be dissuaded from writing and publishing, in addition to works of religious and practical usefulness, some on his favourite subject, the study of the classics. That his love of ancient literature would gain for him the regard of men like Porson and Parr was very natural, also that his success as a teacher would cause his school to be filled with pupils. Belonging to Nonconformist families, many of them yet became highly distinguished in public life. One was Benjamin Disraeli, of whom he used to say, " I don't like him, I can never get him to understand the subjunctive." Others were Samuel Sharpe the Egyptologist, Lord Overstone the banker, Mr. Russell Gurney Recorder of London, and Mr. Milner Gibson a Cabinet Minister.

SIR GEORGE SMITH GIBBES

may be also fairly ranked with the Bath Celebrities. " He enjoyed," says Mr. Monkland in his *Literature and Literati of Bath,* " a very extensive practise for many years." The same genial chronicler also writes of him as not only a man of much skill, but "kind-hearted, liberal in his medical profession, social in his habits and a very agreeable companion." The praise of the writer, however, is not indiscriminate, for though he states that " he was a universal genius and nothing came amiss to him : music, painting, philosophy, chemistry, mechanism ; yet " he adds, " like too many of the genius tribe he was as fickle as he was versatile in his pursuits,

' Everything by turns and nothing long.' "

George Smith Gibbes was the son of the Rev. George Gibbes, D.D., rector of Woodborough, in Wiltshire. From a school at Southampton he proceeded to Exeter College, Oxford, and graduated B.A. in 1792. He was then elected a fellow of Magdalen, took the degree of M.B. in 1796, and of M.D. three years afterwards. Several instances of the same

date suggest the remark that Lord Salisbury's recent complaint
on visiting Oxford was not so applicable then as now. "I
always think," said the Chancellor, "that the science of
medicine has scarcely received among us the tribute it ought
to receive among sciences which rest upon observation.
It is the most sober, the most absolute, the most positive of
all sciences. Others give wide play to the imagination, but
scientific imagination is the snare of scientific men. If you
indulge in it by the bedside of a patient the patient dies."

Forcible as these words are, they appear to indicate the
tendency, if real, of the close of the nineteenth rather than
that of the eighteenth century. The experience of Gibbes
and many of his contemporaries at Oxford appears to have
been practical rather than imaginative and the history of
other medical men who did good work in Bath bears similar
testimony. Becoming a fellow of the Royal College of
Physicians the new alumnus devoted himself to the ailments
especially requiring his attention in the city of the springs.
Here, in 1800, he published his first *Treatise on the Bath
Waters*, and, in 1803, his second, both above the average of
works on the subject. In 1804 he was elected physician to
the Bath (Mineral Water) Hospital; some years later he
successively delivered his Harveian oration before the college,
obtained the appointment of Physician Extraordinary to
Queen Charlotte, and was knighted by George IV. The last
of these honours was conferred in 1820. In addition to the
private pursuits and accomplishments mentioned by Mr.
Monkland, he was much interested in non-professional public
matters, being a magistrate for the county of Somerset, filling
an office in the Bath Corporation, and taking an active part
in founding the Bath Literary Institution. On him devolved
the honour of delivering the lecture at the opening of the

Institution on the advantages of its establishment, which was followed the next year by Mr. Hunter's, *On the connection of Bath with the Literature and Science of England.* Dr. Munk, in his *Roll of the Royal College of Physicians*, states that Sir George Gibbes practised here with distinguished reputation and success many years. About 1835 he quitted Bath and retired to Sidmouth, where he died in 1851, aged eighty. Of the church in that town his son was incumbent, and there may be seen a mural tablet to his memory. One of his most remarkable works was entitled, *Observations on the component parts of Animal Matters, and their conversion into a substance resembling Spermaciti.* This, of course, appeared in his younger days, when chemistry was his ruling passion.

DR. PARRY.

We now come to a name more familiar in the present day than any that have preceded it. No Bath physician of his time had a higher standing than the first Doctor Parry, and throughout the kingdom he had great repute both for his writings and practise. Much of his culture he owed to near kindred and early associations ; his father, the Rev. Joshua Parry, a learned Nonconformist minister at Cirencester, being the intimate friend of Earl Bathurst, who lived near and was the Mæcenas of the time. His college training he received at Warrington, where the society of Dr. Aikin, his daughter Mrs. Barbauld and the Rigby family aided greatly in the formation of his mind. Having begun his medical studies at Edinburgh, he continued them two years in the house of Dr. Denman, a friend of the Aikins and father of the Lord Chief Justice. Prior to his settlement at Bath in 1779 he married Miss Rigby, whose brother at Norwich and nephew in London both attained medical celebrity and who shared all the high tastes of her husband. His practise, small at first as usual, steadily increased until it included a list of patients perhaps larger and more remarkable than that of any other local practitioner in the kingdom. It was the period 1780 to 1816, during which Bath was in the zenith of its fame, and Dr. Parry's memoranda show that many of the British nobility and most distinguished men of the time consulted him. Beginning with receipts for the first year of £39, he notes them for the fifth £239; for the tenth £1,600, and afterwards nearly £3,000. There is a story that during some epidemic he was returning home after a long morning's work when a friend remarked that his waistcoat pockets, of the large fashion of the time, seemed very full, probably of guineas. "Yes," he said, "I believe there are ninety-nine, I may make it a round sum before I get home." Yet Dr. Parry was not mercenary; if he enjoyed success he deserved it; through a long life he studied earnestly; he published many elaborate treatises; he cultivated music, painting and literature, and he devoted much time to works of benevolence and public utility. In 1782 he was elected Governor of the Bath Hospital, in 1800 fellow of the Royal Society, in successive years a member of other learned bodies at home and abroad, and lastly he was honoured with the Bedford Gold Medal of the Bath and West of England Agricultural Society for his varied services during thirty-seven years. The land he purchased on Sion Hill, where he built Summerhill, enabled him to try various minor experiments in agriculture, while a farm he hired in the neighbourhood gave scope for that breeding of sheep and production of wool for which he was celebrated. He died in 1822, after seeing his sons become worthy of their parentage, the elder following the same profession in the same city, the youngest distinguished as a naval officer by Arctic discoveries. Dr. Parry's friends caused a handsome monument to be erected to his memory in the choir of the Abbey Church.

The elder son, Dr. Charles Henry Parry, succeeded his father at Summerhill. He also had a considerable practise and was widely known as an accomplished physician. But he probably distinguished himself more in literature than in medicine, for which his education at the University of Gottingen and his travels in Germany with S. T. Coleridge gave him a strong bias. Pursuing his academic course at Edinburgh he made the acquaintance of Mr., afterwards Lord, Brougham, with whom he long maintained a correspondence. Some of the best years of his life were devoted to the elucidation and confirmation of his father's medical views, which he accomplished by editing and publishing in several volumes his various writings. He was also the author of a work of considerable research, *The Parliaments and Councils of England from William the Conqueror to the Revolution in* 1688, and of a life of his grandfather, the Nonconformist minister, which was edited after his death by his relative, Sir J. Eardley-Wilmot, Bart. Dr. Charles Parry some years before his death retired to Brighton, where he died in 1860 full of years. He was buried in a family vault at Weston, near Bath, several of his daughters having preceded him.

The fame of the younger son was national rather than local. Sir Edward Parry will be known in the annals of England as a distinguished Arctic navigator and the worthy companion of Sir John Franklin. Five quarto volumes written by his own hand in successive years testify to the work those brave men did, their unfailing courage and their patriotic service. Step by step they advanced until they reached the higher posts of their profession, always displaying the qualities that deserved them, receiving at length their knighthood together, and standing, side by side, at an Oxford commemoration for the degree of D.C.L. All this is told with much beauty of expression by the Rev. Edward Parry, in a memoir of his father's life. There we learn that the home of the navigator's childhood continued ever dear to him, and there that his native city was always foremost to do him honour. While the Bath Corporation led other municipal bodies in presenting him with the freedom of their city, the Bath people showed their grateful remembrance by a handsome offering of plate. In all national manifestations, however, the two friends were hand in hand, as when at Oxford the Prize Poem of the year was recited with the lines alluding to their return :—

> " But fairer England greets the wanderers now,
>   Unfading laurels shade her Parry's brow,
>   And on the proud memorials of her fame,
>   Lives, linked with deathless glory, Franklin's name."

DR. BARLOW.

A few readers of these sketches probably remember Dr. Barlow, who for thirty-seven years, until his death in 1848, was prominent in Bath. Born at Mullingar, in the county of Meath, and the son of a distinguished medical man, he was educated for the same profession, attending the schools of Dublin, Edinburgh and London. He practised in Dublin until 1807, when he removed to Bath to begin the career which rendered him one of the most useful and honoured members of the profession. His private practise, although considerable, was surpassed by that of several of his brethren, but his work as physician to both the large hospitals and his various scientific publications gained for him great repute.

He was scarcely ever absent from the hospitals on his allotted day, and at the "United" generally passed from three to four hours investigating the cases of out-door patients and pre-scribing for their relief. The kindness with which he listened to their histories made him a great favourite, though an occasional quickness of manner when he was overburthened with work may have been slightly observable. His real feeling was manifest in the practical direction of all his efforts. No better illustration is needed than the "Flannel Waistcoat Charity" which he established to meet the want of sufficient clothing, and is still one of the most useful in connection with the Hospital.

Among his intimate friends and fellow workers was one who thoroughly sympathised with him in all his benevolent and scientific projects—Mr. J. Soden. They were both ardent Phrenologists, and together founded a local Phreno-logical Society, engaging Mr. George Combe to deliver a course of lectures and enlisting a considerable number of members for the discussion of problems. There could be no better testimony to Dr. Barlow's favourite theories on the subject than his own broad, beautiful forehead, and fine, regular features—all eloquent of his moral and mental qualities. Whether his scientific knowledge of physical deficiencies in the brains of others strengthened his charit-able allowances or not, it is certain that in this respect his example was in unison with his doctrine. It would be easily imagined that when it was proposed to found a Literary and Scientific Institution worthy of the city, he was one of the most active supporters ; nor should it be forgotten that the offshoot which flourishes to this day—the Literary and Philosophical Association—owed its formation in a great measure to him. Of his medical works those in the highest repute were eight valuable treatises in the *Cyclopædia of Practical Medicine* and an *Essay on Physical Education*, the latter having been translated into several European languages. He also published pamphlets on Medical Reform, the Bath Waters, The Study of Phrenology and numerous essays in the Medical Journals illustrating the pathology and treatment of disease. With all his skill and knowledge, however, he could not baffle the great enemy beyond the age of sixty-three. Nearly fifty years have now passed since his death ; many good men have come and gone, but few more worthy of honoured remembrance than Dr. Barlow.

Other ornaments of the medical profession have also passed away in the present century whose memories those who knew them would not willingly let die. A more copious biographer, one with a wider scope than the present, should do justice to physicians like Dr. Daniel Pring and Dr. James Watson, also to surgeons like Mr. George Norman and Mr. Richard Thomas Gore. Knowing and esteeming them all as I did, whether for great professional skill or enlightened public spirit, whether battling with acute disease in the private chamber or giving their noble services in the public hospital, I regret that I must content myself with paying this short tribute to their worth.

CHAPTER XV.

DR. HENRY HARINGTON.

Dr. Henry Harington was fifth in descent from Sir John Harington, Queen Elizabeth's godson. The intermediate descendants having been also connected with Bath it will be right to state first a little of what is known of them. Few families in any city can trace their pedigree through five hundred years and point to a succession of eminent ancestors from the time of the Wars of the Roses to the present century; but this is what a respected member of the Harington family now living in Bath can do.

Sir John Harington, of the Tudor times, died at Kelston in 1612, leaving seven children. His ideas as to education, like many of his other ideas, were peculiar and produced a result he did not anticipate. Although a strong Royalist he is said to have placed his eldest son to be trained by a Puritan, hoping he would see in him and his party so much to dislike as to be confirmed in the old faith. What the young man's impressions were when he returned home does not appear, but it is certain that eventually he became both Presbyterian and Parliamentarian, and was censured accordingly by party writers. He was much liked, however, in the neighbourhood of Kelston, where he inherited his father's estate. As member for Bath in the time of the Commonwealth and Chairman of Sessions for the county of Somerset he was prominent and influential. He married Lady Dioness Ley, daughter of the first Earl of Marlborough, and dying in 1654 left several children, the eldest surviving son being John, his successor.

This John was born in 1627. He also belonged to the
Puritan party, and, on the accession of Charles II., was thereby
in danger of much tribulation. In 1660 Lord Chancellor
Hyde wrote to Lord Poulett for "a true account of all who
had been employed in the late troubles by commission, civil
or military, under the Usurper." "Among some others," he
continues, "information is delivered of John Harington, son
to the late member for the city of Bath, bearing arms by
virtue of commission from the Usurper." This demand and
Lord Poulett's answer are found in *Nugæ-Antiquæ*, written
by a Harington, and have been lately reproduced, in beautiful
facsimiles illustrating the Harington pedigree, by the Rev.
F. J. Poynton, rector of Kelston. Lord Poulett replied to
Lord Hyde that he had submitted his lordship's letter to
Mr. Harington, in which it was stated "whatever the father's
principles led him to, the son was no object for his Majestie's
displeasure." The reply was followed by a curious certificate
as to the good intention of the Kelston squire, signed by
Lord Poulett and twenty other noblemen and gentlemen of
Somerset. The substance was that he did accept a commission from Cromwell, and that the signers themselves had
earnestly entreated him to do so, but it was in order that
they and their families might be secured from the "spoyle
and ruine" they anticipated from the Civil War. "To the
above certificate," says Harington in a memorandum on the
same page in Mr. Poynton's book, "I am indebted for my life
and fortune, which otherwise had been forfeited by the laws
of the land, and hereby I obtained under the seal of England
his Majestie's most gracious pardon."

In preparing for his work Mr. Poynton examined, among
other MSS.,the Records of the City of Bath. He there found
that this John Harington was first chosen, with Mr. James

Ash, member for Bath in 1658. It was four years after his father's death, which is at variance with the statement in *Nugæ-Antiquæ* that he went in 1646 "to dine with the Maior and citizens to confer with them about serving in Parliament as his father was helpless and could not go any more ;" adding that he could not, however, be excused, and that "the Maior promised him and Sir John Horner a horse apiece." "Nor," adds Mr. Poynton, " is the name of Horner for Bath anywhere discernible. In fact the borough seems to have gone short with one member for some years previous to 1658. Has the compiler of the *Nugæ* confounded the representation with that of the shire? It would seem so." Whatever the public duties and trials of this Mr. Harington may have been, he had many of a private nature in connection with his property. As his mother, Lady Dioness, survived her husband twenty years, and Kelston was settled on her for her life, the son lived at Corston, another family estate, though her ladyship spent her time almost entirely in Bath or London. During her absence Kelston became greatly deteriorated, so that when the heir came to his inheritance his fortune was sorely taxed. The claims upon him were very heavy. Married four times, he had twenty children and innumerable grandchildren. Yet he was very generous, a benefactor to many parishes, and always ready with his purse for good public objects. His name is in the list of contributors to the old Bath Abbey Library. One of his wives having property in Marshfield he made a bequest to that parish. Kelston was liberally remembered in his will, and the vicarage of Weston was re-endowed with certain sources of income which had been alienated by some ancestor.

On his death, in 1700, another John Harington, his son, succeeded him at Kelston. In 1725 *he* died and being

K

childless, his brother Henry inherited the estate. This was
the father of the chief subject of the present sketch, by whose
aid, as the eldest son, he disentailed the property. Mr.
Poynton has shown how seriously the family resources had
been reduced from time to time, dating so far back as the
outlay by Sir John "in completing and adorning the great
mansion called Kelston house." Probably for this purpose
two of the manors granted by Henry VIII. were disposed of:—
St. Catherine's Court in Batheaston and Nyland near Glastonbury. Sir John also spent large sums of money in litigation ;
he attempted to recover some ancient manors belonging to
another branch of the family, and he undertook a Star
Chamber suit against his wife's relations, the Rogers's of
Cannington. Again, the manorial estate of Corston, which
the frugality of Sir John's son, the Parliamentarian, had added
to the family resources, was, in 1693, diverted to the use of
another branch. Thus were the acquisitions of one generation lost by the bad management of another. The more
immediate cause of the sale of Kelston by the father of Dr.
Harington of Bath, appears to have been the heavy charge
on the estate for the legacies and marriage portions of the
owner's younger brothers and sisters. He clung, however,
to his ancestral property till 1759, when, finding he could no
longer support his position, he availed himself of his power
to sell. The estate was bought by Mr. Hawkins, an eminent
surgeon, afterwards Sir Cæsar Hawkins, baronet, who pulled
down the large stately mansion and built a smaller one. Dr.
Pocock, the antiquary, happened to be in Bath during the
demolition, and describes in his tour the grandeur and great
solidity of the old edifice. The last owner retired to Bath,
where he spent the remaining years of his life, enjoying the
society of his son. He died in 1769 at the age of eighty-
three, and was buried among his ancestors at Kelston.

At length we come to the life of Dr. Henry Harington, "whose memory," Mr. Poynton justly says, "still lingers in Bath as of one long known and very highly esteemed there." "It comes under our notice," he adds, "accompanied at first by sad reflections If we grieve over the demolition of the ancient and beautiful home, what must be our regret for the last Harington born within its walls, baptised in the old parish church and associated with all its ancestral surroundings. It seems hard that the only surviving son should never himself enjoy the property, but should find himself, on coming of age, with no power in family affairs because his elder brother had joined his father in barring the entail."

Still there was much to reconcile him to his lot. The long, painful struggle with strained circumstances was ended. The reverse had not been caused by the follies and vices which had ruined so many wealthy families. The estates had not been wasted by costly election contests or gambled away on the turf or at the card table. In addition to the father's unsullied name there were his own pleasant professional prospects and circle of congenial friends. No man was better able to say, "My mind to me a kingdom is." Not destined to be Squire of Kelston, he chose the work of life most conducive to the enjoyment and usefulness of life. Holy Orders had been thought of, but he wanted wider scope than they would have allowed him, and after the usual course at Oxford he studied medicine. His first settlement was at Wells, where two of his uncles (Hudlestones) were successively rectors of St. Cuthbert's Church. Here he practised eighteen years, earnestly cultivating all the time his love of music.

In 1757 he removed to Bath, where he followed a medical uncle, Dr. Edward Harington. The literary as well as musical society was larger, and he had more inducements to cultivate his talents in both directions. Fifty and sixty years ago one often met in Bath Society those who remembered his genial manners, his agreeable conversation and his rich stores of anecdote. The benevolence of Dr. Henry Harington was known to all the country round. He was warmly interested in the Bath Hospital, now styled the Mineral Water Hospital, to which he was physician. Not only was his house open on certain days to the poor who needed his advice, but he willingly wrote it to those at a distance who were unable to come.

His facile pen was never more successful than when appealing for charitable objects. To his love of literature testimony is given by various writers of the time. There was a Rev. Samuel Rogers who published a Latin version of *Gay's Elegant Fable* of the shepherd and philosopher. He dedicated the book to "the ingenious, learned and judicious" Dr. Harington, and mentions his literary merit as one of his claims to distinction. Mr. Monkland in his pleasant little volumes on *The Literature and Literati of Bath* describes Dr. Harington among a knot of good talkers at Bull's Library, a favourite place of resort, in his accustomed chair, with his full-bottomed wig, his three-cornered hat and full of animation though quite blind and approaching his ninetieth year. Of his wit there is a specimen in his well known epigram in the Abbey Church :

> " These walls adorned with monument and bust
> Show how Bath Waters serve to lay the dust."

His political proclivities may be inferred from one of his toasts :

> " Here's to Rex, Lex and Pontifex,
> A toast no loyal heart rejects :

The King in safety all protects
The Church to future bliss directs.
May knaves who plot the State to vex
Find Law provides for all their necks."

Milder and more in accord with his usual mood were his lines on

THE THREE ENGLISH PHILOSOPHERS.

"Three wondrous sages midst these eras born
Revered for knowledge, Albion's isle adorn.
One called forth Science as she slumbering lay,
And led the dawn of intellectual day.
The next through life immersed in Thought profound,
Toiling for Truth search'd Nature's ample round.
The third reviewed with new enlightened soul
Improved all past and perfected the whole."

In the time of Dr. Harington, and notably by his efforts scientific music was much cultivated in Bath. For some years prior to his settlement here the concerts and oratorios had obtained considerable repute. William Herschel and his gifted sister Caroline, the Linleys—"the nest of nightingales" beloved by Dr. Burney, with a few others were heard of everywhere. The passionate love of music which Harington had cherished from his earliest years was probably one strong reason for his removal to a city where it would find ample scope. Rauzzini had become Director of the public concerts, Incledon was articled to the Director, Braham lived in his house, Madame Mara and Mrs. Billington were as great attractions then as Madame Catalani and others were afterwards. A catch club had been popular, but was beginning to decay. Harington, with the assistance of two friends the Rev. John Bowen and the Rev. Thomas Broadhurst, both of whom I knew well, formed out of its remnants the Bath Harmonic Society. He also published a long series of musical compositions, much admired in their day, especially the glees and anthems. Perhaps he gained the greatest fame by his *Eloi* or *The Last Words of our Saviour*, which was sung for many years on Good Friday in the Abbey Church and other churches in Bath. The versatility of his mind on various subjects is shown in works as different from each other as the *Ode to Discord* and the *Ode to Harmony*, the *Witch of Wokey* a ballad in the old English style, and the *Geometrical Analogy of the Catholic Doctrine of the Trinity*. Nor did these numerous works prevent his interest in various city matters. As trustee of his mother, he contracted for the erection of Northumberland buildings. It was in one of these houses he lived some years until his death, and there he gathered his congenial friends around him to share his hospitality. He was a member of the Bath Corporation many years, and filled the offices of alderman, magistrate and mayor. On his death in 1827 at the age of eighty-nine, he was buried with his ancestors at Kelston, but an elegant monument was erected to his memory in the Abbey Church with a long classical inscription, six lines of which indicate his leading characteristics :—

> Medicus solers et fidelis
> Poeta lepidus ;
> Musicus sciens et peritus ;
> Magistratus, gravis, justus et acer ;
> Erga suos amantissimus ;
> Erga omnes comis et benevolus.

Further knowledge of the life and works of this excellent man may be obtained from various memoirs, notably from one in the third volume of the *Bath and Bristol Magazine,* published in 1834. The author signs himself Philo-Musicus, the real name being probably the Rev. Thomas Broadhurst, an intimate friend and most genial fellow-worker in the Harmonic Society and other kindred objects. He states that Dr. Harington "married the amiable and accomplished Miss Musgrave, of Oxford," by whom there were four children, hree sons and a daughter. The eldest son, Edward, was Mayor of Bath in 1745, and having taken up a loyal address from the Corporation was knighted by George III. Sir Edward was the author of several spirited and ingenious publications. One of the most interesting in Bath was *A Schizzo on the Genius of Man,* in which the merits of Thomas Barker, who had recently acquired fame by his picture "The Woodman" were particularly considered. Dr. Harington's second son, Henry, was a Prebendary at Norwich, where he was popular and useful as a preacher, and where in 1799 he published the second edition of a remarkable book *Nugæ·Antiquæ,* relating chiefly to his distinguished ancestor of Queen Elizabeth's time. Sir Edward's son married a Somersetshire lady of fortune, Miss Bave, descended from the eminent physician noticed in a former sketch, and his grandson was a clergyman in recent times and of great repute for benevolence at Exeter. He lived till 1881, was Chancellor and Sub-Dean of Exeter, an intimate friend of Bishop Philpotts and, being possessed of ample means, enjoyed the privilege of doing much practical good, especially to his poorer clerical brethren. He thoughtfully remembered in his will the poor of Kelston, where he was buried in the old family vault.*

* The connection of the Baves and Haringtons is very amply described by Mr. Poynton in the work I have often referred to

CHAPTER XVI.

SIR W. HERSCHEL AND CAROLINE HERSCHEL.

That Bath should be at all noted for scientific men has been a matter of some surprise. How contrary to the *Genius Loci* would be the exclamation of many who knew it only as a fashionable place. They would expect perhaps some musical taste and love of art, but not the patient, plodding, studious habits required in the pursuit of science. That a distinguished Astronomer and the Father of English Geology should be found in a city famed for dancing and card-playing, whose visitors were believed to worship chiefly at the shrine of Pleasure, would seem passing strange.

Yet a little inquiry would show that the fact was not new.

---

on the parish of Kelston. The description is commenced in page 78 with an elaborate chapter entitled, *The Baves of Bath and of Barrow Court, Tickenham, co. Somerset, allied to the Haringtons, both of Kelston and Corston, in the same County.* This chapter is followed by an exhaustive pedigree of the Baves and copious summaries of their wills, from the time when Dr. Samuel Bave settled in Bath in 1640 to the death of Dr. Anthony Bave of Wootton-under-Edge, in 1738. The first Dr. Bave of Bath bought Barrow Court some time before his death, and bequeathed it to his son Anthony, with contingent remainder to another son, Charles, who was also devisee of his father's house and gardens in Bath and property in Gloucester, sole executor of his mother's will and inheritor of lands at Tickenham. That a Bath physician of the seventeenth century should have been in a position to found a family as thus described is noteworthy in connection with the local medical history of the period.

It would be seen that in almost every period of the history of Bath, science has had its votaries there. The mysterious springs alone would have given an impulse to investigation, and brought thoughtful men intent on more than common aims. Century after century, from the time of Adelard and John de Villula to that of Herschel and William Smith, such men have appeared, as these pages testify, quickened themselves and quickening others. Within twenty-five years of recent times two of the largest scientific societies in the kingdom, the British Association and the Bath and West and Southern Counties Society, have each held two meetings at intervals in Bath, and nowhere have they been more warmly welcomed, nowhere more successful as to numbers, earnestness and practical results.

The first of the names at the head of this sketch belongs rightly to national rather than local history. But Herschel began his astronomical career in Bath, spent some of the best days of his life here, and by his great discoveries added to the reputation of the city. His early history, like that of many remarkable men, illustrates the influence of difficulties in forming character and ensuring ultimate success. The family were of Jewish origin, the heads of three successive generations being called Abraham, Isaac and Jacob, but all became Christian confessors. Abraham, expelled from Mahren, his place of residence in Germany, on account of his Protestantism, was the great uncle of the astronomer, whose father was originally a farmer near Leipsic. The farmer, excelling in the national aptitude for music, gave up his farm to teach what he knew so well, and was able to develop considerable musical talent in all his ten children.

William, the future astronomer, was born at Hanover in 1738, and came to England when twenty-one to earn his living by his father's profession.   Having intellectual tastes he had been provided at home with a French tutor, under whom he had made considerable progress in logic, ethics and metaphysics.   But his studies were interrupted by the poverty of his family, and at fourteen he was placed in the band of the Hanoverian Regiment of Guards, a detachment of which he accompanied to Yorkshire.   After many struggles with adverse fortune he attracted the notice of Lord Darlington, who engaged him to instruct a military band then forming for the Durham Militia.   Having fulfilled this engagement, he passed several years in the West Riding, giving lessons in the principal towns, and employing his leisure in improving his knowledge of English, acquiring Italian, and improving his Greek and Latin.   In 1765 he gained the situation of organist at Halifax.   There also he taught music and directed oratorios and concerts.   And there, moreover, with a view to master the theory of harmony, he taught himself mathematics, which led ultimately to his great astronomical investigations.

It was in the following year, 1766, he removed to Bath.   He was accompanied by his elder brother, who, with a sister, be- came his companion for many years.   The brothers were both engaged by Mr. Linley for the Pump Room Band, and William also obtained the situation of organist to the Octagon Chapel, which was very advantageous as leading to a profitable range of public and private engagements.   Caroline, an admirable woman, poor, patient, self-denying, self-educated, found employment first as her brother's leading solo singer at his various concerts, also in training the trebles and copying the scores, afterwards in aiding him to perfect his astronomical instruments and to "sweep the heavens" from the little garden at the back of the home in New King Street.   This work of perfecting the instruments by the brother and sister is one of the most interesting in the records of science. We have seen that Herschel's thirst for knowledge of the heavenly bodies had been stimulated by his mathematical acquirements. After working twelve or fourteen hours a day at lessons to musical pupils, or conducting concerts and oratorios, he sought relaxation in studying optics. He borrowed from a friend in Bath a two-feet Gregorian telescope which delighted him so much that he commissioned a friend in London to buy one of larger dimensions, but found that the price was beyond his means. By no means discouraged, he resolved to construct the complicated machine with his own hands, and after repeated disappointments succeeded. In the year 1774 he had the great pleasure of seeing the planet Saturn through a five-feet Newtonian reflector of his own making. There could now be little doubt as to his future career.

And now old things were changed. Musical engagements were gradually relinquished. Time was found for cultivating the acquaintance of scientific men in Bath. For some years the city had had a Philosophical Institution of which Herschel was a member with a few other remarkable men. It failed to succeed, however, and another was formed, the original minute book of which is now in the possession of a Bath citizen, Mr. Frederick Shum, who has favoured me with a sight of it. Thence I learn that of this new Institution Dr. William Falconer was president, and that on the 3rd of January, 1799, Mr. Herschel and Sir William Watson were received on the ground that they had been members of the former Institution. The success of Herschel in his earlier construction of telescopes impelled him to "try his hand" at larger ones, seven, ten, and even twenty feet in length. Eventually he began a regular survey of the skies by means of a seven feet reflector, in the course of which he remarked

that a star recorded as fixed was progressively changing its
position, and by prolonged attention he was enabled to
ascertain that it was a hitherto undiscovered planet. The
Royal Society at once awarded him their annual gold medal
and elected him a Fellow. In compliment to the king he
named the planet Georgium Sidus ; continental astronomers
chose to designate it first Herschel, afterwards Uranus. The
king, however, showed his appreciation by at once granting
a salary which enabled the discoverer to give up the musical
profession and devote the rest of his life to astronomy.
What he afterwards did ; how he quitted Bath to be near the
king at Slough and was knighted in due time ; how he
constructed new instruments, made fresh discoveries, and
was duly honoured by Oxford and other seats of learning;
how he trained his son to follow in the same glorious path,
winning admiration by religious worth as well as scientific
eminence; all this may be learned from the biographers of
the period. His portrait appropriately adorns the reading-
room of the Bath Institution.

Sir William married in 1788 the daughter of Mr. Baldwin,
a London merchant, a most amiable woman whose jointure
relieved him from all pecuniary care ; they had the one
son just mentioned who was born in 1792. The king continued his sincere friendship for many years, granting him
£2,000 twice for the completion of a giant reflector in
addition to £200 a year for repairs and his salary as
Astronomer Royal. His majesty was among the many
distinguished visitors who came to Slough to see the reflector,
being accompanied on one occasion by the Archbishop of
Canterbury whom he helped through the great tube, saying
"Come my Lord Bishop I will show you the way to Heaven."
Herschel's biographers all write of him as possessing the

qualities of truly great men, kindness, modesty, simplicity and readiness to explain. His family affections were unusually strong, endearing him to his widowed mother and many other kindred whom he assisted. In 1807 he had a severe illness which permanently impaired his strength and caused him to take frequent intervals of rest at Bath and other places. He lived, however, till 1822 when he died at Slough in his eighty-fourth year, where he was buried. Lady Herschel survived him ten years.

CAROLINE HERSCHEL.

Mention of this distinguished woman is made in the preceding sketch which is given chiefly as it appeared in the original series. It was not at first my design to write a separate memoir, but having now more scope I cannot withhold a few outlines of one of the most remarkable lives in the annals of science. Bath may well be proud of Caroline Herschel; humble as her position was during the time she lived here, her path was ever onward and upward; day by day, unknown to the world, intent only on the work of the hour, she laid the foundation of a world-wide fame which will long endure the tests of time.

In the large family of the Herschel brothers and sisters at Hanover, she was the eighth child and fourth daughter. Born in 1750, she came to Bath in 1772 to assist her brother in the musical engagements to which he was then devoted. Her father being in the same profession had given her a few violin lessons which relieved her from the household drudgery imposed by her mother, and enabled her to take part in his pupil's concerts. But his untimely death made fresh efforts necessary; first she attempted to learn dressmaking in order to earn her livelihood, and then endeavoured to qualify herself as a governess by practising fancy work in hours taken from sleep. It was at this period that her brother William, to whom from childhood she had been strongly attached, offered her a home at Bath. She readily accepted the proposal and threw all her energies into everything that could advance his interests. For singing at his concerts she prepared herself by imitating the violin parts with a gag between her teeth, and is said to have " gained a tolerable execution before she began to sing."

These particulars I owe chiefly to the *Dictionary of National Biography,* its authority being Mrs. John Herschel's *Memoirs and Correspondence* of her relative. It is there stated that Caroline's brother besides giving her two singing lessons daily taught her English and Arithmetic, though her studies were impeded by continual demands for aid in his astronomical pursuits. She herself says, " The summer of 1775 was taken up with copying and practising music in addition to attendance on my brother when polishing mirrors, since by way of keeping him alive I was constantly obliged to feed him by putting food into his mouth ; I also read novels to him while he was at work, sometimes stopping to lend a hand so that in time I became as useful a member of the workshop as a boy in the first year of his apprenticeship. As I was to take part in the oratorios, I had for a whole twelve-month two lessons a week from Miss Fleming, the celebrated dancing mistress, to drill me for a gentlewoman ; God knows how she succeeded." The brother aided the preparation by giving her ten guineas with which to buy a dress, the result being that on her first appearance she was pronounced " an ornament to the stage" and received much applause. She sang as first treble in the Messiah, Judas Maccabeus and other pieces, at Bath and Bristol, sometimes five nights in the week, but declined an engagement for the Birmingham Festival, having resolved to appear only where her brother conducted. Their last public performance was at Margaret's Chapel, Bath, on Whitsunday, 1782.

This was prior to their removal to Datchet in consequence of the appointment by George III. mentioned in a preceding page. At Datchet, Caroline's training for astronomy, which was begun at Bath, was pursued with greater vigour, though she very unwillingly abandoned music. She called herself "a mere tool which her brother had the trouble of sharpening," but some one remarked that "that there was temper in the tool which made it invaluable." She not only acquired the necessary knowledge to perform simple calculations and keep the records of his multitude of observations in perfect order as long as he lived; she also learned the details of those observations with such success that she began to "sweep the heavens" on her own account with a small Newtonian reflector.

In the first year at Datchet she discovered three remarkable nebulæ, one of them the well-known companion to the Andromeda nebula. In the intervals of her attendance on her brother, often through the watches of the night till day began to dawn, she brought the stars of the *British Catalogue* into zones of one degree each for his "sweeps," and prepared all his papers for the *Philosophical Transactions*. In ten years, between 1786 and 1797, she discovered eight comets, five of them with undisputed priority; one was afterwards famous as "Enckes comet." For her "Reduction and Arrangement in the form of a Catalogue of all the Star Clusters and Nebulæ observed by Sir William Herschel" she received the Astronomical Society's Gold Medal in 1828. "This laborious work," says the *National Biographical*

Dictionary, was styled by Sir David Brewster, "an extra-ordinary monument of the inextinguishable ardour of a lady of seventy-five in the cause of abstract science. Although never published it was the most valuable of her under-takings, because indispensable to the review by her nephew, Sir John Herschel, of the northern nebulæ. Miss Herschel was created an honorary member of the Royal Astronomical Society in 1835 and of the Royal Irish Academy in 1838."

Turning to domestic subjects, her brother's marriage in 1788 and his death in 1822 were probably the most trying events of her English life. Not that she thought the marriage unwise, but the change from her home with him to solitary lodgings cost her severe pangs, though it was bravely borne and she worked with him cordially as before. Her devotion to him was simply boundless and after his death was transferred to his son; even the success she gained was regarded as caused by her connection with Sir William, not as the reward of any efforts of her own; and it was to Sir John Herschel as his representative that the same unselfish allegiance was given. In all her little money matters there was the same forgetfulness of self; it was not till she was nearly forty years of age she thought herself free to spend according to her own liking and then it was in consequence of a salary of £50 a year granted to her by the king as her brother's assistant. In the shock caused by his death she resolved, friends thought unwisely, to go back to Hanover. When she left England she made over her little funded property £500, saved by her frugal habits, to her brother Dietrich whom she had nursed at his house in the Markstrasse till his death, and Sir William's legacy of £100 a year enabled her to do more for needy relatives. Some years before her departure she spent a short time at Bath to set in order the house of her brother Alexander, a teacher of music. Her later years were cheered by many attentions. All men of science passing through Hanover called to see her. Her ninety-sixth birthday was marked by Humboldt's transmission to her, in the name of the King of Prussia, of his gold medal for science. On the succeeding anniversary she entertained the crown prince and princess with great animation for two hours, even singing to them a composition of her brother William. She lived long enough to receive Sir John Herschel's *Cape Observations*, the completion of his great celestial survey, and then, January, 1848, passed calmly away in her ninety-eighth year. Her coffin contained, at her special request, a lock of her beloved brother's hair, and the inscription on the tomb-stone, adjoining that of their parents, was composed by herself to " commemorate her participation in his immortal labours."

The story of the family will not be complete without a few lines on Sir John Herschel. He was born at Slough in 1792, when the household was full of triumph for recent discoveries and the completion of another grand telescope. An astronomical atmosphere marked all his earliest years and gave direction to his studies. At Cambridge he was Senior Wrangler and Smith's Prizeman, and soon afterwards in conjunction with Peacock and Babbage, reconstructed Lacroix's *Treatise on the Differential Calculus*. In 1816 he began to examine the double stars, aided by James South, with whom he worked several years. The result of their joint labours, shown in many wonderful discoveries, was presented in a Report to the Royal Society, and acknowledged by the presentation of the gold medal of the Astronomical Society, and the astronomical prize of the French Academy.

L.

Nor was John Herschel content with working out former researches. He earned fame gradually in other fields, in galvanism, chemistry, mathematics and electricity. It had fretted his father's spirit that in the cloudy climate of England he could only work successfully even with the best telescopes about 100 hours in the year. *He* could not go to the Cape but his son could and went, taking his wife and children, remaining away four years, and concluding the resurvey of the skies for which he had been long preparing. Well might the civilised world ring with applause of this noble instance of self-denial, especially when in the true spirit of greatness he declined the compensation offered by Government for his expenses. Large honors were however awarded him ; he was made a Baronet, a D.C.L. of Oxford, and Lord Rector of Marischal College, Aberdeen, with other marks of distinction. During the thirty years that followed, his works as an author would alone have made him eminent. His *Outlines of Astronomy* passed through eight editions, a success due not only to its scientific teachings but to the revelation of his own bright, genial, truthful, poetic and reverential nature. On this, Dr. Stanley, the Dean of Westminster, was eloquent when, in 1871, the author having gently passed away in his eightieth year was fitly laid by the side of Newton in the grand old Abbey. Speaking of the religious excellence of his friend Dr. Stanley, remarked, " Not with high-vaulting words, but with deep humility he saw in the unity of science, the unity of one supreme Life and Power, habitually entering into the spirit of those sublime words, " The Lord our God is one Lord."

CHAPTER XVII.

DR. WILLIAM SMITH AND CHARLES MOORE.

DR. WILLIAM SMITH.

There have been many William Smiths all over the world, but only one for whom Bath has been celebrated. Few general readers are aware either that there was such a celebrity in the gay city, or, if so, what was his title to distinction. Few know that our William Smith was the Father of English Geology, that he long lived in and around Bath, directing the formation of the Somersetshire Coal Canal, and that while thus employed he began the discoveries which raised him eventually to the scientific rank he occupied.

A hundred years have now passed since he began his work in the beautiful valleys around Bath. His nephew and biographer, Professor Phillips of Oxford and other writers have traced with loving hands the progress of geological science in the interval. My task is simply to mention a few incidents illustrative of the life of a very remarkable discoverer, and a singularly clear-minded, right-minded, unselfish man. He was born in 1769 ; his father, an intelligent mechanic was descended from a race of farmers who owned through many generations small tracts of land in Oxfordshire and Gloucestershire. This parent died when he was eight years old leaving him and other children to a gentle and affectionate mother who was intent on giving them as good an education as possible, though it seems there was no better than that of the village school. William, however, passed to the care of a paternal uncle, one of the farmers of the family, so very practical that he was not at all disposed to tolerate the boy's early taste for collecting "pundibs," Terebratulæ, and "pound-stones," used as pound weights by dairy women. The good farmer was better satisfied when his nephew showed an interest in draining and improving land, though it was only after urgent entreaty he could be induced to part with a little money for the purchase of books on the rudiments of geometry and surveying.

Between the ages of thirteen and eighteen the growing youth prosecuted irregularly, with no instruction or sympathy, yet earnestly and successfully, the studies to which his mind had been awakened. He began to draw mechanical objects and attempted engineering calculations, thus recommending himself to a worthy neighbour, Mr. Webb of Stow-on-the-Wold, who had been employed to make a complete survey of their native parish of Churchill for the purpose of inclosure. At once Smith became his assistant, and a very useful engage-ment it proved to both parties, for although Webb, like his pupil was self-taught, and but slightly acquainted with public works, he possessed considerable mechanical skill, and his practise included much now given to engineers, while his generous disposition allowed full scope to Smith's aspirings. "Speedily entrusted," says his biographer, "with the manage-ment of all the ordinary business of a surveyor, he traversed in constant activity the oolitic lands of Oxfordshire and Gloucestershire, and the lias, clays and red marls of Warwick-shire; visited the Salperton tunnel on the Thames and Severn canal, and examined the peculiarities of a boring for coal in the New Forest. All the varieties of soil in different districts were particularly noticed and compared with agricultural and commercial requirements of the locality, not merely for present professional needs, but to be treasured in a mind capable of combining them afterwards."

In 1791 Mr. Webb transferred to his young friend the survey of an estate at Stowey in Somersetshire. No railway then, and perhaps no coaching there, he had to walk all the way from Gloucestershire, carefully observing and recording what he saw. In 1792 and 93 he was occupied professionally at the High Littleton Collieries, near Bath, where again he studied surrounding soils and made memoranda for models of strata arranged in the order in which nature had placed them. His ability and perseverance induced some gentlemen of the neighbourhood to consult him about one of the numerous canals talked of at the time, their more immediate object being the transit of coal from the Radstock district. If not at once equal to the occasion Smith soon became so; he studied all the schemes for conquering inequalities of level, inclined planes, caissons and locks, procuring some instruments and inventing others, resolved to compete creditably for the honours within his reach. Nor were the committee of the canal insensible to his merits or unequal to the occasion; when their Bill had received the sanction of Parliament they deputed two members of their body to accompany him as their engineer on a tour of inquiry into the construction, management and trade of other navigations. The journey extended to nine hundred miles, occupying nearly two months; by one route the party reached Newcastle, by another returned through Shropshire and Wales to Bath; and while the two shrewd coal-owners lingered to inspect every invention interesting to themselves, the embryo geologist noted every aspect of every part of the country to see how far his own theories were borne out. In future years, from time to time, he published as results of his observations a succession of maps and descriptions of strata. Of six such publications in 1815, 16 and 17, there is an elaborate account

in the *Edinburgh Review* of the date of 1818. The author
mentions one of the maps as " the first work of the kind that
had ever appeared in England, the production, after the
labour of more than twenty years, of a most ingenious man
who had been singularly deficient in the art of introducing
himself to public notice."

The journey with the two directors was taken in 1794,
when Smith was twenty-seven years old. He lived till 1839,
reaching his seventieth year, eventually with much distinction
but after many vicissitudes. The incidents of the interval
may be rapidly sketched, for in truth what has been said as
to his early life explains the reputation he gradually acquired.
It was the right application of his remarkable qualities during
his surveys, his journeys on foot, and engineering conferences
that gave him such a rare amount of valuable knowledge.
Professor Phillips fully shows this in the story of his life, of
which I have here made use, and to which I can never turn
without admiration.   I remember that the young self-taught
man attracted the few inquiring spirits interested in the
geology of Bath, the Rev. Joseph Townsend, the Rev.
Benjamin Richardson, and Dr. James Anderson, and induced
them to join him in recording facts and constructing charts.
I remember that the middle-aged man enlightened the
princes and potentates of agriculture : Mr. Coke of Norfolk,
Francis, Duke of Bedford, Lord Hardwicke, Sir John
Johnstone, Mr. Pusey, visiting them at their homes, inspect-
ing their great estates and showing the influence of strata on
vegetation.   I remember that the old man, at length suffering from his want of worldly wisdom and having sold his
cherished little property near Bath, had to part successively
with his books, his instruments, the museum he had collected,
and even the home where he welcomed his friends. But I

also remember the gleams of comfort which cheered him from time to time; no large accession of worldly means it is true, though kindness in this respect was not withheld; though Government acknowledged his services to the country by a pension and private friends were considerate; but what chiefly smoothed his downward path was the testimony borne to his honour by the highest authorities in the realm of his favourite and at length prospering science.

It is pleasant in conclusion to recall some circumstances connected with that testimony. One of the great benefactors of science in the early part of the century was Dr. Wollaston, a relative and friend of a gentleman well known in similar paths in Bath, the Rev. Leonard Blomefield. Dr. Wollaston invested £1,000 for "promoting researches concerning the mineral structure of the earth and rewarding those by whom they should be made," and the first year's income was devoted to the acquisition of a die for a medal bearing the head of the founder. In 1831, the Trustees, who were the Council of the Geological Society, passed a resolution "that the first medal of fine gold be procured with the least possible delay and presented to Mr. William Smith in consideration of his being a great original discoverer in English geology and especially of his having been the first in this country to discover and teach the identification of strata and to determine their succession by means of their embedded fossils." The interest of the presentation was greatly increased by the fact that the president was Professor Sedgwick, "an original thinker and faithful observer," who said at the interesting ceremony that he had tracked Mr. Smith's footsteps through Wiltshire and the neighbouring counties with his maps in his hand learning from him as his master. After wishing that the stern lover of truth, Wollaston himself, "before whose dark eye all false

pretensions withered," could have been present, Sedgwick
proceeded: " I would appeal to those intelligent men who form
the strength and ornament of this society whether there was
any room for doubt or hesitation that we ought to place our
first honour on the brow of the Father of English Geology ? "

The British Association, founded at York in 1831, was a
source of great pleasure to Smith. Always warmly welcomed
by his brethren, to himself, says his nephew, "the return of
the meetings was like the revival of spring to the vegetable
world." At Dublin, in 1835, he was received with special
kindness by the Provost and Fellows of Trinity College, which
conferred on him the unexpected honour of the Degree of
Doctor of Law. That he had reached his sixty-seventh year
did not diminish the pleasure felt by him and his friends,
while through the world of science generally it was felt that
never was title more deserved, for had he not promulgated
some of the grandest laws of nature ? Except on the summons
to these meetings, he now rarely quitted his hermitage at
Hackness in Yorkshire, where he spent six of the calmest and
happiest years of his life as the highly valued land steward on
the large estate of Sir John Johnstone. At length, believing
his work was done, he retired to Scarborough, though he
proved able to attend several more meetings of the Association,
one of much interest in 1836 at Bristol, when I had the
pleasure of seeing him enjoy the wit and eloquence of his
friend Sedgwick. In 1838 he accepted a commission from the
Government to examine, with Mr. de la Beche and Mr. Barry,
the principal quarries of the kingdom, prior to the selection of
stone for the new Houses of Parliament. In 1839 he consented
to go to one more meeting at Birmingham. But man proposes
and God disposes. Visiting an old friend at Northampton on
his way he was seized with illness. The summons was short

but decisive. His vigorous constitution yielded quickly. In a few days there was a peaceful end to an eminently useful life.

CHARLES MOORE.

The subject of this sketch is described in a memoir to which it will now be indebted as " *the* foremost geologist of Somerset and *one* of the foremost in England." This remark by so indefatigable a votary of the same science as the Rev. H. H. Winwood, will be considered amply sufficient to place Charles Moore next William Smith in the roll of Bath Celebrities. Here he spent nearly fifty years of his life in the unceasing study of scientific facts; on this city he conferred lasting benefits by the development of its geological surroundings and the formation of his beautiful museum ; and by a wide circle of men of science he was regarded as an eminent authority on doubtful questions.

It may be not unfrequently noticed that those men are the most successful who have had the least outward assistance in early life. Charles Moore was the son of a respectable printer and bookseller in the town of Ilminster, and his training had reference to the business of his father which was probably favourable to mental culture. But, besides this, and what would now be considered a short and limited education in the local schools he had few advantages, the lot of standing behind a counter seeming to be that to which he was destined. Thus, about the year 1837 he was engaged by Mr. Meyler, a well-known bookseller of Bath, with whom he remained some years, but on the death of his father he returned to Ilminster for a time to aid the family in retaining their home.

This temporary residence in his native town appears to have greatly favoured the bias of his career. Mr. Winwood has

shown how it reawakened tastes which had been cultivated in
his school-days, and partially revived at Bath amidst the
claims of business. The neighbourhood in which he had
been brought up is remarkable for its geological phenomena ;
"few districts can boast," says the author of the memoir, " of
such medals of creation as a short ramble would disclose in
the Upper Lias strata around his native town." Even the
walls of the Commercial School with which he was so familiar
were built of Ammonites and Belemnites, the latter locally
called "Ladies' fingers," which proved as attractive to him as
the "Pundibs and Poundstones " of Oxfordshire, were to his
predecessor William Smith. "In my school-boy days " he
writes in one of his early papers " my half-holidays were often
spent in collecting the Ammonites, with which the beds in
the Upper Lias strata abound, for the purpose of rubbing them
down to show their starry chambers." But it was not until
the return of Charles Moore to his favourite haunts after the
Bath interval that the dormant taste was thoroughly revived.
No doubt his intelligence had become more keen and strong ;
he could observe the wonders of creation with a more earnest
desire to know their origin, the "how" and the "why" of
what he saw. In a speech at the Bath meeting of the
British Association in 1864, he related an Ilminster incident
which occurred twenty years before as contributing to the
reawakening of his interest, and leading to scientific results of
great importance. "An old civic building," he said, "near
the School-house in which he had passed his early days was
being renovated, and two boys were amusing themselves with
a pebble or nodule they had found in the rubbish. This in
rolling from one to another separated, and by a lucky chance
the pieces were looked at and preserved. In the centre, and
naturally at the point of separation was a beautiful fish of the

extinct genius Pachycormus." "This," adds Mr. Winwood, "was the first beginning of that magnificent collection of fishes which now enrich the Bath Museum. Before finally leaving his native town, he had accumulated most of the characteristic fossils of the district, and by short visits there, a few days at a time, he made himself thoroughly acquainted with its physical and stratagraphical geology."

In 1853 Charles Moore returned to Bath, a more ardent student of Nature, and happily with the prospect of being able to devote his life to the work. He had become engaged to a lady of congenial disposition in Widcombe Crescent, whose means allowed his relinquishment of business, and he was married to her soon afterwards. The leisure he thus acquired enabled him not only to distinguish himself in the world of science but to take a prominent part in Bath public life, especially in the political conflicts of the day, when he advocated consistently what he deemed the cause of progress. For many years he was known as an able and useful member of the Town Council, where his opinion was often sought on such questions as the supply of water, the causes of the local land-slips and the varied quality of the great oolite beds to which the city owes so much of its beauty. It may be easily imagined how, as he became known, he was valued by the various scientific societies of the district. To the Bath Institution he was an invaluable member, sparing neither time nor strength in promoting its interests, as his life-long work the Museum so amply testifies. What an instructive companion he was in the excursions of the Field Club and at the meetings of the Somersetshire and Natural History Society many of their members can well remember. Nor should it be forgotten that with all these claims upon him the higher duties of life were faithfully

discharged; he had too much simplicity of character to
obtrude professions and manifestations, but in all weathers,
morning and evening, he frequented his place of worship;
teaching in the Sunday School for many years and aiding
every organisation for charitable purposes.

It may be thought that what has now been said does not
show that Charles Moore rose to the height of a Bath
Celebrity; we therefore turn again to Mr. Winwood's memoir.
There we find abundant proofs of the high position he established by long, arduous, successful and disinterested labour
through many a time of trial and difficulty down to the latest
moments of his life. As no language of my own would be
adequate, even if I were personally acquainted with the facts,
I may be allowed to quote extracts from the memoir merely
as indications of what was done in the way of papers read
before Field Clubs, Archæological Societies, British Association Meetings and other gatherings. Respecting a paper at
Bath in 1852 on the *Palœontology of the Middle and Upper
Lias,* which referred to Moore's former researches in the beds
at Ilminster, Mr. Winwood writes :

" Until very recently those beds were supposed to belong to the
Inferior Oolite, and he claims to have placed them in their true
position, as underlying and distinct ; asserting that from his
intimate acquaintance with the Lower Lias Beds at Twerton, and
those of the Inferior Oolite in the neighbourhood of Bath, he was
able to show that they hold not only a distinct position but also a
fauna peculiarly their own. It was in this paper that he alludes
to the discovery of that marvellously rich yellow Limestone band
in the Upper Lias, only from 4 to 5½ inches thick, called the
" Saurian, Fish and Insect bed," from which he obtained his
beautiful Pachycormi, now deposited in the Bath Museum and
still awaiting some specialist to describe. It was from this
nodular Limestone also that he uncovered his " Baby Saurian "

as he called it, the Pelagosaurus Moorei (Deslongchamps), the story of the finding of which he graphically told to the writer of the present notes ; and the history given in a subsequent paper on the " Middle and Upper Lias of the S. W. of England," (Som. Arch. and Nat. Hist. Soc. Proceedings, vol. xiii, p. 181, 1865-6)— one among the many instances of this man's patient industry and indomitable perseverance."

" Elected a Fellow of the Geological Society of London in 1854, he contributed five valuable papers to their journal. The first in 1860, "On the so-called Wealden beds of Linksfield and the Reptiliferous Sandstones of Elgin," directed attention to the similarity of appearance between these Linksfield shales with their limestone beds, and those of the Bone bed series (at the base of the Lias) at Pylle Hill near Bristol, at Aust Passage, and at Penarth, also at the Uphill cutting on the G.W.R. The lithological resemblances were well marked ; and he recognised the " White Lias " the " Cotham Marble," the " Bone bed," and the Gypseous clay bands of the S. country in the quarry at Linksfield. The palæontological evidence, moreover, supported his correlation of these beds. As to the Cornstone at Linksfield, on which the above mentioned beds rest, he thought they were of Triassic date, as he had observed on the flanks of the Mendips and elsewhere stone of a similar aspect belonging to the Trias and occasionally yielding remains of reptiles and fishes. In this paper he mentioned his discovery of reptilian and mammalian teeth near Frome, in a fissure containing a Triassic deposit, and ventured to correlate them with the reptilian remains found at Lossiemouth, and therefore the probable Secondary age of the latter."

" The result of his many years work amidst the Secondary rocks of the district was laid before the Geological Society on March 20th, 1867, under the title, "On Abnormal conditions of Secondary deposits when connected with the Somersetshire and South Wales Coal-basins ; and on the age of the Sutton and Southerndown series."

" In this paper, giving his reasons for the abnormal character of the Secondary formations on the N. of the Mendips, he speaks of the difficulties attending the investigation of his subject and the length of time occupied ; corroborates Godwin-Austin's view of an old land area near Frome, and shows that this may be looked for in the Mendip axis of elevation, by his discovery of Mammalia, Reptilia, and terrestrial Mollusca that once inhabited this land area in Rhætic and Liassic times.   The barrier of land, thus interposed to the incursion of the waters of the Secondary seas, modified the physical features of the whole line of country between Frome and a portion of S. Wales, thus accounting for the extreme tenuity of the Secondary deposits to the N. of this barrier as compared with those on the S.   With the one exception of the statement of his views as to the Basaltic dyke, this contribution will remain the best authority on the geology of a portion of England surpassed by none in geological interest ; and will serve as a mine of information to many a future explorer of that particular district, as it has done to many a past one.   This paper alone was sufficient to establish his reputation as one of the leading geologists of the day."

" Charles Moore was a frequent attendant at the Meetings of the British Association for the Advancement of Science, and read several papers before Section C.   My earliest acquaintance with him was in the year 1863, shortly after my arrival in Bath, when we went together to the Newcastle Meeting as two of the local Secretaries for the Meeting to take place the following year in Bath ; and in the Report of the Transactions of Section C, presided over by Warington W. Smyth, F.R.S., is a short abstract of Moore's paper " On the equivalents of the Cleveland Ironstones in the W. of England."   He had traced these Ironstone bands from Lyme Regis to Yeovil and Bath.   In the following year, in the midst of his arduous labours as one of the local Secretaries at Bath, he found time to lay before Section C, then under the Presidency of Prof. Phillips, the specimens of Saurians, Fish and Cuttle-fish he had discovered in the Upper Lias at Ilminster; and the mammalian and fish-teeth (70,000 in number) obtained from the greenish clay which filled the fissures at Holwell, and the remains of the extinct animals from the drift that surrounded Bath. The President said that the Section had heard one of the most interesting and instructive addresses that could be possibly given to the British Association. They had expected a most interesting communication from Mr. Moore, but not to the full the great treat he had given them, illustrated as it was with specimens of his own discovery of the greatest possible value and interest. Sir Charles Lyell, who was also present, spoke of Moore's discoveries in the Mammalian drift of the Bath basin as rendering essential service to science, alluding especially to his finding the male and female musk sheep in that neighbourhood."

"On February 15th, 1882, the evening Meeting was set apart for Charles Moore and myself, when he was to have communicated his latest investigations on the "Eozoon and Micropalæontology," embodying some of his recent microscopic researches in the Palæozoic rocks. Death, however, had taken away my geological friend, and the pen of the earnest, hardworking student of nature had ceased to write; he had gone to his rest, literally worn out and a victim (may we not say a martyr?) to the cause of science, for which he had laboured and for which he lived. How well I remember the closing scene, or at any rate the last hours spent with him in endeavouring to elucidate the fibre mystery. Possessed with the idea that even in the earliest rocks of the earth's crust he could trace the presence of organic life, he had selected the room in the Institution where the least chance of any adventitious or external accidents could interfere with his researches; he had prepared some glass slides coated with glycerine over-night, these we were to examine the following morning microscopically and compare the results of the night's capture with the residue he proposed to test after decalcification of the rock by hydrocloric acid in the morning.

The specimen so tested was a slice of the Laurentian rock containing the so-called *Eozoon Canadense.* I was particularly struck with the zeal of the man, who, labouring under a most distressing cough at the time, and being asked whether he did not feel the cold (I was chilled to the backbone during the time of the investigation in the Lonsdale room at the Institution), replied, No, I don't, but suppose my enthusiasm has kept me warm. These were the last words I ever heard him utter; in a fortnight after this he was gone. Bath knew him no more—a simple green mound in the pretty little Unitarian burial ground at Lyncombe marks his resting place by the side of one of his sisters, and it is to be hoped that some appropriate record will be erected there to mark the last home of one of Bath's most scientific and hard-working students of nature ere all traces be lost. But his memory remains, and his name, linked with Walcott, William Smith and Lonsdale, will be handed down to posterity as that of a man whose good work in the scientific investigation of the wonders of nature any city may be proud of. *Si queris monumentum circum-spice*—The Moore Museum, purchased after his decease by his fellow citizens for a thousand pounds, and secured to the city of his adoption by those who appreciated his work and honoured his memory, is a memorial of the scientific labours of a man whose scientific acquaintance it was my great privilege to make, and whose presence seems to be with me as I busy myself amongst the cases that contain the results of his life-long work."

Mr. Winwood gives at the end of his interesting narrative the titles of twenty three "Papers and Communications" by his friend and fellow labourer.

CHAPTER XVIII.

THE TWO WOODS, GAINSBOROUGH, AND WILLIAM HOARE.

THE TWO WOODS.

A stranger in Bath, observing its handsome buildings, would naturally suppose that the city could boast of a long roll of architectural celebrities. But this can hardly be said; it is remarkable how few there have been in the two centuries since the city began to attain eminence in respect to its buildings. Striking likewise is the fact that those few have been so far above the average of their professional brethren in the provinces of any country as were the two Woods of Bath. Walter Savage Landor, in a note to his *Imaginary Conversation between Pericles and Sophocles*, says of Queen Square and the Circus, that "there is nothing in Rome, or the world, to equal them." Perhaps this is exaggerated praise, but everyone knows that Macaulay wrote of Bath as "that beautiful city which charms eyes even familiar with the works of Bramante and Palladio." For my present purpose, however, there is sufficient force in a recent moderate remark of Lord Grimthorpe, "by attending to the true principles of art the two Woods changed Bath from a mean-looking town to the most beautiful in England."

It is true that fault has been found with the interiors of the houses. Critics have complained that, in many cases, outward effect is obtained at the cost of comfort and convenience. We are told of dark, narrow staircases; of some rooms ill-shaped, others badly lighted, and a want of varied accommodation. But without admitting that this gives a

M

correct idea, we yet remember what the Woods had to do;
not to build a number of detached houses, each having
sufficient space for ample individual requirements, but to
erect the streets, squares, crescents and circuses of a city.
For such an object diminished internal advantages, to some
extent, were unavoidable. Those who are acquainted with the
works of the Woods in country situations can testify that
there they proved they knew, as indeed is evident in their
city work, that "good architecture is not wrapped up in a
front wall," but is visible within as well as without and fulfils
its true object in securing the full amount of comfort possible
in the circumstances of the case.

There is a valuable book, not so well known as it ought to
be, *The Municipal Records of Bath*, by Austin J. King and
B. H. Watts. It has an essay on "the Renaissance of the
City," in which an explanation of some leading characteristics
is given in the statement that "they were due to a
Triumvirate." The individuals were Ralph Allen, Richard
Nash and John Wood, who, though each playing a distinct
part, yet aided in producing the general result. Allen, as was
told in a former chapter, came from Cornwall to Bath in 1711
as a clerk of the Post office, and in the next two decades rose
rapidly to a position of great influence. Previously the Bath
stone, since so celebrated, had been comparatively little
worked; Allen, as his means increased, bought quarries and
began a vigorous trade in their contents. At the same time
there was a great demand for more and better houses; people,
some of great distinction, came from all parts of the country
and looked in vain for suitable homes. The Cornish postmaster, having a sharp eye for every kind of talent, brought
Wood to Bath. It was about the year 1722, and together
they planned such magnificent piles of buildings as would

require all the stone that could be worked in a life-time. For Wood was more than a skilful architect, though qualified to delight future ages by enduring monuments of genius ; he was "an administrator of a type rarely met with." "The stagnation of the building trade in Bath " (says the writer on the Renaissance) " was so great in the seventeenth century that competent workmen were not to be had there. Wood brought excavators from some great waterworks, masons from York-shire and carpenters from London." It was he who introduced into the West of England even such simple appliances as the lever, the pulley, and the windlass, to the vast relief of the builders, who had previously no other method of hoisting their heavy stones than that of dragging them up with small ropes against the sides of a ladder.

It may be asked what the other member of the Triumvirate, Nash, did to aid the work and fame of Wood. The answer is that no man knew better than Nash what the wants of the City were as to good dwelling houses and public buildings. Whatever his moral failings may have been, in consequence of the inferior education and circumstances of the period, his mental capacity was undoubted. Hence there were constant cogitations with him on designs in quick succession for the Parades, Queen Square, the Circus and other great works. Certainly it was with Wood that Nash took counsel respecting the Bath Hospital, which he had so much at heart, though Wood himself by his business talent conquered the great difficulties about the site, and made no charge for anything he did in connection with the structure. But, still, it was with and for Allen that Wood was chiefly concerned. Mr. Peach states that his first work was in connection with the Postmaster's town house ; not that he was the original architect of it, but employed to make great additions and

alterations.   Twenty years afterwards, about 1735, Allen,
having acquired considerable wealth, and wishing to make
his quarries productive, resolved to build a large house on the
Prior Park estate, with regard to which he had the advantage
not only of Wood's genius in the designs but also of his skill
and knowledge as to working the stone.   For no one knew
so well the true method of excavation, how to treat the oolite
so that it should stand weather, and how to adapt the grain
to the required position.   He had other good clients, notably
the Duke of Chandos, for whom he built Chandos Court ; he
restored St. John's Hospital, and canalised the Avon between
Bath and Bristol, an undertaking in which many had failed,
and was peculiarly arduous to him with his other great works
on hand.   Among the houses he built in the neighbourhood
were Eagle house, Batheaston, the Shockerwick mansion, and
what Mr. Peach justly describes as " the exquisite house at
the head of the sloping avenue at Bathford."

In one character certainly the great architect did not excel—
that of an author.   His *Description of Bath,* in two volumes,
is marred by absurd credulity as to past history, and egotistical
exaggerations of various kinds.   Of the little that is known
of him personally it is said that he was a proud, sensitive man,
with a great dislike of all shallow pretentions, but with so
little worldly wisdom as to have comparatively scanty means.
His house at Batheaston, however, where he lived at the close
of his life, and his general position in the neighbourhood,
caused his appointment as a county magistrate.   He and his
son both died at Batheaston, the elder in 1754, the younger
in 1781, and both were buried near the altar of the Church of
Swainswick.   Of the younger Wood the information given by
various writers is even more meagre than that of the father.
It is remarkable that the latter never mentions him in his

account of the works they had jointly on hand for so many years. But the fact that they were on good terms may be inferred from the evident harmony of their procedure and the fact that they both lived and died in the same house at Batheaston. The chief buildings, for which the younger Wood had the principal responsibility, appear to have been the Circus, York Buildings, Brock Street, Royal Crescent and the Assembly Rooms. The father, we have seen, died in 1754; the Circus was begun about 1760; York Buildings, 1762; Brock Street, 1765 ; the Royal Crescent, 1767 ; the Assembly Rooms, 1769. What other architect in any provincial town could boast of having erected in such quick succession so many magnificent piles of buildings, destined to command unstinted admiration through many a long year? At the end now of more than a century the Crescent in particular is as impressive as it ever was. "Beautiful for situation," there is a combination of simplicity and classic grandeur in the noble range of mansions which once seen can never be forgotten. The Assembly Rooms also, occupying half an acre of ground in the centre of a hilly city, yet with no step throughout; its lofty, well proportioned rooms all admirably suited to their various purposes ; no wonder that the world of fashion thronged them so long. We think of the inscription to Sir Christopher Wren's honour in St. Paul's Cathedral and remember how appropriate the word "Circumspice" would have been in a monument to either of the Woods in the city they adorned. But there is no marble to their honour in Abbey, crescent, circus or square. Neither did any local biographer pay a tribute to the struggles and successes of those two preeminently remarkable men. No one knows whether they speculated unwisely in the works they undertook or lost money in other ways. All we are told is that the father could not have been rich, and the son died very poor, his widow having even come to want. What a melancholy termination of such a story!

GAINSBOROUGH.

Passing to celebrities in painting it hardly need be stated that although, as in other cases, my task is limited, I am far from forgetting what Bath owes to those who are not in my list. Undoubtedly the reputation of the city has profited by the labours of many in various professions who, without attaining the first rank, did their work thoroughly well. Several of the most celebrated, whose lives are here sketched, only began their career in Bath, studying, practising persevering, till they could enter on the great arena in London, where their full power was developed.

Foremost among the painters was Gainsborough, one of the undying names in the history of English art. Happily he has not wanted faithful chroniclers of his life and works, one of whom Allan Cunningham in *Murray's Family Library*, gives a pleasant account of his early history. "Born," he says, "in 1727 at Sudbury, in Suffolk, his family were of old standing, well-to-do and of unblemished respectability. His memory and his love of art are still cherished in the eastern county, where a beautiful wood is shown four miles in extent, whose ancient trees, winding glades and sunny nooks inspired the exquisite taste for landscape painting which was developed in after life. Scenes are pointed out where he used to sit and fill his copy-books with pencillings of flowers and trees or whatever pleased his fancy, and it is said that those early attempts of the child bore a distinct resemblance to the mature works of the man."

When ten years old he had made some progress in sketching, and at twelve he was a confirmed painter, though his devotion to the art and the deficiency in those times of early education prevented anything like good general cultivation. Encouraged by the advice of friends, who saw his earliest attempts and believed " the boy was a genius," his father sent him to London to study under Hayman, one of the companions of Hogarth. Grignon, the engraver, who knew him well, informed Edwards, author of the *Anecdotes of Painters*, that Gainsborough received the first rudiments of his art from Gravelot, another celebrity of the time. He remained in London four years and then returned to Sudbury to make such a beginning as the Fates would allow. In one respect they favoured him ; he was universally acceptable as a companion in consequence of his pleasant manners, his handsome person and his lively conversation. In another respect he was also fortunate. Seated one day sketching in the woods, a young lady appeared on the scene to whom he showed his work. Miss Margaret Burr was of Scottish extraction, then only in her sixteenth year, but in addition to the charms of good sense and good looks possessed an annuity of £200. Gossips in the neighbourhood added what they thought another attraction. She was the natural daughter of an exiled prince, a parentage she herself was rather proud of in future years. Whether Gainsborough cared for the distinction or not, he wooed and won the lady ; she made him a kind and faithful wife. Leaving Sudbury they began life together in a small house at Ipswich at £6 a year, resolving to do the best they could.

This, at first, was merely painting a few local portraits. Gainsborough's fame slowly increased and interested a neighbour of some repute, Philip Thicknesse, governor of

Landguard Fort and well known in Bath, where he spent much of his time. He was a vain, selfish man, but probably wished to gratify the artist as well as himself by giving him a commission to paint the fortress with the port of Harwich and the neighbouring hills for the price of 30 guineas. The picture was engraved, and contributed to make Gainsborough known, but he was now in his thirty-first year ; he had exhausted the faces and the scenery of Ipswich and his talents demanded wider scope. Thicknesse, who then played the part of patron, though afterwards a false friend, was of the same opinion and advised his removal to Bath. This was in 1758, when there appeared to be an opening in Bath for all kinds of talent. At first there was but little encouragement ; people cared little for painting, not even the more educated who admired the Greek and Italian architecture of the two Woods. There had been comparatively little foreign travel to give any love or even knowledge of the great masters whose works had created a new intellectual world in the older cities of Europe. Gradually, however, young men came to Bath ; aiming first at what was most likely to give employ-ment—portraiture, and, though well qualified for higher work, willing to wait patiently. Such was the case with Gainsborough. He began in the Abbey churchyard, but soon removed to Ainslie's Belvedere, where he could enjoy a beautiful view of Hampton Rocks, his favourite sketching ground. Charging at first only five guineas for a portrait, he spent the intervals of the sittings in studying the fine trees of the neighbourhood ; notably one near the London road, still standing, and called Gainsborough's elm. His studio being soon sought by discerning visitors, he ventured to hire a house in the Circus. Men of eminence at the Bar and the Senate ; women, distinguished on the stage and the

orchestra ; all were charmed, both with his social qualities
and artistic skill. For full length figures his price rose to
50, 70, and 100 guineas. There, in the Circus, he painted
Lord Chancellor Camden, Bishop Hurd, Miss Linley,
Sheridan, Richardson, Garrick, Burke, Sterne, Quin, and
many others. As one of the earliest members of the Royal
Academy he often sent up pictures by Mr. Wiltshire of
Shockerwick, a prosperous London carrier, who always
refused payment on the ground that he loved pictures too
well to make a charge. The artist, however, prevailed upon
him at various times to accept six of his works. Some idea
of their ultimate value may be formed from the fact that
when at length the treasures at Shockerwick were sold, the
National Gallery secured two, the " Parish Clerk " (a venerable
man at Bradford-on-Avon) for £500, and "The Harvest
Wagon " for £2,500. There was also a portrait of Quin,
which went elsewhere. About the same time " The Sisters,"
from another gallery realised £9,975.

The connection of Gainsborough with Mr. Wiltshire leads
me to introduce selections from an interesting account of the
Shockerwick estate and the Wiltshire family, in *Bladud*, the
Bath Society Paper. The information is due to the researches
of Mr. Peach. My extracts have a two-fold interest, the
mansion of Shockerwick having been built by the elder Wood,
whose memoir precedes that of Gainsborough in these pages.
I have pleasant recollections of representatives of three
generations of the Wiltshire family.*

---

* "Shockerwick derives its name from Adam de Socherwicke,
who lived as early as the reign of Henry II. He held it of the
Bishop of Bath as part of a knight's fee. After passing from
the Socherwicke family the manor with Batheaston, Bathford,

Great as Gainsborough's fame was as a portrait painter, his own delight was in landscapes. To his sitters he was often brusque and independent ; to Nature a most patient and joyous scholar. Cunningham says "he was like a poet divided between two mistresses, paying to the one cold visits and giving to the other a warm heart." It is certain that the Bath people did not care for his landscapes. In vain they saw his studio full of charming views of the most beautiful objects in the neighbourhood. They were willing to pay

---

and much besides, came into the possession of the Hosate (now softened into Hussey) family, whose principal seat was called Husei and then Hussey Court, standing on or very near the present mansion. In the reign of Philip and Mary the manors were held by Thomas Earl of Northumberland. Hussey Court then suffered from neglect, until in 1667 Shockerwick was sold, with Batheaston, to James Lancashire ; and from that time until about eighty years after, when Shockerwick passed into the possession of the Wiltshire family, not much can be found recorded of it. The Court had become a ruin, scarcely one stone standing upon another, and the Park little better than open fields. Then, with the Wiltshires, came the great transformation, the revival of all that was picturesque and beautiful in the charming domain."

"The Wiltshire family, like Allen and others, of whom we are so proud, were of mean origin (perhaps 'humble' is the word.) The first of the family whom we trace is Thomas Wiltshire, who died in 1648. He left a son Walter, who had two sons, Walter and Julyan ; the former of whom died in 1719, the latter in 1721. This Walter was the man known as the lessee of 'Wiltshire's Rooms.' Besides other issue he left a son John, who, with Walter (our local *worthy*), was the founder of the vast carrying business, which owed its later development to Walter. This

liberally for likenesses of themselves ; farther than that their love of art did not go. So after spending 14 years in Bath he removed to London. This was in 1774. What he did there to found the English school of which the nation is now so proud, may be seen in the chief galleries of the country. This sketch, therefore, may well be confined to the earlier features of his life. One, however, prominent throughout, which ought to be mentioned, was his passionate love of music. This made him acquainted with Thicknesse ; they

important business, which opened up the resources of the city, and brought it within reach of the metropolis and every part of the country, taken in connection with Allen's stone trade and his rare munificence, together with the genius of the two Woods, made Bath what it is. Walter Wiltshire was the progenitor of worthy successors, who, down to the latest occupier, · John Wiltshire in recent times, worthily sustained the chivalrous character, the generous nature, and the beneficent disposition, by which the first Walter of Shockerwick was distinguished. This Walter, in conjunction (more or less) with his father John, acquired the ancient domain of Shockerwick and other property, between 1740 and 1750.   About the latter year he engaged Wood the elder to lay out the grounds, and to design and build the mansion—one of his most characteristic achieve· ments. Walter Wiltshire, like Allen, was a gentleman by nature. If he lacked the dignified reserve, the mental grasp, and the gentle *hauteur* of Allen, he was imbued with the same desire to do good—to dispense his bounty with judgment, and so far as his means justified. Walter Wiltshire built No. 1, Broad Street, in which he transacted his business and conducted his correspondence in chief; at his classic little seat at Shockerwick he delighted to dispense his hospitality with a gentle courtesy and a bounteous hand."

began their friendship by playing the violin together at Ipswich. Here I remember that much may be learnt about Thicknesse in an interesting paper by Mr. F. Shum on "Gainsborough and his connection with Bath," read before the Literary and Philosophical Association, and afterwards printed, in 1875. As to the painter's affection for music, Allan Cunningham says that he allowed his house to be infested with all sorts of Professors save bag-pipers. He loved Giardini and his violin, Abel and his viol-de-gamba, Tischer and his hautboy, and was in raptures with a strolling harper from the Welsh mountains. The poet's account of the great artist's house in the Bath Circus is full of interest. Surrounded by numerous friends he lived in good style, entertained hospitably, and was kind to all who needed assistance. In London his generosity increased with his prosperity. That he had failings may be easily imagined. One of them was jealousy of his illustrious rival, Reynolds. But it wore away before the end of life came, when he seems to have well made his peace with the world generally. He died in London in 1788, in the sixty-first year of his age. He had thought much of the event and often talked quietly about it From Sheridan, for whom he had great regard, he obtained a promise to attend his funeral. To Reynolds he sent quite at the last to ask him to come and take leave of him. There was the old friendly, cheerful tone at this memorable meeting. "Ah!" said Gainsborough suddenly, "we are all going to heaven, and Vandyke is of the company;" then instantly fell back and died.

WILLIAM HOARE

may be said to have competed at Bath successfully with Gainsborough, who both found and left him there enjoying great repute. Hoare, like his contemporary, was a native of Suffolk, the son of a prosperous farmer who gave him an excellent education. The boy developed at school so great a talent for drawing that he was allowed to adopt art as a profession. Beginning in London under Grisoni, an Italian master, he proceeded to Rome to complete his studies at a time when an English student in the Eternal city was a novelty. His father was ruined by the South Sea Scheme, and the son, thrown on his own resources, maintained himself by making skilful copies of famous works which were sold easily. After spending nine years in Italy he returned to London hoping to paint historical subjects or, failing in the attempt, to gain a living by portraits. In both he failed at first, yet ventured to marry a Miss Barber, who, having connections in Bath, induced him to settle there. At once his prospects brightened ; he soon obtained ample and profitable work. The author of the memoir in the *Dictionary of National Biography* says that "for many years he was without a rival," alluding to the time before Gainsborough. Among the distinguished visitors who sat to him was the elder Pitt, who presented his portrait to Lord Temple in 1754 and wrote in high terms of the artist's powers. That the Bath Corporation thought highly of them was shown by a commission they also gave for a portrait of the great statesman for the Guildhall when he had ceased to be a Member for the city. The Pelham family were Hoare's special patrons ; many of them sat to him and they probably encouraged his study of crayon drawing. In this he succeeded so admirably that his works in crayon were perhaps more highly esteemed than those in oil. Maintaining his connection with London he frequently contributed to the small Exhibitions of the time. He was one of the artists who attempted to establish an academy in 1755.

Thirteen years later he and his friends succeeded ; the Royal Academy was established under the immediate patronage of the king, who signed William Hoare's diploma as an original member.   He was a man of scholarly tastes and enjoyed the personal friendship of many of his eminent sitters, together with that of Ralph Allen and the visitors at Prior Park.   His death occurred in 1792.   He left a numerous family ; of one son, Prince Hoare, the well-known artist and dramatist, some account will now be given ; a daughter married a brother of Sir Richard Hoare of Stourhead.   Fortunately Bath possesses several works of her famous artist.   Besides the portrait of Lord Chatham there are others of Christopher Anstey, Beau Nash, Samuel Derrick and Governor Pownall.   Of less merit, though to a certain extent interesting, are "The Pool of Bethesda" in the Octagon Chapel, Bath, a large picture of the Saviour in St. Michael's Church in the same city, and "Medical Men Examining Patients" in the Mineral Water Hospital. The National Portrait Gallery contains the Duke of Newcastle, Lord Chesterfield, Lord Temple and Pope, all in crayons, and a full length of the Duke of Grafton in oil.   Many of his portraits were engraved.

There were two artists of the name of Prince Hoare in Bath ; one a sculptor, the brother of William, and who executed the bust of Beau Nash in the Pump Room, the other already mentioned as the son of the Royal Academician. Prince Hoare, junior, was born at Bath, in 1755, educated at the Bath Grammar School, and instructed in art by his father. In 1772 he gained a Society of Arts' premium and went to London to learn at the Royal Academy.   In 1776 he visited Rome, studying under Mings with Northcote and Fuseli as fellow pupils. In 1780 he returned to England and exhibited at the Academy a classical picture called "Alceste," and a picture of Sir Thomas Lawrence when a child. He ceased to exhibit after 1785, and devoted himself chiefly to dramatic writing. His first play, a tragedy *Such things were*, was acted in Bath in 1788, and repeated in London for the benefit of Mrs. Siddons. "His best known production," says the author of the memoir in the *Dictionary of National Biography*, was the farce, *No Song, no Supper*, which became very popular. A long list of other productions, some of great merit, extending over many years, is given in the same work. The offices he filled indicate, as well as his numerous works, that he was a man of varied accomplishments. For some years he was Foreign Secretary to the Royal Academy ; well known also as a fellow of the Society of Antiquaries and of the Royal Society of Literature, to which he bequeathed his library. He died at Brighton in 1834.

CHAPTER XIX.

THOMAS BARKER AND BENJAMIN BARKER.

An advertisement has lately appeared repeatedly in the *Athenæum* of a want to purchase some oil paintings of certain artists, among those named being Gainsborough, Constable, Reynolds, Opie, and "Barker of Bath." To the English public the last name is less known than most of the others, though sixty and seventy years ago it was in great repute with connoisseurs, and the pictures with which it was identified were by no means of an ephemeral character. There were three Barkers connected with Bath ; Thomas, the subject of this sketch, the most distinguished, Benjamin his brother, so far honoured as to be called the English Poussin, and Thomas Jones, the son of Thomas, who attained considerable celebrity after his removal to Paris and London.

Various circumstances combined to make Thomas Barker the one chiefly remembered. His talent was pre-eminent, his local training most interesting, and he studied and painted in Bath through a very long life. He was a native of Ponty-pool, the son of an erratic artist who had been employed there in some Japan works, and removed to Bath, when his children were young, in search of further employment. The works in the Welsh town gave his sons their earliest ideas of art before poverty impelled them to dash off little pictures at Bath with the chance of gaining means of subsistence. The pictures were seen in a small window in what is now called Cross street, Kingsmead, by a well-to-do coachmaker, as good as he was prosperous, a Mr. Spackman, who went into the house, inquired who did them, and on satisfying himself that Thomas deserved encouragement, undertook the charge of his training. His first care was to give him a good, sound education. Then after some years he sent him to Rome for a course of study in art. How that paved the way for his success, what a tone of classic refinement it gave to his works, is known to all who are acquainted with them.

Spackman was judicious in allowing the youth's faculties to expand as a preparation for Rome. They not only expanded ; they gave proof of extraordinary genius which could not fail to profit by the varied influences awaiting him. That he attained at his very early age, in a provincial town, such an envied position might well encourage his generous patron. We are told that though Etty at thirty-five could only get £25 for a large, grand picture, painted on commission in Italy, Barker before he was twenty easily obtained considerably more for even small works. Sir Edward Harington, in his enthusiastic pages of *Schizzo*, eulogising the genius of Barker, states that he was not nineteen when he painted " The Woodman." A later writer, Mr. Frederick Shum, points out that the same subject employed his pencil at three different periods, each picture surpassing the preceding. The first was a woodman in a thunderstorm, painted at the age of fourteen, after a picture by Gainsborough, and, being exhibited by Spackman in an early collection, realised a considerable sum. The second, about two years later, represents the same man returning from his labour with his dog on a winter evening ; it was sold by Spackman to Mr. Rogers of Southampton, a well-known collector, for five hundred guineas, and thirty years ago was in the possession of Lord Powlett. The third, painted at the age of twenty-one, showing the old patriarch going forth on a snowy morning, met with extraordinary success ; it was sold in the first place to

N

Machlin for five hundred guineas, and exhibited by him with the result that he was offered a thousand for it.   It was also engraved by Bartolozzi so that it might be known all over the country, and then worked in worsted by Miss Linwood and hundreds of ladies.   Did ever artist rise to fame more quickly ? For this picture Barker had two sources of inspiration—the old man himself and Cowper's poem, " The Task."   The old man lived at Claverton many years and was much respected by the worthy Rector, Richard Graves, author of the *Spiritual Quixote*.   In later life the intervals of his work as a woodman were occupied in the garden of Mr. Howse of Lyncombe, in which parish he spent the close of his life.   He was buried in the little Unitarian cemetery adjoining the garden where he worked, and his name—George Kelson—is graven on the stone over his remains.   The poetic inspiration was in the simple lines of Cowper :

> " Forth goes the Woodman, leaving unconcerned
>   The cheerful haunts of men, to wield the axe
>   And drive the wedge in yonder forest drear,
>   From morn to eve his solitary task.
>   Shaggy and lean and shrewd with pointed ears,
>   And tail well cropped, half lurcher and half cur,
>   His dog attends him."

Barker, before his departure, became known as the painter of the Woodman, not only in all art circles but in every part of England.   Abroad he employed himself in visiting the best Italian galleries, copying the old masters and sketching from nature.   At Rome he endeavoured, in conjunction with his friends Eastlake and Flaxman, to organise a society of English students.   It grieved him that in so great a centre, where France had a good school and provided handsomely for it, where Germany and even Belgium had classes, England with all her wealth and power did almost nothing. But while a generous public spirit prompted his organising efforts, many a tale was told of his industry and perseverance in everything relating to self-improvement often at considerable risk. Against the advice of his friends he persisted in going out to sketch on the Campagna in the fierce heat of the mid-day sun until he was disabled by a *coup de soleil* Then he found retreats in the grand old palaces where he studied far-famed frescoes, and laid the foundation of a success in that branch of art which his contemporaries had laboured in vain to reach. For good as are many similar works in England, costly as were those of Leslie, Stanfield and others in Buckingham Palace and the Houses of Parliament, it is believed that Barker's "Massacre of the Sciotes by the Turks " in the house he built for himself in Bath will endure when they have faded away.

His experience of a sun-stroke on the Campagna did not teach him wisdom. He often walked to Tivoli with a huge folio under his arm and lingered till the heavy dews from the stagnant marshes made his homeward walk dangerous. At length he was compelled by illness to return to England, where he was warmly welcomed by his good friend Spackman and others who were interested. Perhaps no better estimate could be formed of his versatility and artistic power than that which was obtained by successive exhibitions of his works in Bath. At the time Spackman began them, before he went to Rome, people exclaimed " What a wonderful boy," while some of the best judges in the country joined the chorus, and when, after a lapse of years, the fruits of study and experience had increased his fame, the days on which the works were shown were like public holidays. For some reason he declined

joining the Royal Academy; not even his friend Lawrence
could persuade him to do so; but he sometimes sent
pictures to it, and for half a century exhibited at the British
Institution; thus the public were prepared for the later
collections at Bath.   It was a grand occasion when, the gallery
of his new house on Sion Hill being completed, he and his
brother joined their forces, brought together some of their
best productions and invited the world to see them.   Newspapers told of innumerable strings of carriages containing
the élite of the country round, from Bowood to Brockley
Combe, and from Berkeley Castle to Badminton.   This was
early in the century.   Other exhibitions followed of the works
of Thomas Barker alone.   One was devoted to the Battle of
Waterloo with the scene of " Up Guards and at them."   On
another day visitors were invited to see " The Trial of Queen
Caroline," when the crowds were greater than on the
opening of the gallery.   But popular as such pictures were,
they gave a less perfect idea of the genius of the artist than
his quiet works, such as " Sunset," " The Morning Star,"
" Lansdown Fair," Diogenes in Search of an Honest Man,"
· " The New Zealand Chiefs," " The School of Euclid," and
" Poor Mary the Maid of the Inn."   It was known that, while
his powers were quickened by the society with which he mixed,
his hosts were delighted with the brightness he brought to
their homes.   For he was not a man of small resources; his
variety of information, as well as his genial manners made
him welcome wherever he went.   To lovers of art, like Lords
Lansdowne, Egremont and Stafford, Sir W. Cockburn, Mr.
Smith Pigott and Mr. Rogers, the tales he had to tell, the
experiences he was able to relate, gave much zest to his
conversation.   There is an anecdote that, on going to dine
with Lady Jervis in Bath, he was shown what was called a

fine old Rembrandt, bought by her mother at Southampton, which Barker, recalling his copying days, had no difficulty in identifying as his own work. A similar story is told of a dealer in London extolling to him and a friend who accompanied him to his shop the merits of a supposed Correggio, " a genuine and undoubted work of the master."

Correggio was indeed a master to Barker ; for many years he made him his model ; but he was able to convince his friend that the picture before them was of much later date ; there happened to be a distinguishing mark showing that he himself was the painter. Barker's great love for both Rembrandt and Correggio did not prevent abundant original and independent effort. The short list already given might be extended to one of several pages, and if a life worthy of him should ever be written there ought to be many a pleasant illustration of scenes that inspired him. " Poor Mary the Maid of the Inn " has been mentioned. I owe much of the information in this sketch to an interesting lecture on Barker given by Mr. Frederick Shum thirty years ago at the Bath Royal Literary Institution. His knowledge of Barker and of many of his friends enabled him to give the anecdotes I have already quoted, and he happened to know the history of the picture of " Poor Mary." " The question has been mooted," he says, " whether the ballad by Southey was suggested by the picture or the picture by the verses. I am inclined to think neither statement correct." Both Southey and Barker were acquainted with Sir Foster Cunliffe and visited him and Lady Cunliffe at their hospitable mansion in South Wales. In the neighbourhood was a poor deranged girl, often to be seen wandering about the ruins of Tintern Abbey. One day when Barker was riding in the carriage with Lady Cunliffe they caught a glimpse of her seated upon a bank in a romantic spot far from any dwelling, the very type of melancholy. Barker, deeply affected by her appearance, obtained from Lady Cunliffe the particulars of her history, in return for which she stipulated for a sketch of the girl, and, when an opportunity offered, obtained from Southey after a similar recital his description in verse.

We have had glimpses of Barker's prosperous days ; we must now glance at those of his declining life. For them, unfortunately, he made no provision ; though his earnings were large his outgoings were larger. Like so many of his brethren he had but little worldly wisdom, so that, when a change of circumstances came, things quickly went from bad to worse. If people wanted to see his pictures they found he had sold all the best; if they wanted to give a commission he would only condescend to portraits where he was unknown, and for other subjects the inward fire had become extinguished ; he had in fact neither strength nor spirit to paint. A few friends did all they could to cheer him ; there had been a grant of £100 by the Government in 1846, when Sir Robert Peel was Prime Minister; but this was inadequate to the wants of the family, and a further effort was made privately. Nothing could be more depressing than his domestic circumstances. Towards middle life he had married a Miss Jones, who for some time fully shared his prosperity. But soon after they settled at Doric house her health gave way, and for sixteen years she never left it. Laid aside mentally as well as bodily, she ceased to be the cheerful companion of former days, so that how desolate his home became can be easily imagined. It has been mentioned as a good trait in his character that he was always devotedly attentive to his afflicted wife, never failing in any of the tender assiduity of a nurse. She sat to him for the Magdalen in his fine picture of the " Resurrection," and in happier years entered thoroughly into all his objects of interest.

Specimens of his works abound in the city he loved, throughout Somersetshire, and in the adjoining counties. Not many are to be seen in public galleries; only one in the National Gallery "A Landscape on Somerset Downs," but several in the South Kensington Museum, notably, "Sheep Washing," "Lansdown Fair," and a " Boy Extracting a Thorn from his Foot."   He died at Bath in 1847 at the age of eighty.

BENJAMIN BARKER.

The other brother from Pontypool was also assisted generously in early life by Mr. Spackman, but not to the same extent as Thomas. He appears to have fought his way upward with much less aid in various respects though with results highly honourable to him and to Bath, where he eventually settled.   Neither   Sir   Edward   Harington's *Schizzo* with all its information about the Barker family, nor *The Dictionary of National Biography* gives any particulars of his education.   But the lecture of Mr. Shum, already referred to, gives interesting facts as to his later history ; and I may be allowed to repeat some of them here, because they have the value given to a great extent from personal knowledge and increased by discriminating judgment.

"The works of Benjamin Barker," says Mr. Shum, " were of valued merit, but the best will bear comparison with those of any artist, and whatever may be the position which our English school may attain they will be found worthy to grace our choicest galleries.   Although at first sight there does not appear much in his pictures yet, the longer you view them, the better you are pleased and the more you see to admire.   Two small landscapes of his which have been more

or less before me for the last twenty years I never tire of
looking upon ; they are full of poetry and to a contemplative
mind suggest a thousand thoughts."

"His pictures generally were more carefully painted than
his brother's and more highly finished. The elder Barker
possessed the greater power and manifested more versatility
of genius ; yet he was more unequal and less uniformly
pleasing. His was the freer and bolder hand, Benjamin's the
more careful and delicate. In all his paintings you may see
his taste in the selection of subjects, a scene either beautiful
in itself or suggestive to the imagination. Although his
reputation was not proportioned to his merit, yet among his
patrons were some of the best judges of art ; of whom may be
mentioned the Marquis of Stafford, Lords Egremont, Essex
and Dartmouth. Neither of the Barkers had much tact in
matters of business, but Benjamin had more than his brother.
He not only obtained handsome prices for his works but
realised a good income from teaching. He chose a beautiful
site for a villa in Bathwick hill and was the first to build
there. Among the numerous visitors attracted to his pleasant
residence was Queen Charlotte, while staying in Bath. Some
said she went to see the pictures ; others that it was to see the
kitchen, which was reported to be a model one." During the
years 1813-20 he was a large contributor, chiefly of landscapes, to the Water-colour Exhibition in London, also,
though less in number, to the British Institution. Three of
his water-colour drawings may now be seen in the South
Kensington Museum. After enjoying a fair share of prosperity
in Bath he removed to Totness, where he suffered a lingering
illness and died in 1838 at the age of sixty-two.

A third Barker has been mentioned, Thomas Jones, the son of Thomas. Born in Bath and first educated by his father he was sent to Paris in 1834, became a pupil of Horace Vernet and remained in his studio several years. He exhibited frequently at the Salon ; on one occasion "The Beauties of the Court of Charles II.," for which he received a gold medal. Many medals were also awarded him by provincial towns in France. For Louis Philippe he painted "The Death of Louis XIV.," which was destroyed in the Revolution of 1848, and for the king's youngest daughter, the Princess Clementina, "The Bride of Death," for which he received the Cross of the Legion of Honour. The inspiration of this picture was a deeply affecting death-bed at Bath in the house of a family to whom the artist was much attached. On his removal to London he painted pictures for the Exhibition of the Royal Academy, where his portraits were admired, especially one of Mr. Disraeli, now in the possession of the Queen. Subsequently he dealt chiefly with military subjects, going to the great battlefields of the time for scenes. These works, says *The National Biography*, are faithful and impressive records of the most memorable events of the Crimean and Franco-German campaigns. Thomas Jones Barker died in London in 1882 at the age of sixty-seven.

Bath continued the nursery of good painters many years, but those who attained great eminence did so after their removal to London. Of these one of the most celebrated was Sir Thomas Lawrence, P.R.A., who, born at Devizes in 1769, was placed at an early age under an artist here, probably William Hoare. When only thirteen he received prizes from the Society of Arts for copying in crayons the "Transfiguration" by Raphael, supporting himself while working up to future distinction by painting half-guinea likenesses of the fashionable people of Bath.   Sir Frederic Leighton, one of his successors in the Presidency, is connected with Bath by early residence ; his parents lived many years in the Circus.   A beautiful monument designed and erected by him to the memory of his mother adorns one of the suburban cemeteries. A lately deceased distinguished academician, Mr. Long, was born and educated here ; he also began his successful career as a portrait painter ; in addition to the earlier works possessed by fellow citizens in private dwellings, there is at the Guildhall a portrait by him, in his later style, of Mr. William Hunt, several times Mayor of Bath, painted by public subscription.   Of not a few other recent local artists it may be said that but for the greatly increased competition of the nineteenth century they also would have become Bath Celebrities, for most of them spent their lives here with good repute and fair success.   Ford, Jagger, Sheldon, Syer, Duffield, Hardwick, the Hardys, Maddox, Rosenberg, all deserve honourable mention in the local annals.   They are succeeded by men and women who in their day are also doing good work.

Chapter XX.

FOUR DIVINES—HALES, CARTE, JAY, KEMBLE.

It would be strange if among the Celebrities of Bath there were no divines. That there would be a large number would not be expected by any who know the circumstances of the city. It would not be just, however, to suppose an amount of religious indifference sufficient to discourage considerable pulpit eminence.

At various periods there have been able and excellent ministers in Bath. They were somewhat known in the eighteenth century; more in the nineteenth; men of learning, piety, eloquence, and practical usefulness. Still, except in a few instances, they have not been Celebrities, destined to leave their mark on the city and be a light to future generations. Bath has, however, been the training place for divines of rank as well as laymen. Three instances will be remembered. Canon Fleming, now of London and York, was preacher at All Saints'; the present Dean of Windsor was curate of Walcot; and the late Archbishop of York was incumbent at the Octagon Chapel. My present chapter will contain sketches of the " ever-memorable " John Hales, the Rev. Thomas Carte, the Rev. William Jay and the Rev. Charles Kemble.

The Ever-memorable John Hales.

The fact that this title was first given by high authority and continued in successive centuries indicates celebrity. Born in Bath in 1584 and receiving his classical education at King Edward's School, Hales was one of its earliest and most distinguished scholars. " His proficiency in grammar learning," we learn from the *British Biography*, "was so early that at thirteen he was sent to Corpus Christi College in Oxford, and soon became Fellow of Merton." There he was noted for "subtle disputations in philosophy, eloquent declamations on history, and exact knowledge of Greek," the latter qualifying him, first to read the Greek lecture in his college, and afterwards to be Greek Professor in the University. He was also chosen by Sir Henry Savile to assist in his edition of *S. Chrysostom* and by the University to deliver the oration at the interment of Sir Thomas Bodley, the founder of the Bodleian Library.

Having taken Holy Orders he accompanied King James's ambassador, Sir Dudley Carleton, in 1618 to Holland as his chaplain. How long he acted in this capacity, or continued to officiate as a clergyman, does not appear, but frequent mention is made of his great interest in theological questions. An intimate friend of Chillingworth, he shared the strong desire of that eminent man "to see religion freed from whatever did not belong to it, and cultivated in its primitive purity and simplicity." One of his contemporaries remarks that he went to Holland a Calvinist and returned an Arminian, and when a friend who saw him reading *Calvin's Institute* remarked that he thought he had got beyond that, he answered, "In my younger days I read it to inform myself, I now read it to reform him." His engagement with Sir Dudley Carleton led to his taking an active part at the Synod of Dort. On his return he was appointed Canon of Windsor, but steadily refused any further preferment, "choosing rather a good conscience." Towards the close of life his pecuniary trials were great. He kept his library as long as possible, but was at length compelled to sell it, live in very small lodgings and put up with scanty fare. He died at Eton in 1656 at the age of seventy-two. Anthony Wood writes of him as "sincerely pious, of the strictest integrity, charitable to the utmost extent of his means, and of the most amiable and engaging manners." In 1659 his works were published with the title *Golden Remains of the Ever-memorable Mr. John Hales*, and in subsequent years other productions of his pen were distinguished by the same appellation.*

---

* One of Mr. Peach's Bath books is a fine copy of the early edition of the *Golden Remains*. Its value is increased by a few annotations of recent date, one being an extract from the register of Hales's baptism, May 5th, 1854, from the register of St. James's parish, Bath. There are also printed cuttings from Bath newspapers containing letters caused by some local theological discussions. The following is signed Francis Barham, who was known as a learned and benevolent man; he writes as a peacemaker: "It may befit us sometimes to revive the memories of great worthies who have flourished in Bath in the good old times. Amongst these worthies John Hales, with whose name the title 'ever-memorable' is constantly associated occupies a conspicuous place. The reason why he is so called and why his *Remains* are called *Golden Remains* is principally because he was one of the most illustrious pacificators of his age and country. While most scholars, divines and politicians were eager if not violent for the triumph of particular sects and parties, John Hales rose to that holy universalism of truth which views them all as necessary parts in the whole system of things—as indispensible wheels in the organised clock-work of society, not to be destroyed but regulated and harmonized. He therefore urged the pacification of sects and parties, Jews and Christians, Catholics and Protestants, Conformists and Nonconformists, and proclaimed the principles of civil and religious toleration and

The estimation in which Hales was generally held is shown by his influence at the Synod of Dort. A series of his letters to the English Ambassador on the proceedings of the Synod are given in the *Remains*. There also may be found the remarkable sermons which Chillingworth is said to have prized as "most precious for setting forth the great religious questions of the day clearly and courageously." One proof of the success Hales sometimes met with in his efforts for conciliation may be found in the good understanding between him and Archbishop Laud, to whom he is said to have owed his appointment to the Canonry at Windsor. Differing so widely on theological and ecclesiastical questions they could yet see in each other grounds for mutual respect, though not even Laud could induce Hales to accept other preferment than the canonry. He would aid the Archbishop in his controversy with a Jesuit, but he would not, directly or indirectly, sanction what he believed to be wrong.

THE REVEREND THOMAS CARTE.

Thirty years after the death of Hales, Thomas Carte was born, the son of a Prebendary of Lichfield. His celebrity in Bath was as Reader in the Abbey Church, a political controversalist and a prolific historian. Though styled "Reader" in the Abbey, he was in fact Rector of Bath, and it was from

---

liberty long before they were generally understood. He believed the true church to consist of truly pious persons in every denomination, the Bible to be the only true confession of faith and subscriptions to particular human creeds to be the cause of division and antagonism. In this respect he agreed with Jeremy Taylor in his *Liberty of Prophesying* and Archdeacon Blackburn in his *Confessional*."

a sermon preached in that capacity his chief notoriety dates. This was on the thirtieth of January, 1714, when the Jacobite party was still strong in the city. Carte being at their head, lost no opportunity of defending the Stewarts, and now vindicated Charles I. with respect to the Irish massacre. He was answered by the Rev. Henry Chandler, Minister of the original Nonconformist congregation in Bath, then denominated Presbyterian, now Unitarian. Several letters followed on both sides which, being published, acquired more than usual importance as the antagonists were both able men.

Carte, however, had a greater trouble before him. On the accession of the House of Hanover he refused to take the oaths of allegiance. He even threw aside his clerical habit and assumed the character of a layman, acting for some time as secretary to Bishop Atterbury. In 1722, either in speech or writing, he had so far committed himself as to be accused of high treason, a reward of £1,000 being offered for his apprehension by the Government. There was a story that an officer was sent from London to arrest the Jacobite offender, and that in order to escape he jumped from the window of the Rectory house in full canonicals. At all events he was compelled to quit England, but he was welcomed in France, introduced to men of learning and position, and gained access to the best libraries of Paris. Thus he was enabled to pursue his historical researches which eventually resulted in several important works. While thus engaged, Queen Caroline, wife of George II., who had much sympathy with scholars, arranged that he should return to England.

Some writer has remarked that Carte was weak rather than wicked; certainly he had the esteem of many who differed from him; he counselled forbearance if he did not always practise it, saying often " there will be mistakes in divinity

while human beings preach, and in government while mortals
rule." The chief of his many works was a *History of England*
in four volumes. His *Life of the Duke of Ormond* was also a
work of much repute. Bishop Warburton said of him "You
may read Hume for eloquence, but Carte is the Historian for
facts." At his death he left his mass of papers to his widow who
married a member of the Church of Rome by whom, Mr.
Jernegan, they were sold for a considerable sum to the University of Oxford for the Bodleian Library. His great wish was to
bring his History, which ends in 1564, down to the Revolution, for which purpose he says he had taken great pains in
copying innumerable documents in England, Scotland, and
other countries. The various intrigues of the Court at the
end of the reign of Charles II., were his chief subjects of
investigation. One of his biographers states, that while the
papers were in Mr. Jernegan's possession, the Earl of Hardwicke paid £200 for the perusal of them, and Mr. Macpherson
£300, to use them as materials for his historical work.

THE REV. WILLIAM JAY.

A striking contrast to Thomas Carte, but undoubtedly
celebrated, because singularly able and eminently useful, was
William Jay. He was born in 1769, the son of a Wiltshire
stonecutter, and in due time apprenticed to his father, with
whom he worked in the erection of Fonthill Abbey. The
Dissenting minister of his native village, Tisbury, noticing
his studious disposition, recommended him to the Rev.
Cornelius Winter, of Marlborough, who received him as a
pupil. Jay not only studied earnestly, but preached in the
neighbouring villages when only sixteen years of age, always
attracting crowds to hear him. On leaving Marlborough in 1788
he preached a series of discourses for the Rev. Rowland Hill,

at Surrey Chapel, London, where the fame of the boy-preacher filled the large building. His first settlement was at Christian Malford near Chippenham, whence he removed to Clifton to officiate in an Independent chapel belonging to Lady Maxwell. It was in 1791 that he removed to Bath, where he enjoyed great popularity during the long period of sixty-two years. The writer in *The National Biography* says "his style was simple, his manner earnest, and his voice remarkably good." John Forster calls him the "prince of preachers," Sheridan "the most natural orator he had ever heard," and even so fastidious a critic as Beckford describes his mind as "a clear, transparent stream, flowing so freely as to give the idea of its being inexhaustible." For many years he supplied Surrey Chapel for six weeks at a time. Some of his works had a large circulation. *The Mutual Duties of Husbands and Wives,* ran to six editions ; *Morning Exercises* to ten ; and the *Evening Exercises* had also a considerable sale. He died in 1853, in the house in which he had long lived, No. 4, Percy place, at the age of eighty-four.

Mr. Jay retired from the ministry of Argyle chapel where he had ministered more than half-a-century in 1853. The event was followed by the secession of a part of the congregation who built a Chapel in Charlotte street, which in compliment to their former pastor they named Percy chapel Many tributes to his memory appeared after his death, one in recent times by Mr. Peach in the first volume of his *Historic Houses,* which I may introduce here as remarkably faithful and comprehensive.*

---

*"It is a proof of Mr. Jay's rare qualities that for so long a period he maintained his influence over a large congregation, unimpaired almost to the last. He was a man of fine courage,

O

THE REV. CHARLES KEMBLE.

Few Bath benefactors are remembered with more gratitude than the munificent restorer of the Abbey Church. And Mr. Kemble had other strong claims as a clergyman and a citizen; his memory will be long respected for his earnest ministrations in the pulpit and his services to many useful institutions. But by his work at the Abbey he did spontaneously for the noblest building in the city what few men could do and what no other man would have done.

---

great ability, and possessed preaching power of a high order. These were attributes which enabled him to win and hold that ascendancy over his people, which he used with a moderation and wisdom that marked the character of the man. Mr. Jay devoted himself exclusively to his ministerial duties, turning neither to the right nor to the left after other pursuits. In relation to the Church, to politics, and the exciting questions of the day, during his long and honoured life, his conduct was characterized by great caution, candour, and sound judgment; and he always acted towards those with whom he differed in opinion, on the principle that there are generally two, if not more, sides to every question. Mr. Wilberforce no doubt was attracted towards Mr. Jay by this breadth of character and eclectic taste. It may be thought that Mr. Jay clung with too much tenacity to the position he had so long filled. It was natural that a man of so much energy and intellectual vitality should be unwilling to admit the decaying powers and enfeebled physical ability which had become painfully apparent to others, and that he should resist the proposed assistance proffered by his congregation. He did not object to an assistant, but a co-pastor was to him highly distasteful. 'If,' he said, 'two ride on horseback, one must ride behind.' The reply to which was very simple, namely, that as to a co-pastor or

Charles Kemble was born in 1819. His father and grand-father were opulent tea merchants in London. His father died when he was six weeks old leaving no other child. For a long time it was doubtful whether he could be reared, so delicate were his infancy and childhood. But first the care of a judicious mother, then the wise training of grandfather and uncles, brought him up. He always spoke of his grandfather very gratefully, attributing to his influence the business habits he found so useful in after life.

Not these, however, nor yet the prospect of considerable wealth, fixed young Kemble's destination. His strength of

---

assistant there could never arise a dispute as to which place Mr. Jay was to occupy. The end was that during the closing years of his ministry he had the aid of a coadjutor of singular eminence, in the person of Robert Alfred Vaughan, a man of great accomplishments. Mr. Vaughan came to Bath in 1848, and re-moved to Birmingham in October, 1850, where he remained until 1855. He died in 1857, too soon for the church of which he was one of the brightest and most gifted ministers ; and for literature, on which he left the impress of his power and learning in various essays, and in that remarkable work, *Hours with the Mystics.* His sermons were full of exquisite thoughts, showing deep reading and immense diligence. We believe that Mr. Jay, before he died, was brought by reflection and by what he discerned around him, to believe that something more than praying and preaching were indispensible in a pastor ; that a knowledge of his people, of their thoughts, and habits, and personal lives was needful, and that it was desirable to meet and see them in their homes as well as in his chapel. This he did not do, and the fault was not all his own. He had grown up with a system which did not insist so much upon pastoral care and general regard for the flock, as upon pulpit exhortations and long prayers."

character and religious convictions made him resolve to devote himself to the ministry of the Church of England. His mother, still anxious about his health, accompanied him to Oxford, where he passed through the usual course until his ordination in 1842. His first settlement was as curate at Stockwell in a new church without a district. Soon afterwards the incumbent resigned and he succeeded him, forming with judgment and carrying out with energy various plans. For the rapidly increasing population he obtained a new parish consisting of part of Lambeth and containing 7,000 people. He also immediately built schools for 400 children at the part of the parish farthest from the church and provided Sunday services for the parents.

On another large work in Stockwell Mr. Kemble soon fixed his heart—a second church. Governed by no sectarian feeling, but by earnest interest in the spiritual condition of his fellow creatures, he erected the needed building at his sole cost. He was thus engaged when Mr. Simeon's Trustees made him the offer of the Rectory of Bath. Strong as the ties were which bound him to Stockwell after seventeen years of constant work, he yet felt it right to accept the invitation. Here he commenced another service of fifteen years, and continued it with the same fidelity and large heartedness which he had always shown. Removing in 1859 he found three objects to be carried out if possible. (1) The separation of St. James's Parish from the Abbey Parish, (2) the restoration of the Abbey Church with more space for worshippers, and (3) the re-building of the National Schools.

The first was accomplished, and an income of £300 with a house provided for the vicar of St. James's. The rebuilding of the schools had to be given up, partly in consequence of the establishment of a School Board. But the restoration of the Abbey and the blending of the nave with the choir were carried out with great vigour. Besides substantial repairs of considerable magnitude, it was deemed right to undertake ornamental works appropriate to the dignity and importance of the edifice. The beautiful groined ceiling of Bath stone, the east and other windows, Prior Bird's elegant little chapel, the reredos, all testify to the spirit which characterised the plans. From the beginning Mr. Kemble was cordially aided by an energetic committee and the support of the city generally. It was felt that no sectarian or political differences should prevent a united effort for doing what was needed to such a fine old, historic, national monument. On the seventh of May, 1864, at the first public meeting called on the subject, the Bishop of the Diocese presided, the Mayor of Bath, a Nonconformist, moved the first resolution, which was seconded by the Rector, and the entire proceedings were in all respects worthy of the occasion. The total cost exceeded £30,000, about one-third being provided by Mr. Kemble and his family, the remainder by public subscription. The fine coloured window in the transept was put up at the expense of Mrs. Elliott, who also paid for the restoration of Bishop Montague's tomb. The east window originated with the Bath Literary Club, one of whose members collected from comparatively few friends the amount of the cost, about thirteen hundred pounds.

Nearly ten years passed before the Restoration was completed. Through the whole time neither Mr. Kemble's energy nor generosity ever flagged. He attended to all the details with the committee, meeting any pecuniary difficulty arising from unexpected wants and encouraging public efforts by his munificent example. Nor did this engrossing occupation preclude his discharge of many other duties; his functions as Rector of the parish, the Royal United Hospital, of which he was President several years, the Mineral Water Hospital, where he filled the office one year, and long acted as Governor, the Victoria Park Committee, the School Board and other institutions had the benefit of his unremitting service. Amid so many engagements in the year 1873, illness arrested him. He had lately completed a new edition of a Hymn Book which he originally compiled before coming to Bath. An attack of bronchitis was followed by symptoms of heart disease which laid him aside for some time. At length in August, 1874, the summons came ; it found him ready ; the flame of life flickered a few weeks and all was over. He was buried in the Abbey Cemetery with every mark of respect from the ministers of all denominations, the Corporation of the city and the people at large.

CHAPTER XXI.

BISHOP BAINES AND BISHOP CLIFFORD.

It may have been obvious that the reputation of nearly all the eminent men of whom I have written has not been merely local.   Their names if not their works, their positions if not their histories have been well known to a considerable extent, thereby increasing their claim to grateful local remembrance. This was the case especially with the two prelates whose histories have been selected for the present chapter.   Closely connected with Bath by official ties they were heard of and respected in distant countries while their own sympathies had a range of corresponding extent.

It is impossible to write of such men without remembering this leading characteristic of the Catholic Church.   Macaulay, fifty years ago, said that "the members of her communion were certainly not fewer than a hundred and fifty millions, whereas all the other Christian sects united scarcely amounted to a hundred and twenty millions."   Probably in the interval the proportion has become still more favourable on the Catholic side ; at all events there is, happily, a growing disposition to regard not only numbers but great antiquity, marvellous vitality and undoubted practical usefulness as reasons for deep interest in one of the foremost religious agencies of the world.

The preceding chapter of divines, short as it is, illustrates the variety of the human mind.   Hales was a broad Churchman, so broad that, though his learning and ability would have given him high station, he declined all preferment. Carte was a high Anglican, so high that the Government of

the day ordered him to be arrested for treason and he, while
still a clergyman, refused to wear clerical habits.   Jay was a
Nonconformist, relying for means of usefulness in the world,
neither on ordained sacramental observances nor any other
obedience to state requirements, but on simple, powerful,
practical preaching, such as would affect the conscience and
daily life.   Kemble, a clergyman of the Established Church,
but in sympathy with all sincere Christians, devoted himself
and his opportunities to the right preservation of a noble
historic religious edifice and to general means of doing good
in the city where his lot was cast.   After saying what has to
be said of Bishop Baines and Bishop Clifford I propose to
introduce notices of two other members of the clerical profession, Mr. Warner and Mr. Hunter, who being chiefly
remarkable for public services outside the lines of that profession, and perhaps differing from all the others in some
respects on religious matters, are additional instances of the
prevailing variety of human thought.

Peter Augustine Baines was born in 1786 at Pear Tree
Farm, near Liverpool.   In 1798 he quitted his home with
three brothers to study divinity in Hanover.   It was at the
English Benedictine Abbey of Lambspring, but in about four
years his studies were interrupted, the property suffering
the fate of war, being seized by the Prussian Government.   The students were scattered, and Baines, returning
to England, joined a mission near York connected with
the Benedictine College of St. Lawrence, Ampleforth.
When he had passed through the usual gradations to the
priesthood and occupied fourteen years as a teacher in the
college he was selected to take charge of the mission at Bath,
where his exceptional gifts were fully recognised.   The author
of the memoir in the *Dictionary of National Biography* says

"he was conspicuous for his eloquence as a preacher, his vigour as a controversialist, and above all the charm and dignity of his personal bearing."

Six years afterwards Dr. Baines was consecrated as a bishop, still continuing his work in Bath. Soon, however, he fell into serious ill-health, and being advised to travel, visited Rome with a few friends, who kindly accompanied him. "He came," says Cardinal Wiseman, in the fascinating chapter on Leo XII in his *Recollections of the last four Popes*, "with an interior abscess working on an enfeebled frame, hoping that change of climate might do more than medicines or their administrators. He was not disappointed ; the mild climate, the interesting recreation, and perhaps still more, the rest from the labour and excitement in which he had lived wrought a visible change for the better ere the return of spring. A delightful summer spent between Assisi and Porto di Fermo completely re-established the health which he had travelled to seek." One advantage of this visit was an intimate acquaintance with the reigning pontiff Leo XII, who was much interested in him, not only on account of his social qualities and great abilities, but as a member of the Benedictine brotherhood to which Leo himself belonged, and whose interests he had much at heart. Cardinal Wiseman's further account of the steps by which Bishop Baines gained celebrity, as well as of some striking personal characteristics must form part of this sketch :

"By degrees the reputation which he had acquired in England began to spread in Rome ; several noble families in which he had been intimate at home were in Rome, and gave many others the opportunity of becoming acquainted with him ; and he had a power of fascinating all who approached him, in spite of a decided tone and manner which made it difficult to differ from him in opinion. He had sometimes original views upon a certain class of subjects; but on every topic he had a command of language, and a clear manner of expressing his sentiments, which commanded attention, and generally won assent. Unfortunately, this proved to him a dangerous gift. When he undertook great and magnificent works, he would stand alone : assent to his plans was a condition of being near him ; any one that did not agree, or that ventured to suggest deliberation, or provoke discussion, was easily put aside ; he isolated himself with his own genius ; he had no counsellor but himself ; and he who had, at one time, surrounded himself with men of learning, of prudence, and of devotedness to him, found himself at last almost alone, and fretted a noble heart to a solitary death.

"At the period, however, to which this chapter belongs, these faults could scarcely show themselves to any great disparagement of his higher and better powers. In the course of the ensuing winter he was able, though contrary to the opinion of his friends, to appear in the English pulpit, which, as we shall see, Leo XII opened in Rome. The church, which was nearly empty when preachers of inferior mark occupied it, was crowded when Bishop Baines was announced as the orator. Many people will remember him. He was happiest in his unwritten discourses. The flow of his words was easy and copious, his imagery was often very elegant, and his discourses were replete with thought and solid matter. But his great power was in his delivery, in voice, in tone, in look, and gesture. His whole manner was full of pathos, sometimes more even than the matter justified ; there was a peculiar tremulousness of voice, which gave his words more than double effect, notwithstanding the drawback of a provincial accent, and occasional dramatic pronunciations. In spite of such defects, he was considered, by all that heard him, one of the most eloquent and earnest preachers they had ever attended."

It is not surprising that in these circumstances Dr. Baines

was destined by Leo XII to be the first English cardinal. The fact that they were both Benedictines influenced the Pontiff who told Monsignor Nicolai that he had been " looking around for a member of the order on whom to bestow the hat of restitution."

With this view Leo, having made suitable inquiries as to fitness in various respects, desired that as a preparatory step Baines should remove from his private apartments in Rome to the Benedictine monastery of San Callisto and wear the Episcopal habit of his order. Cardinal Wiseman states he was assured on good authority that this having been done the Pope renewed the offer but it was declined; why, we are not told; only that "the bishop would have been made a cardinal not on national grounds but as a Benedictine, though the thought of travelling so far for a fitting recipient of the dignity was generous and broad and undoubtedly formed the basis of the nomination of an English cardinalite in the ensuing Pontificate."

In one of the passages I have quoted referring to " magnificent works " there is probably an allusion to the great enterprise of Prior Park in which certainly courage may have been more conspicuous than prudence. What was accomplished there, however—the purchase of the estate, said to have been the noblest day-dream of his life and the establishment of the college, for which a want had long existed, amply confirms Dr. Wiseman's statement as to the influence the Bishop had acquired by his abilities and high character. The titled and wealthy Catholics of England saw in him no common man ; they believed him capable of doing much to restore their church to what they conceived to be its right position in the country ; and if a Protestant like Macaulay could be so deeply impressed with the vital power

of that church as to write the celebrated eulogy, in which he
states that "the proudest royal houses are but of yesterday
when compared with the line of the Supreme Pontiffs," can it
be wondered that noblemen and gentlemen should gladly
support one of their prelates whose aspirations were so high?
Hence on returning from Rome after the death of Bishop
Collingridge, whose coadjutor he had been at Bath, hastening
back, we are told, with the added responsibility of Vicar
Apostolic of the Western district, he proceeded to carry out
his plans as to Prior Park. The new buildings arose; the
college succeeded, at least for a time; men who attained
much eminence were trained in it; the indefatigable bishop
continued to preach in Bath with his accustomed eloquence
and gathered around him occasionally at Prior Park the
friends of the students and the *élite* of Bath. But all that
had been done caused a load of anxieties and obligations
which oppressed him till the close of his life "fretting a
noble heart to a solitary death." This came with unexpected
suddenness in 1843 at the age of fifty-seven. Very numerous
were the testimonies of respect and affection. At the lying
in state upwards of thirteen thousand persons passed round
the catafalque. Besides the memory of his great personal
services he left numerous controversial writings, pastorals
and lectures. He was interested in art and much as he loved
Italy he had a great admiration of the city and scenery of
Bath. I remember standing with him in the portico of
Prior Park when, looking at the varied landscape stretched
out before us, the richly covered hills, the city embosomed
among them, the Avon winding peacefully for many a mile,
he said "I know nothing more beautiful in Italy or anywhere."

Prior Park is so often mentioned that I add a few particulars. The following description appeared lately in a London morning paper :—

"Prior Park is situated at the head of a long, well-wooded vale on a brow which commands a beautiful view. It derives its name from the fact that it once belonged to the priors of Bath Abbey. The original house as it now stands was built by Wood for Ralph Allen, who was the original of Fielding's Allworthy in *Tom Jones*. It is a handsome Palladian structure with a central portico, two large wings and connecting arcades ranged in a semi-circle. The front descends in terraces to a stream and pool, which are spanned by a bridge, built in the form of a temple. The house is built of Bath stone, darkened by time, and the effect of the pillared front and the porticoed entrance is very fine. It came to the Roman Catholic Church by gift, and is now used as a residence for the Bishop of Clifton, and a college for the education of aspirants to Roman Catholic orders."

To this I subjoin a short history of the property. It belonged to the ancient monastery and included on that side of Bath three Combes, Widecombe, Lyncombe, or the Watery Valley, and Smallcombe in the Parish of Bathwick. Ralph Allen's purchase was a portion of the Widecombe, adjoining his stone quarries, where the Prior of the Monastery had possessed a park which supplied it with venison, and a grange or farm with the usual produce for such an establishment. This portion was called the Prior Park estate after the dissolution in the time of Henry VIII, when it was purchased by Humphrey Colles, then transferred to Matthew Colthurst, and ultimately to Fulke Morley from whom it descended by kinship to the Duke of Kingston. From him it devolved through the female line to the Meadows family, who assumed the name of Pierrepont, the head of which family was created Earl Manvers.

Allen acquired the estate in the full tide of his prosperity. He wanted a house corresponding to it, but he also wanted to show what effect could be produced by the stone from his adjoining quarries.   It has been stated in the Memoir of Allen that after the death of Bishop Warburton in 1779, Lord Hawarden who married Allen's niece succeeded to the property and lived there till he was followed by his son who died without issue in 1807, when the connection of Prior Park with the Allen family ceased.   The house was afterwards void or had only occasional tenants until 1817.   Then Mr. Thomas, a Bristol merchant, came and remained nine years.   In 1827 Bishop Baines was placed in possession, very much as the result of the great efforts made by himself to buy the property for a high-class educational establishment.   Two wings were built for distinct classes of students, and called respectively St. Peter's and St. Paul's College.   Great spirit was thrown into the undertaking, and for some time the prospects were encouraging, but at length heavy clouds intervened, the expenses could not be sustained, the college was broken up and the estate let.   A succession of tenants occupied it for some years, the longest being Mr. Thompson, a Nonconformist gentleman from a distance, who became a member of the Bath Corporation.   In 1856 it was again vacant, and bought by Bishop Clifford, a most generous effort for the revival of a thoroughly efficient Catholic College.

From the additions and improvements which have been made in the interval, now thirty-seven years, it may be inferred that there has been a fair amount of success.   Two elements have certainly not been wanting : unceasing interest on the part of the noble-minded prelate who accomplished the purchase and the high character of successive presidents and assistants.   If Bishop Baines was instrumental in adding considerably to the original structure of Ralph Allen the wings and arcades for the college and the commencement of a beautiful chapel, Bishop Clifford caused a completion of much that was unfinished and infused from year to year a spirit of the greatest value.

It is probable that exaggerated ideas prevail as to the mansion. Handsome as it is externally the interior is far from being what might be supposed. Wood is said to have been much more particular about accommodation for the horses for the establishment than for the inmates of the house. Allen, though in some respects unassuming, was fond of state ; his horses were richly caparisoned and he seldom drove with less than four. It was one of the follies of the times promoted by the man whom the Corporation was so weak as to consider King of Bath. And while Wood did not give his employer a single good room in the centre of the house his care for the horses and even for the pigeons and poultry was excessive. Still the sight of the noble facade, with its magnificent flight of steps and the other architectural surroundings, adorned as they all are by luxuriant vegetation, are worth a long journey to see and will always form one of the greatest attractions of Bath.

BISHOP CLIFFORD.

While these pages are passing through the Press, I hear of the death of this distinguished prelate. Although Clifton was his habitual place of residence he spent much time at Prior Park, and his intimate connection with it would alone justify a tribute to his memory here. But he was also well known in Bath, much interested in its various scientific societies and especially useful in throwing light on doubtful questions relating to its Roman antiquities and other matters of local history.

The *Athenæum* justly says that Bishop Clifford was in many ways an uncommon man ; by descent indeed almost a curiosity. He was the second son of the seventh Baron Clifford, of Chudleigh who married the daughter of Thomas Wild who, being left a widower, took orders in the Church of Rome and eventually received a Cardinal's hat. Hugh Clifford was thus the extraordinary instance of a Cardinal's grandson, and there is reason to believe that had he lived a little longer he would have enjoyed the dignity conferred on Dr. Wild. So long ago as the early fifties Dr. Oliver in his *Collection illustrating the history of the Catholic Churches in the West of England,* predicted that Dr. Clifford would become a prominent character in the community.

He received part of his early education at Prior Park, at the time when Bishop Baines lived at the mansion, and he was in constant intercourse with him until his death. The next resident prelate was Archbishop Errington, with whom he had the warmest friendship, as is shewn by the desire to be interred by his side in the corridor adjoining the college chapel. Bishop Clifford's love for Prior Park, begun in early life, continued to the end. He was accustomed to say that wherever he was, through the long period of sixty years, no place had greater charms for him. In addition to the surpassing beauty of the landscape and the historic associations, which no one could appreciate better than himself, there would be his attachment to successive heads of the college, men of no ordinary intellectual and religious worth.

Great therefore must have been his sorrow when, in 1856, the vicissitudes came which broke up the college and deprived the catholics of the beautiful estate. But great also were his courage and energy, when, after the changes of nine years, he obtained funds for buying back the property and re-establishing a high class seminary. Mention was made of his efforts by Dr. Hedley, Bishop of Newport, in his sermon at the Mass prior to the interment. " No one," he said, " could tell how generous and large hearted the deceased prelate was ; no one would ever know how much the place where they were assembled owed to him." As one of the audience I felt indeed it was only necessary to look around on the rows of noble pillars, the ceiling, the windows and other accessories, all in the exquisite style and proportions of an Italian cathedral, to feel the force of the preacher's remark. And while this was evidence of the care, skill and cost with which additions had been made through successive decades, thoughts would crowd upon the mind of the constant care for the educational objects of the establishment and of the love which every member of it cherished for the benefactor.

The contiguity of Clifton made Dr. Clifford's frequent visits to Bath easy. And here a large circle of friends were always glad to welcome so genial and accomplished a visitor. Apart from his episcopal duties many objects of interest in the city had a share of his regard, especially the antiquities, on which he occasionally gave lectures at the Institution. It would be easily imagined by all who knew the tendency of his mind and his intimate knowledge of Rome that the uncovering and development of the magnificent baths within his diocese would be watched by him with peculiar pleasure. On this and other kindred subjects he was always regarded as an authority by the various archæological societies with which he was connected at Bath and Bristol and in the counties of the district, while his charming simplicity of style and manner attracted all sects and parties and led to the formation of many friendships. But every one knew that it was to the church of his fathers his most ardent affection and constant

P

service were given.   Year by year it was seen how buildings
arose, institutions multiplied, congregations increased, under
the fostering care of the indefatigable bishop.   Yet preaching
was not amongst his accomplishments, in consequence of a
slight physical hesitancy.   His eminence in the church, however, caused him to be selected for the sermon at the funeral
of his intimate friend Cardinal Newman.   Few dignitaries
were better known in Rome; he had the rare privilege of
being consecrated to his bishopric at the Vatican ; with
Pius IX he appears to have been for a long time a special
favourite, and that Leo XIII had sincere regard for him is
said to have been shewn by a willingness to give him the post
of English adviser when Cardinal Howard left Rome.   This
would have been unwelcome to him in consequence of the
strong ties of Clifton and Prior Park.   One reason for the
Pope's desire to have such an adviser would probably be his
thorough knowledge and excellent pronunciation of the Italian
language.   It has been even said that Bishop Clifford could
preach well in Italian though not in English.

It should be gratefully remembered that the strong religious
affections which have been mentioned were combined with
much independence of character.   Dr. Hedley mentioned
this in his eloquent sermon with reference to Dr. Clifford's
objection to the celebrated dogma of the immaculate conception for which the Pope required the acceptance of the
Church.   The preacher attributed the objection to a broad-
mindedness acquired by Roman experiences, to mingling
with the most learned theologians and men of the widest
intellects, and to constant contact with the great stream of
Catholic thought.   " The Catholic Church," said Dr. Hedley,
" though an immutable Church was not silent and dead, like
some stony sphinx of the Egyptian desert silted up by the

sand of ages; no, her immutability was the accompaniment of perpetual life." "Dr. Clifford," he continued, "recognised this, and saw that, unalterable as the Church was, there was nevertheless in her the development of leaf and the bursting of flower from year to year and century to century." Another writer remarks that "he aimed at leading his flock by gentle suasion and high example rather than by enforcing blind obedience to the voice of authority.

Prior Park had seen many remarkable gatherings. Statesmen, Philosophers and Philanthropists had often met there in genial conclave. But never probably within that beautiful pile of buildings had there been such a grand and solemn spectacle as on Friday, the eighteenth of August. The preceding circumstances had touched many a chord of loving sympathy. It was known how the good Bishop had gone on with his work until he had found it necessary to submit to an operation. It was known how he wished for it to be performed in the quiet of Prior Park with the aid of his personal medical attendant, Mr. King. It was known how a London specialist had been so successful that strong hopes of recovery were entertained, but how in a few sad days other symptoms appeared, and, after the last solemn ceremonies, the patient sank to rest. And thus were brought together from Bath and Clifton and Bristol and all the country round that large sympathising congregation. Those who were present will long remember the solemn dirges, the array of dignitaries, the eloquent sermon, the universal sorrow; and many must have returned home thankful for having known so good a man.

Writing on the fit association of the names of Oliver and Clifford as "antiquaries both born and made" the *Athenæum* adds :—

"If archæology was a pastime to Clifford, it was at the same time a serious study. In Wilts and Somerset he brought much research to investigations in local topography, especially as to the sites of battles between King Alfred and the Danes. He was an enthusiastic member of the archæological societies of Somersetshire and Gloucestershire ; but beyond a few papers read at the meetings of these and similar societies, he has left no written records of his opinions and researches. Few modern bishops have produced less 'copy' of any kind. He fought shy, if he could, of that sort of extended 'imprimatur,' in the form of an episcopal preface to a pious volume, which the modern Roman Catholic author appears hardly to be happy without. When religious controversies raged, Bishop Clifford seldom ranged himself as a champion of the opinions he was well fitted by his sense of courtesy and toleration to defend with effect. In 1874, when he published a reply to Mr. Gladstone's anti-Vatican pamphlets, he did so in the form of one of the pastorals which every Roman Catholic bishop is expected to address to his flock at stated seasons of the ecclesiastical year ; and this, perhaps, will remain as a standard little treatise on the civil allegiance of the spiritual subjects of the Pope."

An annotation by the Rev. J. Hunter refers to another Roman Catholic Bishop in Bath who deserves to be remembered, Dr. Walmesley. Mr. Hunter had written of Sir W. Herschel as having done much to strengthen the connection of science with the city and adds :—

" The only other resident of Bath contemporary with Herschel who can be singled out as likely to have encouraged and assisted him, as far as I am informed, is Dr. Walmesley, a Roman Catholic Bishop and vicar of the western district, who lived much in Bath, and died there in 1797. His house was destroyed in the riots of 1780. He is said by Roman Catholic writers to have been 'very eminent as a mathematician and astronomer.' He was also a theological writer; as was his successor, Dr. Baines, the first superior of the great establishment at Prior Park."

Chapter XXII.

ARCHBISHOP MAGEE.

From time to time clergymen of the Church of England and ministers of various denominations in Bath have been celebrated for preaching power, but probably none more than William Connor Magee. On the platform also as well as in the pulpit few, if any, excelled him in impressing, usefully and permanently, the minds and hearts of those whom he addressed. Thoughtful, earnest, fearless, unconventional, he was also painstaking; he spared no labour in being well prepared for what he had to say; though his delivery had at the same time the charm of true eloquence.

In an article on his death the *Times* remarked that Magee was "not born in the purple." But the social position of his family was good, and early influences may account for much in his character. His grandfather, who, after being Bishop of Raphoe, became Archbishop of Dublin, was of much repute for "evangelical" orthodoxy. His father was vicar of Drogheda, he himself being educated at Trinity College, Dublin, where he made his mark both as a scholar and debater. After his ordination he officiated for a time in a Dublin parish, but being obliged to travel for his health he spent two years in Malaga, and on his return in 1847 accepted the curacy of St. Saviour's, in Bath. In 1850 he obtained the incumbency of the Octagon Chapel, where Herschel had been organist seventy years before, and where a fashionable congregation with strong "evangelical" proclivities now assembled.

Although Magee's bias was then quite in the same direction his preaching was sometimes in a strain to which his hearers were unaccustomed, and a few of them quitted the chapel. The incident on his part was one of those indications of mental independence which characterised his life in all its future stages; he thought for himself and acted accordingly. Year by year as he became better known in Bath his popularity and influence increased, so that not only as a preacher but as a platform orator, not only in the city which admired his eloquence but through a large sphere beyond it, he gained much repute. In the *Bath Chronicle* of the two weeks succeeding that of his death there were articles by Mr. Peach entitled " Recollections of Archbishop Magee," with some striking instances of the effects produced by his speeches. Of the exciting questions of the day three are particularly mentioned—Table-turning, Sabbath Observance and Disestablishment. On the last, the orator spoke at a great meeting for two hours in answer to the arguments of the Liberation Society. His speech passed through many editions, and so great was the demand that two hundred and forty five members of Parliament sent to the local publisher for copies.

Thus it was not surprising that Dr. Magee was induced to remove to London. In 1860 he succeeded Dr. Goulburn as minister of Quebec Chapel. Six months later he was presented to the rectory of Enniskillen. In 1868 he became Dean of Cork, Donnellan Lecturer at the University of Dublin, and Dean of the Chapel Royal at Dublin. In 1868 he was made Bishop of Peterborough. Before his removal to Ireland he gained much renown as a preacher before select congregations at Oxford, Cambridge and the Chapel Royal of London, also before large masses of people at the special services at St. Paul's and Westminster Abbey. " Wherever he went," says the *Times*, " he pondered well the subject of his sermon, never trusting wholly to inspiration, but drawing up full notes, in some cases learning his sermons by heart and preaching them as though extempore. His doctrine was of the sort that pleases most Englishmen, going on broad lines, though it is not to be denied that it changed somewhat with the church fashions of the age, so that it might be said of him as of some other prelates, that rising in his profession he became higher in more senses than one." "In one thing," the *Times* adds, "Dr. Magee never changed; he remained courageous in advancing unconventional opinions which were intended to shock prejudices that he loathed and cant which he held in equal abhorrence. He was once asked to interest himself in a carpenter's son who was doing well at a small school, and whom it was proposed to send to a University. 'Let him first graduate as a good carpenter,' answered Magee, ' what becomes of your boasted concern for the welfare of the working classes if you lift a man out of those classes as soon as he shows brains.'" Though this may be mentioned as a proof of rather brusque unconventionalism it surely cannot be quoted as a conclusive argument. There may be many carpenters with brains who are amply equipped for that calling, but few who could become statesmen or archbishops. Why should the few fail to have the chance of rising, not for their own sakes only but for the public weal?

Even a sketch of Dr. Magee would be insufficient if it failed to notice his published works. They consist largely of speeches and single sermons on subjects of public interest, which ensured a ready sale. Few orators find themselves so famous as to hear that so many members of Parliament had sent for a speech as soon as it was published. Much in demand also were the successive volumes of sermons preached in Bath at St. Saviour's Church and the Octagon Chapel;

they passed through several editions rapidly, and soon became out of print. The author of the articles in the *Chronicle*, to which reference has been made, states that the Bishop declined to have them reprinted because they presented his immature convictions ; but many of his former hearers still value them for their depth of thought, striking language, and practical power. The same author remarks, however, that these sermons if compared with a subsequent volume, *The Gospel and the Age*, would be found not only different in style but in essential points of doctrine. This also, he adds, may be said of the sermons delivered at the Dublin Church Congress, when Dr. Magee was president as Dean of Cork, *The Breaking Net*, and *Rebuilding of the Walls*. Of a sermon preached before the British Association at Norwich in 1868, which the present writer had the privilege of hearing, Charles Kingsley said, "It was the most glorious piece of eloquence I ever heard." The great preacher gratified his Bath friends by a visit to that city as Dean of Cork, for the meeting of the Association in 1864. Among his earlier works was an interesting life of his friend, the Rev. E. Tottenham, for some years a popular evangelical clergyman in Bath. Another may be specially mentioned :—A sermon preached at Bath in 1853, *Talking to Tables a Great Folly or a Great Sin*. *Auricular Confession* was the subject first of a lecture in Bath, afterwards of a speech in London, both published in 1852. A local periodical, *Northamptonshire Notes and Queries*, gave, after the Bishop's death, a list of sixty-five works issued during his life, some of them pamphlets, others substantial volumes, many having reached second and third editions. In a memoir prefixed to this list it is remarked that one great characteristic of Dr. Magee was that of a Church Reformer. "In his diocese he put his finger on abuses and abolished them. He never flinched from speaking out plainly and loudly when there was reason for it. As a matter of fact he had a real Irish delight in a contest, enjoying a tilt with popular fallacies and common heterodoxy."

The appointment of Dr. Magee to the See of Peterborough in 1868 was advised by Mr. Disraeli. When asked what he most admired in the preacher, the Premier, who had possibly not often heard his sermons, answered, " He is persuasive." The *Times* remarked, " That was true, but it might perhaps have been truer to say he is disconcerting. He shed new lights so suddenly and vividly on a question that his hearers were frequently taken aback and confessed to themselves that had they seen the matter in this way they would have acted differently. So when politicians were annoyed by the Bishop's exposure of what was bad in their measures they were not necessarily persuaded that those measures ought to be abandoned." With reference to his oratory in the House of Lords the same writer says, " The Archbishop's versatility was the product of a lively Irish character and of a highly trained intellect. He was heard at his best in the Session of 1883, when, speaking on the Cathedral Bill he described with exuberant sarcasm the position of Churchmen unable to remove the abuses of their Church because of Nonconformist or Agnostic enemies who were interested in letting these excrescences grow as germs of a mortal disease. He told the Government that they would not dare to introduce any measure of Church Reform for fear of irritating their great backbone, and he caused general amusement by sketching the probable fate of a Church Bill struggling through the House of Commons amidst amendments moved by certain Irish members. Bishops are not accustomed to speak with such elaborate playfulness as Dr. Magee used on this occasion, nor would many of their right reverend lordships be able to match their late colleague's irresistible manner if they tried to do so. With his large mouth, shaggy eyebrows and twinkling eyes; with his expressive wags of the head and his quick, forcible gestures; with his droll sallies and occasional outbursts of strong emotion he always compelled attention."

Eminent as Dr. Magee was in the House of Lords he never considered that his chief duty was there. He looked upon the administration of his diocese, and even the work to be done in Convocation, as having stronger claims upon him. Still, there can be no doubt that the public came to know him best by what he did and said in the Upper House, and one of his sons has furnished means of increasing the knowledge by a volume of speeches. The first was on the Irish Church Bill in 1869; the last on the Children's Life Insurance Bill in 1890; the chief intermediate subjects being Temperance, Education, Disestablishment, Church Patronage, Cruelty to Animals, the Cathedral Statutes, and the Discipline of the Clergy. To the fact that he was always heard with great interest, and generally with great admiration, there was universal testimony at the time of his death. The journal I have already quoted states justly, " If others surpassed him in erudition and the *technique* of the theologian, he stood above them all in the sagacity of the statesman. Dr. Magee never took a narrow or professionally clerical view of any public question. Much as his eloquence and wit were appreciated by all classes, for he was equally a favourite with popular audiences and with the *élite* of London society, there was something more highly prized by those who loved him best and honoured him most. It was the assurance that he would bring to bear upon whatever subject he had to discuss the powers of a strong and supple intellect working with a manly freedom from sectional prejudices, and apply to the complex problems of daily life, not cut and dried formulas, but an elevated and enlightened common sense."

This was notably illustrated by his treatment of one of the great questions of the day. He would never consent to treat Disestablishment as fatal to the interests of religion. Both as Priest and Bishop he always fought against the idea that the vitality of the Church of England would be impaired by severing its connection with the State. "He thought the connection good for the State, but he was earnest in advising that Churchmen should face the possibility of Disestablishment, and be prepared to make such a measure, if it came, turn to the benefit of the Church. He never quite forgave Mr. Disraeli for having made his Cardinal Grandison, in *Lothair*, sneer at the establishment as a Parliamentary Church ; the words seemed to him to reflect the writer's own private opinions—those of a Gallio who cared not much for churches save in their political uses." Equally independent, perhaps beyond the verge of prudence, was the Bishop on the Temperance question. True he contended that he had been misunderstood with regard to his memorable saying, "I would rather see England free than sober." Still on various occasions he showed he believed that "common sense" was set at nought ; he believed that a good principle was worked in the wrong way, worked so as in some cases to produce evil results. At all events he would not conceal what he felt. A curate in his diocese appeared before him wearing a blue riband in his button-hole. "I suppose you have reflected," said the Bishop, "that if you are respected in your parish you need not sport any emblem to advertise your character as a temperance man ; whereas if you are not respected this piece of blue would only remind people of the Pharisee and

the phylactery." To a lady wearing the same badge he
addressed a similar remonstrance, advising her to discard
superfluous finery. In these instances, as in that of the
carpenter's son already mentioned, the reasoning may not
be conclusive; there may be, many think there is, a good
argument for the temperance badge in the necessity of
testifying against a fearful and destructive evil, but what the
Bishop said was in harmony with his general character for
mental independence and should be viewed in that light.

On the death of Archbishop Thompson it was Lord
Salisbury's turn to advise the promotion of Dr. Magee.
Besides the obvious fact of eminent intellectual fitness there
was that of similarity of theological and ecclesiastical opinions.
It was justly said there were only two objections—the advanced
age and the feeble health of the successor, but it was remembered that many bishops had done and were doing
vigorous work after they had reached threescore and ten, also
that Dr Magee had apparently gained strength since a recent
illness. So he entered on his new duties amid general
congratulations and was enthroned in March, 1891. But he
only lived long enough to show that he wished the line of
duty which had won so much regard in the diocese of
Peterborough and in public assemblies still to animate him.
He presided at a meeting of the Convocation of the Northern
Province when he explained and justified the Clergy
Discipline Bill; he was publicly received at Hull, Beverley,
and elsewhere as he settled down to his allotted work, and he
made preparation for continuing in the House of Lords his
efforts with regard to the painful subject of " Children's Life
Insurance." For the last object he went to London in April
to preside over the committee of the Bill in Parliament, leaving
his family at Bishopsthorpe suffering from influenza, then

prevailing in all directions. Soon after his arrival in town the malady attacked himself; Sir Andrew Clarke and Dr. Walker, of Peterborough, did all they could, but in vain; day by day for a fortnight the patient became worse, and then bronchitis, accompanied by inflammation of the lungs, extinguished all hope. Forseeing the result he insisted on resigning the chairmanship of the Lord's Committee, but retained to the last his strong interest in the benevolent measure he had advocated so well. The death-bed was surrounded by Mrs. Magee and his sons and daughters, who had recovered sufficiently, some to nurse him the last few days and all to pay the final tribute of love. It can be imagined how deep was the sorrow everywhere when the tidings became known, especially in the places which knew him best; in York as soon as the great bell of the grand old Minster proclaimed the loss the diocese had sustained; in Peterborough where he had gained the warm regard of all classes, parties and denominations; in Dublin which cherished the recollection of his early life and was proud of him for his personal work as well as his intellectual greatness; and why should I not add : in Bath, for though thirty years had passed since his work here had ceased, many remained who felt they had lost one who had been to them a wise teacher and a valued friend.

And as this sketch has been written because Dr. Magee ranks among the Celebrities of our city, I venture to mention a somewhat personal incident. At the time of his elevation to the archbishopric I happened to be Mayor of Bath, and knowing the feeling of many citizens on the subject, I prepared an address of congratulation and invited signatures. It seemed to me a time when any theological or political difference should be forgotten, and when men and women should be glad to unite in showing not only a grateful remembrance of the first fruits of ministerial life, but a sincere admiration of the qualities which had led step by step from the pulpit of the Octagon Chapel in Bath, to the throne of York Minster. My suggestion was adopted, the address was numerously signed, I sent it to the Archbishop, and received the following answer :—

> "Bishopsthorpe, York ;
> "27th March, 1891.

"My dear Mr. Mayor,—It was with sincere pleasure that I received the address of congratulation from old Bath friends, at the head of which your name is placed.

"The years which I spent in Bath were among the happiest of my life, endeared to me as they were by unvarying kindness on the part of those to whom I ministered, and by many friendships never to be forgotten, though alas many of those with whom they were formed have passed away.

"It was very pleasant to me to find that there are still so many left who regard with affectionate interest the career of one who for so many years was privileged to live and labour among them. Pray assure them from me how much their kind words have cheered and gratified me, and

> "Believe me,
> "My dear Mr. Mayor,
> "Very faithfully yours,
> "W. C. EBOR."

"Jerom Murch, Esq.,
"Mayor of Bath."

The following letter is from a friend of the author of these Sketches who lived in Bath many years and has always been an eminent advocate of Temperance :—

"Dear Mr. Murch,—I have been from home, and only yesterday read your very interesting paper in *The Bath Herald*, under "Sketches of Bath Celebrities," on Archbishop Magee. In your paper you make several references to his opinions and remarks on the Temperance question. You are not probably aware, or you must have forgotten that Dr. Magee was for some years a *pledged abstainer*. On Monday, June 18th, 1859, Dr. Magee signed the Temperance pledge, after hearing John B. Gough deliver one of his stirring orations in the Bath Theatre, to an immense audience paying theatre prices to hear that remarkable man.

"That was a memorable occasion for the Temperance movement in Bath, as well as an interesting incident in Dr. Magee's vigorous life. The fact is deeply impressed upon my memory. The Theatre was packed with nearly two thousand people, who listened with wrapt attention to the thrilling address of that remarkable man. It was my privilege to be Chairman of that meeting. Dr. Barrett, then Mayor of Bath, moved a resolution of thanks to the lecturer, which was to have been seconded by Mr. Edward Saunders, when Dr. Magee rose in the Dress Circle and asked permission to second it; which being granted, he did in earnest and eloquent words. He afterwards came on to the stage, heartily shook hands with Mr. Gough, confessed his conversion to the Temperance principle and signed the pledge, with, I think, forty-six others, one of whom was the Rev. James Fleming, now Canon of York.

"I think it is due to Dr. Magee's memory to say that the words, ' I would rather see England free than England sober,' and which have been so much commented upon and so much misrepresented, was not said in relation to *Teetotulism*, but was said in regard to the ' Permissive Bill ' or ' local option ' which he was urged to take up. And the clear and intended meaning of what he said was, that he would rather see England free to work out her own emancipation from the thraldom of drink by voluntary effort and moral suasion, than see her made sober by Act of Parliament or compulsion. That fully accords with his bent of mind and general teaching ; and his objection to wearing the badge of blue was not an indication of his repugnance to, or

dislike of total abstinence, but an objection to parading it
outwardly before the world—a feeling very much participated in
by many of the oldest and staunchest Temperance reformers.

"Knowing how fair you are in your criticisms, I thought it
right to trouble you with these remarks as to one phase of that
remarkable man's life and teaching.

"I remain, dear Mr. Murch,

"Sincerely yours,

"R. P. EDWARDS."

"Hadleigh House, Hammersmith, W. ;

"May 1st, 1893."

Honourable mention is made of Dr. Magee's eloquence in
the House of Lords in a recent article in the *Daily News*
on the oratory of that Assembly, which the writer thinks
worthy of great praise when called forth on great occasions.
After eulogising especially Lords Lyndhurst, Ellenborough,
and Derby of past times, and the Duke of Argyll, Lord
Salisbury and Lord Rosebery of the present day, he adds :—

"Perhaps the House of Lords in our time never had a more
powerful and eloquent debater than the late Bishop of Peterborough and Archbishop of York, Dr. Magee. The unfortunate
thing was that Dr. Magee, being a Bishop, could not find full
scope in the House of Lords. He ought to have been a front
bench politician in the House of Commons. There he could have
made his mark as a political orator. In the House of Lords he
missed it—necessarily missed it; he could not help himself; he
was a Bishop. There is a mediæval Bishop told of, if we
remember rightly, by Montaigne, who was not allowed to fight in
a battle with the weapons of a knight, and who rushed into the
fray and knocked his foemen down with a club. But the Bishop
of Peterborough could not well use a heavy club in the mimic
frays of the House of Lords. Dr. Wilberforce, once best known
as the Bishop of Oxford, contrived somehow to get better scope

for his very remarkable eloquence in the House of Lords. But we do not think he had the originality, the freshness, and the force of Bishop Magee. There have been many eloquent speakers of late years as in former years among the Archbishops and Bishops in the House of Lords, but the field of their eloquence is peculiarly circumscribed. They have to speak rather when they may than when they will or would, and eloquence in a political assembly does not thrive under such conditions."

Q

CHAPTER XXIII.

CHRISTOPHER ANSTEY, REV. R. WARNER AND REV. JOSEPH HUNTER.

We are now come to literary celebrities of the eighteenth and nineteenth centuries. It will not be inferred from the absence of previous separate treatment that Bath had no eminent authors until now. It will be remembered that from Adelard of the Norman period to the Falconers of the Georgian there were many who kept the lamp burning. But it will also be remembered that they gained their general repute in other ways, chiefly as divines and physicians, and were classified accordingly.

A similar explanation may be given as to the literary celebrities of whom sketches will be given in this and the remaining chapters. They are six : Christopher Anstey, Richard Warner, Joseph Hunter, William Napier, Walter Savage Landor, and William Beckford. Nearly all were known otherwise than for distinction in literature ; Anstey as a man of fashion, Warner as a clergyman, Hunter as a Noncon· formist minister, Napier as a distinguished General, and Beckford as the lavish builder of Fonthill. All, however, were eminent as authors; and if Napier and Beckford were less conspicuous than the others in that capacity, if Napier's fame as a General and Beckford's as Lord of Fonthill over-shadowed their reputation as men of letters, still Bath claims them as among her literary celebrities ; one wrote in her neighbourhood a great work, the *History of the Peninsular War*, the other, besides being the author of *Vathek*, possessed here one of the largest and most valuable private libraries in the kingdom.

Mr. Warner, in his literary recollections gives a select list of Bath Literati of modern times with short memoirs of the more distinguished. And Mr. Monkland, in his pleasant little volumes, gives nearly two hundred names. But both lists indicate rather the prevalence of literary taste and industry than anything like eminence in authorship. Undoubtedly the society of Bath in the last two centuries has been brightened and elevated by an intellectual infusion to an extent unusual in provincial towns. And there is another remarkable circumstance ; probably few places in the kingdom have been so much referred to in books by popular writers. Macaulay praises not only the architecture of Bath, but "the beautiful city which the genius of Anstey and of Smollett, of Frances Burney and Jane Austen has made classic ground." And while the mine worked by Fielding in *Tom Jones,* Sheridan in the *School for Scandal,* Graves in the *Spiritual Quixote,* Bulwer in *Paul Clifford,* and Dickens in *Pickwick,* proved so rich, others were opened in the regions of science, history and archæology. It will be seen, however, that the Bath writers who obtained celebrity, they whose works were destined to live the longest and form part of the best national literature were, with a few exceptions, not so remarkable for works on local subjects as for those of general interest.

CHRISTOPHER ANSTEY

may be considered one of the exceptions. He was a Bath Celebrity because he wrote the best book which had been published on Bath Life. The son of the Rev. Dr. Anstey of Trumpington, he was born in 1724 and educated at Eton and King's College, where he was distinguished as an elegant scholar. So far however as University distinctions were concerned he was unhonoured ; he began a Latin speech in

the public schools with a sarcastic allusion to some unfair
treatment he thought he had received, and for that speech he
was rusticated.   In the epilogue to the *Bath Guide* he play-
fully refers to the event :

> "——Of Granta, sweet Granta, where studious of ease,
> Seven years did I sleep and then lost my degrees."

His academic achievements at Cambridge were creditable.
Having early succeeded to a scholarship he distinguished
himself by his Tripos verses for the " Commencement " in
1745.   He also gained University reputation by a Latin poem
on the Peace of 1748.   On the death of his mother he
succeeded to the family estates, resigned his fellowship,
married a daughter of Mr. Calvert the wealthy brewer, and for
some time combined the cultivation of letters with the pursuits
of a country gentleman.   In 1762 he published, in conjunction
with Dr. Roberts, of King's College, a translation of Gray's
elegy into Latin, which, says the writer in the *National
Biography*, " had the advantage of Gray's criticism and elicited
an interesting letter from the poet which is given in an edition
of Anstey's works."

About this time he went to Bath for medical treatment
after a serious illness.   He recovered ; the city and its society
pleased him, and he resolved to live here, fixing his residence
first in the Royal Crescent.   But it was necessary he should
return to Trumpington for a time, and he spent the interval
in describing the votaries of folly and fashion he had seen at
Bath with such wit and force and truth that he became
famous at once.   The first edition of Anstey's *New Bath
Guide* was printed in quarto at Cambridge.   Its success was
instantaneous; the booksellers could not supply it fast enough;
all the best writers praised it and all the world of fashion read

it. Gray writes to Wharton; Horace Walpole to Montague; the clever satire is eulogised and the classic allusions are especially admired. Bath was now rising rapidly; the buildings of the two Woods drew crowds of country visitors; and Anstey thus writes to his mother:

" Our neighbour Sir Easterton Widgeon has swore
He ne'er will return to his bogs any more;
The Thickskulls are settled; we've had invitations
With a great many more on the score of relations;
The Loungers are come too. Old Stucco has just sent
His plan for a house to be built in the Crescent;
'Twill soon be complete, and they say all their work
Is as strong as St. Paul's or the Minster at York.
Don't you think t'would be better to sell our estate
And buy a good house here before 'tis too late?
You never can go my dear mother where you
So much have to see and so little to do."

Anstey continued to write at intervals after his removal to Bath. In 1769 he published an elegy on Lord Tavistock who died from a fall from his horse. Another poem, *The Election Ball*, was a contribution to the noted vase of Lady Miller at Batheaston. But neither these nor any of his other works had the freshness and vivacity of *The New Bath Guide*, although he had the stimulus of intercourse with the chief wits of the age. Perhaps there was an adverse influence in the size of his family, for he had thirteen children. Eight only survived him; the eldest son became a barrister of some repute, and inherited considerable literary power, shown in his *Pleader's Guide*, and his edition of his father's works. The elder Anstey died at the house of a son-in-law, Mr. Bosanquet, of Hardenhuish, near Chippenham, and was buried in Walcot Church. There are monuments to him in the Bath Abbey and the Poet's Corner in Westminster Abbey.

His memory is also kept alive by some verses in gilt letters on a tablet in the Pump Room, which he wrote in aid of the Bath Mineral Water Hospital and indicate that there was a side of his character worthy of admiration.

"Oh pause awhile, whoe'er thou art
That drinks this healing stream,
If e'er compassion o'er thy heart
Diffused its heavenly beam.

Think on the wretch whose distant lot
This friendly aid denies ;
Think how in some poor lonely cot
He unregarded lies.

Hither the helpless stranger bring,
Relieve his heartfelt woe,
And let thy bounty like this spring
In genial currents flow.

So may thy years from grief and pain,
And pining want be free,
And thou from heaven that mercy gain
The poor receive from thee."

Among the numerous valuable contributions by Mr. Peach to the periodical literature of Bath was a series of Papers in *Bladud*, in 1886, on some local worthies. One of them contains a passage relating to Anstey's *Bath Guide* which may supply a deficiency in the preceding sketch where perhaps too little has been said of that remarkable book. Mr. Peach remarks :

" It was not only popular during the life of the author, but we believe that a larger number of editions have been published in the present century than even in his life-time. The terms and allusions in the work are obscured by time and change, but it is none the less true that they illustrate more clearly and distinctly the manners and customs of the period than any other local source of information. The ordinary literature of the time does not give us so clear a conception of Bath every-day life as the witty verse of Anstey. Fielding, Smollett and Richardson constructed their narratives and characters out of the depths of their own genius, the light and shade being tinctured more or less by the peculiar manifestations they contemplated. But Anstey, limiting the field of his observation, presents, in the most amusing manner, the realism of the eighteenth century with all the characteristic humbug, hypocrisy, charlatanry and folly which was peculiar to a certain type of the Bath 'Society' of the period." The writer proceeds however to shew that with all its cleverness and instructive power the satire of the *New Bath Guide* has been surpassed in purity and elevation of tone by that of the present century, and instances of this are quoted convincingly from the pages of Thackeray, who, without a touch of grossness, lifts his reader to an atmosphere where

> "Men may rise to stepping stones
> Of their dead selves to higher things."

THE REV. RICHARD WARNER.

Few names are more prominent in local literature than this. Warner's *History of Bath* is in many good libraries in the West of England. Other accounts of the city are remarkably good, notably Mr. Earle's, but Warner's, through nearly a hundred years, has been the most copious, comprehensive and complete. That he was a marvellously voluminous writer is in his case but slight ground of distinction, though he began to write books before he was thirty and continued till he was nearly fourscore. He had, however, other claims; as a clergyman his services were intellectually above the average of those in Bath ; in society he was also valued as a cultivated man ; and in various ways he contributed largely to the higher life of the city.

Richard Warner was the son of a respectable London tradesman, and was born in 1763. He was educated at

Oxford, apparently for the Church, but on leaving the University his inclination was not in that direction. To literary work he was devoted from the beginning, but at one time he strongly desired to go to sea and explore the world. This his father opposed, so he worked in a solicitor's office for a time, writing his first book in his leisure hours. It was evident, however, that a clerical life would be most in harmony with his prevailing tastes. He therefore took holy orders and became curate to the Rev. W. Gilpin at Boldre in Hampshire. Although the rector was in many respects a man after his own heart circumstances soon led him to quit Boldre and remove to Fawley in the same county. Here again he was not destined to stay long ; the place was unhealthy ; the family became ill and were sent to Bath ; and he determined to try to get a professional engagement there. This he did at All Saint's Chapel, where he officiated a short time, and then as one of the curates of Walcot parish till he was appointed curate of St. James's. He held this curacy twenty-three years with much credit to himself and usefulness to his flock, writing rapidly the various works which he published and engaging prominently in the controversies of the time.

In his *Literary Recollections* he admits being largely infected with the *cacoethes scribendi*. Neither success nor want of it appears to have made much difference ; no sooner was one work issued than another was planned and speedily begun. His "maiden volume," as he terms it, appeared in 1789, *A Tour Round Lymington*. He had not then resolved to go into the Church, and was beginning to study law, from which he found relaxation in writing the book. How little he knew of business matters may be inferred from his ordering a thousand copies to be printed "that the demand of the public might be quickly met." Undiscouraged by the disappointment which followed, he "threw," to use his own words, "into the ocean of English Literature within the four succeeding years, another duodecimo, three octavo volumes, a quarto pamphlet, a more substantial bantling of the same size, besides issuing proposals for a topographical work in three bulky folio volumes." These were to contain a *History of Hampshire*, for which he made great preparations, obtaining influential patronage, visiting the Record Office, the British Museum, the English Universities and many other places; but all the labour was lost; he found that his plan would require a very long purse, half a dozen lettered men as assistants and ten years' hard work; so he dropped it.

Of the *History of Bath* there is better record. The author had grown older and wiser and saw more clearly how to succeed. "In the last few years of the century," he says, "he had been so much interested in the Roman antiquities of Bath as to wish to rescue them from the darkness, dishonour and oblivion in which they had long remained." Dr. Harington, one of the Corporation, obtained for him from that body not only the necessary authority but the necessary funds, and in the course of a few months, with the aid of two able friends, he had the remains cleansed and arranged. Many years afterwards they were deposited in the Literary and Scientific Institution, of which they have long been one of the greatest attractions. Warner's ever-ready pen was employed in a description which he published in 1797. All this brought before him the great want of a good history of the city to whose ancient relics he had given so much time. "Again," he says, "I consulted Dr. Harington, and once more received his encouragement with a promise of any assistance he could render." Mr. Cruttwell, his worthy parishioner, and a most excellent printer, agreed to take upon himself

every expense connected with the work and give him half of
any profits.   In the course of two years the history appeared.
Its reception does not appear to have been very flattering,
but gradually it came to be appreciated.   Modern critics
complain of some omissions, notably those relating to
Bathwick and Widcombe, but it should be remembered that
in 1801 those suburbs were scarcely part of the city and by
no means important.   The want of a general index is certainly
a great fault.

Many other works came out in quick succession.   Prior to
the *History of Bath*, the author published in 1792 *An
Attempt to Ascertain the Situation of the Ancient
Clausentium*, in 1793 *Topographical Remarks on the South-
Western Parts of Hampshire*, in 1796 a *History of the Isle
of Wight*, in 1798 *A Walk Through Wales*, in 1799 a *Second
Walk in Wales*, in 1800 a *Walk Through Some of the
Western Counties of England*, and in 1801 *Excursions from
Bath*.   After these came a *History of the Abbey of Glaston*,
in royal quarto, *A Tour Through the Northern Counties*,
Omnium Gatherum, a short-lived periodical, and various
other works, including, *Literary Recollections*, in two volumes.
Amid all these contributions to general literature the curate
of St. James's did not fail to employ the press on religious
subjects.   A keen controversialist, he took part in many of
the discussions of the time, especially Catholic Emancipation,
to which, though a strong Whig, he was decidedly opposed.
Besides several single sermons, he published two volumes of
Practical Discourses.   Some of his works sold well; by
others he must have lost considerably.   For instance, in the
case of *Omnium Gatherum*—intended to be a periodical
publication; with his usual sanguine temperament he
ordered 750 copies, of which only 150 were sold, so the first

number was also the last. His *Literary Recollections*, in two volumes, published in 1830, is a rambling autobiography, chiefly interesting for the memoirs of various eminent friends. He was especially intimate with Dr. Samuel Parr, who often visited him in Bath, and some of whose letters to his "friend Richard" are extremely amusing. The two Dr. Falconers, William and Thomas, are frequently mentioned, Thomas being a great ally, often assisting him in the pulpit and parish of St. James's, and sharing to a great extent his friend's theological and political sympathies. Warner was an uncompromising Whig; he hated war as he hated Calvinism and preached boldly against both. Though not agreeing with the High Church party, he said he could work with them better than with the opposite class.

Some of his works were remarkable for their pungency. Much excitement was caused by two satirical productions, *The Bath Rebellion* and *Bath Characters ;* the latter a series of dialogues upon living characters, the weak spots of each being unsparingly exhibited. Warner was far from blameless in his satires ; he not only used the lash severely but indulged in wit disgraced by vulgarity. Of these various elements were his mind and character composed. He was a type of clergyman which became more and more rare as the nineteenth century advanced and is now scarcely ever met with. That he was in good repute professionally is evident from his long curacy at St. James's and from successive presentations to livings towards the close of his life. In 1817, before he quitted St. James's, he became Rector of Great Charfield, Wilts ; afterwards he was incumbent successively of Timberscombe, Croscombe and Chelwood. He held both Great Charfield and Chelwood when he died in 1857 at the age of ninety-five.

THE REV. JOSEPH HUNTER.

This gentleman was connected with Bath as the respected minister of the oldest Nonconformist congregation in the city twenty-seven years. The Act of Uniformity passed in 1662, causing the ejectment of two thousand clergymen, drove from their livings many in and around Bath which led to the formation of a Presbyterian congregation. By this name it was known until the close of the eighteenth century when, as a consequence of the latitude allowed by the Trust deeds of their chapel, the congregation became Unitarian. Mr. Hunter's immediate predecessor, Mr. Jardine, was so called, but although the subject of this sketch had been led to the same theological conclusions he preferred the more comprehensive name of Presbyterian. His love of antiquity, especially of ancient literature, which he cherished from childhood, gave him eventually the rank of an eminent antiquary. He filled an important post in the Record office of the nation, and wrote a succession of historical works of much value and authority.

Joseph Hunter was born in 1783 at Sheffield, where his ancestors had lived two hundred years. His father, who was a cutler, died when he was very young, and he was placed under the guardianship of a Presbyterian minister. At a suitable age he was enrolled at Manchester College, York, then having its chief Professors the Rev. Charles Wellbeloved and the Rev. John Kenrick, one known as the author of *Eboracum*, the other for his work on Egypt. Both at school and college Hunter spent much of his spare time in antiquarian studies, filling volumes which are still in existence with church notes, coats of arms and monumental inscriptions. His only ministerial settlement was at Bath, where he remained from 1809 till 1833. He published four sermons between 1811 and 1819, which indicate that he was too quiet, thoughtful, and, it must be added, heterodox, to be a popular preacher. But there was a charm in his style, an earnestness in his convictions, and a consistency in his character which accounted for the attachment of a highly intelligent congregation. Not having many pastoral duties he devoted himself largely to literary pursuits; it was at Bath that he collected materials for his most important works, *Hallamshire* published in 1819 and the *History of the Deanery of Doncaster* in 1828 and 1831. These handsome and costly folios were welcomed not only by the most eminent antiquaries of the day, but by country gentlemen of the localities and by book collectors generally, as permanent additions to the literature of the country. At the head of the list of subscribers to *Hallamshire* was the Prince Regent.

Nor were Mr. Hunter's labours in Bath limited to his study. He was one of the chief founders of the Bath Royal Literary and Scientific Institution. No one worked more earnestly in forming its valuable library and giving it a character worthy of the city. In 1827 he gave an interesting lecture on the *Connection of Bath with the Literature and Science of England*. Twenty-six years later he consented, at the request of the Bath Literary Club, to allow them to reprint the lecture, and he added some valuable notes. One of the members of the club, Mr. Long, showed his appreciation of it by having a blank volume of magnificent proportions in appropriate binding filled with successive pages of the lecture and engraved illustrations of its contents, generously presenting the volume to the club library. Another institution, we are told by the *National Biography*, in which Mr. Hunter had much interest was "The Stourhead Circle," "a party of gentlemen residing in Wiltshire and Somersetshire who assembled annually for antiquarian discussion under the hospitable roof of Sir Richard Colt Hoare of Stourhead."

In 1833 he was appointed sub-commissioner of the public records and removed to London. In 1838, on a reconstruction of the service he became an assistant keeper of the first class. He often gave the fruits of his researches to the volumes of the Society of Antiquaries, of which he was a vice-president, and to those of the Archæological Institute. His pen was incessantly occupied; year by year the press teemed with his productions on a great number of historical and biographical subjects. His *Dissertations on Shakespeare's Works*, his *Diary of Ralph Thoresby*, his *Life of Oliver Heywood*, his *Defence of Lady Hewley's Trustees*, his *History of the Bishopric of Somerset*, show the wide range of his intellectual vision. The *Biographical Dictionary* gives a list of thirty-two of his principal works written in Bath and London. His happiness appears to have been in proportion to the gratification of his literary and antiquarian tastes. Writing to an intimate friend who had congratulated him on his seventy-second birthday, he says, "Yours has been a prosperous life and I have no reason to complain of mine. You have done many good works ; I have endeavoured to do the same. Both of us I may say have gained golden opinions from some whose praise is to be valued, and both of us will be found to have left some impression on the age in which we have lived." In 1815 Mr. Hunter married Miss Hayward, daughter of Dr. Hayward, of Bath. They had six children, one of whom, Dr. Julian Hunter, lived in Bath for some years, carrying on good work at the Institution. His father died in 1861 at his house in Torrington Square, and was buried at Ecclesfield, near Sheffield.

CHAPTER XXIV.

GENERAL SIR WILLIAM NAPIER.

Colonel William Napier came to Freshford, near Bath, with his family in 1831, and lived there and at Bath till 1842, when he became Lieutenant-Governor of Guernsey. In Bath he was chiefly known as an earnest and eloquent politician, being, through the eleven years of his residence, one of the foremost speakers at public meetings on the great questions of the day. This caused many applications to him from various important constituencies to represent them in Parliament, but he declined them all on the ground that his pecuniary means were insufficient, and that he could not abstract the time required by his *History of the Peninsular War.* I shall be indebted for most of the information in this sketch to an admirable life in two volumes written by his son-in-law, Mr. H. A. Bruce, M.P., some time Home Secretary, afterwards Lord Aberdare, whose work is enriched with a large number of letters from eminent men and women.

William Francis Patrick Napier was born in 1785, the third son of the Honourable George Napier. His father was sixth son of the fifth Lord Napier, who was descended from Scott of Thirlestane ; hence the family motto, " Ready, aye Ready." His mother was Lady Sarah Lennox, the seventh daughter of the second Duke of Richmond, who it is well known traced his pedigree to Charles II. One of Lady Sarah's sisters married the first Lord Holland and was mother of Charles James Fox ; another sister married the Duke of Leinster and they were parents of the unfortunate Lord Edward Fitzgerald. Lady Sarah's husband, the father of heroes, was himself cast in the true heroic mould. He possessed great powers, mental and bodily, and was distinguished by an integrity and unselfishness then too rare in public life. Thus noble were the family influences on young Napier's mind as he grew up ; his letters to his mother, in Lord Aberdare's volumes, show that they were good seed sown in good ground, and the fruits in after years amply justified all the bright anticipations of his career.

Yet so far as what would be called education was concerned nothing could be more deplorable. William and his elder brother Charles, the hero of Scinde, were placed in a grammar school in their native town of Celbridge, near Castletown. The master was a passionate, ill-judging man, and the scholars were for anything like scholarship by no means remarkable. The martial spirit of the period caused Charles Napier to organise a volunteer corps in the school, which probably gave to both brothers their first idea of military matters. Not minding his lessons, and taking to a great degree his own course, William read everything he could lay his hands on. Romances of all kinds were devoured, *Don Bellarmin of Greece* being his especial favourite ; but history, poetry and travels were all consumed. Conspicuous among his pet subjects were *Plutarch's Lives*, which probably inspired his passionate admiration in after years for the great men of antiquity. At this period he knew and often conversed with Captain Arthur Wellesley, but not, it is considered, then much to his advantage. On leaving school he received his first commission in the Royal Artillery and was soon transferred to the sixty-second regiment. A few months afterwards his uncle, the Duke of Richmond, gave him a cornetcy in the Blues, one advantage of which was that it recommended him to General Sir John Moore, who proved an invaluable friend. When not yet nineteen he obtained a captaincy in part of Moore's Own West Indian Brigade.

Here all that is possible is to take a rapid view of Napier's life before he entered on the literary part of it. In 1807 he served in the deplorable Copenhagen expedition, was present at the siege of that capital and afterwards marched under Sir Arthur Wellesley to attack the Danish forces. Returning to England for a time, he went with his regiment in 1808 to Spain and endured more than his share of the hardships of Sir John Moore's retreat, being thrown into a fever from which he hardly escaped with his life. In 1809 he became aide-de-camp to his uncle the Duke of Richmond, Lord-Lieutenant of Ireland, but soon gave up the appointment to serve in Portugal, where the fates were against him. He was first attacked with violent pleurisy for which he was bled four times a day, and then in the battles that followed he and his brother George were dangerously wounded. The only reward of their zeal and courage was that they were specially selected by Lord Wellington for the brevet rank of major. From Lisbon William Napier was sent to England in the autumn of 1811, and in the spring of the following year married Caroline Amelia, daughter of General the Honourable Henry Fox, and niece to the great statesman, " a lady as remarkable for intellectual vigour as her husband and admirable in every relation of life."

When only three weeks married, and still suffering the effects of his wound, Napier sailed again for Portugal. After the battle of Salamanca he joined the victorious army in entering Madrid, where he remained some time. Early in 1813 he returned to England, but soon went back to the Peninsula, and was engaged in repelling an attack by Marshal Soult, in which he was twice wounded. The

R

greatest battle of the next few years was at Waterloo in 1815, which took place while Napier was embarking at Dover to join his regiment at Brussels. It can be imagined how his spirit would have chafed if he had known what he missed, but he was in time to accompany the British army to Paris where he saw the triumphal entry of Louis XVIII., whom, however, he much disliked. Patriotic as he was, he had great admiration of Napoleon Bonaparte, entertaining the highest opinion of him as a general, and sympathising in no small degree with his courage. About this period Napier attained the rank of Lieutenant-Colonel, and on the return of the army of occupation in 1819 was quartered at Belfast. Here he had an opportunity of purchasing another step, the regimental Lieutenant-Colonelcy, but he was unable to do so for want of means. In vain did a warm friend, Lord Fitzroy Somerset, press the required sum upon him as a loan; he declined it because he could not see his way to repay the money. It might have been thought that an officer of such extraordinary merit, one so highly connected, who had commanded a regiment in several general actions and received three wounds, one of them causing life-long misery, would have had the distinction promptly conferred upon him. But on other grounds he had become disgusted with war, and now as the distinction was not given he retired with a stricken spirit on half-pay to seek in literature the reputation which narrow means and official neglect denied him in his profession.

The beginning of the new era in Colonel Napier's life, when he conceived the idea of writing his great history, is thus described by Lord Aberdare: "After retiring on half pay he took a house in Sloane Street and spent much of his time in painting and sculpture. In these pursuits, as in all others, he showed extraordinary perseverance. As a preparation he devoted himself to the study of anatomy and the Elgin marbles, and his statuette of Alcibiades is a proof of the progress he made. He became an accurate and vigorous draughtsman, was no mean colourist, and in the opinion of eminent artists would have attained the foremost rank of living painters and sculptors had he not been irresistibly drawn towards Literature. Though Art was his principal pursuit he also read largely and mixed much with friends whose thoughts and pursuits were congenial with his own. Still he felt a want unsatisfied, an undeveloped power within him struggling to come forth. At this time Jomini published his work on the *Principes de la Guerre* which contained the first exposi tion of Napoleon's system of warfare. Having studied all Napoleon's campaigns thoroughly, Napier was enabled to write a very truthful review of Jomini's book for *The Edinburgh*. This was in 1821; the negotiations with the editor led him to visit the northern city where he became personally acquainted with Jeffery and other literary celebrities. Soon afterwards he visited Paris and made acquaintance with Marshal Soult, against whom he had fought so bravely. The French hero, not to be outdone in magnan· imity, entered afterwards into Napier's project of the history of the war, and even generously contributed materials for it."

Not, however, till 1823 was the great work begun. Early in that year Colonel Napier was walking with Lord Langdale in some fields now covered with the houses called Belgravia. The friends conversed on Southey's late narrative of the war in Spain and Lord Langdale was so much struck with Napier's remarks that he urged him strongly to write a history himself. The incident was thus stated to his daughter the year before he died. "It was all owing to Lord Langdale; he first kindled the fire within me. I was living in Sloane Street on

half pay, a pleasant, desultory life, enjoying my home and
friends in London, talking to officers I had known in the
Peninsula, consorting with Chantry and other artists and
painting a great deal.   I had never written anything except
the review in *The Edinburgh.*   Langdale asked me what I
thought of turning to as an occupation, saying the review had
proved to him I had powers yet undeveloped.   He argued so
seriously that the late war was my peculiar province, that I
began to think whether I would not try."   On his return to
his house Napier told his wife what had passed, also his
doubts as to being equal to the work, but she encouraged him
strongly, he resolved to attempt the task and immediately
began to collect materials.   His first step was to call upon
the Duke of Wellington, who also encouraged him, saying he
could not part with his own private papers because he
intended to publish them himself, but he would give him
important official documents and answer any questions.   He
next called on Sir George Murray, hoping to get the " Orders
of Movements" and the maps and plans illustrative of the
operations in the Peninsula, but Murray refused on the
ground that he also contemplated writing a history.   It is
remarkable that neither of these men, who were then, in the
opinion of the whole army, the fittest to undertake the work,
did undertake it.   After the publication of the first and
second volumes of Napier's History both relinquished the
idea.   They found that the book was written with such
unparalleled truthfulness and extraordinary animation that
any other narrative would be dull and insipid.

We are now come to a period when London life was found
incompatible with the needful application.   Other circumstances also, of a family nature, made it desirable that country
air and quiet should be sought.   Hence the removal of

Colonel Napier to Freshford in 1831, and the commencement of those political services which made him through eleven years a Bath Celebrity. Nor was it strange that such a man at such a time, though always intent on the work he had in hand, should yet often leave his desk to mingle with the multitude. Notwithstanding his aristocratic connections and military spirit, his heart was ever with the people. For the rank and file of the army he felt as great an interest as for the cause in which they fought together, and the rank and file loved him with a fervour of which he was proud. So as to the masses of the English population; no man knew better either the qualities by which they were characterised or the evils under which they were suffering, and was it possible for him to be a silent spectator of all that passed? A Reform Government was at length in power; a new Parliament had been elected; measures on which the people had long set their hearts came forth; in every town there were meetings and discussions such as had never been known before. Bath was a remarkable instance; the city at large had gained the power, hitherto confined to the Corporation, of electing its representatives, and it had Mr. Roebuck as one of its first candidates. Mr. Roebuck was a friend of Colonel Napier; they had many likes and dislikes in common; they had both a great aversion to the Whig party; they were both in hearty unison with what may be called ultra-radicals, and the hard battle Mr. Roebuck now had to fight made his friend all the more anxious to help him. So that for a long time there was rarely a public meeting in Bath, whether with reference to Mr. Roebuck's contest for the seat or on behalf of some important measure before Parliament, at which Colonel Napier's eloquent voice was not heard.

His first political speech was made at Devizes in May,

1831, at a meeting to vote an address to William IV. thanking him for dissolving Parliament. Again, in September, when it was generally expected that the House of Lords would throw out the Reform Bill, Colonel Napier was at Devizes joining in indignant remonstrance. "It is impossible," says a journal of the period, " to convey an idea to those who were not present of the spirit and fire with which he spoke. As an orator he must be seen and heard to be appreciated. A clergyman who was present remarked, 'such a soldier and such a speaker might lead an army anywhere.'" The fame of these speeches pervaded the country; hence invitations to the orator from all quarters—some to speak at similar meetings, others to be a candidate for seats which had become vacant. He had been invited to contest Bath but preferred that the choice should fall upon Mr. Roebuck. Mr. Bruce gives a letter from Mr. Charles Buller who had been asked to stand for Bridgwater but declined, and now urged Napier to come forward. He answered, courteously, that he was not in a position to make the necessary sacrifice, that he had a large family of children, very little money, and very bad health; moreover, he was engaged in a difficult literary work which required constant attention, his reputation and means of living in a great degree depending on it. He stated that he had given a similar answer to various applications from important constituencies; among them being those of Nottingham, Glasgow, Birmingham, Kendal and Oldham. Of the speeches at Bath his biographer gives striking specimens in those of August and November, 1835, February and May, 1836, and early in 1837, on the subjects of Coercion, Irish Church Reform, Irish Corporation Reform, the Abolition of Slavery, and the Obstruction of the House of Lords. Not always had he the entire sympathy of his audience; many regretted his frequent bitter attacks on the Whigs; critics often observed a strong dash of one-sidedness; but admiration of his eloquence was universal and everyone acknowledged his noble and generous spirit.

Largely as his time was occupied in Bath and other places with political work, Colonel Napier steadily continued his literary labours. In 1838 he wrote for the *Westminster Review* an important article on the despatches of the Duke of Wellington, "wishing to show that a Radical magazine could appreciate the genius of the great soldier." "Nor did he disdain," says Lord Aberdare, "lighter works of imagination," for in April of the same year he contributed to *Bentley's Magazine* a tale called "Griffone," replete with beautiful fancies and imagery. But it was on his history that the powers of his mind were concentrated; and here should he mentioned the valuable assistance he received from Mrs. Napier throughout the progress of the work, but especially in deciphering correspondence. It is best described in his own words. "When the immense mass of King Joseph's correspondence, taken at Vittoria, was placed in my hands I was dismayed at finding it to be a huge collection of letters, without order, written in a crabbed hand, and in three languages, the most important documents being in cipher, and without a key. Despairing of any profitable examination of these valuable materials, the thought crossed me of giving up the work, when my wife undertook first to arrange the letters by dates and subjects, next to make a table of reference, translating and epitomising the contents of each; and this without neglecting for an instant the care and education of a very large family, she effected in a most simple and comprehensive manner, enabling me to ascertain what I wanted at any time in a few moments. She also undertook to decipher the secret correspondence, and not only succeeded, but found a key to the whole. When I related this to the Duke of Wellington he seemed at first incredulous, but ended by saying, "I would have given £20,000 to any person who could have done it for me in the Peninsula." What the great commander thought of the book which had the benefit of these labours has been already stated. How he valued the simple and beautiful dedication can be easily imagined :—

<blockquote>
"To
Field-Marshal
The Duke of Wellington.
This History I dedicate to your Grace because I have served
long enough under your command to know why
the soldiers of the Tenth Legion were
attached to Cæsar."
</blockquote>

At length the task of so many years was finished. Congratulations came from all quarters. Honours the author had previously received in the usual course of events. He had attained the rank of Major-General in 1841 on leaving Bath to take the office of Governor of Guernsey, which he held six years. Relinquishing this, he received the distinction of K.C.B. as a mark of her Majesty's approbation of his services in the command of the island. For some years he was intensely interested in all that related to Sir Charles Napier's Indian successes, writing his life in two brilliant volumes, also copious histories of the conquest and administration of Scinde.

Nothing could be more gratifying than the testimony of brother officers to the value of his great work. Colonel Shaw writes: " Having read your first volume with every attention, I congratulate you sincerely. It is a book which will be read with admiration by the present and by future ages. As a military history nothing in our language can be placed in comparison with it." Major-General Sir W. Campbell says : " I do not think such a history has appeared since that of Xenophon. The writing is beautiful, and, though entirely free from affectation, the author says the best things ; short, pithy, and to the purpose. He flings to the right and left the dirt and filth of prejudice, lays bare the baseness and corruptions of Juntas, and exposes, alas, the madness or imbecility of our own Government." Marshal Soult, with his wonted generosity, said to Colonel George Napier in Paris, " Your brother's work is perfect ; it does honour to his head and heart, and ought to be as satisfactory to the French army as it is to the English."

All this could not fail to cheer the illustrious General in his latter days. And, unfortunately, those days were saddened by events and circumstances which called for the utmost consolation his friends could offer. Within a short time he had to grieve for the death of three brothers, Charles, George and Henry ; also for that of a beloved daughter. And who would mourn more deeply the departure of the Duke of Wellington ? Then came the alarming illness of Lady Napier. It was doubtful, indeed, which would be taken first, his own state was so precarious. The decree was for him ; it came on the 12th February, 1859. But the Angel of Death did not tarry. Of both it could soon be said by their numerous friends :

> " Their peace is sealed, their rest is sure
> Within that better home ;
> Awhile we wait and linger here,
> Then follow to the tomb."

" One of Sir William Napier's highly gifted relatives was Lady de Ros, his mother's sister, and the third daughter of Charles, fourth Duke of Richmond. She married the Hon. William F. de Ros, afterwards Lord de Ros, Governor of the Tower, survived him many years, and died in 1891 at the age of ninety-six. Only three years before her death she published, at the request of many of her friends, her *Personal Recollections of the Duke of Wellington*, which were very favourably received. In a recent review of a new edition the writer states that the work, prefixed as it is by a memoir of the author, together with some of her correspondence, is not only of value historically, but exceedingly interesting and readable. Lady de Ros, as a child, often played with the Princess Charlotte, whom she describes as a frank but extremely indiscreet girl, openly avowing that the two things in the world she most hated were ' boiled mutton and grandmamma.' " I mention the book here says the author of a review in the *Westminster Gazette*, in connection with an anecdote often repeated, of which Lady de Ros gives a correct version. "It is well known that George III. greatly admired Lady Sarah Lennox when both were young. There is little doubt whom he would have made Queen of England if he had been free to marry in accordance with his inclination. About the year 1813, when the King was not only blind but mentally feeble, Lady Sarah was at Court to be presented on some occasion, and her sister relates that her ' name was sent in, but a request came that if she had a second name it might be used, as it was feared the name of Lady Sarah Lennox, his first love, might have an exciting effect upon the poor King. Lady Sarah, however, had no other name, and the King was informed she was to be presented. He immediately inquired if she was pretty, and, on being answered in the affirmative, he further inquired if she was like her namesake and great-aunt, the Lady Sarah Lennox of his young days, and he was told that there was said to be a resemblance. When the evening came, Lady Sarah was taken up to the King, and to her great surprise and consternation he begged her to allow a blind old man the privilege of passing his hand over her features !— this he did, making no remark. Lady Sarah afterwards said she could not refuse, knowing the reason for his request, but she found it a very embarrassing position.' "

CHAPTER XXV.

WALTER SAVAGE LANDOR.

PART I.

Bath was chosen by Walter Savage Landor as his place of residence for many years in consequence of its remarkable beauty. Himself endowed with good health, always robust and vigorous, he had no special need either of its fine air or its healing waters. Although a keen politician like his friend Colonel Napier, he had not the same strong sense of duty as to mixing with the people and joining his voice with theirs. Interested in music he would sometimes look in at the Pump Room Concerts, but it was not in his nature, as it was in Dr. Harington's, to take advantage of a congenial soil and do what he could to promote and elevate the art. Pre-eminent as a literary man, he would still have nothing to do with the literary societies of the city ; public life of any kind he never cared for ; he had gone to live at Florence simply because it was beautiful, and when he was driven from it by domestic troubles he knew no place that would suit him so well as Bath.

The Landor family were long of much consideration in Staffordshire. They could trace their ancestry in that county through three or four hundred years. The father of Walter Savage Landor was a physician at Warwick who twice married heiresses, the author being the eldest son of the second wife whose maiden name was Savage. From her he inherited a handsome fortune, and he was proud of his descent on her side, though, as in the case of Sir Arnold Savage of his *Imaginary Conversations,* the Speaker of the House of Commons, his pedigree was somewhat shadowy. His father

was said to have been "a polished, sociable, agreeable, but
rather choleric gentleman, more accomplished and better
educated than most of his associates, but otherwise dining,
coursing, telling his story and drinking his bottle among the
rest." Thus is Dr. Landor described by Sidney Colvin in
Morley's *Series of English Men of Letters*. To this charming
little volume and to John Forster's copious biography I owe
much of the information I have to give. Having known
Mr. Landor many years I have been interested in
collecting materials for this sketch and grateful for the
renewal of my recollections. It should here be mentioned
that Dr. Landor had another son, Robert, and five daughters.
The son was an amiable, accomplished, and literary clergyman;
he and his brother selected the titles in their father's epitaph,
"*Lepidus, doctus, liberalis, probus, amicis, jucundissimus.*"

Walter's boyhood was happy. He always looked back on
his holidays with especial affection. They were spent partly
in Warwick and very much at one of the two country houses
on the Savage estates. There he first acquired the love for
books, trees, flowers and country places which be cherished
through the chequered years of his future life. At ten he
was sent to Rugby, becoming soon one of the best Latin
scholars. He also enjoyed good English books, and has
recorded his delight at his first purchase of two with his own
money, Drayton's *Polyolbion* and Baker's *Chronicle*; also
that the writer who first awoke in him the love of poetry was
Cowper. Always physically strong, the bookish boy held his
own well in the playground. His strength made him
victorious in boxing, cricket and football. The rivers of
Warwickshire had great charms for him; the Avon, of course,
stimulating poetic thought. In one of his Latin poems he
laments that his eldest son, born in Italy, would not know

and love the English streams which were the joy of his own youth. On leaving Rugby Landor was placed under the charge of Dr. Langley, at the village of Ashbourne, in Derbyshire, whose good qualities he immortalises in the *Conversation of Izaak Walton, Cotton and Oldways.* He writes of " the good parson of Ashbourne who wants nothing, yet keeps a grammar school, and is ready to receive as private tutor any young gentleman in preparation for Oxford or Cambridge, but only one. They live like princes, converse like friends, and part like lovers."

The "good parson" had to prepare his charge for Oxford. In what fine soil he worked is shown by Landor's mention of his acquisitions at Ashbourne. "There," he says, " I made better acquaintance with the Greek writers, especially Pindar and Sophocles, and turned several things of Cowley into Latin Sapphics and Alcaics." He also translated into verse the *Jepthah* of Buchanan, a poem afterwards destroyed, but of which he himself had so high an opinion that he said he could not have improved upon it even after he wrote *Gebir.* He was eighteen when he entered as a commoner at Trinity College, Oxford. It was the memorable year of 1793 which had opened at Paris with the execution of Louis XVI. Landor, though sharing greatly the excitement of the time, was less interested in the French Revolution than in the American Rebellion. " He was a Jacobin," says Forster, "and with exulting satisfaction saw the conquests of democracy; but pantisocracy and golden days to come on earth were not in his hopes or expectation." Still he had sufficient sympathy with the overthrow of monarchy in France to be affected seriously in his studies and position at Oxford. It was at the critical time when many of the best men of the Liberal party were driven to the opposite side by the excesses of the French.

Those who refused to be so driven became marked men ; at
Oxford there were two undergraduates in the list, Southey of
Balliol, and Landor of Trinity, who made themselves
obnoxious by appearing in hall and elsewhere with their hair
unpowdered, the direct advertisement of revolutionary
sentiments. Though he and Southey were thus brought
together and afterwards became great friends, they were not
then intimate, Southey stating that he " would have tried to
cultivate his acquaintance if, like himself, he had been only a
Jacobin, but he was a mad Jacobin." Landor did some good
work as a student in his eighteen months at Oxford, and used
to call the hours passed with Walter Birch in the Magdalen
Walk (of which Addison was so fond) the pleasantest as well
as the most profitable he could remember. The " madness,"
however, of which he was accused caused many social scrapes
and one of them led to his rustication. The President of his
college was compelled to investigate a charge against him of
firing into the rooms of one of the men. Landor was defiant,
refused all explanation and received sentence accordingly.
One of the worst effects of this was the anger of Dr. Landor,
with whom he had not previously been on good terms. Soon
after his return home passionate words were exchanged ; and
the son quitted his father's house, as he declared and believed
" for ever."

Landor had many changes in the next few years. From
Warwick he went first to London where he worked hard at
French and Italian. He had then an idea of settling in Italy,
but this was abandoned in consequence of efforts by his family
to arrange his affairs and obtain a reconciliation with his
father. Although heir to a large fortune he could only receive
a slender income during the life of his mother, to whose
impartial justice towards all her children he bore ample

testimony, and for whom his feelings were always those of gratitude and affection. In London at this time (1795) he brought out his first book, a small volume of poems, now very rare. Another literary venture was a satire against Pitt in the form of *A Moral Epistle* in heroic verse addressed to Earl Stanhope. On leaving London he spent three years in Wales, chiefly at Swansea, the neighbourhood not then being defiled, as now, by mining and smelting operations. Here he studied indefatigably ; among the writers whom he read and pondered were Pindar and Milton ; both contributed to the formation of his mind, but it was for Milton as Republican, poet and prophet, he conceived the enthusiastic reverence which afterwards inspired some of his writings. Mr. Colvin adds that " at twenty and a few following years Landor's life was well suited to the training of a poet. He made his own all that was best in the literatures of ancient and modern Europe, except indeed in that of Germany, which had then been barely discovered in England by a few explorers like Scott, Coleridge and William Taylor of Norwich, but to which Landor neither now nor afterwards felt himself attracted." There must have been something however in *Gebir*, his next important work, that was akin to the spirit of German poetry, for the German scholars, Taylor especially, were all warm in its praise. What is noticeable here is that Landor's poem was written and his studies carried on when he was in immediate communion with nature. To this he thus alludes, contrasting the influences on his own mind with those on his friend Moore :

> " Alone I spent my earlier hour,
> While thou wert in the roseate bower,
> And raised to thee was every eye,
> And every song won every sigh.

One servant and one chest of books
Followed me into mountain nooks,
Where sheltered from the sun and breeze
Lay Pindar and Thucydides."

It has been remarked that Landor's avoidance of "the roseate bower" was not constant. His biographers mention various attachments, chiefly formed in Bath, up to the time of his marriage. Some of them, though short-lived, were strong enough to inspire his muse and bring him often to the city of the springs. Forster says that " on his accession to the paternal estates in 1805, his younger brother found him at Bath with the reputation of very great wealth and the certainty of still greater on his mother's death." His establishment, with carriage and horses, men servants, books, plate, china, pictures; his successive flirtations with " Ione," "Ianthe" and Rose Aylmer, were all much talked of in the city and regretted by those who knew the better parts of his mind and character. Happily his eldest sister, who was his constant correspondent, had some influence over him. It was probably Miss Landor who caused the wasteful outlay at Bath to cease and induced him for a time to live much on his estate at Lanthony, where, however, expense was equally disregarded. Having formed magnificent plans of a mansion and actually begun to build, he determined to clothe the slopes with woods and to cover the sides of the valley with the cedars of Lebanon. " For this purpose he bought 2,000 cones, calculated to yield 100 seeds each, intending to do ten times as much afterwards and exulting in the thought of the two million cedar trees which he would thus leave for the shelter and delight of posterity." Nor was his private enjoyment as a landowner his chief object. The only means of communication in the district were by rough bridle paths and fords, so he set gangs of men to make roads and bridges. Agriculture was miserably primitive and he imported sheep from Segovia, applying to various friends to help him to find tenants who would adopt and teach improved modes of cultivation. As to the population of Lanthony, they were drunken, morose, and impoverished. Why should he not do all in his power to reclaim and civilise them?

Alas! he little knew what he undertook. Repeated disappointments on every side attended his efforts. In social matters he was especially chagrined; there was scarcely a public authority against whom he had not a grievance; even his tenants and labourers turned against him. Summoned on the grand jury of his county, he got into collision with the judge; and, wanting permission to restore for Divine service a part of Lanthony Priory, he quarrelled with the Bishop. One means of relief he had from all these troubles; it was to go to Bath, to mix there with an entirely different set, and renew intercourse with people whom he liked. The attractions of " the roseate bowers" of the Assembly Rooms were especially strong for him and destined now to influence his future life. It was in 1811 he met a young lady at a ball, Miss Julia Thuillier, the daughter of a banker at Banbury, descended from an old Swiss family. Greatly struck, he exclaimed, with all the impetuosity of his nature, " By heaven! that's the nicest girl in the room, I'll marry her." And this time there was no long wooing, no misunderstanding, no apologetic retreat us in former instances; marry her he did with little loss of time. But the adage " marry in haste and repent at leisure " would have been applicable here. The little wife was sixteen years younger than her husband and at first, with her bright smiles and lively spirits and golden hair, she did very well; they,

S

therefore, both went to Lanthony and hospitably received
visitors including his mother and sisters and Southey and
his wife. But Lanthony was rapidly ruining him; he soon
discovered it, went for a time to Jersey, and resolved to live
in France, to which, however, Mrs. Landor strongly objected
and in a temper developing too surely. Arguing one evening
with more than usual petulance she taunted him before her
sister with their disparity of years. His pride took sudden
fire; he rose at four the next morning, crossed the island on
foot and was soon under weigh for the coast of France in an
oyster boat alone.

But neither the joyful nor sorrowful incidents in Landor's
life prevented literary work. In 1810 he printed two Latin
odes and began two important works, his *Idyllia Heroica*,
also in Latin, and his *Count Julian*, an English tragedy,
published by Mr. Murray. In 1811 he wrote another tragedy,
Ferranti and Giulio; but a discouraging letter from
Longman's caused him to put it into the fire, and he told his
friend Southey that in future whatever verse he was foolish
enough to write should have the same fate. In 1812 Mr.
Murray brought out another very different production, *A
Commentary on Memoirs of Charles James Fox*, in answer
to *Trotter's Memoirs* and setting forth the author's views on
books, mankind and government. Towards the close of 1813,
about the end of the Lanthony period, he published a comedy,
called *The Charitable Dowager*, the proceeds of which he
destined for the relief of an old acquaintance in Spain to
whose hospitality he was indebted when visiting that country.

Here I cannot do better than introduce Mr. Sidney Colvin's
retrospect, after detailing the troubles at Lanthony and the
departure from Jersey. "Up to the date we have now
reached, 1814, Landor's career seems to present a spectacle

of almost as much futility as force. His resplendent gifts and lofty purposes had been attended with little solid result either in the practical or the intellectual sphere. In the practical part of life he had thus far conspicuously failed. The existence he had planned for himself was one totally different from that which had fallen to his lot. Bent upon walking in the paths of serenity he had nevertheless trodden those of contention. With a high standard of intercourse and behaviour he had been involved in ignominious wranglings with his neighbours. Born to wealth and eager to employ it usefully he had experienced nothing but frustration and embarrassment. Tenderly chivalrous towards women, he had turned his back in anger upon his young wife. Neither in the other sphere of human activity, the intellectual and imaginative sphere, which to him was in truth the more real and engrossing of the two, had Landor as yet done himself anything like justice. Posterity, if his career had ended here, would probably have ignored his writings, or have remembered them at most as the fragmentary and imperfect productions of a powerful spirit that had passed away without leaving any adequate memorial. Several years had still to elapse before he addressed himself to that which was destined to be his great and vital task in literature, the writing of the *Imaginary Conversations.* His life until then had been continually unsettled and his efforts uncertainly directed."

From the coast of Brittany, after leaving his wife, Landor made his way to Tours. He found a resource at once in composing a Latin mythological poem, in which some of his Welsh tormentors were pilloried. "Of his quarrel with his wife," says Colvin, "he writes like a gentleman, doing justice to her conduct during the trying experiences at Lanthony.

He even proposed to hand over to her all his remaining fortune, reserving only £160 a year for himself, but adding that 'every kind and tender sentiment towards her was rooted from his heart for ever.'" Hearing, however, after a while, that she was very ill, his natural good feeling returns, he loses his resentment entirely, and writes to comfort her. The result, with the aid of friends, was reconciliation; Mrs. Landor joined him at Tours early in 1815, and they proceeded later in the year to Como where they lived three years. At Como their first child, a boy, was born and christened Arnold Savage, after the Speaker of the House of Commons, Landor's supposed ancestor. Within a few years a girl and two more boys were added to the family. One of the father's brightest features was his constant interest in his children ; his love for them as they grew up was intense ; no sacrifice was too great to be made for them ; no companionship preferred to theirs. But again his evil genius unsettled him ; he was compelled to quit Tours in consequence of a quarrel with an Italian poet who summoned him before a magistrate for some opprobrious verses. In vain did the magistrate try to do impartial justice ; Landor insulted him, threatened him with a thrashing, and was ordered to quit the country.

Then, after spending two months at Genoa he settled at Pisa, remaining there till the summer of 1821. Shelley and Byron were both in the same town about that time, but he had then no personal acquaintance with either. For other eminent English poets, Southey, Coleridge, Wordsworth and Walter Scott, he had much admiration, and though he never liked Byron he afterwards formed a high opinion of Shelley. But it was in the political opinions of the period he now took the deepest interest. The great Continental upheaval of 1821-22, the struggle against tyranny in Greece, Spain,

Naples, Lombardy, and Vienna had his warmest sympathy.
Never did he write nobler verse ; all domestic disquietude, all
pecuniary anxiety became merged in passionate love for the
cause of freedom. To Italy he addressed a stirring oration
on representative government ; to Corinth, a poet's eulogy on
the defeat of its Turkish oppressor ; to Albion, degenerate
Albion, an Englishman's reproaches for

" Mocking at the thirst of Holy Freedom in its agony."

Expelled from Pisa he took refuge at Florence and worked for
many years at his *Imaginary Conversations ;* but yielding at
length to what he deemed unbearable family troubles he fled
back to England, renewed old friendships a short time in
London, and eventually settled in Bath, a period which, with
some account of the Florentine life and of the more immediate
cause of its termination, I reserve for another chapter.

CHAPTER XXVI.

WALTER SAVAGE LANDOR.

PART II.

Landor's sympathies with the insurgent populations of
Southern Europe extended beyond his residence at Pisa ;
they were cherished also at Florence where some of them
found expression in the *Imaginary Conversations.* There
was much now in outward circumstances to favour his
literary work ; he loved the city and its surroundings, he had
his home in the beautiful palace of the Medici ; and he
found in his children inexhaustible sources of enjoyment.

His occupations at Florence were diversified by that of a
picture collector. Soon after his arrival he began to avail
himself of the opportunities afforded him. "He formed,"
says Colvin, "his own opinions in connoisseurship as in
other things and acted upon them with his usual confidence
and precipitancy." He was one of the earliest modern
admirers of the pre-Raphælite masters, whose works were
then in no demand, and innumerable specimens, with those
of other schools, passed through his hands. "He liked his
rooms to be denuded of nearly all furniture except pictures,
covering the walls with them from floor to ceiling. A
generous giver, especially in later years, he was fond of
sending away a guest the richer for a token from his
collection."

Landor was visited at Florence and afterwards at Fiesole
by many friends whose companionship he valued. One of
the most welcome was Francis Hare, with whom an encounter
of wit was always a great delight. "Both men of amazing

knowledge and memory, their self-confidence was about equal; they often disputed but never quarrelled. In one of his letters to his mother, who continued to write affectionately to him up to the time of her death, he remarks how often he had been applied to for introductions since he published the first volume of the *Conversations*. His biographers mention Hogg, Kirkup, Leckie, Hazlitt, Leigh Hunt, Crabb Robinson, Lord Houghton, and many others as being courteously received and highly gratified. Those who visited him when he lived in the Medicean palace could not fail to associate him with that historic edifice, which however the poet had ere long to quit in consequence of a rupture with the landlord, the living representative of the Medici family. He had accused this gentleman, whose reputation was not high, of tempting his coachman to leave him; on which the Marquis called, entered the room where Mr. and Mrs. Landor and Mr. Kirkup sat and strutted in without removing his hat. He had scarcely advanced three steps from the door when Landor walked up to him quickly, knocked off his hat, took him by the arm and turned him out. "You should have heard," said Kirkup, "Landor's shout of laughter at his own anger, inextinguishable laughter, which none of us could resist." It was followed by a letter to the Marquis announcing that he should quit the house at the end of the year.

We next find the poet at the charming villa Gherandesca, which he had bought at Fiesole. It had been the home of Boccaccio, whom he considered "the greatest genius of Italy or the Continent." The years he spent there seem, on the whole, to have been the happiest of his life, so great was his enjoyment of his children and his classic grounds. His love of animals had now full play; besides the great house-dog

Parigi we hear of the cat Cincerello, a tame marten, a tame
leveret, and all manner of other pets.   Amid the groves of
olive and cypress within his gates he loved to look down
along the sweep of Valdarno, or towards the distant woods
of Vallombrosa, or the misty ridges above Arezzo.   His own
means would not have sufficed to buy this beautiful place,
but he had a generous friend at Florence, Mr. Ablett, who,
knowing his wish for it, insisted on advancing the required
amount; he would take no interest, and only consented to
be repaid after some years when Landor had saved the
amount out of his annual savings.   In writing to his sister,
telling her the story of Mr. Ablett's unexpected kindness,
and of the roses, arbutuses and bay trees he was planting, he
says: " My country now is Italy, where I have a residence for
life and may literally sit under my own vine and my own fig
tree, having some thousands of the one and some scores of the
other."   But though all this made him happy for a time, and
the outbursts of passion became more rare with advancing
years, he was still subject to them.   He had a quarrel with
the police about some plate of which he had been robbed ; he
thought the men inefficient, his language was so violent that
he was ordered to leave Tuscany, and he did actually retreat
as far as Lucca.   But a courteous letter to the Grand Duke,
with the intercession of Lord Normanby, the English
Ambassador, and other friends, cleared up the matter; the
order was revoked and the offender returned in triumph.

Landor's letter to his sister was written on New Year's Day,
1830. .It was just after the death of his mother who had died
at the close of her eighty-fifth year.   " Her great kindness to
me," he says, " throughout the whole course of her life made
me perpetually think of her with the tenderest love."   She
had told him that she hoped he would come to live at Ipsley

after her death, enjoy the place as she had done, and lead the life of an English country gentleman. But he insisted now on his sisters continuing there, and declining to allow the place to be let or the contents to be sold for his own benefit. He was satisfied to remain for a time at least in his Italian home. His manner of life was favourable to the composition of his great work and that of other minor works. He was to be met at all seasons rambling alone in old clothes and battered straw hat upon the heights around Fiesole, repeating audibly what was in his thoughts. In 1831 he brought out a revised selection of his earliest poems. In 1832 he came to England after an absence of eighteen years, enjoyed the visit himself and gave pleasure to many friends. Crabb Robinson entertained him hospitably in London, taking him to see Flaxman one day, Charles Lamb another, and Coleridge a third. He next went to Cambridge to make the personal acquaintances of Julius Hare, and agreed to contribute to a new periodical, the *Philological Museum*. His sisters, of course, claimed him at Ipsley, as did his friend Ablett at Lanbedr, with whom he paid flying visits to Southey and Wordsworth. Returning home by Belgium, the Rhine, the Tyrol and Venice, he saw many other friends, and early in 1833 was back again among his children, his pet animals, and his pictures at Fiesole. His thoughts of the poets he had seen in England found vent in an ode to Wordsworth, and stanzas on the death of Charles Lamb addressed to his sister. The ode begins :—

> " We both have run o'er half the space
> Listed for mortals' earthly race ;
> We both have crost life's fervid line
> And other stars before us shine ;
> May they be bright and prosperous
> As those that have been stars for us ! "

The three last stanzas to the mourning sister have a truthful beauty :

> " His gentle soul, his genius, these are thine ;
> For these dost thou repine ?
> He may have left the lowly walks of men ;
> Left them he has, what then ?
> Are not his footsteps followed by the eyes
> Of all the good and wise ?
> Though the warm day is over, yet they seek
> Upon the lofty peak
> Of his pure mind the roseate light that glows
> O'er death's perennial snows.
> Behold him ! from the regions of the blest
> He speaks and bids thee rest."

The short remainder of Landor's life at Fiesole was fruitful. His *Examination of Shakespeare,* his *Pericles and Aspasia,* and his *Pentameron and Pestalogia* formed a trilogy of books of much value. " The last was published in 1837, when a great change had come over his life ; he had said farewell to his beautiful home ; he had turned his back upon his wife and children ; and returned to live alone in England. To this he had been driven by renewed dissensions. The household, below the surface, had long been inharmonious and ill-ordered. A husband absorbed in his own imaginings ; a wife agreeable to anyone but him ; children devotedly loved but allowed to run wild. If Landor's bursts of passion were violent, they met with more than their match in his wife's persistent, petulant opposition. The immediate cause of his departure appears to have been the language addressed to him by Mrs. Landor in the presence of their children, notwithstanding all his remonstrances. This he felt to be demoralising to them and humiliating to himself, and, resolving to endure it no longer, he left his home in the spring of 1835, spent the summer by himself at the baths of

Lucca, and then came back to England." Two years which elapsed before his settlement at Bath he gave chiefly to London, Clifton and Lanbedr. His pen in the interval was as busy as ever; the *Conversations*, an Irish squib in verse, a political pamphlet addressed to Lord Melbourne, and last touches to *Pericles and Aspasia* fully occupied him. Friends on both sides of the family endeavoured to bring about some kind of arrangement between the husband and wife, so far at all events as to give Landor intercourse with his children. At one time it was proposed they should meet him in Germany, and he travelled to Heidelberg expecting to see them there; but they never came, nor were any of the other plans found practicable. Letters and presents were exchanged occasionally between the father and children; twice or thrice in the coming years they came to visit him in England, but henceforth they were practically lost to him. With his wife's relations living in this country he continued on perfectly cordial terms. His wanderings after his return to England ceased with his final settlement at Bath in October, 1837.

He lost no time in making generous arrangements for his family. His estates of Lanthony and Ipsley were yielding £3,000 a year, of which, however, mortgages absorbed £1,400. On leaving Fiesole he settled it with farms and gardens, which were almost sufficient for the support of the family, on his son Arnold. To Mrs. Landor he made over two thirds of the income he had been accustomed to spend while they were all under one roof, reserving to himself only about £200 a year. Finding this, after a year or two in England insufficient, he increased it with another £200 from savings he had accumulated, and on this income he was perfectly content to live in the solitary home which he made for himself in a Bath lodging.

After stating these facts Mr. Colvin proceeds to show that
his solitude was not morose or devoid of consolations. In
Bath, foremost among the friends whom he found after his
own heart was Colonel William Napier, with whom for years
he spent part of almost every day. He enjoyed the tender
devotion of his wife's niece, Miss Stopford, afterwards Lady
Charles Beauclerk, as well as of another young lady, Miss
Paynter, now Lady Sawle, a relative of the Aylmer family to
whom he was attached. As time advanced he valued the
society of new friends, especially those, who like Mr. Empson,
Mr. Frederick Shum, Mrs. Lynn Linton, and others, were
interested in art ; one feature of such friendships being its
constancy ; and although at times he was dictatorial there
was generally an innate courteous gentleness which made his
society extremely agreeable. To this the present writer can
testify as the poet's conversation through many years was a
privilege he can never forget. Biographers have placed on
record the annual visits to Landor's Bath home of his literary
friends ; they occurred chiefly on his birthday, when Dickens,
Forster, and Carlyle cheered him together or alternately with
their company. His hospitable nature is shown in an
invitation to Tennyson :

> "I entreat you, Alfred Tennyson,
> Come and share my haunch of venison.
> I have, too, a bin of claret,
> Good, but better when you share it.
> Though 'tis only a small bin,
> There's a stock of it within.
> And as sure as I'm a rhymer,
> Half a butt of Rudesheimer."

Quite as characteristic this as Sir Walter Scott's invitation
to his son-in-law, Mr. Lockart, who was staying near and

writing an article for the *Quarterly Review*, Sir Walter
happening to have some Whig visitors at Abbotsford.

> " Irrecoverable sinner,
> Work what Whigs you will till dinner,
> But be here exact at six
> Smooth as oil with mine to mix.
> Sophy may come up to tea,
> Our table has no room for she.
> Come the gum within your cheek
> And help old Peveril of the Peak."

Landor's favourite place of habitual exercise was the Bath
Park. Living in S. James's Square, or one of the adjoining
streets, the access was easy. Day by day he and his clever
dog, Pomero, were seen in the pleasant grounds taking their
accustomed morning walk. No one thought the majestic old
man less impressive because " muttering his wayward fancies
he would rove," dressed in a rusty brown suit, bulged boots
and battered hat. And everyone noticed the " noisy, soft-
haired, quick glancing, inseparable Pomeranian companion,
though few knew he had been one of his master's favourite
pets at Fiesole, and was now really the delight of his life.
" With Pomero," we are told, " he would prattle in English
and Italian as affectionately as a mother with her child ; " he
would tell you that the dog had the brightest eyes and most
wonderful tail ever seen, that he was the wisest and most
beautiful of his race. Believing this, Landor spoke of him
jocosely as a kind of sagacious elder brother, whose opinion
had to be quoted on all occasions before he would deliver
his own ; and the visitor, who saw the sensible creature
curled up in his basket till his master began to laugh, and
then spring up and bark to show his sympathy, would half
believe in the brotherhood. In the afternoon, the poet, accompanied by Pomero, having had his simple dinner on viands
often procured and sometimes cooked by himself, walked

several miles in all weathers, having especial preference for
the suburb of Widcombe, in whose beautiful churchyard he
resolved to be buried. From seven in the evening, after the
simplest possible tea, he generally read till late at night.
If he went into society at all, it would be to meet a party of
three or four at dinner at the house of some old friend,
where he was sure to be seen and heard to the greatest
advantage. I remember on such an occasion being delighted
with his response to some praise of a poetess whose writings
were better known at the beginning of the century than now,
Mrs. Barbauld. He repeated whole stanzas from memory,
and asked joyously what modern writer had produced
anything better.

At intervals Landor continued to use his pen with much
vigour. One of his employments was to assist his friend
Forster in bringing out a complete edition of his works.
Much time was occupied by his correspondence with the
Literati who have been mentioned, and with such friends as
Lady Blessington, at whose house he was a frequent guest.
The cessation of intercourse with Southey when his mind
gave way in 1839 was a great grief to him. Francis Hare he
had lost previously. Then followed in quick succession the
death of his generous admirer, Ablett, his affectionate brother
Charles, and his greatly attached friend Lady Blessington.
" All these deaths," Mr. Colvin writes, " would naturally have
prepared Landor's mind for his own had he stood in need of
such preparation. But he had long faced that contingency
with the same composure with which others are encouraged
to face it in his own tender and heroic admonitions." Of
each successive birthday as it came round he felt as though
it might naturally be his last. It was on the morning
after his seventy-fifth that he wrote and read aloud before

breakfast those lines which he afterwards prefixed to the volume called *Last Fruit off an Old Tree*.

> " I strove with none, for none was worth my strife,
>   Nature I loved and next to Nature Art.
> I warmed both hands before the fire of life ;
>   It sinks and I am ready to depart."

But the patriarch lingered on. He had passed eighty when a dangerous illness came, and at his request I called upon him. He then told me with infinite pathos how much he longed to be released. I said what I could to comfort him ; other friends did the same, and he rallied sufficiently to write and talk much as usual. Alas ! if the future could have been foreseen, continued life in his case would have been considered anything but a blessing. The tale is too sad to be told here minutely ; enough that other writers have detailed the melancholy incidents. I need only add that he quarrelled with a lady, wrote verses which were deemed libellous, left Bath to avoid the consequences of an action at the Assizes, and actually returned once more to Florence.

Thus ended a residence in Bath of twenty-two years. He found his wife and children at the villa in Fiesole, of which he was so fond. At first there was contentment, but dark clouds soon came again. Some of his old friends looked coldly upon him in consequence of the Bath scandal, among them the English Minister, Lord Normanby, which wounded him to the quick. Time had not lessened former domestic incompatabilities, and in addition there were now pecuniary hardships which disabled him from living elsewhere. Mr. Browning the poet, then at Florence, exerted himself to interest friends and relations in England to meet the difficulty. It was met ; five years more of life were granted ; his children tended him at the last, and in September, 1864, " the indomitable spirit was spent, the old lion was at rest."

CHAPTER XXVII.

MR. BECKFORD.

PART I.

Among the sales of English Libraries recorded in literary history, one of the most remarkable was that of Mr. Beckford at Hamilton palace in the year 1882. The books were for a long time in spacious rooms in Lansdown Crescent, Bath, sharing with the choice pictures the admiration of the visitors who were generously allowed to see them. They were bequeathed by the owner to his son-in-law, the Duke of Hamilton, and on his death in 1844 were removed to Scotland to be added to another collection of considerable value, all being sold by auction forty-two years afterwards. The sale attracted much attention in consequence of the beauty and rariety of many of the lots and the high prices they realised. In Bath it formed a subject of conversation at the Literary Club, several of the members having, like myself, often seen the well-filled shelves in Lansdown Crescent, and it occurred to me that an evening of the Club might be given to a paper on some of the incidents in Mr. Beckford's life.

The suggestion was adopted ; I wrote and read ; and the substance of my contribution is in the following chapters, very much as it was then given. My chief sources of information were a biography in two volumes, believed to be by Mr. Cyrus Redding, and some articles in the *Athenæum* and the *Gentleman's Magazine* for 1844. Why the biography was anonymous cannot be easily understood ; Mr. Redding was well known in Bath as the editor of a local newspaper, the *Bath Guardian* afterwards the *Bath Express* and the author of a book of some repute on wines. He knew Mr. Beckford, and his collections, and the memoir, though not of a high class, appears to be trustworthy. The recent memoir in the *National Biography* is a good condensation of what had been written previously, but contains no new facts. It states justly that the catalogues of Beckford's library and his Fonthill collections contribute much to the knowledge of his tastes and character. It also refers to the remarkable criticisms in Lockhart's review of his letters in volume iv. of the *Quarterly* and an article by Tiffany in volume xc. of the *North American Review.*

Beckford's education and early circumstances had of course much influence on his mind and character. The son of the celebrated Lord Mayor of London, he was only eleven years old when his father died, leaving an immense fortune. To a good private tutor, appointed by his mother, he owed much sound knowledge of the classics with other acquirements intended to fit him for a high position. The strong individuality of his future life was shadowed forth by various decided tastes, notably a love of Eastern fiction so absorbing that by the advice of his father's great friend, his own god-father, Lord Chatham, the *Arabian Nights* were hidden from him. Another incident also indicates a favourite study. When he was in his fifteenth year he spent a month with Lord Chatham at Burton Pynsent in Somersetshire. The evening family parties included the future statesman, William Pitt, then of the same age as William Beckford, and those parties were enlivened by recitations. On one occasion Beckford was asked to recite a speech of considerable length which he had translated from Thucydides and learnt by heart. He obeyed with great readiness, excelled both in action and emphasis,

T

and delighted his venerable host, who laid down his crutch (having then a fit of the gout) and embraced him, saying to his son, " May you, my boy, some day make as good a speaker." What the son became all the world knows, how brilliant in the Senate, how commanding in the Cabinet; but it is said of the two youths at this time that while quietness, discernment, and accuracy were with Pitt, genius, imagination, and energy were with Beckford. Fortunately for the young orator he was not always flattered. In the same year he visited his relations, the Duke and Duchess of Queensbury, in Wiltshire. There also he displayed his oratorical powers, but the Duchess—a very stately old lady—thought him deficient in etiquette. Once he failed so lamentably that her Grace rang the bell and ordered the servant to bring the family Bible, where she found a passage applicable to the case, which she requested him to read, saying, " There it was young man that I learnt my manners."

Mrs. Beckford having a prejudice against the English Universities, sent her son for his further education to Geneva. He lived there with her relation, Colonel Hamilton, his studies being still directed by the wise tutor who had been with him from the beginning. In addition to a course of lectures on civil law, mention is made of some lessons in riding and fencing. But the chief good of his residence in Switzerland was in the companionship of a few able and eminent men. He learnt much from Saussure, one of the earliest Alpine explorers and from Bonnet the great naturalist. With a literary family named Huber, who were fond of falconry, he contracted a great intimacy. Noteworthy visits of the period were to the Grand Chartreuse, of which he wrote an admirable account, and to the philosopher of Ferney then in his eightieth year.

Prominent among young Beckford's educational influences was the noble gallery of pictures formed by his father. The interest he took in them and the knowledge he acquired of their merits, were shown by the first book he wrote. This was *A History of Extraordinary Painters*, the exact date cannot be ascertained, but it was before he went to Geneva, when he was about seventeen. The more immediate cause was that the pictures at Fonthill were shown by an ignorant woman who made all kinds of strange blunders. He therefore wished to provide, first an accurate catalogue, and then some account of the masters; in connection with which he largely indulged his sarcastic humour. He had followed the housekeeper in her rounds with strangers; he had chuckled while she dilated before a picture by Rubens on what she called "the skill of Og, of Basan" or the colouring of "Watersouchy, of Amsterdam;" and Beckford, in this book, while giving really admirable descriptions of the masters, made great fun of the stories swallowed by the rustic sight-seers.

Returning from Switzerland in 1778 he visited various relations. One was Lord Courtenay at Powderham Castle, near Exeter, who had built a tower in his park which Beckford admired, and was probably suggestive to him in future years. Another relative was the Hon. George Hamilton, then member for Wells, who lived at Bath in the Royal Crescent, and was celebrated for his love of planting. Some months having been occupied in seeing a succession of great houses, old castles and fine scenery, and the traveller not being yet of age, he was advised by Lord Chancellor Bathurst, under whose legal care he had been placed, to take the grand tour. Accordingly he and his tutor proceeded to the Continent, where his mind was greatly impressed by much that he saw.

Not, however, in the Low Countries nor in Germany did he chiefly find congenial objects ; they awaited him in the classic beauties of Italy. To friends in England the tutor reported that, do what he would, he could not restrain his pupil's love of eastern lore ; stolen moments were constantly given to it, and all possible objects were made subservient. Then was it that the thoughts and images accumulated which found expression soon afterwards in *Vathek*, though time was also found for the preparation of another book, *Dreams, Waking Thoughts and Incidents.* Thus before he was twenty-two he may be said to have been the author of three remarkable works, an instance noteworthy in the early life of a man of large fortune.

On Mr. Beckford coming of age after his return from the grand tour, the event was celebrated with great rejoicings at Fonthill. His Oriental tastes were gratified by adding to the plans for feasting all classes a brilliant illumination of the house and grounds. Thousands of lamps were lighted on the lawn, in the wood, and along the banks of the river ; fireworks, bonfires, and musical entertainments provided regardless of cost. Lord Byron, in *Childe Harolde*, had called Beckford " England's wealthiest son," so by the poet at all events these rejoicings would not have been thought strange. Soon afterwards the rich man came to Bath again, and like Walter Savage Landor met his future wife at a ball. The attraction was Lady Margaret Aboyne, an amiable woman, who died within three years, leaving two daughters. Beckford felt the loss so acutely that his friends advised him to enter political life and follow his father's example by strengthening the popular Chatham party. His tastes were altogether different ; he cared nothing for party struggles and distinctions, yet at length he consented to sit for Wells, succeeding his relative,

Mr. Hamilton of Bath, from 1784 till 1790, when he was returned for Hindon. This seat he resigned four years afterwards by accepting the Chiltern Hundreds, thus terminating finally what had been the mere semblance of political life, and leaving more time for the enjoyment and, as he thought, the improvement of his property. We shall see that if he succeeded in one object he failed in the other.

Prior to his marriage Mr. Beckford took another journey on the continent with equipments such as are now never heard of. In addition to his old tutor and a staff of servants, he engaged an artist, a musician and a medical man, three carriages and several led horses and out-riders; accordingly while the cavalcade was sometimes supposed to belong to one imperial personage and sometimes to another, the hotel bills had everywhere an imperial complexion. But what is most remarkable as bearing on his future life is that notwithstanding all this luxury of travelling his mental aims were always prominent and his love of nature supreme. Never neglecting opportunities of acquiring knowledge, they were all the more welcome if, as in the case of an ancient palace or a venerable monastery, they gave scope for historic research or poetic feeling. Nothing, however, delighted him like fine scenery; he revelled in the glories of the Alps and the Tyrol. While other companions took long rides he drew Cozens the artist into the woods to admire the wild flowers and sketch the huts of the peasantry. Though charmed with much that he saw in the Italian cities; the missals at Siena, the sculptures at Florence, the ruins at Rome; finding at Venice especially abundant gratification of his Oriental taste; he yet turned incessantly to nature for refreshment and inspiration. At this time he wrote several poems, far inferior to his prose it is true, but proving his

sincere love of country life. In some lines on leaving
Fonthill, after describing the changes of the seasons and
various rural objects he says :—

> " But though the scenes you now deplore
> With heart and eye be your's no more,
> Though now each long-known object seem
> Unreal as the morning's dream,
> Yet still with retrospective glance
> Or rapt in some poetic trance,
> At will may every charm renew,
> Each smiling prospect still review,
> Through memory's power and fancy's aid
> The pictured phantoms ne'er shall fade."

The departure from Fonthill would remind those who are
old enough of the celebrated sale which took place more than
seventy years ago. It had been announced a year previously,
but postponed in consequence of the purchase of the Abbey
and domain by Mr. Farqhuar for £330,000. A guinea
catalogue was issued, of which it was stated in the
Gentleman's Magazine 7,200 copies were sold ; other writers
give the number as high as 10,000. The sale occupied
thirty-seven days, though it did not include many things
which Mr. Farqhuar had arranged to take and many more
which Mr. Beckford had reserved for the house he had
bought at Bath. It was attended by a great concourse of
people from all parts of England, from various European
capitals, and even from the United States ; a large number
with no intention of buying, but merely desirous of seeing
the place.

Who can now realise what it was ? As a private residence,
is there anything like it in our own country or any other ?
Perhaps those who know York Minster and Westminster

Abbey can form the best idea of the exterior. Standing on more ground than either, yet presenting the grandest features of both; with magnificent woods as a background, its size alone was impressive. In the interior, the central saloon occupied a space of 330 feet, as great a distance as can be seen at once in Westminster Abbey—the lofty windows, arches and pillars relieved by every imaginable means. It was worth a long journey to see the stained glass in the windows when the sun threw their colours on the crimson carpet, contrasting them with the vivid green of the lawn seen through the open doors, doors as high as a moderate sized house. Looking up you saw galleries a hundred feet above, leading to what were called nunneries. Looking around, mirrors in all directions reflecting the landscape for miles, and amplifying the vistas of the saloon itself. At every step the attention was arrested by choice books, china, paintings, cabinets, natural curiosities, silk hangings and costly furniture. While enjoying all this Beckford's mental sources were ample and varied; music had been one of them from childhood, and he continued to cultivate it. His improvisations on the piano delighted his visitors, and he rarely went to London without enjoying a good concert. Reading occupied a large part of every day, enabling him to form a judgment of every new book worth attention. Of planting he was passionately fond, ample scope being found in his broad acres, nineteen hundred within the park wall and three thousand around it. His gardens testified alike to his love of botany and his excellent taste, for whatever he did was accordant with nature. A great employer of labour; to him innumerable families owed their means of subsistence. If he spent money lavishly on the Abbey, he did not waste it on the turf or at the gaming table.

Among the thousands who flocked to Fonthill for the sale
in 1822 many asked why it was sold. It was known generally
that there had been a great loss of property somewhere, but
it was thought that vast wealth remained. The truth is that
Beckford had spent as if his wealth had been absolutely
inexhaustible. On his father's death he came into possession
of an income exceeding one hundred thousand a year, and
an accumulation amounting to nearly a million. One tower
employed four hundred and sixty men, day and night,
through an entire winter, the torches used by the workmen
being visible to travellers for a long distance. When, in
consequence of such foolish haste, this tower fell, another was
ordered, which soon shared the same fate, the owner, it is
said, regreting that he had not been present to see the sight.
Not content with his Wiltshire erections, he built a palace at
Cintra, "that glorious Eden of the South" eulogised by
Lord Byron.

> "There thou too, Vathek! England's wealthiest son,
>   Once formed thy paradise, as not aware
>   When wanton Wealth her mightiest deeds hath done,
>   Meek Peace voluptuous lures was ever wont to shun.
>   Here didst thou dwell, here schemes of pleasure plan
>   Beneath yon mountain's ever beauteous brow,
>   But now, as if a thing unblest by man,
>   Thy fairy dwelling is as lone as thou."

The building at Fonthill alone cost £273,000, exclusive of
the stone and timber from the estate and of the wonderful
wall around the park, seven miles in circumference and twelve
feet in height. But neither this outlay nor that required for
the roads and plantations would have compelled the sale.
Very early his property began to suffer from two causes:
great mismanagement and adverse Chancery suits. A large

West Indian estate which had been in his family sixty years was taken from him in consequence of defective title, while he had to pay the heavy costs of long litigation. The success of the plaintiff in this case led to other attacks of the same kind, some of which he consented to terminate by buying off the litigants at enormous sacrifices. Then came the great fall in West Indian property generally, involving a rapid diminution of income several successive years. While the earlier losses were going on he was yet able to maintain a princely establishment, including a physician, a professor of music, and other gentlemen of education. He also gave great regal entertainments, the most notable being occasioned by the visit of Lord Nelson and Sir William and Lady Hamilton, and he could still keep open house for half the county. But when the heavier trials came he bowed to necessity, considered for some time whether to live in a smaller house at Fonthill or seek a suitable one at Bath, and eventually decided on Bath. Some of the incidents of his residence here will be related in the next chapter.

Chapter XXVIII.

MR. BECKFORD.

Part II.

The paper for the Literary Club adverted to in the first part of this sketch was entitled "Recollections of Mr. Beckford." Although he had brought from Fonthill the exclusive tastes and habits which had grown upon him, yet glimpses were caught in Bath of what he was and did after his removal. Pedestrians would meet him in quiet places, sometimes walking, often on his pony, and various people had to communicate with him on matters relating to books, pictures, furniture, gardening, planting and building. His remarkable individuality naturally made such means of knowledge more thought of than they would have been in ordinary cases.

I first saw Mr. Beckford's house in Lansdown Crescent in the year 1833. He had then lived there ten years, during which he had built the tower on the adjoining hill. He had also bought most of the land between the Crescent and the hill, a distance of about a mile, in order that his grounds might be as spacious as possible. Here he resumed his love of planting, for which the neighbourhood became indebted to him, there being a great want of trees and his selection always such as the soil and situation required. His love of pure, natural beauty extended to the smallest objects. Along the private walk which led up to the tower he produced a great variety of picturesque effects. At one turn you came upon thickets of roses, at another beds of thyme, marjoram and other aromatic herbs, interspersed with ferns and wild flowers. The immediate approach to the tower was marked by trees and shrubs suited to its architectural character, in which his Italian and Oriental tastes were obviously blended.

Mr. Beckford greatly enjoyed the air and views of Lansdown. Riding or walking he was attended by his favourite dogs and two grooms, intelligent elderly men. At intervals he was seen in the Bath Park, to which at that time I gave much attention as one of the committee of management. My employment then was that of converting an exhausted stone quarry into something like a dell by planting Coniferæ. It was the only thing of local public interest for which Mr. Beckford was known to care; every afternoon while the work lasted he came to see what progress had been made. In reply to some pleasant remark on what I was doing I said how glad I should be to receive any advice from him. He was by no means unwilling to give it, although at first his manner was reserved. He spoke of the effects of contrasts in similar situations, not so much in the trees themselves as with reference to the line of sky and the surrounding objects. On one occasion he asked if I had seen his plantations around the tower, adding that he thought the library would interest me. "Pray go," he said, "at any time; you will forgive me if I don't offer to meet you; my health is uncertain, and I shrink from some states of temperature; besides you probably know that the world and I have taken leave of each other."

It was easy to conjecture why Mr. Beckford forsook the world. Until he came to Bath he had lived in a sphere different from any he could find within a large radius here. Never accustomed to mere local society, never prone to cultivate friendships, he only accepted the acquaintances which his birth and position brought him. They were generally people distinguished by rank, either in this country,

as in the case of the Hamiltons, Queensburys, Effinghams,
Dorchesters and Chathams, or in Portugal where his
intercourse with the royal family was frequent. He was
remarkably proud of his own descent from royalty; it was
shown in a genealogical tree in the vestibule of his house in
Lansdown Crescent, which, if I remember rightly, began
with Edward III. He could put up with the loss of Fonthill;
he could submit to a great reduction of his establishment;
he could reconcile himself to the impossibility of more regal
entertainments; but he could not form fresh ties altogether
different from those of a long life; and, having great
resources in his own mind as well as in the costly and
beautiful things which he retained, especially his books, he
preferred seclusion. This may be understood without being
defended; those who have right views of social duty would
assuredly not defend it. On the other hand we may think of
the peculiar circumstances of such a life, the training, the
education, the early indulgence; and the result of those
considerations would probably be the question, how should
we ourselves have acted if we had lived under similar
influences?

On availing myself of Mr. Beckford's invitation I was a little
disappointed in the plantations around the tower, although if
I had known the hill before they were made I might have had
a different feeling. A dull, flat piece of ground, open to the
west wind; nothing but a careful selection of trees would have
made it interesting or answered the owner's purpose. But the
building and its contents were well worth many a visit, showing
the most exquisite taste in all respects, as well as the most
thorough provision for intellectual enjoyment. It is pleasant
to remember the various rooms; some full of books; others
of vases, pictures, and cabinets; everything in the best Italian

style, harmonising with the architecture. There was a room called the chapel; bouquets of the loveliest flowers were on the tables, a few choice pictures adorned the walls, while upon a pedestal of Siena marble, in a niche panelled with Egyptian porphyry and lighted by a dim cupola, was a delicate piece of sculpture, St. Anthony with the infant Saviour in his arms, and the Oxford motto "Dominus Illuminatio Dea." All this is gone; no trace remains within the building of what the owner did; but the view from the top is still as glorious as when he enjoyed it; reaching to Fonthill in one direction, and the Welsh mountains in another; the waves of the Severn, some fifteen miles off, sparkling when the sun shone, and the Greville monument close by telling its tale of the Great Rebellion; all as if to show how enduring nature is, how evanescent the work of man.

In my conversations with Mr. Beckford he was by no means reticent on topics mutually interesting. From the work of planting and landscape gardening we were led to authors on such subjects and thence to other paths of literature. He mentioned the kind of books I should find at the Tower, and on my first visit I made myself acquainted to some extent with their general character. Although not numerous they were rare and elegant; binding, paper and type vying with the contents. Spanish and Portuguese books abounded; of French authors there were some choice specimens; and I wondered what many an English Divine would have thought of the theology in all languages. A writer in the *Times*, after relating how Mr. Beckford's books "followed him from Fonthill to Bath," and how they crowded every room of his house, none but the owner knowing where to find them, adds "but *he* always knew; his memory was as wonderful as his judgment and he was a buyer till he died." The book he was reading at the time of my first visit was *Wiseman's Lectures on Natural and Revealed Religion.* It was open on the table at which I sat and had marginal notes in Mr. Beckford's writing on almost every page. This was the habit of his life. At the sale at Fonthill in 1823 large prices were obtained for books thus enriched. And at the Hamilton sale in London a volume of *Beckfordiana,* being a transcript of the various notes on margins and flyleaves in his library, sold for £156. To all book collectors the interest was so great that every work was examined with a view to the discovery of manuscript notes, and any that contained them sold for as many pounds as, if unannotated, they would have produced shillings.*

It has been said that with all Mr. Beckford's lavish expenditure he was not a bad man of business. To what

---

* One of the most interesting of the lots at the Sale was the quarto *Gibbon,* in six volumes, containing ten pages of M.S. notes by Mr. Beckford, who thus concludes his criticism :—

"The time is not far distant, Mr. Gibbon, when your almost ludicrous self-complacency, your numerous, and sometimes apparently wilful, mistakes, your frequent distortion of historical truth to provoke a gibe or excite a sneer at everything most sacred and venerable, your ignorance of the Oriental languages, your limited and far from acutely critical knowledge of the Greek and the Latin; and in the midst of all the prurient and obscene gossip of your notes, your affected moral purity perking up every now and then from the corrupt mass, like artificial roses shaken off in the dark by some prostitute on a heap of manure ; your heartless scepticism, your unclassical fondness for meretricious ornament, your tumid diction, your monotonous jingle of periods, will be still more exposed and scouted than they have been. Once fairly kicked off from your lofty, bedizened stilts you will be reduced to your just level and true standard.—W. B."

extent this is true of the general management of his property, either English or West Indian, we have few means of judging. With regard to works of art whatever he did was marked by great decision ; he would not haggle with others nor would he allow others to haggle with him. That he knew the real value of things may be fairly inferred by his great knowledge and experience ; that he did not hesitate to make a fair profit especially when he parted with anything he prized, was well known. His *Letters on Italy* he sold to Mr. Bentley the bookseller for £500, £400 in cash and the remainder in a bill. The bill he passed to his agent ; the cash he invested in a sweet picture by Gerard Dow ; but soon, not liking the high finish, he sold it for £500. His biographer states that the National Gallery paid him £800 for a Perugino which only cost him 50 guineas. More than forty years ago I received a call from the Marquis of Lansdowne, who told me he had come to Bath on behalf of the Government to see some pictures in Mr. Beckford's collection. He had in view more particularly the St. Catherine by Raphael, and the Doge of Venice by Bellini. There was this remarkable circumstance : the owner had no other specimen by the same masters ; the National Gallery was without one of either. No one, therefore, would blame Mr. Beckford for asking from the Government much larger sums than he gave ; and they were given without any of the long negotiations he disliked. Knowing now as we do the increased value of such works, there is no doubt that the Government on this occasion made a good investment.

I remember another instance of Mr. Beckford's decision. At one time he had serious thoughts of leaving Lansdown Crescent. He had increased his collection so largely that even his two houses united by the arch became insufficient.

But perhaps a still stronger reason was that he allowed himself to be worried by grievances unavoidable with other houses near. The evil now, in his own words, was that he was "perpetually annoyed by the ticking of some cursed jack, the jingling of some beastly piano, bells of horrid tone perpetually tinkling, and so on." It happened that the owner of the neighbouring Summerhill property, Dr. Parry was then willing to sell it, and, although less secluded than he wished, yet as the grounds reached nearly up to his own plantations around the tower, he proposed to buy it. Mr. English, of Milsom Street, who told me the story, was commissioned to offer a certain price and to obtain an answer within twenty-four hours ; Dr. Parry, however, asked for longer time for consideration and the matter dropped.

Whether it was before or after this that Mr. Beckford added the third house I fail to remember. At first he did not intend to use it, saying that his object was merely to secure greater quiet, but it soon became full of costly and beautiful things. He also made openings in the walls of the drawing-room story which showed a fine vista extending the entire length of the three houses and the arch. The grandeur of these rooms, quiet as it was, contrasted with the simplicity of others for his private use, especially his bedroom, with its little narrow uncurtained bed, reminding one of the Duke of Wellington's answer at Apsley House with regard to his own ; on hearing the remark that there was no room to turn, he said, " Turn, turn, when one wants to turn it is time to turn out."

Another contrast was of a different kind but not less striking. It was the ugly dwarf Pero stationed in the vestibule of the house with no apparent duty whatever. The visitors were admitted by the hall porter and passed on to a servant in the interior, while this wretched looking object sat in his armchair grinning. One explanation of the incongruity was that Mr. Beckford's taste was in many respects Oriental, and that he liked to perpetuate as much as possible the customs of feudal times and ancient families. Among the strange characters in *Vathek* is the dwarf Bababalouk, a combination of Caliban and Sancho Panza, if such can be imagined, uniting immense conceit with a hideousness of person less than human. In Portugal the author was intimate with a distinguished family, the Marialvas, relations of Don Pedro, who took him one evening to the theatre where he saw in the stage box the light-complexioned Countess of Pombion with a black dwarf negress on each side of her, as if to show how very fair she was.

I conclude with a rapid survey of Mr. Beckford's achievements in authorship. His *Memoirs of Extraordinary Painters* have been mentioned. The *Quarterly Review*, Vol. li., says of them that " they would have excited considerable attention under any circumstances, as a series of sharp and brilliant satires on the Dutch and Flemish schools, the language polished and pointed, the sarcasm at once deep and delicate." In his twenty-second year came the tale of *Vathek*. Originally written in French, editions were published both in Paris and Lausanne. Translations appeared in successive years in England, some for which he was not responsible. Lord Byron says of it that for correctness of costume, beauty of description, and power of imagination it is unsurpassed. " As an Eastern tale," the poet adds, " even Rasselas must bow before it ; the Happey Valley will not bear a comparison with the Hall of Eblis." Then came the book of travels written in one of his journeys. Of this the world was almost entirely ignorant until fifty years afterwards Mr. Beckford reprinted it with additions in two volumes under

U

the title of *Italy, with Sketches of Spain and Portugal.* One
object of the reprint was to vindicate his claim to certain ideas
which had been adopted by other authors, consciously or
unconsciously, to whom he had allowed a perusal of the
unpublished work.   Rogers is said to have read it before he
wrote *Italy ;* Thomas Moore to have been indebted to it while
writing *Rhymes on the Road,* and even Lord Byron to have
had it in his mind when he formed the general plan of *Childe
Harolde.*

In 1796 and 1797 Beckford wrote two novels for the purpose
of satirising the fictitious literature of the day.   First, *The
Elegant Enthusiast with the interesting emotions of Arabella
Bloomville.*   By the Right Hon. Lady H. Marlow.   Then
Amezia, a Descriptive and Sentimental Novel.   By Jacquetta
Agneta, Mariana Jenks of Bellegrave Priory in Wales, with
criticisims anticipated.   Though full of sparkling humour it
would be impossible to appreciate these clever " Burlesques "
without some knowledge of the absurd romances they were
intended to cut up.

The author's genius always appeared to the greatest
advantage in works descriptive of nature and art.   As in his
early books on *Italy,* so in his later eloquent account of his
Excursion to the Monasteries of Alcobaca and Batalha the
ruling passion is manifest.   Those works also furnish the best
clue to the character of his mind and the philosophy by which
he was governed.   The Quarterly Reviewer, writing in 1834,
speaks of " His spirit so capable of the noblest enthusiasm
and so dashed with the gloom of over-pampered luxury yet
ever and anon stooping to chairs and china with the zeal of an
auctioneer, reminding one of the Lord of Strawberry Hill ;
though here all we have is on a grander scale.   The Oriental
prodigality of his magnificence shines out even in trifles ;

Beckford buys a library where Walpole cheapens a missal; one is as superior to the other as Fonthill with its York-like tower embosomed among hoary forests was to the silly band box on the road to Twickenham." "Beckford," adds the writer, "is a poet and a great one, although we know not that he ever wrote a line of verse. His rapture amidst the sublime scenery of mountains and forests, in the Tyrol especially and in Spain, is that of a spirit cast originally in one of nature's finest moulds; and he fixes it in language which can scarcely be praised beyond its deserts—simple, massive, nervous, apparently little laboured, yet revealing in its effect the perfection of art. Some immortal passages in Gray's letters and Byron's diaries are the only things in our tongue that seem to us to come near the profound melancholy and yet picturesque description of these extraordinary pages." Long before this passage was written Beckford had composed the lines on quitting Fonthill, given in a former chapter, and long afterwards some verses were published entitled *A Prayer written at Fonthill.* Short as it is it yet reveals something of the inner life of the author. The last three lines are given in the inscription on his tomb in the Lansdown Cemetery.

" Like the low murmur of the secret stream
    Which through dark alders winds its shaded way,
My suppliant voice is heard :—ah do not deem
    That on vain toys I throw my hours away !

In the recesses of the forest vale,
    On the wild mountain, on the verdant sod,
Where the fresh breezes of the morn prevail,
    I wander lonely, communing with God.

When the faint sickness of a wounded heart
    Creeps in cold shudderings through my sinking frame,
I turn to Thee ! That holy peace impart
    Which soothes the invokers of Thine awful name.

Oh, all pervading Spirit ! sacred beam !
  Parent of life and light ! Eternal power !
Grant me through obvious clouds one transient gleam
  Of thy bright essence in my dying hour ! "

That hour came at length, in 1844, after eighty-five years of life.   His illness was short ; it found him at home, comforted by his favourite daughter the Duchess of Hamilton.   Long before his death he ordered his tomb of Aberdeen granite and directed that the coffin should be placed within it so as to be above the ground.   He wished to lie under the shade of his tower near a favourite dog, but the dog being there and the ground unconsecrated the interment took place at the Abbey Cemetery, and the tower and its grounds were sold by auction. Then the Duchess of Hamilton, shocked at hearing that her father's beautiful little domain was to be perverted to tea gardens bought it back, gave it to the parish of Walcot for a cemetery, obtained the Bishop's consecration after the removal of the dog and ordered the remains of the former owner back to the spot he loved.   There he lies amidst the trees and shrubs he planted, surrounded also now by the fellow men from whom in life he was divided.   There they all sleep side by side, the same sun shining upon the quiet graves in summer's heat and winter's cold ;   and there the visitor who wishes to see the last resting-place may see the fervent aspiration,

                    " Eternal Power !
Grant me through obvious clouds one transient gleam
  Of thy bright essence in my dying hour ! "

Chapter XXIX.

MISS LINLEY.

I had written the last line of the sketch of Mr. Beckford and supposed I had fairly completed the series when I thought of some regretable omissions. Pondering once more on what had chiefly conduced to the reputation and prosperity of Bath in the Eighteenth Century it occurred to me that I had not done sufficient justice to Music and the Drama. Probably I mentioned the Miss Linleys and Mrs. Siddons in connection with the lives of men like Ralph Allen and Dr. Harington, patrons of whatever elevated mankind, but I was then too intent on such luminaries of the Bath firmament as they were to write about the bright particular stars, Miss Linley and Mrs. Siddons.

And yet these were undoubtedly for a considerable time very prominent influences as Bath Celebrities. That I should even seem to underrate the share which eminent women had in building up the fame of the city would be unpardonable. No one should forget that, if Society here took its tone chiefly from bright and beautiful leaders of fashion, it was also elevated by literary ladies who made the city classic ground, and still more by musical and dramatic ladies who raised its enjoyments to a high level. That Miss Linley and Mrs. Siddons belonged to Bath there can be no doubt; in the second and third decades of the century few families were better known here than that to which the eminent vocalists belonged, and a life-long boast of the great actress was that she was "a child of Bath." My task in connecting them with my local roll will be lightened, as in the case of many others, by the work of those who have gone before me. Every good biographical dictionary for many years has contained information respecting the ladies who, trained in Bath, charmed large audiences in every part of the kingdom.

At an early period Miss Linley was associated with her sister Mary at public concerts. Thomas Linley, their father, was the son of a carpenter, and born at Wells in 1732. As a lad he was sent to Badminton, the seat of the Duke of Beaufort, to do some work in the way of his father's calling. There he had much pleasure in the singing and playing of Thomas Chilcot, the organist of Bath Abbey Church, which led him to resolve to become a musician. Chilcot, struck with his ability, undertook to teach him the elements of the science, and afterwards got him sent to Naples to study under Paradies, a man eminent at that time. On his return he settled in Bath as a singing master, soon gaining the position, as we find from Parke's *Musical Memoirs*, of being " almost unrivalled in England." In addition to the work of teaching a large number of profitable pupils, he gained the post, then very enviable, of Director of the Public Concerts of Bath, in which his daughters aided him considerably, the eldest, Eliza, afterwards Mrs. Sheridan, being his *prima donna*. He had a large family, most of whom were eminently musical, so that they were called by Dr. Burney in one of his published letters " the nest of nightingales," and as their fame spread through the country they were in request for concerts, oratorios, and musical festivals in all directions.

The two sisters were especially popular at Oxford ; both beautiful and much attached to each other, there was an inexpressible charm in seeing and hearing them together ; and while country squires and their families poured in from the surrounding country whenever their coming was announced, the members of the University—dons, tutors, professors, undergraduates—fairly lost their heads. Both sisters were charming, but Elizabeth, or Eliza, as she was commonly called, was distinguished by her exceptional beauty of person and rare sweetness of voice. An interesting memoir in the fourth volume of *The English Illustrated Magazine* contains the following passage :—

"Her beauty has been immortalised by the genius of Gains-borough and Reynolds, and chronicled by many and divers pens ; from Horace Walpole who spoke of it as being ' in the superlative degree,' to John Wilkes who called her, ' the most beautiful flower that ever grew in Nature's garden.' Whilst even the birds bore their testimony to the unrivalled sweetness of her voice, as is shown by the following anecdote taken from a newspaper of the year 1770 :—' At a Salisbury music meeting the beginning of this month, while Miss Linley, a young lady from Bath, was singing the air in the oratorio of *The Messiah*, ' I know that my Redeemer liveth,' a little bullfinch that had found means by some accident or other to secrete itself in the cathedral, was so struck by the inimitable sweetness, and harmonious simplicity of her manner of singing, that mistaking it for the voice of a feathered chorister of the woods, and far from being intimidated by the numerous assemblage of spectators, it perched immediately on the gallery over her head, and accompanied her with the musical warblings of its little throat through a great part of the song.' "

About this time the father received his title of Doctor, which probably helped him to gain a footing in London, where in 1774 he became joint-manager of the Drury Lane oratorios. Still, he retained his home at Bath, where all his twelve children were born, Eliza having first seen the light at No. 5, Pierrepont Street. At the time of the London engagement

she was probably married; Sheridan is spoken of as his son
in-law in the following year, when Linley composed the music
to "The Duenna." It was produced at Drury Lane and
obtained the then unparalleled run of seventy-five nights.
Such great success and the general prospects of the family
induced Sheridan to urge their remóval to London, and they
quitted Bath in 1775. Linley joined his son-in-law soon
afterwards in buying Garrick's share in Drury Lane, the
music of which he directed fifteen years. All contemporary
writers concur in giving him a high position as an English
composer. Dr. Busby, in his *Concert Room Anecdotes* relates
a striking instance of the correctness of his judgment in vocal
matters. Dr. Burney calls him "a masterly performer on
the harpsichord," and says "his style of composition was
formed on the melodies of our best old English masters."
His works were very numerous, some of the most popular
being music to songs and airs of Sheridan's, notably in "The
School for Scandal," "The Beggar's Opera," and "The
Monody on the Death of Garrick."

It is obvious that Linley had some fine qualities which were
inherited by his children, but there were the usual shadows
of human imperfection to chequer his path and provoke
adverse criticism. I shall presently have to refer to a
mercenary spirit shown in connection with Miss Linley's
matrimonial affairs, which caused much excitement in Bath,
but the troubles he had to contend with at the close of
his life were numerous. His health was undermined by
monetary difficulties complicated with those of Sheridan.
Though he lived to see several of his children attain
eminence, he lost nine out of the twelve before his death.
His eldest son, Thomas, a pupil of Dr. Boyce, was celebrated
as a violinist and composer, leader of his father's orchestra in

Bath, and a charming solo player. His anthems are very beautiful. There is one, " Let God arise," with orchestral accompaniment, written for the Worcester Festival of 1773, which has extraordinary merit. This son was drowned in 1778 whilst on a visit to the Duke of Ancaster at Grimsthorpe, and buried in the Duke's vault. A portrait of him, together with his sister Mary, Mrs. Tickell, by Gainsborough, is at Knole, in the gallery of Lord Sackville. Dr. Linley died in 1795 and was buried in Wells Cathedral, where a handsome monument also commemorates his two celebrated daughters, Mrs. Sheridan and Mrs. Tickell, and a grandchild.

The family particulars now stated may aid the reader to realise the circumstances in which Eliza Linley was placed prior to her marriage. She was about sixteen when the Sheridan family came to settle in Bath ; the houses were not far apart and similarity of tastes and pursuits soon led to intimacy. Sheridan's parents possessed considerable ability ; his father, greatly interested in the drama, was the competitor and even rival of Garrick ; his mother wrote pamphlets, novels and dramas of much merit. One of her comedies " A Trip to Bath," never either acted or published, is said to have "passed with her other papers into the hands of her son Richard, and after a transforming sleep like that of the chrysalis, to have taken wing in the brilliant form of 'The Rivals.'" The first friendship was between Miss Linley and Miss Sheridan ; they became inseparable companions and then the two brothers of the latter, Charles and Richard, both fell in love with the great attractive power without knowing the sentiments of each other. Charles failed to make a conquest ; Richard succeeded, partially at first and subject to many anxieties. Mr. Penley in his work on the *Bath Stage* says: "He constituted himself a sort of guardian over his enamorata, presuming to advise and direct her in various matters in which she was nearly concerned. They used to meet in what are now the Institution Gardens, where Sheridan appears to have warmly protested against any encouragement being given to a certain Captain Mathews, who persecuted her with his attentions and worked upon her feelings by threatening to destroy himself unless she listened to his suit. As a matter of fact this Mathews was a married man and a thorough scamp; Sheridan proved to Miss Linley what his true character was and as danger seemed imminent proposed that she should fly to France with him and take refuge in a convent till it was overpast. Though the flight appears to have been conceived and carried out in a platonic spirit there was nevertheless a ceremony of marriage gone through at Calais, Miss Linley remaining in the convent until she was taken away by an English doctor from Lisle who placed her under his wife's charge. There her father found the fugitives; he appears to have taken the matter more coolly than was expected, while even in Bath though it was the veritable 'School for Scandal' the story of the runaways was fully believed; on which Mrs. Oliphant pertinently remarks, 'We doubt whether such faith would be shown in the hero and heroine of a similar freak in our own day.'"

But the end was not yet. Sheridan had to face both his own and Miss Linley's relatives. His father was strongly opposed to the engagement and his brother Charles thought he had been shamefully treated. The greatest difficulty was with the latter, whose anger was so great that a duel was expected and, it is believed, only prevented by the interposition of the sisters. Strangely, however, the brothers were reconciled by the attitude of a common enemy, Captain Mathews, who assumed a position of deadly antagonism on hearing of the success of one of his rivals. He inserted an advertisement in a Bath newspaper posting Sheridan as "a liar and scoundrel for having insinuated charges derogatory to his character and that of an innocent young lady." On seeing this Charles and Richard forgot their enmities, started for London to send a challenge to Mathews and met him in Hyde Park, but being interrupted adjourned to a tavern where a fight with swords took place in which Mathews was vanquished, begged for his life and obtained it. Some altercation caused a second duel on Kingsdown near Bath ; after a few passes the combatants both fell and both swords were broken, but Mathews, having the advantage this time, required Sheridan to ask for his life and on his refusal gave him wounds which at first appeared fatal but only confined him for a time to his bed. Many months passed before the formal marriage in 1773. To this Dr. Linley consented, but Sheridan's father objected. The bride's father atoned in some measure for his conduct in regard to his daughter's matrimonial affair with Mr. Walter Long, an elderly gentleman in Wiltshire, to which I have referred, and about which Bath Society were greatly exercised. Dr. Linley had encouraged the wealthy suitor in spite of many offers from younger men ; Miss Linley was strongly adverse and at length persuaded her admirer to relinquish his suit. This so enraged her father that he threatened the gentleman with an action for breach of promise of marriage and would have had it tried at the Assizes but for the generous conduct of the disappointed lover who at once settled £3,000 on the lady he had lost. All this took place some time before the affair between Sheridan and Mathews on which the play of "The Rivals" was founded and of which a permanent memorial was given in the characters of the comedy. "It was Miss Linley," Mr Penley

says, "who supplied the idea of the romantic Lydia ; Captain
Paumier, Sheridan's second in the duel on Kingsdown, was
Sir Lucius O'Trigger ; Mathews the original Bob Acres ; Mrs.
Malaprop some ignorant, pretentious person frequenting the
Pump Room ; Sir Anthony Absolute the elder Sheridan, and
Faukland the hero himself." The play was first produced at
Covent Garden in January, 1775, three years after the
marriage, and at Bath in the following March.

Of the married life of Mr. and Mrs. Sheridan little is known.
What he was as a public man ; how soon he rose to fame, if
not to fortune, is fully recorded. Very early he distinguished
himself as described by his friend Moore :—

"The orator, dramatist, minstrel, who ran
    Through each mode of the lyre and mastered them all."

Within seven years of the flight to Calais and the duels which
followed, his wife was seen among the brilliant crowd in
Westminster Hall, immortalised as Reynolds's St. Cecelia,
"the beautiful mother of a beautiful race," listening to her
husband's wonderful speech at the trial of Warren Hastings.
Her letters in *Moore's Life* show that she entered with true
wifely feeling into Sheridan's various pursuits, though by no
means sympathetic with him in the tastes and habits which
his friends regretted. There was a purity and elevation in her
character which he admired but failed to imitate. In all the
sisters of the Linley family a vein of sincere, unpretending
religiousness raised them above the temptations and
difficulties of their lot and gave them a simple dignity which
the world might envy. One of them who has not yet
been mentioned, Maria, was a striking instance of this;
she also had an exquisite voice, and excelled particularly
in sacred music. She died early, and shortly before her

death, after a touching conversation with some of the family, gave vent to her " strong aspiring hope " by raising herself in bed and singing with all the sweetness of former years a portion of the anthem, " I know that my Redeemer liveth." The physician who attended her was so overcome that he left the room, saying "She is, indeed, an angel."

But it was Mary Linley, afterwards Mrs. Tickell, who also died comparatively young, to whom circumstances gave her elder sisters choicest love. They were more together in the bringing up, generally inseparable on public professional occasions, and always thoroughly sympathetic. Mr. Tickell, who lived some time at Beaulieu, Newbridge Hill, near Bath, was grandson of Addison's friend, Thomas Tickell, and one of his daughters became the mother of John Arthur Roebuck. The strength of the attachment of his wife was shewn by Mrs. Sheridan's adoption of the children, and her beautiful care of them until her own death, which occurred after a long illness in 1792, at the age of thirty-eight. She left some lines on the death of her favourite sister which, while characterised by much intellectual grace, reveals what deserves to be well remembered of her inner life. The writer, after dwelling on her beloved sister's high qualities, concludes by invoking her spirit to aid in the training of the eldest daughter—

> " And, oh, let *her*, who is my dearest care,
> Thy blest regard and heavenly influence share ;
> Teach me to form her pure and artless mind,
> Like thine, as true, as innocent, as kind ;
> That when some future day my hopes shall bless,
> And every voice her virtue shall confess,
> When my fond heart delighted hears her praise,
> As with unconscious loveliness she strays.

' Such,' let me say, with tears of joy the while,
' Such was the softness of my Mary's smile ;
' Such was *her* youth, so blithe, so rosy sweet,
' And such *her* mind, unpractis'd in deceit ;
' With artless elegance, unstudied grace,
' Thus did *she* gain in every heart a place !'
   ' Then, while the dear remembrance I behold,
Time shall steal on, nor tell me I am old,
Till, nature wearied, each fond duty o'er,
I join my Angel Friend—to part no more !' "

The chapter in *Moore's Life of Sheridan* relating to the death of his wife contains valuable testimony from one who knew them both. It is followed by some of Mrs. Sheridan's letters to her life-long friend, Mrs. Lefanu of Dublin, first mentioned in this sketch as her husband's eldest sister, then unmarried, at Bath. But long after the publication of *Moore's Life,* so recently as 1887, other letters have come to light still more illustrative of the mind and character of the charming vocalist. Many of them are given in an interesting article by Miss Matilda Stoker in the volume of the *English Illustrated Magazine,* already quoted, preceded by an account of the preservation of the letters :—

" When the fire broke out which destroyed Drury Lane Theatre in 1809, all the papers which could be found in Sheridan's private room were hurriedly packed into barrels, and carried away. Some of these barrels were, in the confusion, thrust into neighbouring cellars ; where they remained undisturbed for over sixty years— after which lapse of time they were brought to light and examined in the hope of their containing documents of interest. This hope proved to be well founded, for amongst the heterogeneous mass of papers was discovered a series of most interesting letters addressed to Sheridan by his first wife, the beautiful Eliza Linley.

"There is a special fitness in their appearance at the present time. A statement made long ago, and perhaps forgotten, has been repeated and endorsed by a recent biographer of Sheridan—to the effect that by his conduct he succeeded in completely alienating the affections of his wife. Such a statement, if made at all, should have been supported by the most indisputable authority, and in the absence of such authority we offer the testimony of Mrs. Sheridan herself, which will be found wholly inconsistent with the sinister suggestion.

"The letters cover a period of twenty years—commencing at the time the young couple returned from France after their secret marriage there in 1772, and ending at the date of Mrs. Sheridan's untimely death in 1792. Those which we especially put forward in support of our opinion belong to the last ten or twelve years of their married life, when surely, there would have been some indication of such a change of feeling as that alleged, had it taken place."

I now introduce Moore's testimony in writing on the death of Mrs. Sheridan :—

"There has seldom, perhaps, existed a finer combination of all those qualities that attract both eye and heart than this accomplished and lovely person exhibited. To judge by what we hear, it was impossible to see her without admiration, or know her without love; and a late Bishop used to say that 'she seemed to him the connecting link between woman and angel.' Jackson of Exeter, too, giving a description of her, in some Memoirs of his own Life that were never published, said that to see her, as she stood singing beside him at the piano-forte, was 'like looking into the face of an angel.'

"The devotedness of affection, too, with which she was regarded, not only by her own father and sisters, but by all her husband's family, showed that her fascination was of that best kind which, like charity, 'begins at home;' and that, while her beauty and music enchanted the world, she had charms more intrinsic and lasting for those who came nearer to her. We have already seen with what pliant sympathy she followed her husband through his various pursuits—identifying herself with the politician as warmly and readily as with the author, and keeping Love still attendant on Genius through all his trans-formations. As the wife of the dramatist and manager, we find her calculating the receipts of the house, assisting in the adaptation of her husband's opera, and reading over the plays sent in by dramatic candidates. As the wife of the senator and orator we see her, with no less zeal, making extracts from state-papers and copying out ponderous pamphlets—entering with all her heart and soul into the details of elections, and even endeavouring to fathom the mysteries of the Funds.

" They had, immediately after their marriage, passed some time in a little cottage at East Burnham, and it was a period, of course, long remembered by them both for its happiness. I have been told by a friend of Sheridan, that he once overheard him exclaim-ing to himself, after looking for some moments at his wife, with a pang, no doubt, of melancholy self-reproach, 'Could anything bring back those first feelings?' then adding, with a sigh, ' Yes, perhaps the cottage at East Burnham might.' In this, as well as in some other traits of the same kind, there is assuredly any-thing but that common-place indifference which too often clouds over the evening of married life. On the contrary, it seems rather the struggle of affection with its own remorse."

The first four of the following extracts are from letters to Mrs. Lefanu and selected from those given by Moore; the remainder are to Sheridan himself, and published with others by Miss Stoker :—

"LONDON ; June 6.

" I suppose we shall not leave town till September. We have promised to pay many visits, but I fear we shall be obliged to

give up many of our schemes, for I take it for granted Parliament
will meet again as soon as possible. We are to go to Chatsworth,
and to another friend of mine in that neighbourhood, so that I
doubt our being able to pay our annual visit to Crewe Hall. I am
glad to hear my two nephews are both in so thriving a way. Are
you still a nurse? I should like to take a peep at your bantlings.
Which is the handsomest? have you candour enough to think
anything equal to your own boy? if you have, you have more
merit than I can claim."

"PUTNEY; August 16.

"My sister desired me to say all sorts of affectionate things to
you, in return for your kind remembrance of her in your last. I
assure you, you lost a great deal by not seeing her in her maternal
character—it is the prettiest sight in the world to see her with
her children—they are both charming creatures, but my little
namesake is my delight—'tis impossible to say how foolishly fond
of her I am. Poor Mary! she is in a way to have more—and
what will become of them all is sometimes a consideration that
gives me many a painful hour. But *they* are happy, with *their* little
portion of the goods of this world—then, what are riches good for?
For my part, as you know, poor Dick and I have always been
struggling against the stream, and shall probably continue to do
so to the end of our lives, yet we would not change sentiments
or sensations with . . . . for all his estate."

"DELAPRE ABBEY; December 27.

"I am still a recluse, you see, but I am preparing to *launch* for
the winter in a few days. Dick was detained in town by a bad
fever—you may suppose I was kept in ignorance of his situation,
or I should not have remained so quietly here. He came last
week, and the fatigue of the journey very nearly occasioned a
relapse, but by the help of a jewel of a doctor that lives in this
neighbourhood, we are both quite stout and well again (for *I*
took it into my head to fall sick again, too, without rhyme or

V

reason). We purpose going to town to-morrow or next day.
Our own house has been painting and papering, and the weather
has been so unfavourable to the business, that it is probable it
will not be fit for us to go into this month; we have therefore
accepted a most pressing invitation of General Burgoyne to take
up our abode with him till our house is ready."

"LONDON ; May 23.

" I hope in a very short time now to get into the country.
The Duke of Norfolk has lent us a house within twenty miles of
London ; and I am impatient to be once more out of this noisy,
dissipated town, where I do nothing that I really like, and am
forced to appear pleased with everything odious to me. God
bless you. I write in the hurry of dressing for a great ball given
by the Duke of York to-night, which I had determined not to go
to till late last night, when I was persuaded that it would be very
improper to refuse a Royal invitation, if I was not absolutely
confined by illness. Adieu. Believe me, truly yours."

Miss Stoker's selection from the recovered letters is preceded
by an account of what she terms " the enviable position of
Mr. and Mrs. Sheridan soon after their settlement in London
—*his* intimacy with the Prince Regent and the foremost
statesmen of the day, and her cordial reception by the leaders
of society " :

" We now see by his side a gifted wife, endowed with every
charm which could adorn society, or make a home happy. They
were no longer the unknown couple whom, a short time previously,
the beautiful Duchess of Devonshire hesitated about asking to
her house. She was now to find that even the brightest star of
rank and beauty was doomed to pale before the sun of wit and
genius.

" In the midst of this whirl of success and dissipation however,
we find those feelings still fresh and warm, which time and

circumstances too often dull. The following few letters of hers to him—the earliest of which was written after years of married life, the last, almost on her death-bed—speak for themselves on that point. The tender familiarity of expression ; the small details of her everyday life which abound, show that she felt she was writing to one who returned her love, and for whom the most trivial incidents which concerned her had an ever-new interest."

"MY DEAREST LOVE,

"I shall call at the office for the chance of seeing you, tho' I am afraid it will be in vain. But I write again to beg you would come to us in the Evening, for indeed, my dear Shery, I am never so happy as when you partake my amusements, and when I see you cheerful and contented with me. Your note had a tinge of Melancholy in it that has vex'd me, because I know my own heart, and that it has not now a thought or wish that would displease you, could you see it. I shall not, therefore, enjoy this party to-night unless you are of it. We shall not go from Mrs. Nugent's till half-past ten, I dare say. The girls are to come in the coach to me there by ten to go with us, and I shall direct them to call at the House of Commons for you. God thee bless my dear one, believe that I love thee, and will love thee for ever."

The following letters were written when she was expecting her last child, whose birth only preceded her own death by a short time, and which seems not to have very long survived her. Her failing health had for some time been a cause of much anxiety to her family and friends :—

"*Friday evening.*

"I HAVE been so engaged, dear S., with Mons. Valliant's *Travels into Africa* to-Night I quite forgot the hour, and now it is too late for the post, and to-morrow there is none, and I am afraid you will be frightened, so I send this by the coach to tell you that I had a better Night last Night than I have had a great while, and have been finely all to-day. So don't neglect Business of Consequence to come sooner than you intended.

. . . .

"God Bless you, dear S.,

"Yours affectionately,

"E. A. S."

"*Sunday morning.*

"Dear S.,

"I hope you received the letter I sent by the coach Friday Night, which would prevent your anxiety about me, and hinder you from leaving Town perhaps at a very inconvenient time. I write this on the supposition, to assure you that I have been better these last days than I have been a great while.

. . . .

After all, dear S., however I may suffer, and certainly I do, and must continue to do—there is nothing to be alarmed at. It is natural for my spirits to be weakened at times, but since the cause is known it ought not to frighten you, or make you unhappy. I have been particular in my account that you may be easy on the subject."

Ill as she was at this time, she still took an interest in his business, and knew all that was going on. In the same letter she goes on to say :—

"I see Mrs. Siddons is announced. Have you brought her to reasonable terms ! Or is it enormous ? I want to know, too, why *Cymon* is withdrawn, and how have you managed with the Duke of Bd. about the opera ? Tom is very well. Shoots gulls all the morning, and has read aloud to us every evening, but, indeed, it is not the life he ought to lead, and I am very uneasy about him at times. Have you done anything about Dr. Parr ? God bless you, dear S.

"Ever yours affectionately,

"E. A. S."

The following letter possesses an additional and pathetic interest as bieng most probably the last she ever wrote to him:—

"MY DEAREST DICK,

"I had a better night than usual last night, and Dr. Bain, who has this moment left me, says my pulse is better to-day than it has been these ten days. He confessed at last it was but ninety-four. He was unwilling to tell me because he thought it might make me too bold; but you may depend on my prudence. God bless you. I am happy to send you this good account, and shall still be happier to see you and my dear cub to-morrow. It tries me sadly to write.

"God bless you."

It may be thought that the saying "Whom the gods love they take early" is applicable to Mrs. Sheridan. Certainly if she could have seen or known all the miseries of her wretched husband's later years her lot would have been terrible. But there is reason to believe that if those miseries could not have been averted by her influence in the management of his affairs and the regulation of his conduct they might at all events have been lessened. And could she have been allowed a glance into the distant future; could she have seen how her darling "Tom" avoided the snares into which his father fell and recruited the fame and fortunes of the family, what a happy day it would have been for her. Mr. Thomas Sheridan was universally liked; and his son, Richard Brinsley, of Frampton Court, Dorsetshire, long ranked amongst the magnates of his county, sitting in Parliament many years, first for Dorchester and afterwards for Shaftesbury. His son, Algernon Brinsley, succeeded to the estate.

Other descendants of the poor lady who in early life rejoiced in the title of the "Maid of Bath," have occupied high positions. Thomas, her only son, married Lady

Elizabeth Callender (afterwards Campbell) by whom there were four children. (1)—Caroline, a woman of surpassing beauty, who married first the Hon. Mr. Norton, and secondly Sir William Sterling Maxwell. (2)—Lady Dufferin, afterwards Countess of Gifford, mother of the Marquis of Dufferin and Ava, English Ambassador at Paris and Ex-governor of Canada and India. (3)—Lady Seymour, Queen of Beauty at the Eglington Tournament, then Duchess of Somerset, her husband being First Lord of the Admiralty, and a very able though eccentric man. (4)—Richard Brinsley, mentioned in preceding paragraph, who married in 1835 the only child of Sir Colquhon Grant, of Frampton Court, and died not long ago. A more remarkable list of grandchildren it would be difficult to produce. There must have been something very good in the stock from which they sprung. If it be true that the good qualities in families may generally be traced to the mother there is much to take note of here.

Chapter XXX.

MRS. SIDDONS.

I have remarked that the great tragic actress was accustomed to call herself a " child of Bath." Of course she did not mean that she was born in Bath; her birth-place was Brecon, in South Wales, in the year 1755. Her father was Roger Kemble, the progenitor of a distinguished race and the manager of a respectable dramatic company. Beginning chiefly as a vocalist, Sarah Kemble soon found she was fitted for a more serious line and resolved to attempt tragedy. At eighteen she married Mr. Siddons and appeared with him at various places in the North of England, obtaining considerable reputation.

Two years afterwards she was invited to try her powers at Drury Lane. Her first part was Portia to Gárrick's Shylock, but her reception was not flattering. "She is certainly very pretty," said one who saw her, " but then how awkward and what a shocking dresser." Mr. Penley remarks "this would have been dispiriting to most beginners, but it only moved Mrs. Siddons to greater care and more persistent efforts." In 1778 she and her husband left London and were engaged for the Bath Theatre, her début being as Lady Townley in "The Provoked Husband," and her second appearance as Mrs. Candour in "The School for Scandal." John Palmer was then manager; at first he was not very favourable to her, and she complained that she had not sufficient scope, the fact being that comedy was not her forte, and the leading parts were as usual given to the lady on the staff who had prior claims. By degrees, however, her abilities were recognised. She worked herself steadily into

good repute and was allotted a succession of important
characters. Twice she delighted the audience by repeating
Sheridan's Monody on Garrick. Her salary was the modest
amount of three pounds a week, which was considered
respectable in those days though the labour was so great.
For not only were the duties at Bath very onerous and
exhausting in consequence of the number and variety of
plays performed, Palmer was also proprietor of the Bristol
Theatre, and the company had to go to and fro, meeting
constant demands for freshness and energy with little time
for rest. The author of the *History of the Bath Stage* adds,
" It was a hard though good school, but Mrs. Siddons's heart
was in her work and she heroically laboured to gain success
by hard study, striving both to satisfy the public and make
progress in her profession."

Through four successive seasons Mrs Siddons continued at
Bath. When we look at a list of her performances the
prevailing feelings are admiration and astonishment. There
would be also pain and sorrow if it were not known that the
public gradually appreciated her powers and that they were
rewarded substantially as well as by popular applause. She
had also an opportunity of bringing out her sister,
Miss Kemble, who then became another " child of Bath " and
whose first appearance was long remembered in the city.
Mrs. Siddons took her benefit soon afterwards when a great
crush occurred. The performances were " Jane Shore " and
" All the World's a Stage," with a concluding address to the
audience. Room was found by " laying the pit and boxes
together and reserving the front rows of the gallery for the
gentlemen of the pit, an innovation for which the actress made
the most humble apologies." On this occasion she realised
£124, and on a similar one at Bristol a few months afterwards

£100. Again in the following year, 1782, when her benefit night came round at Bath, the same arrangements for accommodation were necessary, and the profit was £146 with an additional sum of twenty guineas presented as a compliment at the box office.

These proofs of public favour, together with the great improvement in acting which her experience was known to have produced, led to overtures from London. Mrs. Siddons attributed the invitation in a great measure to the celebrated Duchess of Devonshire, whose acquaintance she had made at Bath, and who always spoke highly of her. " At all events," she said, " it was a triumphant moment to me when I was invited to Drury Lane, remembering, as I did, my dismissal some years before." The truth is that her fame had reached London from various sources, and her engagement was largely due to the influence and exertions of the elder Sheridan, whose son had become proprietor of Drury Lane. It will be remembered that Richard Sheridan had a sister for whom Miss Linley had great regard and to whom, as Mrs. Lefanu, she, when Mrs. Sheridan, wrote the letters from which I have given extracts in the preceding sketch. A daughter of Mrs. Lefanu thus describes in after years the part her grandfather, old Mr. Sheridan, took in bringing Mrs. Siddons to London. The description appears in Mr. Penley's *History of the Bath Stage* :—

" While at Bath for his health, Mr. Sheridan, senior, was solicited to go to the play, to witness the performance of a young actress, who was said to distance all competition in tragedy. He found, to his astonishment, that it was the lady who had made so little impression on him some years before in the ' Runaway ;' but who, as Garrick had declared, was possessed of tragic powers sufficient to delight and electrify an audience. After the play was

over he went behind the scenes to get introduced to her in order
to compliment her.   He said : 'I am surprised, madam, that
with such talents you should confine yourself to the country ;
talents that would be sure of commanding, in London, fame and
success.'   The actress modestly replied that she had already tried
London but without the success which had been anticipated ; and
that she was advised by her friends to be content with the fame
and profit she obtained at Bath, particularly as her *voice* was
deemed unequal to the extent of a London theatre.   Immediately
on his return to London, he spoke to the acting manager of Drury
Lane, strenuously recommending her to him.   Upon her being
engaged, he directed her, with a truly kind solicitude, in the
choice of a part for her first appearance.   With the usual
preference of a young and handsome actress for a character of
pomp and show, she inclined to that of Euphrasia, in 'The
Grecian Daughter,' but the juster taste of Mr. Sheridan determined
her in favour of the far more natural and affecting character of
' Isabella ; ' and the judgment with which the selection was made
was amply confirmed by the bursts of rapturous applause."

Mr. Palmer did all in his power to retain the Bath favourite.
Negotiations proceeded for some time but were finally unsuccessful.   Mrs. Siddons pleaded the duty devolving on her
of improving the circumstances of her family.   She had three
daughters growing up, whom she pointed to when taking
an affectionate farewell of the Bath Theatre as her "three
reasons" for relinquishing an engagement which had been
so pleasant and useful to her.   Her salary at Drury Lane
would be immediately ten guineas a week with a prospect not
only of speedy increase and excellent benefits, but good
engagements elsewhere in the vacations.   Within two years
the salary was raised to nearly £25 a week, and applications
came to her from all parts of the kingdom for performances
whenever she was able to leave London.   A writer in the

Encyclopædia Britannica remarks that on the night of her re-appearance at Drury Lane, which was marked by the greatest enthusiasm, she took possession of the tragic throne on which for thirty years she reigned without a rival. To the favourite characters in her early days were now added those for which she gained most celebrity in after life. Portia has been already mentioned ; in quick succession there were Constance, Isabella, Rosalind, Hermione, Imogene, Desdemona, and above all Queen Catherine. Anyone who has seen the engraving of a scene in this play from the painting by Harlow, in which the magnificent figure of Mrs. Siddons is seen surrounded by other members of the Kemble family, can form some idea of the wonderful spectacle. No wonder that the great intellectual variety thus afforded from month to month and year to year commanded the admiration of all ranks and classes from the throne to the cottage. George III and Queen Charlotte often engaged the gifted actress to read plays at Windsor—a source of honour rather than emolument, but still too rarely granted in those days. She was invited to the houses of the nobility and gentry, partly for the same purpose, but very much that they might enjoy her society, and she was always gratified when she gave pleasure to the humble audiences of country towns. On one occasion the gentlemen of the long robe were so charmed with a classical performance that they requested her acceptance of a purse of a hundred guineas. Amidst all these gratifications she never forgot that she was a "child of Bath ;" and that the feeling was mutual was shown by the enthusiasm with which she was received when she re-visited the scene of her first triumphs several times towards the close of her career. In 1799, as soon as her coming was announced every seat was taken in the Theatre for each of the six or eight performances in which she was to act, and on the night of her benefit, which was graced by the personification of Zara in the " Mourning Bride," the scene was unprecedented. People literary fought for places ; the uproar was so great that hearing was impossible. Mrs. Siddons therefore retired, and waited till some degree of quiet was restored, when she returned and began again from the beginning. Twice more at intervals she came to Bath and played with great spirit, but the end was drawing near ; she had realised a handsome fortune and enjoyed the satisfaction of knowing that she had the love and respect of a large circle. Her retirement was in 1812, but she lived till 1831.

Mrs. Siddons was as remarkable for her good judgment as for her kind feeling, and long experience of dramatic life gave great value to her opinion. An instance is given in Donaldson's *Recollections of an Actor* where, after quoting a statement by Gerald Griffin that Kean was going to America and Macready talked of entering the Church, the author writes :—

" This idea was very probable, as Macready was educated for the Church ; and it was owing to Mrs. Siddons's suggestion that he embraced the stage. When the elder Macready was away at Newcastle, his son was home for the holidays ; and Mrs. Siddons was at that time on a starring visit to the north. The leading actor of the theatre not suiting the Queen of Tragedy, she requested the manager to allow his son to undertake the part of Biron, in ' Isabella.' The anxious father was shocked at the request, and replied with dignity that he intended his son for the Church. ' The Church ! ' exclaimed the great actress : ' have you any interest—any patron ? ' ' None whatever,' answered Macready, senior. ' Well, then, your son will live and die a curate, on £50 or £70 a year ; but, if successful, the stage will bring a thousand a year.' The wily manager took the hint ; allowed William to appear; and from that period he got advanced, till, in 1817, he burst on a London public, where a fortune has crowned his efforts."

I have mentioned as one reason for writing on the Miss Linleys and Mrs. Siddons that Bath owed much of its prosperity at one time to Music and the Drama. It should not be forgotten that other members of the Kemble family enjoyed a large share of the reputation gained in the local nursery. Both John and Charles often acted here and were highly distinguished; various circumstances combined to give John the rank among his brother actors of "the noblest Roman of them all." This title would be conceded by all who knew the Kemble portraits, for while Gainsborough's Mrs. Siddons in the National Gallery conveys a just idea of her commanding qualities, Sir Thomas Lawrence's John Kemble, reproduced in so many engravings, gives the true conception of him. His education was excellent, his knowledge of French particularly good, he surpassed all his brethren of the stage in dignified bearing and distinguished manners, making him a welcome visitor to men like Talma in Paris and the *élite* of London society. "In private life," says Donaldson, "his costume, his fine Roman head, his clerical proclivities, and his austere and stately manner gained for him a position which no actor ever achieved before or since; and when he appeared as Pizarro in 1798 his Rolla fairly stamped him the first tragedian of the age." The play ran for thirty-two nights, the longest run then known, its great popularity being mainly due to the combined talents of the two brothers, and of Mrs. Siddons and Mrs. Jordan. The "noblest Roman" retired in 1817. His farewell address at Edinburgh was written by his friend and admirer, Sir Walter Scott. He lived till 1823, and his career was closed

at his villa on Lake Leman at the age of sixty-six ; " thus,"
says Donaldson, " was the stage deprived of Coriolanus,
Brutus, Cato, Rolla and Zanga, for all those parts died with
him."

To return to Mrs. Siddons, if her brother's noble figure
could not be forgotten neither could her own. Those who
are acquainted with Crabb Robinson's *Diary* know what
impression it produced, together with her acting for many
years on minds of the highest intellectual culture. The more
marked characteristics are thus described by her biographer
in the *Encyclopædia Britannica* :—

" The symmetry of this great actress's person was most
captivating. Her features were strongly marked, but finely
harmonised ; the flexibility of her countenance was extraordinary,
yielding instantaneously to every change of passion ; her voice
was plaintive, yet capable of firmness and exertion; her articulation
was clear, penetrating and distinct ; above all she was completely
mistress of her powers, and possessed that high judgment which
enabled her to display all her other qualifications to the greatest
advantage. One of Mrs. Siddon's highest, if not her very highest
endowment, was the power of identifying herself with the
character which she personated. The scenes in which she acted
were to her far from being a mere mimic show ; so powerfully did
her imagination conjure up the reality that the tears which she
shed were those of bitterness felt at the moment. From her frown
of proud disdain and scorn the very actors themselves shrank
with something like terror. Her greatest characters were
Katherine in ' Henry VIII,' and Lady Macbeth, in which she
manifested a dignity and sensibility, a power and pathos never
equalled by any female performer. Lastly, Mrs. Siddons was
truly an original ; she copied no one, living or dead, but acted
from nature and herself. In all the relations of life her conduct
was most exemplary."

Many of the present generation can testify to the esteem in which Mrs. Siddons was universally held. In former years one often heard from those who knew her not only of the unrivalled charm of her acting but of the never-ceasing kindness of her heart. In Bath sixty years ago, when I first knew the city, her memory was cherished with remarkable affection; letters were shown, written when she was young and handsome, full of the winning frankness which was among her chief characteristics. That all parties respected her is shown by her correspondence with Mrs. Hannah More. The poet Campbell, who was well acquainted with her and wrote her life, in doing justice to many noble qualities, remarks, "She was more than a woman of genius, her benevolence made her the pride of her sex and an honour to human nature." Long will the memory of her life be green with all who value the wide-spread elevating influences such a life can give.

It can be easily imagined in what high estimation Sir Walter Scott held the Kemble family. Especially must "the noblest Roman of them all" have had a strong attractive force for the immortal poet and novelist. What more natural therefore than that John Kemble should ask that his retirement from the stage at Edinburgh should be honoured by the address to which I have referred.

> " As the worn war-horse at the trumpet's sound
> Erects his mane, and neighs and paws the ground ;
> Disdains the ease his generous lord assigns,
> And longs to rush on the embattled lines,—
> So I, your plaudits ringing in mine ear,
> Can scarce sustain to think our parting near,—
> To think my scenic hour for ever past,
> And that these valued plaudits are my last.

But years steal on, and higher duties crave
Some space between my acting and the grave ;
That, like the Roman in the Capitol,
I may adjust my mantle ere I fall.
My life's brief act in public service flown,
The last, the closing scene must be my own.
Here then adieu ! while yet some well-graced parts
May fix an ancient favourite in your hearts—
Not quite to be forgotten even when
You look on better actors, younger men ;
And if your bosoms own this kindly debt
Of old remembrance, how can mine forget ?
Oh, how forget how oft I hither came
In anxious hope !—how oft return'd with fame !
How oft around your circle this weak hand
Has waved immortal Shakespeare's magic wand,
Till the full burst of inspiration came,
And *I* have felt, and *you* have fann'd, the flame !
By mem'ry treasured, while her reign endures,
These hours must live, and all their claims are yours.
O favour'd land, renown'd for arts and arms,
For manly talent and for female charms,
Could this full bosom prompt the sinking line,
What fervent benedictions now were mine !
But my last part is play'd, my knell is rung,
Whene'er your praise falls falt'ring from my tongue,
And all that you can hear, or I can tell,
Is—friends and patrons, hail, and fare ye well ! "

FRAGMENTS OF LOCAL HISTORY.

CHAPTER

   I. ST. JOHN'S HOSPITAL.

  II. THE ROYAL MINERAL WATER HOSPITAL.

 III. OTHER HOSPITALS AND DISPENSARIES.

 IV. THE ROYAL LITERARY AND SCIENTIFIC INSTITUTION.

  V. THE UNCOVERING OF THE OLD ROMAN BATH.

 VI. THE NEW BATHS OF 1868 AND 1889.

VII. THE THEATRE ROYAL.

VIII. THE NEW MUNICIPAL BUILDINGS.

W

FRAGMENTS OF LOCAL HISTORY.

CHAPTER I.

ST. JOHN'S HOSPITAL.

From various causes the charitable institutions of Bath are among its objects of foremost interest. Their number is large and altogether they are well managed, well supported and extremely useful. Two are of considerable antiquity; St. John's Hospital dates back to the twelfth century and St. Catherine's to the fifteenth. One, the Mineral Water Hospital, is almost, if not quite, unique; I am not aware of any similar establishment connected with the Continental spas, and certainly none in England can be compared with it as to the large utilisation of mineral springs.

These institutions have been fully described by various competent writers, but in much of the work of which I propose to treat Bath Celebrities were largely concerned. I wish to show in connected form the direction taken by their public spirit and its effect upon the character of the city. With respect to a few recent matters of local history, personal knowledge may possibly enable me to place on record a few things which, though comparatively unimportant now, will be regarded with interest in future years.

The institution now before us is not a solitary instance of old English philanthropy. Venerable as St. John's Hospital is, there were organisations in Bath for the relief of the sick poor of even an earlier date. Traces of them may be found in various ancient "Fragments" from the first dawn of Christianity in Roman and Saxon times down to its fuller development in these latter days. Mr. Hunter, in his treatise *On the connection of Bath with the Literature and Science of England,* relates a tradition that the poor were especially cared for in the earliest official administration of the waters. Pious and benevolent women are said to have devoted themselves to the work of attending upon them, and it is matter of history that in the seventh century King Osric founded a nunnery near the springs.

Another Saxon king, the warlike Offa, has the credit of establishing a *Xenoclochium,* or hospital for the reception of discharged strangers who had travelled to Bath for the benefit of the waters. We are told that it may have been from a desire to make some practical atonement for pouring his troops into Somersetshire that he provided the curative asylum. Offa's institution, however, disappeared prior to the twelfth century, which was marked in Bath by the erection of a building near the hot bath for seven lepers. It is scarcely probable that they lived permanently on that spot for two reasons: lepers were generally forbidden to live within the boundaries of towns, and the Bath sufferers certainly had a chapel, if not a house, outside the walls in Holloway. An ancient record designates it the chapel of "St. Mary extra muros," in the parish of Widcombe, which was not then a part of Bath. The hospital was maintained for this and other purposes more than six hundred years. It ceased to exist in 1786 ; how the funds were appropriated for a long time does not appear, but in 1825 the Court of Chancery decreed that they should be handed over to the Mineral Water Hospital.

We now come to the establishment of St. John's. So many narratives of this have been written that another may seem superfluous. Here, however, it is peculiarly desirable to connect the oldest charitable institution in Bath with the Celebrities of the time of its foundation. It originated with Reginald Fitz-Jocelin, the fourth in the list of Bishops of Bath and Wells at a period when local government assumed a more definite and practical shape than it had known under the Norman *régime*. Reginald succeeded the celebrated Bishop Robert after an interregnum in the See of nearly nine years, caused by the unsettled state of ecclesiastical affairs. To Robert, a man of extraordinary ability and energy, the County of Somerset was chiefly indebted for its two noblest churches, St. Peter's at Bath and the Cathedral at Wells. He appears to have had much influence with King Stephen, gaining his assistance in important measures for the organisation and endowment of the diocese, and giving in return powerful political support. Mr. Hunter, in his notes to his translation of the *History of the Bishopric of Wells*, referred to in a former page, gives an idea of the troubles as well as the successes of Bishop Robert. On one occasion he was seized in his palace in Bath by a party of the adherents of the Princess Maud, who had come from Bristol for the purpose, and carried him off to that city; soon, however, to come back again.

Reginald succeeded Robert in 1174, founded the hospital shortly afterwards, and dedicated it to St. John the Baptist. No such useful and generous act would have been possible but for the successful administration of his predecessor. Robert had not only settled satisfactorily the grave official questions in dispute between Bath and Wells, but made the revenues of the See partly available for charitable objects.

Accordingly, Reginald Fitz-Jocelin endowed his new Hospital, St. John's, with certain defined property in lands and houses, and with a tithe of the hay of so much of the domain of the monastery as was under episcopal control. To these endowments the then Prior Walter, added a tithe of the remainder of the hay and of all the bread, cheese and flesh produced by the lands in the possession of the monks, who in return for their liberality were allowed the control of the Institution. But a time came when succeeding bishops found the pecuniary arrangements inconvenient, so in the fourteenth century the original grants were quashed and a definite sum of one hundred shillings was ordered to be paid to the master and brethren from the bishop's bailiff.

A little more must be said of Fitz-Jocelin. In some respects he was one of the most remarkable men of the century. Notwithstanding his foreign name and his Italian education he was English by birth, connection and position. His father was Jocelin de Bohun, Bishop of Salisbury ; his own first appointment was that of Archdeacon of Salisbury, and through life he filled high offices in Church and State. Strongly devoted to Henry II, he was employed by him on various important missions, in one of which he pleaded before the Pope the king's innocence as to the murder of Thomas à Becket. Unfortunately it was alleged that he himself had persecuted the Archbishop, against whom he was known to have had feelings of resentment because his Grace, for some insufficient reason had excommunicated his father, the Bishop of Salisbury. The charge of persecution was brought prominently forward when it was proposed he should be made Bishop of Bath and Wells ; also another charge which, if true, would have been his misfortune rather than his fault, that he was the son of an ordained priest, an idea that greatly scandalised the high churchmen of the day. But as he was able to trace his parentage to a period anterior to his father's ordination and to clear himself from the other offence the king succeeded in gaining the Pope's consent to his appointment.

No sooner was he enthroned at Wells than he took vigorous steps for the benefit of the diocese. One striking feature of his administration was his energetic treatment of temporal as well as spiritual matters. To those who knew his personal proclivities, how he mingled with the laity and shared their amusements, this was not surprising. A man who in early life had distinguished himself in hawking, and, at a later period, obtained " a royal charter granting to him and his successors the right of keeping sporting dogs throughout all Somerset," such a man was not likely to be a one-sided ecclesiastic. Another charter obtained by him made Wells a free borough. That he long continued a favourite at Court was evident from the fact that at the coronation of Richard I (1189), he walked on one side of the king when he ascended the throne, the Bishop of Durham being on the other. But what is most noteworthy here is his care as to the foundation of St. John's Hospital. It was one of his first works after his consecration ; he drew up wise and generous rules for its management ; and he endowed it with what at that time was considered a liberal sum. The vital power it has had is seen in the fact that although it has suffered from an amount of wrong doing which would have wrecked many charities it is now, after seven centuries, more useful than ever. The founder's intimacy with State affairs caused his frequent absence from the diocese, and in 1191 he was elected to succeed the Archbishop of Canterbury, but died before the appointment could be completed. He had gone down to Wells to secure the election of his kinsman, Savaric, as his successor, and in returning received a stroke of apoplexy at a manor in Hampshire, belonging to the Bath Monastery. His interment took place near the high altar of the Abbey Church of Bath.

On the dissolution of monasteries there was a great change in St. John's Hospital. For some reason it was not subject to the dissolving act and became vested in the Crown. Queen Elizabeth being on the throne, then consolidated all the churches of Bath into one rectory and granted the presentation of them together with the patronage of St. John's to the Mayor and chief citizens, subject however to the rules and orders of Reginald Fitz-Jocelin.

Alas, for human nature and the honour of the old city this led to a deplorable state of things. The revenues had now increased greatly ; a strong temptation was offered to the civic governors, who shamefully fell into it. First they appointed the Mayor for the time being Master of the Charity ; then successive Mayors divided the greater part of the proceeds amongst themselves and the Corporation. Small indeed was the portion that went into the hospital chest ; hence the paupers were discharged, divine service was discontinued, and the Chapel became, first a Post-office and afterwards an ale-house. Such was the state of things when Queen Elizabeth, amongst other good deeds on behalf of the city, ordered a brief to be issued for raising money "to rebuild the ruinated Hospital of St. John."

Meanwhile, there were further changes. One year the speculators carelessly omitted to present to the office of Master which caused the patronage to lapse to the Crown. This was shortly after the restoration of Charles II, but the king did not long retain it, though he lost no time in presenting his chaplain, John Rustatt, who soon died, and Charles, glad to find favour with the Corporation in those troubled days, gave them back the patronage. But they proved as corrupt as ever; no pity moved them for the poor brothers and sisters whom they had dislodged, and, believing they were now safe from all attacks, they continued their iniquitous embezzlements. Dishonest men, however, often fall out; they did so; and the old adage was verified though in unforeseen ways. Sundry quarrels caused the office of Master to be taken from the Mayor and become elective. One of the Chapman family being chosen under the new *régime* required the Mayor to account for certain fines and rents. And more than this; John Chapman, Master, filed a Bill in Chancery against John Clement, Mayor, demanding full particulars of the Charity and the production of all deeds and writings concerning it.

Here we have the turning point of the lamentable story. The case was argued fully in 1713 before Sir John Trevor, Master of the Rolls, who at length gave an important decree reversing all recent proceedings. He ordered that the interests of the brothers and sisters should be clearly recognised and that the master *with their consent* might renew leases on lives, the fine not to exceed one year's value for each life. The proceeds were to be divided in fair proportions; two-thirds to the Master for his own use and for certain specified repairs; the remainder to the inmates in equal shares distributed monthly. The judge also directed authoritative surpervision; the Lord Chancellor, the Master of the Rolls, the Bishop of Bath and Wells, and others, or any two of them were to be visitors and the chapel was to be immediately rebuilt. This was done at a cost of £540 and the edifice dedicated to St. Michael. Much care was taken to define the duties and privileges of the Master. He was to have the power of nominating and putting in poor brothers and sisters, but only in strict accordance with the judge's decree as to qualifications. The following masters have been appointed since the death of Rustatt, the chaplain of Charles II :—

Joseph Glanvil	...	1666	John Chapman, D.D. ...	1791
William Peake	...	1680	James Phillott ...	1816
William Clement	...	1683	W. J. G. Luckman ...	1865
John Chapman, D.D.	...	1711	R. E. Whittington ...	1892
William Chapman, D.D.	1737			

This outline of the history of St. John's Hospital might have been filled in with innumerable details. But enough has been said to show how great were the evils of irresponsible government in unprincipled hands through several centuries. That similar tales might have been told of corporate bodies in every part of the kingdom was one strong reason for the comprehensive Municipal Reform Act of 1836. But even that did not secure to the poor, for whose benefit Fitz-Jocelin founded his Hospital, all they could fairly claim. The system of granting leases on lives for limited fines failed to allow the full value of the property to be realised. Once more, therefore, the Court of Chancery was appealed to ; another Bill was filed praying for a better scheme of administration, and arguments were heard on four following days before Sir George Turner and Lord Justice Knight Bruce. On the twenty-second of December, 1864, Sir George Turner gave the decision of the Court. " It is in evidence," he said, " that the annual value of the property, if in hand, would amount to about £12,000 and that under the present system it does not yield more than sufficient to pay the yearly sum of about £27 to each of the twelve poor brothers and sisters, a system which, as producing such results, ought not to be allowed to continue. Therefore the prayer of the citizens must be granted ; none of the property must be let in future on the payment of fines as at present, but only on the best terms which can be obtained." At the same time equitable arrangements were made with the existing holders of leases; their respective interests were fairly valued, each was to pay a moderate rent for a fixed number of years and then the property was to revert to the Trustees of the Charity.

Little remains to be said. Details were wisely arranged. No difficulty arose as to religious distinctions. Candidates of all persuasions being eligible as recipients the same principle was declared applicable to Trustees. In this spirit the affairs of the Hospital are, it is believed, consistently worked with corresponding success. As in the year 1851 the Hospital was decreed by Lord Chancellor Truro to be a municipal institution, the patronage, by an order dated 1853, was vested in Trustees of the Municipal Charities of Bath. That their work in future with regard to this ancient institution will be heavy is obvious from the fact that, according to Vice-Chancellor Malins, in 1876 the houses alone belonging to it then numbered more than two hundred.

On the first of July, 1878, it was my duty to officiate, as Mayor of Bath, at the re-opening of the Hospital after a closure for repairs. A goodly company assembled at the Guildhall and proceeded with civic ceremony to the unassuming building near the Baths. It was interesting to contrast the strong feeling of responsibility which then prevailed with the indifference of some former periods and the scandalous perversions of others. A prominent part in these opening proceedings was taken by the clerk to the Trustees, Mr. Edward Turner Payne, on whose death Mr. E. Newton Fuller succeeded to the office. From him I learn that the Rev. W. J. G. Luckman resigned the office of Master in July, 1892, and the Rev. R. E. Whittington was elected to succeed him. I find also that six men and seven women are now inmates of the house, being provided with all that is necessary, and eighteen men and seventeen women receive ten shillings per week each as out pensioners. The qualifications of candidates in both cases are that they have attained the age of fifty-five, that they have resided or paid rates in Bath for at least three years immediately prior to the date of election, and that they have not been in receipt of parochial relief for the twelve months also immediately preceding that date.

The reader has seen that at the beginning of the eighteenth century the Master of the Hospital filed a Bill in Chancery to compel the Mayor of Bath to render a financial account and produce books and papers relating to the foundation. There happens to be a curious record showing that at a much earlier period, so far back as that of Edward VI, a system of unworthy concealment was practised too powerful even for a body of Royal Commissioners. The record is contained in a handsome volume by Mr. Emanuel Green, printed for the Somerset Record Society, and entitled, *Survey and Rental of Chantries, Colleges and Free Chapels.* Subjoined is a *facsimile* of the page in which the incident of 1548, the fruitless visit of the Commissioners to the Hospital, is given in the quaint words of the time, which are a "Fragment of Local History" significant as to the difficulties the Reformation Government of the day had to contend with.

Decanatus de Bathe.

187. The Paryshe of Saincte Michell by the Bathe w'in the Citie of Bathe.

Lyghte foundyd w'in the paryshe churche ther.

One annuall rent to be levied and receyued of the Issues and Revenues of a teñt w^t thappteñnces scituate in Walcote strete w'in the saide Citie nowe in the tenure of William Abyam . vj$d$.

Memord.

Ther is an hospitall callyd Saincte Johans Hospitall w'in the saide paryshe, having landes, teñtes and hereditam'es thervnto belonging of the clere yerely value of xxvli. xiij$s$. viij$d$. ob.

The hospitall was erected (as y^t is saide) for the relief of vj poore men, and one priest or maister to sve them, havinge their contynuall lyving upon the same.

This hospitall is annexed to the paryshe churche of saincte Michelles aforesaide and the pson of the saide churche is maister of the same Hospitall.

The residue of the pffectes ar imployed and receyved by the saide Maister.

The ornamentes of the Hospitall ar estemyd wo^{r}the,—xv$s$. ij$d$.

No fundacon shewed, neither wolde the Maister appere.

CHAPTER II.

THE ROYAL MINERAL WATER HOSPITAL.

This Institution was founded in 1736 with the title of "The Bath Hospital." It was called either by that name or " The Bath General Hospital" until the middle of the present century. "General" was a misnomer as the cases under treatment were limited to those which required the Bath Waters, although patients from all parts of the kingdom were eligible. Another hospital had arisen and gained the name of " United ; " several small institutions for a variety of complaints having been blended. Hence the designation Mineral Water was given to the older hospital, the term " Royal " being prefixed to both by authority, and in recognition of the support they had received from various members of the Royal Family.

In the first chapter of these Fragments I mentioned what had been done for the sick poor of Bath prior to the establishment of St. John's Hospital. We may now glance at the organisations which came into existence between the twelfth century when St. John's was founded, and the eighteenth to which we are now come. The chapel in Holloway, intended for lepers, of which notice has been taken, appears to have been succeeded by another, the donor being one Walter Hoseate, who also gave an endowment for its support. About this time some connection seems to have been formed with an institution for idiot children by whom Hoseate's chapel was used, and for whom an asylum was built near it.

In the fifteenth century a worthy Prior of Bath, John Cantlow, built a third chapel on the same spot, and in the nineteenth a worthy Rector of Bath, Charles Crook, enlarged it. It was to this chapel Leland, the traveller, thus drew attention in his *Itinerary*, " Or ever I came to the bridge over the Avon I descended a rocky hill full of springs, and on this hill is a long street where is a chapel of St. Mary Magdelene." Mr. Wood, in his history, mentions the asylum for idiot children which was probably always small, but is represented by him as in his time only a poor cottage kept by a nurse with a stipend of £15 per annum. The number of inmates seems to have corresponded to the dimensions of the dwelling ; in 1863 it was only one. But about twenty years afterwards a successful effort was made to connect it with another having the same object, also a considerable endowment. The Bath Charity Trustees concurred in an arrangement by which both the houses were given up and thirteen children located in one more healthy on Combe Down, the funds of the institutions being equitably adjusted. These appear to have been consider-able, consisting of much valuable land and £10,000 consols, three-fourths of the latter having belonged to the Bath Asylum in Belvedere. In order to place the United Charity on a permanent basis the Trustees secured twenty acres of land on Claverton Down for the erection of a house. The institution is made in some degree self-supporting by a small payment from the friends of the children.

The next hospital in chronological order has two names, " St. Catherine's " and " The Black Alms." The first is probably due to the fact that St. Catherine was the patroness of the whole city of Bath. The other owes its origin to the colour of the garment ordered to be worn by the inmates in memory of the death of the founder, Edward VI. In former years there was a third name, " The Bimberries," the house being in Bimberry Lane, in which two sisters called Bimburie were said to have founded an older hospital.

Edward VI was undoubtedly the founder of the institution now in question. His endowment was for two objects : a Grammar School and " the maintenance of ten poor folk for ever." Certain " messuages, tenements, lands, rents, &c.," formerly belonging to the Monastery were made over to the Corporation for both purposes. In 1872 the government of the two institutions was changed; that of the school devolved on the Charity Commissioners and that of the Hospital on the Bath Charity Trustees. It was then arranged that the Governors of the school should receive the entire income derivable from the property of the old foundation and pay a fixed annual sum of £280 to the Trustees of the Hospital. For a long time the living of Charlcombe was held by the Master of the school, but the Corporation Reform Act required that it should be sold and the connection dissolved.

It appears that the same fraudulent spirit as we have noticed with regard to St. John's Hospital also affected the Grammar School and St. Catherine's. The strong arm of the law was necessary to restrain and punish the offending Governors, but at length, the reforms of modern times and the appointment of responsible boards produced a good effect. When the Royal United Hospital was built in 1825 the old building of St. Catherine's Hospital was pulled down and the present structure erected. At present there are fourteen inmates, all women, each receiving five shillings per week. The traditional black cloak is given to every inmate on her election with the understanding that when needful it must be renewed at her own cost. The weekly allowance of money is five shillings, and to this is added annually coal to the value of fourteen shillings. At the back of the Hospital there is a garden and much care is taken to make the abode conducive to the comfort of the inmates.

There is yet another ancient foundation which ought to be included in these narratives, Bellot's Hospital, but it must be reserved for a future page; the more immediate subject of the present chapter is the Mineral Water Hospital. This was founded to meet the wants of the poor in all parts of the kingdom whose cases required the use of the waters, but at the beginning the poor of Bath were not admitted, it being supposed that they could go to a free bath from their own homes. For a long time indigent men and women afflicted with disease were accustomed to flock to the springs with no means of paying either for any modes of cure or even for food and lodging. So grievous was the state of things that Parliament interfered and passed an Act requiring Justices of the Peace to give licenses to poor people to travel to Bath and have the use of the waters gratuitously. The result was that the city became inundated with beggars; fortunately the Act was only for a limited time and when it expired in 1714 was not renewed; still the evil continued and both residents and visitors were "at their wits end" to find a remedy.

Then was conceived the idea of a Refuge. A few benevolent persons formed the plan of a temporary home near the springs. Beau Nash and Dr. Oliver were especially prominent in their advocacy of the scheme. It was also taken up by some distinguished visitors, notably Lady Elizabeth Hastings, Sir Joseph Jekyll and Mr. Henry Hoare. But many years elapsed before the object was accomplished; contributions were few and small; many people thought that the parishes to which the poor belonged should care for them; and when objections of this kind had been met, others arose as to the site and plans for a building. At length, in 1739, these also disappeared; Mr. Gay, whose name is perpetuated in the

X

well-known street, gave the site; Mr. Wood the eminent architect undertook to give, free of cost, the plans and superintendance; and Ralph Allen promised £1,000 and all the stone required for the building.

Much was done to interest the wealthy and influential classes of the kingdom in the undertaking. It had gradually assumed a national character, promoted for the benefit of a wider and more deserving section of the poor than the travelling beggars who infested Bath. Eminent medical men gave their best aid towards the cure of the patients, and a large business-like Committee attended to various practical matters. One thing was to arrange that Beau Nash should submit the plans for the inspection of George III and the Royal Family ; another to obtain from Parliament an Act of Incorporation. In July, 1738, the foundation stone was laid by the Hon. William Pulteney, afterwards Earl of Bath. Twelve months afterwards the first officers of the Hospital were appointed, consisting of Mr. Thomas Carew, President ; Dr. Oliver, Deputy President and Physician; Dr. E. Harington and Dr. Rainey, additional physicians; and Mr. Pierce, Surgeon. Meetings of the Subscribers for this and other purposes were held at the "Rummer Tavern" until January, 1741, when the building was so far completed that the Governors assembled in it. But it was not until May 1742 that it was opened for the reception of patients.

The Charity was incorporated by the Act of Parliament under the name of the President and Governors of the Hospital or Infirmary at Bath. Ninety-one Governors were originally named, who were to be succeeded on their decease or resignation by others elected at a General Court. Besides these any persons might become Governors by contributing £40. Thus constituted, the Institution prospered. The medical men spared no professional effort, and other influential citizens collected money largely. Oliver Goldsmith's *Life of Nash* bears testimony to his unwearied efforts. In six years, besides his own gift of £100, he paid £2,100 to the Treasurer, collected by him. Ralph Allen also added considerably to his original gifts.

In 1795 two additional wards were built which enabled the Governors to meet for some time the applications for admissions, and later a great advantage was gained by the construction of baths in the house. Previously the patients had been conveyed to the public baths in a kind of Sedan chair; now they had the means of cure almost at the bedside. For this it was necessary to obtain a special Act of Parliament allowing pipes to be laid in the streets for conveying the water from the springs.

Many years afterwards when sanitary matters were better understood it was considered that the recovery of the patients would be quickened and their comfort greatly increased by the addition of day rooms. The limited site on which the Hospital was built, no more land being then obtainable, had not only caused the confinement of the patients to the rooms in which they slept, but compelled those who could take exercise to find it in the streets. The premises adjoining the Hospital were the house and garden of the Bath Rectory, and the Governors considered that if a more suitable residence for the Incumbent could be obtained, and the site utilised for the requisite additions, there would be great mutual benefit. Negotiations with this view were commenced in 1840, when it was understood the property was for sale, but they failed; they were renewed in 1846 and were again unsuccessful, nor was it until 1856 that all difficulties were surmounted. Meanwhile the Governors had deliberated frequently on a proposal to remove the Hospital to an entirely new site ; suggestions of several were fully discussed, and one of them, a part of the Freeman's Estate in the Lower Common, appeared desirable. But before deciding it was deemed right to obtain professional opinions as to the effect of the transit of the water to a considerable distance upon its temperature and quality, also as to the respective merits of different sites. Professor Maskelyne, of Oxford, reported on the first question, and Mr. Mitchell, Civil Engineer, of London, on the second ; the result being that the Governors considered that the risk of failure in various respects would be too great to justify them in taking a step of such magnitude.

The course was now clear. No time was lost in proposing extensive additions. A special committee were appointed to act with the energetic President, Mr. Long, and the public responded promptly. The cost of the new building, together with that of the Rectory premises, amounted to £20,000 ; it was defrayed chiefly by donations, but to some extent by a sacrifice of capital. The addition comprised spacious Day Rooms for the patients of both sexes, a commodious and beautiful chapel, for which special gifts were made, a Board Room, a Dispensary, and, in the rear, an Exercising Ground. The largest benefactor was Mr. J. Brymer, who gave £1,000 for a Ward in memory of his brother, to be called Archdeacon Brymer's Ward, and £500 for the chapel, in addition to £250 to the building fund. Mr. Brymer died suddenly before the completion of the building. His great interest in the Hospital received honourable mention in a copious historical narrative by Dr. Falconer, who says " It is impossible to mention his munificent donations without expressing deep sorrow at the loss which not only this, but numerous other valuable charities of Bath have sustained by his sudden decease. The warm interest he felt in the object and his large-hearted liberality in connection with it will be long and gratefully remembered."

Dr. Falconer records that

" The Committee to whom the ordering and management of all matters relating to the new building and the alterations in the old one were delegated, consisted of the following Governors :—

> The President for the time being.
> James S. Brymer, Esquire.
> David Johnston, Esquire.
> James Heywood Markland, Esquire, D.C.L.
> Jerom Murch, Esquire.
> George Monkland, Esquire.
> Randle Wilbraham Falconer, Esquire, M.D., and
> William Long, Esquire.

The Physicians and Surgeons of the Hospital were as follows :—

> *Physicians*—Thomas Sanden Watson, Esq., M.D.
> Randle Wilbraham Falconer, Esq., M.D.
> Charles Coates, Esq., M.D.
> *Surgeons*—Richard Francis George, Esq.
> George Leighton Wood, Esq.
> John Stothert Bartrum, Esq."

The foundation stone was laid on the 4th of June, 1859, by Viscount Portman, Lord-Lieutenant of Somersetshire, assisted by Lord Auckland, Bishop of the Diocese, Mr. Long being President of the Hospital, and Dr. Falconer, Mayor of Bath. In addressing the audience Lord Portman trusted that donations to the object would not be confined to the counties which chiefly benefited by the Institution, Somerset, Gloucester and Wilts, but that the more distant ones from which patients came would do their part. The Mayor, Dr. Falconer, remarked that though a national charity it had its claims upon every citizen of Bath, inasmuch as it was the public and faithful exponent of the virtues and efficacy of the springs to which the importance of the city was

mainly attributable. And the President, Mr. Long, stated
that since the Hospital was opened in 1742 nearly 40,000
patients had been received, of whom 11,535 had been restored
to their homes cured and 19,293 relieved ; adding that by
means of the new erection 20 additional beds would be
supplied, and if the liberality of the public were continued 100
more patients could be passed yearly through the Hospital.
A large social gathering on the invitation of the President
concluded the great interest of the day.

Two years passed and Bath had another Hospital festival.
The building was completed in July, 1861, and a distinguished
company assembled at the opening. There had been a change
of President and Mayor, but the Lord-Lieutenant and the
Bishop were the same, and repeated their valuable assistance.
With regard to the President it was considered by the Governors
at the beginning of the undertaking that instead of adhering
to the custom of electing a new one annually, it would be
well to have the office filled for a longer period during the
work and what related to it. Mr. Long was therefore chosen
the three first years for the first half of the period, and the
writer of the present pages the three next for the second.
Mr. Thomas Jolly now filled the office of Mayor. As at the
former ceremony of laying the stone a large number of
citizens met at the Guildhall and walked in procession to
the site, headed by noblemen and gentlemen of the county
with the Corporation and City Magistrates. After the presentation by various ladies of valuable and suitable offerings,
divine service was celebrated, including an impressive sermon
by the Bishop ; then a handsome collection was made and
the congregation, the general public and the patients, to
the number altogether of about a thousand, met in Archdeacon
Brymer's Ward to hear the addresses. Finally there were

many congratulations at the luncheon party of the President in the new Board Room on the great forward move which the Institution had made.

That there was good ground for these it is scarcely necessary to show. Not only had health, comfort and convenience been largely promoted; room had been made for twenty additional beds. Thirty-three years have now passed since the new wing of the Hospital was opened, during which it has been found that all the pleasant anticipations then formed have been realised. The record of cures has been highly satisfactory, while the pecuniary support has not been diminished either by the lapse of time or the other very numerous appeals for charitable objects. Fulfilling predictions made at the opening ceremony that other advantages would be gained from time to time, the Governors have built a house in the exercise ground for cases requiring separate treatment. Twenty-five beds have been added since 1885, making the number altogether 171, being 101 for men and 70 for women. The expenditure of the last year was £4,977 3s. 8d., which was somewhat higher than that of average years in consequence of various alterations and improvements, including the introduction of the electric light. Towards the annual cost of the Hospital a comparatively small amount is contributed in subscriptions; in 1892, though larger than formerly, it was only £672; the deficiency being met as usual by the income from endowments. The annual subscriptions would probably be greater if, as in the case of most other Hospitals and Charities, the admission of Patients was obtained by the recommendation of subscribers; here it is only necessary that certificates should be furnished of the fitness of the case.

The last Report of the Hospital compares its operations at different periods. In the first five years of the Institution the total number of patients was 636; fifty years later, 1793 to 1797, in the same period, 1,617; after another fifty years, 1843 to 1847, 2,789; again in the five years from 1888 to 1892, 5,875. In the first period the patients cured or benefited were 62 per cent. of those admitted; in the second, 72 per cent; in the third, 79 per cent; in the last nearly 93 per cent.

The following statement shows the national character of the Charity :—

Counties from which Patients have been received during the past Six Years :—

Middlesex ...	...	... 1382	Northampton	...	...	33
Somerset ...	...	... 747	Salop ...	...	...	23
Gloucester...	...	... 723	Norfolk ...	...	...	20
Surrey ...	...	... 659	Lancashire	..	...	20
Wilts ...	...	... 475	Suffolk ...	...	...	18
Hants ...	...	... 353	Leicester ...	...	...	17
Berks ...	...	... 313	Montgomery	...	...	15
Glamorgan	...	... 287	Lincoln ...	...	...	14
Kent ...	...	... 270	Radnor ...	...	...	13
Monmouth	...	... 264	Bedford ...	...	...	13
Devon ...	...	... 231	Cambridge	...	...	9
Dorset ...	...	... 219	Durham ...	...	...	9
Oxford ...	...	... 137	Derby ...	...	...	8
Sussex ...	...	... 122	Denbigh ...	...	...	8
Essex ...	...	... 106	Huntingdon	...	...	7
Hereford ...	...	... 94	Carmarthen	...	...	6
Bucks ...	...	... 91	Nottingham	...	...	6
Warwick ...	...	... 72	Cardigan ...	...	...	4
Herts ...	...	... 64	Cheshire ...	...	...	4
Worcester...	...	... 55	Pembroke...	...	...	3
Stafford ...	...	... 49	Northumberland	...	...	2
Brecon ..	...	... 42	Carnarvon	...	...	2
York ...	...	... 35	And 1 each from 4 other Counties.			
Cornwall ...	...	... 34				

Ireland ... 24 | Scotland ... 10 | Jersey ... 3 | Guernsey ... 2

THE PRESIDENTS OF THE HOSPITAL FROM ITS FOUNDATION.

1739	Thomas Carew, Esq., First	1781	The Earl of Ailesbury
1740	President	1782	The Earl of Camden
1741	Hon. General Wade	1783	The Lord Rodney
1742	Ralph Allen, Esq.	1784	Abel Moysey, Esq.
1743	The Bishop of Bath and Wells	1785	The Hon. J. Jeffreys Pratt
	(Dr. Ed. Willes)	1786	The Lord Vernon
1744	The Earl of Chesterfield	1787	The Earl of Mansfield
1745	Francis Colston, Esq.	1788	The Earl of Nugent
	H.R.H. Prince of Wales	1789	The Lord Primate of Ireland
1746	The same		(Lord Rokeby)
1747	The same	1790	The Marquis of Bath
1748	The Duke of Beaufort	1791	The Lord Harewood
1749	The Duke of Bedford	1792	The Earl of Chesterfield
1750	The Lord Viscount Palmerston	1793	The Bishop of Durham (Dr.
1751	The Lord Viscount Dupplin		Shute Barrington
1752	The Duke of Devonshire	1794	The Lord Viscount Weymouth
1753	Nathaniel Curzon, Esq.	1795	Sir R. P. Arden, Knt.
1754	The Marquis of Rockingham	1796	The Duke of Northumberland
1755	The Hon. Sir John Legonier	1797	H.R.H. Prince of Wales
1756	The Lord Ilchester	1798	H.R.H. Duke of York
1757	The Duke of Kingston	1799	The Lord Gwydir
1758	The Right Hon. Wm. Pitt	1800	The Marquis of Stafford
1759	The Marquis of Carnarvon	1801	Wm. Gore-Langton, Esq.
1760	The Archbishop of Canterbury	1802	Wm. Dickinson, Esq.
	(Dr. Secker)	1803	The Lord Bishop of Bath and
1761	The Lord Chancellor (Lord		Wells (Dr. Beadon)
	Henley)	1804	The Lord John Thynne
1762	The Duke of Marlborough	1805	John Palmer, Esq., M.P.
1763	Sir John Sebright, Bart.	1806	The Earl Manvers
1764	Walter Long, Esq.	1807	The Earl of Pembroke
1765	The Earl of Lincoln	1808	T. B. Lethbridge, Esq., M.P.
1766	The Duke of Beaufort	1809	Wm. Dickinson, Esq., M.P.
1767	H.R.H. Duke of York	1810	The Earl of Bridgwater
1768	The Duke of Montague	1811	The Duke of Leeds
1769	Sir Lawrence Dundas, Bart.	1812	The Earl of Guildford
1770	The Earl of Kerry	1813	Sir Benjamin Hobhouse, Bart.
1771	John Smith, Esq.	1814	Sir James Mansfield, Bart.
1772	Rev. Mr. Hethrington	1815	Lieut.-Colonel Palmer, M.P.
1773	Rev. Dr. Domville	1816	The Lord Bishop of Gloucester
1774	The Duke of Devonshire		(The Hon. H. Ryder)
1775	The Duke of Leeds	1817	John Parish, Esq.
1776	Henry Hoare, Esq.	1818	Sir T. Shelley, Bart., M.P.
1777	The Lord Clifford	1819	Lieut.-General Popham
1778	The Bishop of Bath and Wells	1820	Chas. Knatchbull, Esq.
	(Dr. Chas. Moss)	1821	Sir Walter James, Bart.
1779	The Earl of Guildford	1822	Charles Phillott, Esq.
1780	The Earl of Spencer	1823	The Earl of Brecknock

1824	The Earl of Liverpool
1825	The Lord Bishop of Bath and Wells (Dr. G. H. Law)
1826	E. B. Portman, Esq., M.P.
1827	Sir William Draper Best
1828	John H. Smyth-Pigott, Esq.
1829	The Marquis of Lansdowne
1830	The Lord Bexley
1831	E. A. Sanford, Esq., M.P.
1832	John Wiltshire, Esq.
1833	George E. Allen, Esq.
1834	Wm. Miles, Esq., M.P.
1835	The Earl Manvers
1836	The Lord Carrington
1837	The Lord Jas. O'Bryen
1838	The same
1839	The same
1840	Joseph Neeld, Esq., M.P.
1841	Sir Orford Gordon, Bart.
1842	Sir W. R. S. Cockburn, Bart.
1843	The Ven. W. T. P. Brymer
1844	The Duke of Beaufort
1845	The Lord Wm. Powlett
1846	The Lord Bishop of Bath and Wells (Dr. Bagot)
1847	The Marquis of Thomond
1848	G. W. Blathwayt, Esq.
1849	Philip Bury Duncan, Esq.
1850	The Lord Viscount Midleton
1851	Major-General Daubeney
1852	William Sutcliffe, Esq. J. H. Markland, Esq., D.C.L..
1853	The same
1854	The same
1855	Thomas H. King, Esq.
1856	The same
1857	William Long, Esq.
1858	The same
1859	The same

1860	Jerom Murch, Esq.
1861	The same
1862	The same
1863	The Lord Bishop of Bath and Wells (Lord Auckland)
1864	Major Thomas R. Baker
1865	David Johnstone, Esq.
1866	The same
1867	The Earl of Cork
1868	The Rev. H. M. Scarth
1869	Henry Duncan Skrine, Esq.
1870	The Lord Bishop of Bath and Wells (Lord Arthur C. Hervey)
1871	The Duke of Beaufort
1872	The Rev. C. Kemble
1873	Major Ralph S. Allen. M.P.
1874	The Marquis of Bath
1875	G. D. Wingfield Digby, Esq.
1876	James Watson, Esq., M.D.
1877	The same
1878	The same Jerom Murch, Esq.
1879	Major Ralph S. Allen
1880	The same
1881	The same
1882	The same
1883	The same
1884	The Lord Brooke, M.P.
1885	Major Ralph S. Allen
1886	Major-Gen. J. Gordon Jervois
1887	The same
1888	Major-Gen. R. Q. Mainwaring
1889	The same
1890	The same
1891	The same
1892	The same
1893	The same

CHAPTER III.

OTHER HOSPITALS AND DISPENSARIES.

BELLOT'S HOSPITAL.

We have now to go back to the seventeenth century to pick up a Fragment relating to Thomas Bellot and his Hospital. If strict chronological order had been maintained, this subject would have been treated in the last chapter, but the stream of local history will not suffer from its introduction here. The circumstance that Bath, like most old places, had two kinds of hospitals in former times, one for the cure of disease and another for the relief of poverty, prevents an unvaried adherence to the chronological rule.

Thomas Bellot's name has been well-known in Bath nearly three hundred years. He lived at the time when many old institutions either assumed a new form or vanished altogether. Himself, one of the middle classes, though steward of the Queen's household, Bellot so far partook of the spirit of the age as to promote various large-hearted undertakings. We have seen what he did for the Bath Abbey Church; we shall now see how he founded a Hospital, and can appreciate the lines written by Sir John Harington in his punning epistle to Bishop Montague:

> " Hospitals, baths, streets and highways
> Sound out the noble Bellot's praise,
> 'Cause he was pious and hath given
> Much, whose reward shall be in Heaven,
> Let bounteous Bellot take the palm
> And after age his name embalm."

His position at Court brought him into intercourse with Lord

Burleigh from whom he received both sympathy and co-operation in his objects at Bath. In the year 1609 he bought an estate in Wiltshire for £300, endowing with it his Hospital in Bell Tree Lane, at the corner of the "Bymburye" lands, for twelve of the poorest strangers who should be in Bath for the benefit of the waters. We have seen that the national interest in the Springs was indicated by the act passed in the reign of Elizabeth giving the free use of them to strangers who should travel to Bath, and who flocked thither in great crowds to the annoyance of the inhabitants. It was to provide a home for some of the most destitute of these that Bellot founded his Hospital; for although the parishes through which they passed were compelled to relieve them on the journey, their lot on their arrival was most deplorable. Another benevolent person, Viscountess Scudamore, followed up Bellot's action by bequeathing an annuity of £8 in trust to the Corporation for the payment of a physician to advise poor patients who used the baths gratuitously.

The original building continued until 1859 when, after the winters of two hundred and fifty years, it was taken down and replaced by the present structure. A drawing of the extremely picturesque gateway of 1609 is given in Mr. Peach's *Rambles about Bath*, and suggests many a "longing, lingering look behind" on other similar relics, but the comforts of the present abode are undeniable. An attempt was made about the time of the rebuilding to incorporate the charity with the Mineral Water Hospital, but resulted in its continuance with larger aims as a separate institution, under the management of the Municipal Trustees. The annual income is about £220; the Hospital is open for the reception of patients from Lady-day to Michaelmas, or longer if the funds permit, and each inmate, of whom there are eleven when the house is full, receives a weekly payment of two shillings and sixpence. A new bath has lately been erected within the Hospital for the benefit of the patients ; they have also the use, in common with other poor persons who obtain orders from the Mayor or any medical man, of the ancient bath appropriated to the lepers.

ROYAL UNITED HOSPITAL.

It is remarkable that generous as were some of the endowments in Bath prior to the middle of the last century no one seems to have contemplated organised relief for cases of casual illness or accident. Lepers were provided for ; Idiots had a home and a nurse ; Strangers needing the waters were assisted ; Poverty in its ordinary phase was lightened by weekly allowances ; but the sickness that, sooner or later, visits every poor man's dwelling was uncared for. Even from what was then the *new* " Bath Hospital " where a hundred patients were to be admitted for such relief as the waters could give, even from this the inhabitants of Bath were excluded, and it was not until after many years that the exclusion was removed. With the increase of the population, came greater heed to the varied wants of the indigent. It was seen that surgical and medical aid ought to be provided for labouring people disabled by illness. Then in 1747, just nine years after the Mineral Water Hospital was opened, a scheme was commenced for supplying " the villages of Walcot and Widcombe with medicine gratis." Probably the city parishes were omitted as being better cared for ; at all events this was the first of the various movements which after many years culminated in the United Hospital. It was regularly designated " The Pauper Scheme," not contemptuously, but as showing the real object, the term giving less offence then than it does now. Captain Rowland Mainwaring, to whose *Annals of Bath* I am indebted for information at this part of my narrative, states that "afterwards the scheme increased very much, in consequence of which, not only many sick persons were restored to health but often preserved from distress and ruin."

A certain amount of good fellowship has always been useful in promoting charitable objects. In the earlier days of the Mineral Water Hospital the Governors partook monthly of "a friendly dinner" at an adjoining hostlery at three o'clock, much to the advantage of the institution. In like manner the friends of the new "Pauper Scheme" met once a month at the Bear Inn, "when and where," as the notices expressed, all well wishers were invited to "attend and give their assistance towards promoting the design." Mr. Warner gives an account of the origin somewhat different from that of Captain Mainwaring. He does not mention the "*villages* of Walcot and Widcombe," but says that a hospital was founded for the diseased poor of the parishes of St. Peter and St. Paul, St. James, Walcot and Bathwick. As, however, the date is the same, 1747, it is probable that the efforts were contemporaneous, some difficulty having been found in including *at first* all the poor of the rapidly increasing city, though eventually the whole benefited. The words "founding a hospital" cannot mean here providing board and lodging, because for many years—nearly half-a-century—relief was given to the sick only, either at the counter of a dispensary or at their own houses. Probably the labour of visiting from house to house was one of the chief reasons for hiring or buying a house in 1792, and opening it with plans enlarged in other respects under the name of the Bath City Dispensary and Asylum. It had been a tavern, was situated on the Lower

Borough Walls, and being now, as Warner says, "fitted up commodiously for the excellent purpose," helped to concentrate the benevolent efforts which had been previously disunited. For the first seven years, from 1793 to 1799, the number of out-patients increased steadily from 638 to 1,536, the in-patients being in the former year 140, in the latter 113.

But very useful as this City Dispensary was, it yet failed to meet a great want. There was no provision for the case of serious accidents which, as the city increased, became, like other claims on public benevolence, more numerous. Amongst the eminent surgeons by whom Bath was raised to a high position in the last decades of the last century was Mr. James Norman, father of Mr. George Norman, who contributed still more largely to the surgical reputation of his native town, and it is remarkable that, whereas the father projected the Casualty Hospital in 1788, and was its sole professional support for many years, the son largely originated and through a very long period was the most important medical officer of the United Hospital, so called because thirty-six years afterwards the Casualty was united with the Dispensary and one building erected for both. The building secured for Mr. James Norman's project is said to have been "a comfortable house in Kingsmead Street, where the sufferers from accidents had good surgical assistance and the necessaries of life afforded them till they recovered." Here the good work was carried on with varying support, often saving the lives, and always lessening the sufferings of the inmates, until the great increase of cases and the dilapidated state of the house, suggested an effort for a larger building and the union of both institutions. Happily Mr. James Norman lived to see this accomplished. Captain Mainwaring in his *Annals of Bath* thus mentions what he did. "By great zeal in the discharge of his duties toward the inmates of the establishment, aided by economy in its management, effectual relief was afforded to all casualties occuring in Bath and its vicinity, at a period when from the extensive buildings in progress, dangerous cases were of frequent occurrence. His active benevolence also subsequently established the Puerperal Charity which affords to numerous poor women able assistance in the time of their utmost need. He had long retired from active life, but retained to the last the respect of all who knew him."

It was in 1822 that the union of the "Infirmary" and the "Casualty" was fully discussed. Early in 1823 it took place, the trustees and subscribers of both having consented. One great object, in addition to better accommodation for the poor, was the more effectual advancement of medical and surgical knowledge. There were many reasons why there should be virtually a school in Bath in which young students and the profession generally might gain knowledge and experience. That this would be made a great point of might be inferred by all who knew Mr. George Norman, his own love of his profession and his generous wish to impart to others what he knew himself. With reference to his share in the preliminary arrangements, he spoke thus on the presentation of a testimonial thirty years afterwards. The "Hospital" he said, " in which you have placed this memorial of me (his bust), is dear to me from the circumstance that I was appointed by the representatives of the Casualty Hospital to meet the late Mr. Hastings Elwin, on behalf of the Infirmary, to discuss and recommend the terms on which the two should be united. The result was submitted to general meetings of the subscribers of both charities ; it was substantially adopted, and soon afterwards the public caused the erection of the building we are now in, with an establishment which has afforded an amount of benefit we could scarcely have anticipated." The sum required for the new building was estimated at £5,000, exclusive of the cost of the ground and furniture. . The Corporation contributed £1,000, the members for the city £100 each, and the public generally in proportion to their means. Timely aid was given by a special sermon at the Abbey, and a grand musical festival in the same building; the collection after the sermon by the bishop was £121, and the proceeds altogether £419. The first stone of the new building was laid in August, 1824, and the Hospital was opened for patients in June, 1826.

More than three-score years have since passed, and what is *their* history? Not very eventful, but one of constantly increasing usefulness. This might have been expected if only from the character of the medical and surgical staff. Amongst Mr. Norman's pupils was Mr. Gore, a name always to be honoured in Bath, who, at an early period, assisted his teacher at the Hospital, and ultimately succeeded him, devoting his best energies to the close of a long life. With them were associated Dr. Barlow, Dr. Falconer, Mr. R. Wilson Browne, Mr. Soden, and others of much reputation in former years—all now gone. Nor have those who followed and are now living, whom it would be invidious to specify, failed to sustain the high reputation of the Hospital. A succession of able committees, fortunate in the rule of their presidents, have introduced from time to time various improvements, especially in the character of the nursing. Of the great value of Mr. Norman's services through more than half a century, evidence was given in 1857 by two remarkable presentations —one, a silver salver, from the working classes, value forty guineas, subscribed for chiefly in pence; the other, a beautiful marble bust, by Behnes, with a purse of £200, from other

Y

classes. The salver was presented at a crowded meeting at the Guildhall, when the sons of labour poured forth their gratitude to their benefactor for his ever kind attention, and Mr. Norman spoke of the interest he had always felt in his poorer patients. Thirty years afterwards the bust was presented at a large gathering of citizens in the Hospital; on the pedestal it is stated to be the gift of Mr. Norman's friends as a public and lasting testimony of their admiration and gratitude for his eminent services to the poor of the city, first at the Bath Casualty Hospital, and then at the Bath United Hospital during a period of fifty years.

The next noticeable event is the erection of the Albert Wing in 1864-5. On the death of the Prince there had been a strong wish that Bath should possess some suitable memorial of him. After much discussion no plan seemed better than an enlargement of the Hospital, which had been long urgently required. One statement by the president, Mr. Kemble, will give some idea of the want: "Fifty years ago 170 patients were received within the Hospital, and externally 1,522 attended to; whereas last year the in-patients numbered 1,025, and the out 11,151." "But," he added, "we wanted more than a wing, we wanted the light and air of heaven to cheer our patients, we wanted to clear the ground on which the old houses around were standing. In order to do this we had first to deal with the owners of the property, and then to solicit the aid of the Corporation, who unanimously consented to accept for their large piece of ground the moderate sum of £2,000; honour therefore to that body from all who have at heart the welfare of the suffering poor." This was said at the ceremony of laying the foundation stone—a beautiful spectacle—on a May morning. Flags waved from the houses, the Abbey bells rang out

merrily, Freemasons assembled in large numbers with full
craft adornments, headed by the Provincial Grand Master of
Somerset, Major Adair; the Corporation, the clergy and
Nonconformist ministers, the principal citizens were there as
part of a long procession, while the poorer classes showed
unmistakeable interest in the scene. Having the honour to
be Mayor, I gave utterance to the general hope "that, in
erecting the building and obtaining more space for light and
air around it, we were showing in the best manner our respect
for the memory of a truly benevolent man." It was pleasant
to find that the Queen appreciated the feeling of her subjects
in Bath; the committee were allowed to adopt in future the
designation of the *Royal* United Hospital; and her Majesty
graciously suggested the inscription on the plinth of the
handsome marble bust of the Prince in the entrance hall of
the new building: "*His life sprung from a deep inner
sympathy with God's will, and therefore with all that was
true, beautiful and right.*"

Every history, great or small, has its lights and shadows.
In this instance the shadows came, not at once, but too
surely. When the new building was advocated, some feared
it might entail serious pecuniary anxieties. They thought
that though the first cost might possibly be met, the annual
income would be inadequate to the additional expenses.
And so it proved; indeed the income had itself been
diminished by drafts on the capital to make up deficiencies
in the fund for the building. Thus in 1865-6, the committee
had to make urgent appeals, and these not succeeding to the
requisite extent, fêtes, concerts and other amusements also
falling short, a bazaar was held on a large scale. It was in
April 1866, and proved successful; the Lord-Lieutenant
presided at the opening; the ladies of the city attracted

crowds to their stalls ; and the public bought with a liberality
which added £2,000 to the exchequer.   When, however, the
work was over, a few friends pleaded that now was the time
to see whether the income and expenditure could not be
brought into accordance.   A committee of investigation were
appointed who sat many weeks, obtaining the cost of every
article of consumption and comparing it with returns from
other hospitals.   At length they issued an elaborate report
recommending certain economies, which were adopted, but
too soon the funds again proved inadequate, showing that
such an institution, liable to so many claims, at uncertain
times, cannot expect to be long free from financial anxiety.

There was a striking instance of the claims in the memorable Widcombe Bridge accident in 1877.   A somewhat slight
wooden structure crossed the river Avon, near the Old bridge
in Bath, shortening the distance from the adjoining Great
Western Railway Station to the showyard of the Bath and
West of England Society, then holding its hundredth
anniversary meeting.   A train had arrived from Salisbury
bringing a large number of passengers who crowded upon the
bridge.   If they had passed on without interruption they
would probably have been safe, but there was a stoppage at
the exit end, the weight was concentrated in the centre and a
deafening shriek proclaimed what had happened.   All were
immersed ; a few nearest the banks struggled out ; and fifty
were rescued, but five were drowned.   Nearly all the rescued
were taken to the hospital, where most of them remained and
received the greatest skill and kindness until removed to
their homes.   Four, however, succumbed to the injuries they
received, making the fatal cases nine.   I had occasion to visit
the Hospital daily and could testify to the admirable treatment.   Looking back after an interval of sixteen years I feel

that if those who distinguished themselves in those wards were not among the Celebrities of Bath they were certainly among its foremost worthies.

The progress of the Hospital in recent years has been considerable. Patients have increased, curative processes have been improved, and additions to the wards and alterations of the building have been carried out. As the result of a fund commenced by a member of the medical staff, a house opposite the hospital has been taken for cases requiring separate treatment. The Rev. E. Handley, having succeeded to the office of President, exerted himself successfully to establish a Nurses' Institute ; guarding against any additional charge to the Hospital, and hoping for an improvement of its funds by the earnings of the Nurses. His anticipations have been realised and the other results are satisfactory. Very obvious also has been the gain of the addition of a spacious children's ward. Built at the top of the house, and reached by a lift, it commands an extensive view of the surrounding country, and in various ways fully answers the benevolent purpose. There have been frequent additions by generous contributors of means for the improved treatment of various cases. A kind-hearted naval officer, Captain Murray Dixon, lately bequeathed £1,000 for the foundation of an Antiseptic Ward and a lady gave £900, the interest to be spent on orthopædic appliances.

It is not generally known that this Institution is open not merely to the poor of Bath but to those of a very large district around the city, including a radius of twenty miles, the benefit being recognised by special collections in Churches and liberal annual subscriptions. While I am writing a pleasant instance of rural recognition come from the village of Brinkworth near Chippenham, as the result of the annual

Harvest Thanksgiving in the Parish Church. It is thus announced in the *Bath Herald :*—

" The gift from Brinkworth this year was larger than ever. It filled the accommodation provided by three vans, and the procession of assistants engaged in unloading what appeared to be about a hundred packages. They reminded one of a scene in the *Arabian Nights.* Waist high were stacked baskets of rosy apples, pears, plums, melons, &c., neatly packed with flowers. The list of the unusally fine vegetables was remarkable. There was also a liberal supply of poultry and game."

Doubly acceptable was this generous present in consequence of the accession of patients caused the week previously by a terrible disaster in the Box Tunnel. Probably the sympathy of the Brinkworth villagers with the work of the Hospital had been strengthened by hearing that nine sufferers had been conveyed there and were receiving every possible attention.

The last return (that for 1892) of the number benefited by the Hospital amounted to 1,158 in-patients and 9,813 out-patients, total 10,971, being an increase on the year of 1,475.

PRESIDENTS.

W. Gore Langton, Esq., M.P. ...	1803—1847
P. B. Duncan, Esq., M.A.	1848—1862
Rev. C. Kemble, M.A.	1863—1873
R. W. Falconer, Esq., M.D. ...	1874—1881
Col. J. Randle Ford	1882
Rev. J. Murray Dixon, M.A. ...	1883—1885
John Stone, Esq.	1886—1888
Rev. J. Murray Dixon, M.A. ...	1889
Rev. E. Handley, M.A.	1890

HOMŒOPATHIC HOSPITAL.

First established as a Dispensary in 1849, this Institution became a hospital for the reception of patients ten years afterwards. Its objects are the medical relief of the sick poor on Homœopathic principles, both out-door and in-door cases, also the training of nurses. The earliest physicians of the Dispensary were Dr. W. Luther and Dr. D. C. Laurie ; the chief founder of the Hospital Mr., afterwards Dr., Newman, who had been some time settled at Wells. The first locale of the Hospital was Chapel House, Queen Square, which was furnished with ten beds, but in 1870 the Midland Railway Company required the premises, and in 1872 No. 1, Duke Street was acquired. At the time of a recent report the number of in-patients was 85, and the attendances on out-patients were 6,167. There is also "The Hahnemann Free Dispensary" in Abbey Street, where attendance to the sick poor is given daily. Nor must "The Hospital for Women," a useful institution of recent origin and on the same lines, be omitted. It has six beds, the occupants of which pay something towards the expenses.

In conclusion, we glance at the other Dispensaries which follow the older lines. There are three for ordinary cases: the Eastern, the Southern and the Western. There is also one for complaints of the Eye and Ear, established in 1837, and another for diseases of the skin, of the date of 1861. Besides these are several institutions for lessening the effects of accidents, and illnesses or infirmities, such as the Bath Créche, the Convalescent Home, and the Humane Society for cases of drowning.

The Eastern Dispensary is the oldest of the three first mentioned. It was established in 1832, and draws its numerous patients from Walcot, Lansdown, St. Saviour and Bathwick. The Western Dispensary meets the wants of the populous parishes of Weston, Trinity and part of St. Paul's, while the Southern supplies Lyncombe, Widcombe, Combe Down and other parts. With regard to all these institutions the tribute of an old resident is due for the earnestness with which they are worked and their unspeakable usefulness to the poor.

CHAPTER IV.

THE BATH ROYAL LITERARY AND SCIENTIFIC INSTITUTION.

As the traveller enters Bath from the Great Western Station one of the first buildings which attracts his eye is that of the Institution. Its handsome classic portico is not crowned by an elevation of corresponding dignity though the interior is spacious and convenient, but the scene that opens on the view is striking. The public gardens immediately around, the Italian façade of the North Parade on one side, and the sketch of hill, wood and sky beyond the slowly winding Avon, make up a charming landscape on a bright sunny day. "Beautiful for situation" would the traveller say of the building, "but an unfortunate mistake" would a citizen reply; for if it had been in the centre of the city instead of on the verge, a brighter tale might have been told of the Institution. The situation has been decidedly adverse to its prosperity.

How the mistake was committed will be related presently; first as to preliminary points. The Institution originated in the third decade of the present century with a few gentlemen whose tastes differed from those for which Bath was chiefly noted. Not that the city had been devoid of literary and scientific ornaments; these pages have testified to the reputation of many at various periods. And it can be imagined how glad some of them would have been, literary men like Harington and the elder Falconers, scientific men like Herschel and William Smith, if they could have had the meeting place of more recent times. The women, too, Mrs. Piozzi with her wit, Lady Miller with her Frascati vase,

Jane Austen, Madame d'Arblay, Frances Burney, Harriet Bowdler, Mrs. Radcliffe, Helen and Sophia Lee, what a pleasure it would have been to all of them if such a centre had existed.

The Founders had chiefly in view a high class library and a good room for lectures. They also made a point of space for a museum, for antiquities and for works of art. In 1820 an event occurred which turned their thoughts definitely to the object ; the original Assembly Rooms which stood on the sight of the present building were burnt down. They were the property of Earl Manvers to whom application was made as to whether he would be willing to erect such a building as was needed, and if so on what terms. The result was a liberal proposal by his Lordship to devote the sum of £4,000 which he had received for the insurance of the premises together with the value of the old materials, estimated at £1,000 towards the required suite of rooms. He also consented to grant a lease at what was then considered a moderate rent for a long term of years. This induced the promoters of the undertaking to decide on the spot. Probably they did not fully consider how inconvenient it would be in future years when popular support would be needed more than it then was. The situation was healthy and respectable, the terms were regarded as liberal and practicable, and, foreseeing difficulties as to other localities, they resolved to proceed.

Subscriptions were invited and terms of membership agreed upon. But before entering into financial particulars let us glance at the earlier steps. Of these an interesting account is given by the Rev. Joseph Hunter in his lecture on the *Connection of Bath with the Literature and Science of England*. He appears to have drawn up a scheme for a minor Institution so far back as 1812 ; the chief object of which was the formation of a good public library; he "mentioned it to a few friends but it was thought by them impracticable and nothing more was heard of it." The next movement was in 1819 by Dr. Barlow, who had recently settled in Bath and contemplated a grand scheme to be carried out by raising £30,000 in proprietary shares of £50 each and incorporating the holders *under a legislative charter.* Mr. Hunter of course thought the plan too magnificent to succeed, but joined Dr. Barlow and a few other gentlemen, in asking public attention to it. They met once a month for some time, but dropt off one by one, so that before the close of 1820 it was seen that nothing so costly could be accomplished. Then Dr. Barlow proposed another scheme on the basis of a £6,000 subscription, and Mr. Hunter, a third, limiting the capital to £4,000, the site to be at the end of Johnston Street, Mr. Hunter going so far as to have "plans and elevations prepared by a skilful architect." At this stage of the affair the destruction of Lord Manvers's building occurred; the Rooms had not been popular as a place of public amusement, and those in the upper part of the town were considered sufficient; but the noble owner possessed so much good property near that he was willing to consent to a handsome edifice for a good public object.

Added, however, to the terms I have mentioned, were the reasonable conditions that he should approve both of the Design and the Trustees. The term for which the building was to be held was forty years, from June 24th, 1825, subject to the annual rent of £250 for the first twenty years and £300 for the remainder of the term. The Trustees were Sir John Kean, Bart., Sir John Coxe Hippisley, Bart., Sir John Palmer Acland, Bart., Rev. Thomas Leman, Francis Ellis, Esq., Hastings Elwin, Esq., and Charles Dumbleton, Esq.

They proposed raising "a sum of eight thousand guineas, by the sale of four hundred shares of twenty guineas each for the purpose they had in view." Of the sum thus raised £1,000 was to be a perpetual reserve fund, partly as a guarantee for the payment of rent; the remainder was to be expended in books, maps, apparatus, furniture and other requisites. Each proprietor was to make an annual contribution of two guineas; strangers were to be admitted for the same payment, and it was hoped that these payments, aided by the interest on the reserve fund with the rent of the vaults under the rooms and the profits of courses of lectures, would be sufficient. But with regard to the amount of capital it was soon seen that the promoters would be disappointed. At the end of six months only one hundred and sixty shares had been taken, and a few friends became responsible for the remaining forty. The Corporation of Bath gave a hundred guineas. The Marquis of Lansdowne was elected President, and several literary men Vice-Presidents.

The Committee chose as their first Chairman the Rev. Thomas Watson. With him were associated for the special purpose of forming the Library, the Rev. Joseph Hunter, Dr. Davis, Mr. P. B. Duncan and Mr. Wilkinson. The sum of £1,200 was allotted for the work; some time was occupied in spending it, and meanwhile the building was opened to the members: This took place in January 1825; an inaugural lecture was delivered by Sir George Gibbes in the presence of Lord Lansdowne, the Bishop of Bath and Wells, and other persons of distinction; and a dinner which followed was graced by speeches from three poets of the neighbourhood, Thomas Moore, George Crabb and William Lisle Bowles.

Much judgment was shown by the Library Committee in

the purchase of books. Their chief desire was to obtain those which had gained a place in the literature of Europe. Dictionaries of high character were bought, and preference was given, in many cases, to rare and costly books rather than those which members might have in their own houses. The fine set of the *French Transactions* was secured at the sale of Mr. Beckford's library at Fonthill; Lord Lansdowne obtained valuable Parliamentary publications, and among the welcome presents from various quarters were choice folios of the Greek classics and a magnificent Virgil printed on vellum. Beginning with 1,800 volumes the Committee soon found the number amounted to 2,000. MSS. and autographs of considerable value, the transactions of learned societies, ordnance maps on rollers and even a curious collection of oriental books were added. Good country histories and other works of the same class would be a prominent object with antiquaries like Sir Richard Colt Hoare and Mr. Hunter. In after years contributions of scientific books were numerous. One donor gave *Sowerby's Botany*, another the series of *Annales Des Sciences Naturelles*, another a valuable Herbarium and a collection of good botanical works. As time passed and members of a somewhat different class joined the Institution it was found that the wants of the general reader had not been sufficiently met. A Reading Society therefore contributed annually the books which passed through it, thus filling a set of shelves with the current literature of the day. But the most important accession was in 1869 of the scientific library of the Rev. Leonard Jenyns, 1,200 choice volumes, together with his Herbarium of British plants, forty volumes in folio, all being generously offered on the simple condition that a separate room should be devoted to the gift. The Committee gratefully added a room to the building for its reception, with others for objects which had long claimed more space. Year by year the Jenyns' Library has received valuable additions from the generous donor.

Since the above was written the benefactor has passed away at the great age of ninety-three. The prominent position he filled in the scientific circle at Bath induces me to add a few particulars of his life. His surname was Jenyns until about 1874 when he took the name of Blomefield on inheriting some family property at Fersfield in Norfolk, which formerly belonged to the author of the history of Norfolk. His father was the Rev. George Leonard Jenyns of Botisham Hall, Cambridgeshire, son of John Harvey Jenyns, an alderman of Eye, Suffolk. Botisham had been the property of the celebrated Soame Jenyns, and the inheritance gave Mr. Blomefield's father a good position in the county. His son's scientific tendencies came from ancestors on the mother's side. She was the daughter of Dr. Heberden, Physician to the Royal family, and the sister of another medical man also of high rank in the profession. The elder married a sister of Dr. Wollaston the eminent astronomer, one of whose sons, Dr. William Wollaston, a great friend of Sir Humphry Davy, and often at Botisham was known by his researches in optics and chemistry. Although Mr. Blomefield traced his love of science generally to frequent intercourse with these relatives he states, in an autobiography from which I gain much information, that his fondness for Natural History was due to a great uncle named Chappelow. Both at Eton and Oxford Nature appears to have had more charms for him than Greek and Latin. He says that " even in early life his habits were studious and he was fond of solitary walks, wrapped up in observing, admiring and reflecting." His first settlement as a clergyman was near Botisham, but he was compelled after a few years to relinquish his living in consequence of the continued illness of his first wife. After a short visit to the Isle of Wight he removed to Bath, where Mrs. Blomefield died. This was in 1854; and here he spent the remainder of his life, thirty-nine years.

On leaving Cambridgeshire he gave part of the scientific collections he had formed to Museums at Cambridge and Ipswich. His Herbarium and a large Cabinet of British Shells he took with him to Bath, interesting himself at once in the Natural History of the neighbourhood. In 1855 he succeeded in establishing a Field Club, of which he was President at the time of his death; six volumes of its Proceedings are found to contain about twenty communications from himself. In 1864 he caused a Meteorological Observatory to be set up in the Institution Gardens, and from that period a register has been regularly kept under arrangements for preserving its utility and permanent scientific value. To the interests of the Institution he devoted a large portion of his time, attending its committee meetings regularly, taking special interest in all that related to the Museum and often spending a quiet hour with the books he had given. The value of these can only be known by those who are acquainted with them; some are bound up with MS. letters from the donor's intimate friend Mr. Darwin; one has a copy of verses written by himself, at Eton, on an Arctic Expedition, and all are indicative of that innate love of neatness and order which marked his life. Mr. Blomefield was twice married; his second wife survives him.

His more important works were: *A Manual of British Vertebrate Animals*, published at Cambridge by the Syndicate of the University Press, 1836;

Observations on Natural History, with a Calendar of Periodic Phenomena, 1846 ;

A Memoir of Professor Henslow, brother-in-law of the author, 1861 ;

He also published a *Report on Zoology* read to the British Association in 1864; and one in the Westminster Review on *Yarrell's British Birds,* 1840.

Mr. Blomefield belonged to the following societies :—

Linnean Society (1822) ; father for many years.
Cambridge Philosophical Society (1822).
Zoological Institute 1826 (original member).
Entomological Society 1834 (original member).
Ray Society 1844 (original member).
British Association (1832).
Geological Society of London (1835).
Boston Natural History Society U.S. (1839).
Royal Zoological Society of Ireland (1841).
Ipswich Museum (1849).
Bath Institution (1854) ; Vice President and Trustee.
Bath Field Club (1855) ; President.
Anthropological Institute (1863).

Mr. Blomefield was present at the great dinner at the Freemasons' Tavern, in 1828, in commemoration of the birth of John Ray, Sir Davies Gilbert, President of the Royal Society, being in the chair.

The original formation of the Museum of the Institution was undertaken by Mr. Lonsdale, who generously worked there day by day for years with great skill and success. He laid the foundation of a geological department " by furnishing a local suite of rocks " with corresponding fossils and added a series of British land and fresh-water shells. A nucleus being thus formed, donations rapidly accumulated, making it a geological focus all the more interesting from the discoveries made near Bath by Dr. William Smith. Nor was the Museum deficient in the departments of Botany and Mineralogy; but a collection was soon to be deposited which was probably without a parallel in the kingdom—the magnificent Roman Remains found in Bath. The most important were arranged in the vestibule entered from the classic Portico; others in the corridor leading to the Reading Room. In one of the smaller rooms is a series of Roman coins presented by various friends; another cabinet contains a collection of English coins and medals.

At the earlier periods of the Institution courses of lectures were frequent. Books were then less cheap and accessible than they are now; and people liked to hear able men and meet good audiences. The large room was well filled when Noad lectured on Chemistry, Adams on Geology, Hayden on Painting, Webster on Comparative Anatomy, James Montgomery on Poetry, and Dr. William Carpenter on Physiology. But times gradually changed in this respect; even so competent a Bath citizen as Mr. Cogan with all his knowledge of the Steam Engine and the Electric Telegraph could not long maintain good classes. The large room therefore being disused, proposals were made to devote it to an extension of Geological specimens. It was known that Mr. Charles Moore was forming a remarkable collection and that he would be willing to place it there and add fresh discoveries from time to time on the conditions which I have mentioned in the sketch of his life. The Committee gladly consented and suitable cases were provided. Ere long, however, the space though considerable was insufficient, and Mr. Handel Cossham erected a gallery round the room at a cost of £500. Another instance of liberality was the gift of a Zoological collection

z

consisting of eleven hundred cases of stuffed birds—a great attraction always to the visitors who crowd the Museum on public holidays.

Notwithstanding these favourable circumstances the Institution was never financially prosperous. Year by year for a long time the income was much below the expenditure. Attributing this very much to the burthen of rent the Committee appealed to Lord Manvers, who kindly reduced it to the extent of £100. For a little while the relief appeared sufficient, but the cost of books, papers, officers and repairs was still too large for the income. At length in 1858 a crisis came ; the lease was about to expire and the question arose whether it could be renewed ; the reserve fund was nearly exhausted and even if it were probable to raise another, would it be wise ?

After much deliberation it seemed more desirable to make an effort to purchase the building and thus be free of rent. As Chairman of the Trustees I was requested to communicate with Lord Manvers who was naturally surprised that tenants who could not pay the rent should propose to buy the building. But on looking into the matter his Lordship consented to sell it for the sum of £2,000. Steps were at once taken to obtain the money, with the result that £1,200 was given by members of the Institution and £800 lent on mortgage, thus reducing the rent from £150 to £32. In a few years the mortgage was paid off, and the members had the satisfaction of meeting in their own building under easy financial circumstances. They did not however expect to be free from anxiety in the future ; they knew how precarious support is in such cases ; other societies had been formed in more central situations with better chance of success ; especially did the Bath and County Club in Queen Square gain many of the class who would have joined the Institution; still this was *The Literary and Scientific Institution;* it kept no common lamp burning, though with varying brightness, and maintained a work that could not be spared in Bath.

Although the additions to the building on several occasions were considerable, more have been lately needed. Two auxiliary societies had long possessed a home at the Institution, "The Literary and Philosophical" and "The Bath Field Club." Some others, also claiming kindred, desired a similar advantage; numerous gifts of various kinds also needed consideration. It was therefore proposed to remove the Geological part of the museum to a room to be built in the upper story and to erect a corridor for the General Museum. The kindred societies were to have the use alternately of the large room for meetings and accommodation for books and other things in smaller rooms. This was carried out at a cost of about £1,200.

The Institution has a few ornaments besides its books and antiquities. There are portraits of Sir W. Herschell and the Rev. J. Hunter in the two lower libraries and of Mr. J. S. Duncan and Mr. P. B. Duncan in the vestibule of the Reading Room. Here also are busts of a Duke of Bedford and Sir B. Hobhouse, deposited by the Bath and West and Southern Counties Society, whose library is also deposited in the Institution on separate shelves. Within the rooms are busts of Mr. Hastings Elwin, Mr. Isaac Pitman and the present President, two small classic busts, two casts of Venus and Apollo from the antique, and a cast of the sitting figure of Dr. Johnson in Lichfield Cathedral. On the ceiling of the lecture room are four beautiful paintings of the seasons, which were bought at the sale at Fonthill Abbey.

On the death of Mr. P. B. Duncan, friends far and wide,

especially those in Bath and Oxford, wished to perpetuate the memory of the brothers in some useful way. A sum was subscribed and invested for the benefit of the Institution, as recorded in the subjoined inscription on a brass plate under the portraits of the two brothers which are mentioned in page 12, the portraits having been presented by Mrs. Fraser, wife of the Bishop of Manchester :—

"In Memory of Two Brothers,
JOHN SHUTE DUNCAN, D.C.L.,
and
PHILIP BURY DUNCAN, D.C.L.,
Of New College, Oxford, and the City of Bath,
Who with large minds and liberal hearts
Did good continually,
Winning the Gratitude and the Love of
their University, their Fellow Citizens
and their Friends.

"While many of the societies which they generously aided might claim the honour of perpetuating their names, here at least let it be recorded that they were among the chief Founders and supporters of this Institution.

"As a small tribute of respect to their memories the sum of £500 has been subscribed in various parts of the kingdom and vested in trust for the promotion of the objects to which they were especially devoted, the Library and Museum."

CHAPTER V.

THE UNCOVERING OF THE OLD ROMAN BATHS.

A short account of this work may be appropriate amongst these "Fragments." I therefore propose to give the substance of some documents which appeared at the time. They relate unavoidably to various matters in which the writer was much concerned. It is so likewise with other narratives in various parts of this book, though the aim has been to eleminate personal considerations as much as possible while recording facts that may be interesting to inquirers in future years.

It is known that the existence of the Remains of large Roman Baths had been ascertained a long time. Plans had been published showing very nearly their precise locality as well as their great extent. But how they were to be reached, what depth of soil had to be removed, and other important particulars, no one knew. At length in 1878 there were unexpected discoveries in the course of some drainage work which had been committed to the architectural and engineering skill of Major Davis, the City Surveyor of Works.

The chief object was the construction of a sewer nearly on a line with one which conveyed to the river the water over-flowing from the great spring. In doing so Major Davis found basements of pillars and other things of Roman workmanship, corresponding as to locality with the traditions of the Roman Baths. He made known what he had found to the Society of Antiquaries, to some of whom I was known and who requested me to add any information I could obtain. My correspondent, a Vice-President, stated that the Society would be glad to assist in any well-considered scheme for uncovering the remains.

Much interest had already been excited in Bath by the excavations for the sewer. Tons of lead had been discovered and removed, a fine arch found in one place and masonry for the enclosure of the hot springs in another. One of the incidental works was the restoration of an Old Roman culvert of considerable size which had been closed for thirteen centuries. Through this culvert and other subterranean abysses I penetrated with Major Davis to gain the information the antiquaries required as we found our way through the dirt and darkness. It was difficult with our flickering candles to obtain light enough to see all we were in search of; but it was evident that near us were the hidden treasures. When I emerged it was with the belief that what had been little better than dreams for many hundred years would now be realities, and my companion was still more sanguine. I informed the Vice-President of our joint opinion, promising to communicate at once with friends in Bath who might be disposed to help. Then to request a public meeting of the citizens and generally to obtain as much co-operation as possible.

My first letter was to the Duke of Cleveland, one of the largest owners of Bath property. His Grace answered kindly that if we would make an effort to have the remains uncovered he would give £100. An anonymous friend, hearing what was proposed, immediately gave a similar sum through the Town Clerk. I also received encouraging answers from the then Mayor of Bath, from the Earl of Cork, from Lord Portman and many others. The next step was to request a public meeting, to which I was able to state that between £400 and £500 had been promised. We had now to obtain the aid of owners of the houses which, having been built over the baths, had to be taken down. Some belonged to the Corporation ; one, a large public office, was the property of the Board of Guardians, their place of meeting; and it would be necessary to obtain an order of the Town Council to close an adjoining thoroughfare. The communications with both bodies were satisfactory. Then and on all future occasions the Council took a right view of what the interests of the city required, consenting to the removal of houses and the adoption of all needful facilities. At this time, Major Davis's estimate for uncovering the Remains was about £500. Subsequently it was found that nearly £1,000 would be required, and the Antiquities Committee appointed by the Council undertook to obtain the amount in voluntary subscriptions.

The course of acting being then cleared the Society of Antiquaries kindly sent a donation of £50. An estimate of £847 as the cost of uncovering was accepted from Mr. Mann, though with a prospect of some further expenses. Public interest increased as the houses were removed, the immense deposit of former ages carted away and the magnificent basement of the ancient structure gradually revealed. This work occupied considerable time, during which circumstances occurred causing some anxiety to the Committee. A tradesman in one of the adjoining streets complained of injury to his business from obstruction of the traffic and brought an action for damages. The Committee had of course endeavoured to protect the interest of all parties concerned and, believing they had succeeded, resisted the action and obtained a verdict in their favour. The Lord Chief Justice, however, while admitting that the Committee, engaged in a great public work, had done all in their power and that the verdict was substantially right, considered also that the conduct of the plaintiff had been *bonâ fide* and advised that he should only pay his own costs. This involved a liability of £250 to the Committee, whose pecuniary calculations were upset to that amount ; they felt they could not make a further appeal and therefore settled the matter themselves. As the task of uncovering proceeded the extent of the old Roman establishment became more evident. One important discovery is unfortunately again hidden from public view, a large circular bath adjoining the rectangular bath. There was undoubtedly some convenience in building the new Massage establishment where it is, but a fine opportunity was lost of shewing the grand range of Roman foundations at a glance. Unfortunately the circular bath can now only be seen by those who take the trouble to search for it. Recent proceedings of the Town Council are likely to meet the general wish for the careful preservation of the Remains. It has been resolved to protect them from the weather by a building to be connected with a much enlarged Pump Room establishment. They will probably form the principal contents of an archæological museum in a spacious corridor surrounding the rectangular bath. Meanwhile an efficient committee have been arranging the fragments of figure sculpture and architectural ornament so that they may be seen to the best advantage. They have wisely adopted a distinctive plan of keeping the Classical Remains in the centre, the Ecclesiastical Remains at one end and the Roman bricks and similar antiquities at the other. In the preceding chapter I have mentioned the valuable collection at the Institution ; if this could be added to the recent discovery and placed in the proposed building there would be the great advantage of having all the antiquities under the same roof.

A few extracts from newspapers of the day will convey some idea of the interest excited by the discoveries. The first is from a Canadian paper, *The Montreal Witness*, containing a letter dated April, 1881, by an inhabitant of that province who was visiting Bath :—

"Prince Bladud, said to have been eighth king of Britain some 800 years B.C., may have been altogether a myth, and the story of his recovery a pious fraud, but at any rate the old Romans knew and valued the *Aquæ Solis.* For here, just outside what may be called the mediæval bath, is the veritable *aquarium* into which Roman governors of Britain must have descended 1800 years ago, and to which pilgrims from Rome itself may have come for healing. How grandly those old fellows built. Every stone of the bath proper and of its steps is intact, and also about ten feet in height of the moulded bases of the pillared arches which once formed the surrounding arcades and supported the roof. The leaden lining is there also, a good half-inch thick, and the bronze sluice door by which the bath was emptied. These remains, although long suspected to exist, have only lately been uncovered, and are even now in process of excavation. They lie some 20 feet below the present surface. Bath must have been a place of importance in those days of the Romans. Later on it must have lain desolate, perhaps for centuries ; a wild duck's egg found as it was laid by the bird in a corner of the ruins seems to attest this. And I suppose the history of Bath and of Britain may still run on together till the New Zealander shall come and make a new excavation of the ruins of the Victorian age."

From the *Bath Journal*, May 7th, 1881. Referring to a motion in the Town Council that a house over the Remains should be given up and pulled down, which was carried by a large majority. Two years later, March 1883, another motion for aid of a similar kind, promoting the object more largely was carried with only three dissentients.

"Seldom has a subject been approached by our Town Council with more attention, discussed at greater length, or decided upon

after more careful deliberation than was the request urged by
Mr. Murch at Tuesday's meeting.   It seemed a small matter to ask
the Council to relinquish their right to an old tumbledown house
that was shown to be a nuisance to the bathers and which would
entail a considerable outlay to put in repair, but the contingencies
attaching to its surrender surrounded the question with importance
far greater than would otherwise have attached to it.   The shades
of the antique Romans who once trod the roads and ways of *Aquæ
Solis* and bathed in the perennial springs that then as now gave
life to the city seemed to be in presence as the speaker pleaded
for light to be thrown in upon the newly discovered architecture
and told what long buried treasures the recent labours have
revealed.   He appealed to the scanty allusions made once and
again by the Latin writers as to the importance of the thermal
springs and the general idea of their ancient dignity that was
conveyed by the notices of oral tradition among mediæval authors.
But he showed that no actual proof of this appreciation had ever
been possible.   No works such as the Romans always erected for
their use or enjoyment under similar conditions could be pointed
to as evidence of their high estimation of these waters, and
although many discoveries showed they valued the neigbourhood
for its beauty and the springs for their qualities, the last convincing
proof was still wanting, the one link in the chain was yet missing.
The remains now being unearthed are the very constructions of all
others most apposite to the point and are made at a juncture
most suitable for their preservation.   To have such remains
placed on view in our midst must redound to the benefit of Bath.
They are not matters of ephemeral interest only, but will continue
to attract the savan, the archæologist and the ordinary traveller,
and will increase in value as persistent study and research throw
from time to time a more distinct light upon all portions of
ancient customs and modes of life.   To the unlettered these
massive blocks of masonry point to a people strong in purpose and
ready in design who spared no pains to protect the waters they

held so dear ; while to the scholar they bring into strong relief a refinement of taste and luxuriousness of indulgence in strange contrast to the stern military character of the nation."

From a letter to the *Times*, by Major Davis, F.S.A. Soon after it was written the offices of the Poor Law Board to which it refers were removed :—

" The Roman Baths of Bath that have during the last five years been partially exposed to view are the most remarkable relics of the occupation of Britain by the Romans hitherto discovered.

The hot springs themselves were found to be protected by an octagonal wall built of massive blocks of stone and cased on the inside with lead of an average weight of 38lb. to the foot (exceeding half an inch thick). A great deal of this lead had been broken down by the falling in of the columns and roofs, indeed the whole area of the springs was filled in with Roman tiles and masonry, sand, and organic remains, on which rested the mediæval floor of the bath known as the King's Bath. Excavations have been made beneath the Pump Room opening out the Roman drains, which are now again utilized ; these run among masonry of almost Cyclopean character.

The greatest discovery has been that of a large bath 81ft. in length, by 38ft. 10in. in width, with steps complete on its four sides, floored with blocks of masonry, on which still remains the original coating of lead. This bath was supplied by the hot mineral water, and had a hatch or sluice of bronze (now deposited in the Pump Room) for conveniently emptying it. The bath is in the centre of a large hall with *scholæ* all round, in length (it is anticipated) 110ft., by an ascertained width of 68ft. 6in. The excavation of this great hall is now in progress, large buildings have been acquired and removed for the purpose, but unfortunately the offices of the Poor Law Board which occupy a portion of the site remain, having been under-pinned and arched under. As the floor of the bath is at a depth of 20ft. below the neighbouring streets, the existence of this building does not prevent the opening out of the bath, although it interferes with the view and prevents the completion of the excavations.

The hall consists of three aisles, the centre being the width of the bath, vaulted by a barrel-vault. This vault sprang from an arcade of clustered pilasters, giving seven arches on either side. The pilasters, 2ft. in diameter, of solid block, stand on Attic bases and plain pedestals, the side aisles or *scholæ* were arched and groined, with attached pilasters along the walls and three recesses *(exedræ* or *stibadia)* 15ft. wide, on each side the hall, two being semicircular, and the third and central, square. In the centre bay of the northern arcade is a defaced piece of sculpture, through which ran the water. Underneath the sculpture is a recess in the steps marking the position of a large sarcophagus (now lost), into which the water was first poured and so overflowed into the bath. The entrance to the great bath is at the western end, by a doorway from a large hall, the precise extent of which is unknown, although I believe I saw its western wall during some excavations I made in 1869.

In the progress of the excavations besides the fine fragments of architectural sculpture we found a metal mask somewhat similar to those discovered by of Dr. Schliemann, several patens and ewers, also of metal, and an engraved tablet, read in one way by Professor Sayce, and in another by Professor Zangemeister of Heidelberg (the greatest European authority on Roman inscriptions), also another tablet in cursive character, not yet satisfactorily deciphered, a large number of coins, bones, and pottery, and last, not least, a teal's egg, evidently in the position laid by the bird against one of the ruined pilasters of the bath in the decayed vegetation that covered the *scholæ*, satisfactorily proving that the city of *Aquæ Solis* (Bath) continued for a lengthened period a deserted ruin after its destruction A.D. 577 by the Saxons."

Chapter VI.

THE NEW BATHS.

If this volume should be honoured in future years by the perusal of inquirers into matters of local history, some " Fragment " may be looked for on the recent revival of the use of the Bath Waters. It is well known that in early times they caused successive races to settle here, that then after a long and dreary period Fashion produced a great revival and that another dark cloud in recent times of shorter duration has been followed by the present signs of prosperity. All this is well known, but perhaps fifty years hence some information may be desired as to the prominent circumstances of the present time and the more immediate causes of the improvement ; to give some idea of these is my object in this chapter.

It was through the middle decades of the present century that the dark cloud to which I have alluded overshadowed the city. Unmistakeable signs of depression were visible on all sides, in every institution and in almost every business for a considerable time. The Baths and Pump Room especially presented a melancholy spectacle to those who were acquainted with the traditions of former years. Not a few citizens remembered how different was the scene as lately as the second decade of the century, when royal and noble visitors had not ceased to come to the springs. At the time in question the Corporation were so discouraged that they offered to let the most valuable property of the city containing its staple commodity, the source of all its historic reputation, the Springs with the Baths and Pump Room, to the highest bidder. Two citizens were found to undertake,

with a courage rare in those days, the task of reviving the
fame of the Bath Waters; but although the rent was moderate
they found that private enterprise was little more successful
than public management; the short lease was not renewed
and the Civic Committee once more did what they could,
but in vain.

A similar tale, though perhaps not quite so mournful, could
be told of the Public Balls and Concerts. Nor is it necessary
to go so far back as the time of Beau Nash for a contrast.
My Sketches of Celebrities have given glimpses of what the
Assembly Rooms were when Mr. Beckford and Walter Savage
Landor at different periods met their future wives in that far
famed rendezvous. But the time had now come when it
was necessary to dispense with a Master of the Ceremonies,
notwithstanding two or three spasmodic efforts, after the retirement of General Jervois, to continue the office and maintain
the ancient prestige. So as to the Concerts and the Theatre;
it is true that there were no Miss Linley and no Mrs.
Siddons to draw country squires and their families into the
city, and perhaps no Sheridan or Harington or Gainsborough
to lighten up society with their genius and wit. But what
may be called the occasional residents in Bath were mainly
of a different class from that of thirty, forty and fifty years
previously; people of distinction who now suffered from
rheumatism, sciatica and gout went elsewhere to be cured;
and though the waters were really as efficacious and the city
was as beautiful as ever yet Fashion had set up her throne in
other places and thither her votaries flocked.

Strange as it may seem, even the introduction of the
railway was prejudicial for a time. Bath had been noted for
its large amount of coaching and posting business; the finest
teams and the smartest equipages had been seen in its

streets. No hotels had been better known and frequented; the York House for its quiet dignity and the White Hart for its picturesque servants had been in great repute throughout the country. Nevertheless stagnation came with the railway; temporary of course but still desolating; part of the York House was converted into a post office and the White Hart was closed, what had so long been the scene of so much animation became devoid of all interest except to those who liked street cries and idle-looking groups.

It need not be supposed that in that dreary time nothing was done to lessen the cloud. To the great credit of the city the Park was made; one of the last visits of royalty that of the Princess Victoria and the Duchess of Kent being marked by the opening in 1832. And from that time to the present an energetic committee have been supported by the Public with more or less success in maintaining this great attraction. Nor were other efforts wanting; although when the Theatre was burnt down, its interest had long been sinking, a Company was yet formed to rebuild it, an account of whose proceedings will be found in a future chapter. Justice also should be done to the trading classes of Bath, who undiscouraged by adverse times continued to excel their brethren of other places in matters of taste and quality; for many years few streets in the West of England were more attractive for the beauty of their shops than those in the city of the Springs.

Still the Springs were comparatively deserted, and the city failed to regain its reputation. At length the questions were asked why it was so? Could nothing be done to bring about a better state of things? Had not the baths become old and shabby and unattractive? Were they such as would allow the variety of treatment required by modern medical science?

And was it practicable to facilitate the use of them as had been done at the Mineral Water Hospital by constructing new ones within easy reach of the patients? Eminent members of the medical profession expressed strong opinions on all these points, and partly on their suggestion the subject was discussed at a meeting of the Town Council. Several circumstances were then favourable. One has been referred to; the disuse of the White Hart premises. Not only were those premises disused ; they were an emblem of desolation unworthy of the city. As they belonged to the Corporation it was thought there would be little difficulty in obtaining consent to utilise the site for a new bathing establishment. A great recommendation of the plan was that the situation was close to the springs, immediately opposite the old baths and the Pump Room, of great value for such a purpose, of little for any other.

At an early period of this discussion it was proposed that either a boarding house or an hotel should form part of the plan. Perhaps it will be allowable to repeat here what was said by the Mayor at a meeting of the Town Council in 1864 after notice had been duly given that the subject would then be introduced. "Having thought much lately," said the Mayor, "of the change Bath has undergone I have come to the conclusion that we ought to make a vigorous effort to revive its prosperity and that we cannot do better than follow the old lines. They consist of making the springs a more prominent feature, turning what is in fact our staple commodity to larger uses, and increasing by every possible means the number of visitors who come to be cured by them. It seems to me that one of our great wants, next to a better bathing establishment, is a building or range of buildings, adjoining the springs so that invalids may enjoy their full benefit. In the palmy days of our city the chief medical

men made a great point of having their patients close to
the baths ; we read of Dr. Peirce's lodgings and Dr. Mayhow's
lodgings, which possessed this advantage, the doctors themselves living in them and giving constant attendance. It is
not expedient now to go into details ; but at our next
meeting I shall propose the appointment of a committee to
consider the subject fully and bring up a report; now
I merely add that I hope the utilisation of the White
Hart premises will be a prominent feature and that whatever is done may be on a scale and in a style worthy of
the city."

This was in June, 1864. In July the Committee were
appointed and in August they brought up their report.
The recommendations were similar to those shadowed by the
Mayor and the discussion that followed was marked by much
unanimity. On a vote being taken thirty were in favour of
the scheme and only five against it, the minority arguing not
so much that nothing should be done as that other measures
were more needed by the city. But as in all similar cases
an opposition was soon organised outside the Town Council
by those who were unaccustomed to take large views of public
affairs. Especially were they alarmed at the proposed
expenditure of £30,000 for carrying out the scheme of new
baths and an hotel. For the Council considered that an
hotel would be preferable to mere boarding houses, and, if
of a high class, would be more conducive to the general
prosperity of the city. The opponents certainly urged with
considerable force that an hotel was too speculative an object
to be promoted by the Corporation out of the rates, although
the new baths might be legitimately within their province.
If I remember rightly the Lords of the Treasury on being
appealed to were of the same opinion. At all events the

A *

result was that a company was formed to carry out the hotel
part of the scheme and the Council voted the funds necessary
for the baths.   Their Lordships sanctioned a loan of £10,000
towards the latter purpose, the estimated cost being £12,160
and the company agreed to raise a capital of £25,000 for the
erection and establishment of the hotel.

It was at first proposed that the hotel should be called
Bathforum House.   The object was to link the present with
the past, the old Roman Forum having been in the locality.
But the practical conclusion arrived at was that the title of
Grand Pump Room would be more appropriate as indicating
the object more completely.   It can be easily imagined that
notwithstanding the favourable circumstances which have
been mentioned, there were many difficulties to be encountered
before progress could be made.   Among them was the
restricted site ; large as it was, more space was required for
the two objects, and the Company had to purchase the
property between it and the corner of Westgate Street at a
cost of about £5,000.   The Corporation had generously
appropriated for the hotel as much of the site of the old
premises as could be spared from the baths, on the principle
that such a building would increase the value of their
surrounding property and the general prosperity of the city.
Other difficulties as to the hotel scheme were connected with
the slow process of obtaining the requisite capital.   Plans
had been adopted, architects appointed, property agreed
for, but at the end of a year only £15,000 out of the
£25,000 had been subscribed.   After a little while, however,
more shares were taken and the deficiency was obtained, in
the usual way, by a loan on mortgage to be gradually paid off
at the rate of £150 per annum.

Three years had now passed since the subject was first

mooted in the Town Council. Not until August, 1867, were the Public assured by the demolition of the White Hart that the work would be really begun. Through the long interval the Press of the city had been earnest and unanimous in advocating the onward movement, and there is so much of historic interest in an article of the *Bath and Cheltenham Gazette,* referring to the demolition, that I introduce extracts from it :—

" A tangible step has at length been taken towards carrying out the long-talked-of and much-agitated scheme for the erection of the Grand Pump Room Hotel on the site of the old White Hart. Such an intimation will be received with satisfaction by every burgess who is capable of taking an enlarged view of the requirements of the city. Nor will this satisfaction be less, when it is remembered that the vexations and disappointments experienced by the promoters, almost from the outset, have been enough to dishearten the most enterprising, or to cool the ardour of the most sanguine. Their progress, if such it may be termed, has been indeed of a Sisyphean character, for no sooner had they got their undertaking to the top of the hill, than the machinations of their opponents sent it tumbling to the bottom. Undaunted, however, by difficulties, they persevered again and again, until they have triumphantly planted their flag on the crumbling walls of the old White Hart.

"The destruction of a familiar object like this is suggestive of many considerations, and particularly of those that relate to the past. A long and ancient history is attached to these premises— a history that carries us back to mediæval times, and even to an earlier period ? Of all the vicissitudes which marked the progress of the city, from time immemorial, the White Hart, or the Hart, has been the silent witness. Changing itself with the requirements of the times, it seems to have undergone various modifications, until it became a building of mark in the city. In a survey made

in the latter half of the seventeenth century, the "Hart Lodgings"
is among the principal buildings delineated.   It was then a three-
gable structure, quaint and picturesque-looking, much more
pleasing as seen on paper than the plain, formal elevation which
is so familiar to the present generation.   Nearly facing it stood
the church of St. Mary-le-Stalle, and between Cheap Street and
Westgate Street the thoroughfare was completely blockaded by
the Bear Inn, whose premises covered nearly the whole of the
present Union Street.   This obstruction between the upper and
lower town, into which the city at a later period was divided,
occasioned great inconvenience, to which allusion is made in
Smollett's *Humphrey Clinker*.   In 1791, the Commissioners under
the Act which had been obtained for improving the streets and
thoroughfares, entered into negotiations with Mr. H. Phillott, the
owner of the Bear, for the purchase of these premises, and
eventually they agreed to give him the sum of £13,500 for the
same.   Under this arrangement the Bear was swept away, Union
Street was built, and thus a direct communication was obtained
between the ancient and modern portions of the city.

"But this was only a fragment of the beneficial changes effected
by the Commissioners.   After the Grand Pump Room had been
erected, it was found that the White Hart projected too far to give
anything like an adequate breadth to the thoroughfare, which was
now often occupied by the carriages of the gentry who frequented
this great focus of fashion.   Hence arose the necessity of coming
to some terms with the owners of the White Hart by which
that building should be set back, and likewise made to harmonize
somewhat with Bath Street, then in course of erection.   The old
gabled front disappeared, as a necessary consequence of these
arrangements, and was succeeded by the one now in course of
demolition.

"This then became the second hotel in the city, and an object of
general pride to the citizens.   The stage coaches, from far and
near, all stopped at the White Hart, and the whole establishment

presented a scene of great animation. Only those can realise it who can look back to the time when might be seen the gaily-painted coach, with its three or four reeking horses, sweeping across the Old Bridge and rattling through the streets, the guard, conspicuous by his scarlet uniform, blowing away lustily at his horn. All was commotion in the hotel then; previous arrivals peered from the windows to see if they could recognize some friend or acquaintance, while from the upper stories looked down the domestics, with their clean white caps, and snowy kerchiefs crossed across their breasts, which made them look like members of some charity school. But with the advent of the railway all was altered, and the magnitude of this change the proprietors failed to realise. No effort was made to adapt the establishment to the altered circumstances of the times; it became more and more deserted; its management worse, and at length its doors were finally closed.

"Everybody knows the subsequent history of the building—what a desolate, in-Chancery looking place it became—how it was regarded as a by-word and reproach—and how many were the uses to which it was suggested it might be applied; but none of which found general favour. The sole practical step taken was that by which the Corporation obtained possession of the whole of the premises, the Charity Trustees and the Batchellor family giving up their portions in exchange for other property. Unchanged, however, in its cheerlessness it still remained. The only life in all the vast pile was the little that pulsated in that small cavern called the coach office. And how long this dismal state of things would have lasted had not the mind of the Mayor suggested the advisability of utilising the site for the erection of an addition to the city bathing establishments, in conjunction with a modern first-class hotel, it would have been difficult to say; but this idea, when propounded, met with general approval, and after undergoing various modifications to suit the exigencies of circumstances, it was finally adopted. There is now every probability of our having an hotel of which the citizens may justly be proud, and a bathing establishment adequate to all requirements."

The building was commenced in May, 1867, and opened within two years. It had been found as the scheme advanced that the proposed accommodation would be insufficient; the Company therefore resolved to enlarge it. For this purpose the capital was increased to £30,000; and two subsequent enlargements of the building requiring a further outlay were made, exclusive of a considerable expenditure by the lessee at his own risk for houses in the adjoining street. These were connected by corridors with the hotel and handsomely fitted up and furnished. Various circumstances had induced the Company to grant a lease of the establishment after some years of unsatisfactory experience of the original plan. Whatever the qualifications of the succession of early managers may have been they had failed, nothwithstanding a steady influx of visitors, to produce adequate pecuniary results; the dividends were small and uncertain and, although quite the same could not be said of the attractions, it was seen that they might be considerably improved. The appointment of Mr. Radway as Manager was followed by greater success, and after steady progress for some time he proposed to take a lease on terms which, while enabling him to work the hotel in a liberal spirit, would insure a regular dividend to the proprietors. Those of the founders who survive have the satisfaction of seeing their original anticipations realised; not only is the hotel with all its enlargements and annexes constantly occupied but the flow of visitors to the city, steadily increasing year by year, has greatly revived its reputation. Nor has the gain been confined to the spirited lessee; all the best hotels have

profited by the improved state of things; another of much
repute has been opened in a good situation; private family
hotels have multiplied; houses and lodgings have been
better let.

Undoubtedly the new baths have conduced largely to these
results. But they were always an essential part of the plan
of revival. It was by combining the two objects of good
domestic accommodation and improved curative processes
that success was aimed at. Everyone who sees the beautiful
suite of baths adjoining the hotel, erected by the Corporation
in 1867, sees also what the city has gained in this respect.
Conveyed by a lift from the bedroom floors, the patient is
not subject to hazardous and comfortless exposure, while the
variety of baths, suited to various forms of complaint, is a
great advantage. An eminent physician acquainted with all
the best establishments in Europe states that he does not
know one which equals this in comfort and efficacy. To
the range of ordinary baths, at the end of a spacious
corridor, was added a swimming bath of magnificent proportions surrounded by dressing-rooms; the architecture of the
entire building being worthy of the ancient city.

When two decades more had passed and faith in bathing
had kept pace with the discoveries of science another set of
baths was required to meet the new wants of the time. Two
members of different professions who knew those wants:
Mr. Freeman of the medical who had made the subject his
peculiar study, and Major Davis, the City Surveyor, greatly
devoted to it, both of whom had visited Foreign Spas were able
to give excellent advice. The result was an additional
building on the opposite side of the road for baths of the
Aix-les-Bains class, baths which are justly said to vie with
that famous establishment " in completeness, luxury and

modern appliances." This building was opened in June 1889, during the Mayoralty of Mr. Freeman by Her Royal Highness the Duchess of Albany. An extract from Mr. Peach's useful book *Bath: Old and New*, published the year previously will show what was then intended and ultimately accomplished :—

"The system of continental treatment to which we have referred is in connection with the baths, known as the King's and Queen's Baths. It will constitute an entirely new department, the approach to which will be from the old circular lobby by a curved corridor leading into a cooling room, 42 feet long by 16 feet wide, lighted from the top. Out of this there are two baths for the process known as the Aix-les-Bains Douche, 14 feet by 10 feet each, having two dressing-rooms attached, so that bathers will not have so long to wait as in the old arrangement, when there was only one dressing-room attached to each bath. Also from this cooling room leads the *Berthold Vapour Bath*, 15 feet by 11 feet, having two dressing-rooms attached, lighted above. Also an *Inhalation-room*, 20 feet by 19 feet; a *Pulverization-room*, 18 feet by 19 feet. These rooms are lighted high up under arched ceilings, and are tiled round, having handsome Roman Tesseræ as flooring. The fittings and appointments are luxurious. A staircase leads from a corridor out of this large cooling room, down to the excavations of the old Roman baths, the covering over of one of which has been the subject of so much angry discussion. From this last-named Corridor there are four new *Reclining Baths*, each about 10 feet square, and a *Wildbad Bath* of approximating dimensions, and also two deep Baths, approached by steps similar to those in the Royal Baths attached to the Grand Pump Room Hotel."

It will be seen by the following list of Annual Receipts at the Baths and Pump Room at intervals of five years how greatly the use of the Bath Waters has increased in consequence of the efforts for revival described in these pages. Does it not also give ground for hope that the same policy, contemplated with regard to the enlargement of the Pump Room establishment, may be likewise followed by results satisfactory to the city?

1865 ...	... £1,668	9 10
1870	... 1,854	18 5
1875 ...	... 2,699	14 9
1880 ...	... 2,717	17 0
1885 ...	... 4,970	3 6
1890 ...	... 7,117	18 8
1893 ...	... 7,353	18 1

Chapter VII.

THE THEATRE ROYAL.

No provincial theatre has been more remarkable than that of Bath as a nursery for the best dramatic talent of the country. It began to acquire this character after the middle of the eighteenth century when the city was rapidly gaining its high modern reputation. People of ample means came to settle here in large numbers, wanting the amusement of the theatre, some as a relief from ennui, others as a change from the ballroom and the card table. Hence latent ability was awakened ; encouragement was given to those whom nature had endowed with special gifts, and while they by this means rose to fame and fortune, local and national interests were promoted.

At first one essential was sorely needed. Everywhere the theatres of the day were of the most miserable description. In Bath there was nothing worthy of the name until the Palmers, father and son, exerted themselves to meet the want. From the time of the Miracle Plays performed in the Churches in the middle ages, lovers of the drama had struggled on with no respectable place to meet in.

What was called a Play Room existed in Bath as early as 1705, but it is surprising that even then the place was tolerated. It was under a ballroom, situated on the site of the present Mineral Water Hospital and belonged to a certain Lady Hawley who shared the profits after paying for "hand-bells, music, attendants, performers and tallow candles." But if the usual accessories were wanting, if there were no proscenium or artistic scenery there were some aristocratic pretensions ; the armorial bearings of the principal subscribers were painted on the walls, and it was found that people who could sit in a cellar with their heads only four feet below the ceiling could also endure the noise of dancers above and the smell of tallow candles below.

At this time the Bath Corporation, with a view to insure some respectability, undertook to grant licenses for rooms. But when strolling companies came unexpectedly or special application was made by citizens they were sometimes so much at a loss as to allow part of the Guildhall to be fitted up. This being found incompatible with civic dignity the lower Assembly Rooms, which stood on the site of the present Literary Institution, were utilised for performances until a large room was found in Kingsmead Street and dignified with the name of the New Theatre.

This ultimately became the Jews' Synagogue and continued so until recent times, but before being so used the *Bath Journal* of February 17th, 1747, announced that the " great room of the Globe Inn, without Westgate, having been made very commodious had been taken by the Bath Company of Comedians." It was there that an illustrious party assembled in 1750, as reported by the same journal: " Thursday in the evening their Royal Highnesses the Prince and Princess of Wales, having drank tea at Ralph Allen's, Esq., went to the Play and saw the Tragedy of *Tamerlane* performed by Mr. Sinnett's company, at the command of the Princess Augusta."

The Messrs. Palmer endeavoured to provide something better than " the great room of the Globe." It happened that a Mr. Hippisley, a London actor of some repute, died soon after issuing proposals for the erection of a respectable house in Bath. The Palmers adopted his scheme, built the theatre in Orchard Street, and opened it in 1751 with the play of Richard III, but their rivals in "the great room of the Globe" improved it and the amusements so successfully that it was impossible to keep up the competition. Much loss was sustained by both parties, and in the end John Palmer bought up the shares of his opponents in their undertaking, and secured the interests of both houses for himself. Mr. Penley, to whose work on the *Bath Stage* I owe these particulars, shows that there was much encouragement to Palmer in the brilliant audiences of the two preceding seasons at the two theatres, though they were not large enough separately to make both succeed. The record states that among the names of the visitors in December, 1749, were "ten peers, nine peeresses, five earls' daughters, fifteen baronets and knights, and altogether a greater number of distinguished people than had been known at any previous season," which is mentioned as a proof that Bath was in a state to insure success to spirited and well directed efforts.

And the Orchard Street Theatre did flourish through fifty years. It was the first scene of that successful nursing of dramatic talent to which I have alluded. There Mrs. Siddons and her brothers first developed their powers ; also Henderson, Elliston, Cooke and many others. There Sheridan met the Linley family, for although the chief arena of the beautiful sisters was the concert room they were always warmly devoted to the drama. Within those walls the future orator learnt many a lesson and not far from them he wrote his famous comedies illustrative of the social life of Bath. That John Palmer spared no effort to deserve success we have seen in reviewing his life. As the audiences increased he made additions to the theatre, and at the close of his career the internal decorations had greatly improved. In his annual journeys to strengthen his company his judgment and experience enabled him to select actors and actresses of character and ability for the audiences at Bath and Bristol. In those journeys it will be remembered his celebrated mail coach scheme originated; the scheme itself, with all the labour it involved, causing him eventually to relinquish his connection with the drama and remove to London.

Towards the close of the century the accommodation in Orchard Street was found very insufficient. There were times when if the house had been twice the size it would have been filled. As early as 1796 the erection of a larger building and the removal to a better situation was seriously considered. But the plan did not assume a practical shape until 1803-4 when a company was formed, the capital raised and Beauford Square chosen as the site. It was carried out on the Tontine principle, the subscriptions being readily taken up; some by the Prince of Wales, the Princess Charlotte of Wales and the Duke of York, the Duke and Duchess of York being regular annual visitors to Bath. Mr. Palmer had obtained a patent for the Orchard Street Theatre some years before, which gave it, amongst other privileges, the title of Royal, which was transferred to the new building on the opening in 1805; so that by means of good management, eminent performers and a careful selection of plays, prosperity was again achieved and the full credit of the "nursery" maintained.

After the varied fortunes of another half-century the calamity, too common with many such buildings, befel the Bath Theatre. On the 18th of April, 1862, the morning of Good Friday, at half-past ten o'clock, smoke was seen to issue from the roof and in less than an hour the entire premises were burnt down. The present writer, walking into Bath from the upper part of the town, and not knowing what had happened, reached the top of Gay Street to see the flames rising fiercely above the houses below. People going to their places of worship had a strange turn given to their feelings, and many like myself could not be satisfied without stopping to see whether total destruction was inevitable and how far the adjoining property would be affected. Happily this was very little injured ; nor was any life lost ; but the lessee was uninsured, and the proprietors suffered considerably, having had the policies much reduced two years previously. All the attempts to ascertain with any certainty the cause of the fire were unsuccessful. On the previous Wednesday night the drama, "Peep o' Day," had been played, and it was at first imagined that some wadding fired during the piece had been left to smoulder among some dresses. But it was found that all the dresses had been removed to Bristol immediately the performance was finished, leaving, as the only other ground of conjecture, the contiguity of a beam of an adjoining brewery which might have ignited.

The prevailing feeling amongst the citizens of Bath was one of doubt as to whether rebuilding was probable. Times had changed ; Bath was not what it used to be, the Continent with all its attractions had been opened, and many English cities were now rivals of the Queen of the West. In addition to these causes there was the later dinner hour, indisposing people for evening entertainments, and, still stronger, the altered religious proclivities of the age sternly forbidding any countenance of the theatre. Still the intelligence and public spirit of Bath, the belief that the drama ought to be, and might be an elevating and purifying agency, would not allow inaction at such a crisis. A public meeting was convened by the Mayor, well attended, and addressed with much earnestness, though for some time the practical results were tardy and insufficient. Then another meeting was called, which, together with individual efforts, proved more successful, so that the requisite capital, about £12,000 was subscribed, the interests of the owners of the shell of the old theatre purchased, and competition invited for the erection of a new one. In this, it is well known Mr. Phipps succeeded, gaining thereby a reputation extremely well deserved and amply justified by the structures he has since built in almost every part of the country. The new Bath Theatre was opened on the 6th of March, 1863, with a very beautiful presentment of the *Midsummer Night's Dream*, leading parts in which were taken by the two Mr. Rignolds, Mr. Robertson, Mr. Marshall, Miss Ellen Terry, Miss Madge Robertson, and Miss Henrietta Hodson; the lessee and manager being Mr. Chute, who had been lessee and manager of the old theatre, and filled the same offices at Bristol.

Mr. Penley has done such ample justice to the recent as well as the former *History of the Bath Stage* that I need not add particulars of the thirty years since 1863. This general remark, however, may be added—that the Theatre, in common with other institutions, has profited by the revived prosperity of the city, noticed in a former chapter, as the consequence of public improvements. And having myself filled, through the entire period since the rebuilding of the Theatre, the office of Chairman of the Company, I cannot withhold an expression of what is due to the present lessee, Mr. Lewis, who has co-operated with the Directors in every effort for maintaining the reputation of the Theatre. Liberal in all that relates to decorative skill, his aim as to the entertainments has been ever high and pure; he has spared no pains to engage attractive talent, and while giving great variety he has shown his preference for the best ideals. In this respect he shares the feeling of the great leader of dramatic taste, Mr. Irving, with whose words at a recent Theatrical Fund Dinner I close this chapter :—

" Surely, we have a drama which in its highest expression cannot be charged with lack of humanity. It is the greatest glory of our dramatic literature that it is the most broadly humanising influence in the world. Sympathy, tolerance, serene and sustaining wisdom are preached in the plays of Shakespeare as they have never been preached in the pulpit. It was a wise man who said that the professional moralist was moral by the strength of his antipathies, but that Shakespeare was moral by the strength of his sympathies. And the poet himself has put his gospel of humanity into words which wear the stamp of immortal truth : ' The web of our life is of a mingled yarn, good and ill together ; our virtues would be proud if our faults whipped them not, and crimes would despair if they were not cherised by our virtues.' That is the profound and intensely human lesson which is taught by the drama, even in its humblest endeavour. And though it may not, like the sister arts, be encouraged by subvention and charter, though it may have still to contend against dulness and prejudice, the stage will continue with ever-increasing dominion to play a conspicuous and an honourable part in the history of civilised mankind."

Chapter VIII.

THE NEW MUNICIPAL BUILDINGS.

In a former chapter on civic government it has been shewn that there was a "Grieve" of Bath as early as the year 907. It is believed that, notwithstanding the changes wrought by the Norman Conquest, the Corporation, in some form, may be traced back to that period. As the chief officers in Saxon times presided over local courts of justice and the coinage of money they must have had a building in which to transact the necessary business. Mr. Irvine, whose knowledge of Bath antiquities is considerable, mentions a tradition of a mediæval hall and suggests that what in later times was called the Old Town Hall might have been added to it. This building is said to have stood in the middle of the street, nearer the Abbey Church than the present building, and to have been surrounded by houses of which some idea may be formed by those who have heard of the adjoining Wade's Passage, which was demolished in the third decade of the present century.

The Old Town Hall is sometimes called Inigo Jones's. Mr. Earle thus designates it and gives the date of erection A.D. 1625. But there are doubts as to whether the eminent architect designed it, and certainly the drawings still to be seen do not indicate his taste and skill. There is less uncertainty respecting the origin of the present building which succeeded it after a lapse of a hundred and fifty years. Great delay was caused at first in consequence of objections to the plans. For nine years, from 1766 to 1775, a succession of architects, including the younger Wood, who competed twice, failed to satisfy the Corporation. Even Atwood, the

B *

city architect, was set aside after having actually had his plans adopted and receiving an order to carry them out. Then came Baldwin, a man of undoubted genius; in vain did the economists of the day enter the lists against him on the ground of increased expense; in vain did they oppose the sacrifice of houses which would have spoilt the site and blocked the thoroughfare; the Corporation were true to their trusts of a city then becoming every year more beautiful. Disregarding even the reproach of previous costly blundering, which was fairly hurled against them, they earned the gratitude of future generations and appointed Baldwin for the work.

Both externally and internally there was much to commend it. The front facing the road is classical and handsome, in harmony with the general architecture of the city. The other façade, adjoining the market, is more simply elegant, but being obscured by surrounding buildings has never been sufficiently appreciated. Of the interior the best that can be said is that it fully answered the purposes of the time when there was comparatively little work to be done and yet a large amount of feasting. The most prominent features are the entrance hall and the staircase leading to the banqueting room and council chamber. The size, proportions and decorations of the banqueting room make it one of the most beautiful in the West of England. Mr. Baldwin doubtless knew that the Bath Corporation were celebrated for their civic dinners, and occasionally entertained the highest personages of the land. It was soon after a banquet given to the Prince and Princess of Wales that His Royal Highness presented to his hosts the silver gilt cup and salver which have graced their table ever since. To drink out of the loving cup is still a ceremony duly honoured on important occasions, while the other presents of plate and the fine historic portraits keep up the remembrance of former times. The council room adjoining is also handsome and well proportioned, but too small for a much enlarged Corporation.

These rooms and the hall and staircase will remain untouched in the new erection. The council room will be used for committees and a larger built for the meetings of the City Fathers. It has been the want of sufficient space in all those parts of the Guildhall devoted to public business which has rendered the new additions necessary. The work of the Corporation, Magistrates, and other public officers has increased very largely since Baldwin completed his structure. There were then no County Courts, no Quarter Sessions, no School Board meetings; the Corporation, the Magistrates, the Committees, all had much fewer duties; the Town Clerk, the City Treasurer, the City Surveyor, the Watch and Police Authorities have suffered, especially in recent years from stinted accommodation. In January, 1891, the Magistrates passed a resolution calling the attention of the Council to the necessity of a better court for the administration of justice. The Mayor in bringing the subject forward dwelt on other great needs, caused by the increase of public business, and proposed the appointment of a committee to consider and report upon the various requirements. These were found to be so numerous that after much deliberation through several months, the Council resolved, with very little difference of opinion, to build two wings, one for municipal offices and another for technical education classes, provision for whom had been lately entrusted to local bodies by the Government.

The adoption of the plan of two wings was in accordance

with special advice. At an early period it was deemed desirable to obtain the opinion on various points of some architect of experience and reputation. The choice fell on Mr. Young who had lately completed new Municipal Buildings at Glasgow. Having visited Bath to inspect the site and confer with the Committee he suggested two schemes. No. 1 provided Municipal Buildings on the south side of the Guildhall, and Technical School Rooms on the north ; No. 2, a block of buildings on the north to include both objects and extending the entire length of Bridge Street. The sites on both sides were in the hands of the Corporation to a great extent, though neither would have been large enough without some addition. Scheme No. 1 was adopted as being preferable both on architectural grounds externally and with regard to interior accommodation.

It has been stated that the Government had entrusted to Town Councils the duty of providing for Technical Education. Fortunately it had also granted means of meeting the expense by a provision in the Local Taxation (Customs and Excise) Act, 1890, and the Bath Council had resolved to appropriate its share of the funds to Technical Education. This would meet gradually the cost of one of the wings, and was a great inducement to the adoption of Mr. Young's more advantageous scheme. Plans were then advertised for ; the competition was to be open to architects generally, and the usual premiums were to be awarded for the three best. Nineteen were received and three selected, one as superior to any ; but before the name of the successful candidate was ascertained this motto only being known) it was necessary to learn the cost of carrying out his plan. The estimate for the south wing, which was to be the first proceeded with, was £22,500, exclusive of the architect's commission, also of properties to be acquired and of various contingencies, which it was calculated would bring the amount up to £31,000. The Council then finally resolved that the work should be undertaken. The envelopes containing the mottoes were opened ; Mr. Brydon of London was found to have earned the first premium, Messrs. Burgess and Oliver of Bath the second, and Mr. Silcock of Bath the third ; Mr. Brydon was appointed.

The next step was to obtain the sanction of the Local Government Board to the required loan, which was granted after a visit of their agent to make due inquiries at a public meeting. Much time was now required for specifications, quantities and tenders, so that it was not until September, 1892, that the tenders could be opened. They ranged from £27,823, by a distant firm, to £22,253, by Hayward and Wooster of Bath, and the lowest was adopted. The latter sum was subsequently increased by £272 in consequence of alterations.

At first an impediment arose which threatened much trouble and delay ; it was contended by those who had opposed the scheme from the beginning, that the building would be too near the Abbey and that the roadway would be inadequate. The Council, though not seeing sufficient force in the objections, endeavoured to meet them by arranging that the wings should be set back several feet from the line of the Guildhall, which was generally accepted at the time as satisfactory. But the final result was that in consequence of a wider dissatisfaction the plans were altered to this extent, both wings were to be diminished in length and the accommodation, which the abstracted space would have given, was to be provided by a curtailment of those parts of the market where the necessary projections would be made.

The altered contract was signed in March, 1893; the demolition of the old houses on part of the site was soon effected, the strong foundations were put in by an army of workmen, and the memorial stone duly laid by the Mayor on the first of June.

The time seemed long between January, 1891, when the Mayor introduced the subject to the Town Council and June, 1893, when the stone was laid, but compares favourably with the nine years occupied in deciding on plans, &c., for the existing building. The inscription on the stone is as follows:—

> THESE MUNICIPAL BUILDINGS
> WERE RENDERED NECESSARY
> BY THE LARGE INCREASE OF PUBLIC BUSINESS
> SINCE THE ERECTION OF THE CENTRAL BUILDING,
> THE GUILDHALL,
> ANNO DOMINI MDCCLXXVII.
> AND THIS MEMORIAL STONE WAS LAID
> ON THE 1ST JUNE, MDCCCXCIII.
> IN THE PRESENCE OF THE MAGISTRATES,
> CORPORATION AND CITIZENS
> OF THE ANCIENT CITY
> BY JEROM MURCH, ESQUIRE, J.P., D.L.
> SEVENTH TIME MAYOR OF BATH.
>
> ————
>
> J. M. BRYDON, F.R.I.B A.,
> ARCHITECT.
> JESSE HAYWARD AND EDGAR WM. WOOSTER,
> CONTRACTORS.
> JOHN STONE,
> TOWN CLERK.

Here I could wish that this narrative should end. Some personal considerations would certainly induce me to close it. But the speaking in connection with laying the stone can hardly be left unnoticed. It expressed what was felt by he chief representatives of the city and county on an event of unusual interest and importance. And if I omitted certain complimentary allusions I should lose an opportunity of saying what is much in my mind at the close of life. It is this: Any services I have been able to render have been amply rewarded by the kindness of the citizens, their prompt and generous support of some public objects, and their patient, earnest co-operation through years of difficulty in others. Let me merely add that there is no common satisfaction in remembering how heartily and successfully men who differ widely on other public questions have worked together in whatever promoted the welfare of Bath. For these reasons I subjoin a few extracts from the local journals describing the proceedings of a memorable day :—

"It was a brilliant day for the ceremony, and the scene was animated. Round the boarding of the site fluttered flags and bannerets, flags were on the churches and public buildings, and the Abbey bells pealed. On the level of the stone was erected a large platform, and there was space on the lower level of the enclosure for several hundreds, which as soon as the public gate was opened rapidly filled. Sightseers gathered outside the boarding to watch the passage of the procession from the Guildhall, and from surrounding windows and roofs, particularly the battlements of the Abbey, others looked down upon the whole scene. The Bath Military Band played for half-an-hour previous to the arrival of the procession, and its music was an effective finish to what may be called the ensemble.

"The Mayor was punctual. The *Athalie* processional march was struck up just on the stroke of noon, showing that the procession had left the Guildhall, where the invited guests had met. It reached the site by a kind of triangular route, Guildhall sergeants with the ancient staves in front, then the Mayor's officer, then the robed mace-bearers with the gleaming maces, next the Mayor, in scarlet gown and gilt chain and the cocked hat of a

deputy lieutenant of the county, after him the Town Clerk, the
Recorder, Judge Caillard, and Mr. Watts as Clerk of the Peace—
all robed, the two judicial functionaries in full-bottomed wigs
and the last with the smaller wig; next the Lord-Lieutenant of
the county, the City Members, the Mayors of Bristol and
Chippenham, wearing their chains of office; Canon Brooke in
black gown; and then a line of Aldermen, Councillors,
Magistrates, officials and citizens.

"As soon as his Worship had taken up his position opposite
the stone, he was approached by

"Ald. Marshall, who, as senior Councillor, said :—It having
been decided after full consideration to provide the necessary
accommodation for the transaction of our municipul business, by
the erection of additional buildings, I, as the senior member of
the Council, on their behalf, have much pleasure in asking your
Worship to lay the memorial stone.

"The ex-Mayor, Mr. J. S. Turner said :—The privilege of being
associated with the senior member of the Council in seconding his
request that your Worship should proceed now to lay the
memorial stone of the New Municipal Buildings, is one I highly
appreciate, especially when I bear in mind the arduous, untiring
and unremitting attention with which you have pursued the
accomplishment of this object—mainly one of your own
conception—during a period extending over two years. You saw
the necessity caused by the greatly increased wants of the city and
remembered that at no distant date an extension of our municipal
boundaries might render the present structure still more
inconvenient. To no living person are the citizens of Bath more
indebted than to yourself for the true development of her
municipal institutions, for the advancement of her material
interests and the assistance given to all movements having for
their object the promotion of her social or literary prosperity. It
is therefore appropriate that your name should be indissolubly and
for all time connected with this historic event in our city's annals,

which you are now requested on behalf of the Council and the citizens to undertake.

"Then the ceremony took place. The great block of stone was hanging by a pulley, the stone beneath containing a cavity for the deposit of a sealed bottle, in which were copies of local papers, with a programme of the intended proceedings, and an account of the reasons for erecting the building engrossed on a parchment scroll. The latter statement was prepared by Mr. B. H. Watts, and also contained a list of the Corporation and the City officials. The Mayor was presented by the architect with a silver trowel, hammer, and spirit level, with which to perform the ceremony. The trowel, which was the gift of the architect, Mr. J. M. Brydon, had an ivory handle and enclosed within a beautifully engraved border were the city arms and a conventional inscription. The level—made of ivory and mounted in silver—was also engraved with the Bath arms and the date of the ceremony and on the polished ebony head of the mallet (which had an ivory handle), was a silver plate with the city arms. These were presented by the contractors. His Worship proved himself to be no *dilettanti* workman, but spread the mortar with vigour, the onlookers watching the process with interest. When sufficient cement had been laid down the stone was slowly lowered, and came down true to the building line. 'I declare this stone to be well and truly laid,' said the Mayor, after giving it the customary taps with the mallet, and then the Abbey bells rang out a brief and joyous peal. This, over, the Mayor resumed :—

"My Lord Cork, the Recorder of Bath, his Honour Judge Caillard, Col. Murray, Mr. Wodehouse, ladies and gentlemen, and my fellow citizens, in addition to the very simple formula which I pronounced just now, that this stone was 'well and truly laid,' I beg to add a few words. I wish to say I believe the entire foundation of this building to be thoroughly good and true. I have observed it from the beginning with great interest and satisfaction. I have seen the wise care of the architect, the substantial work of the contractors, and the constant industry of the workmen. What has been already done appears to me a ground of reliance for the good completion of a noble structure, worthy in all repects of this ancient city. Bath has long needed more space for the transaction of public business ; better courts for the administration of justice, and freer scope for various objects in which the citizens are concerned. I remember also that we build not only for the present, but for the future ; we care for those who will come after us ; they will inherit our great trust of those wonderful springs which are still flowing undiminished either in quality or quantity. By means of these springs, Bath has no common place in English history. By their means it became what it now is, and may become still more important. For 2,000 years they have been known as a precious gift from the Giver of all good, and so long as He continues the blessing ought those who have the charge of it to make their civic policy correspond to it. Let that policy, gentlemen, be wise and generous ; let human skill and public spirit come in aid of the bounties and beauties of nature ; then who shall assign a limit to the prosperity of Bath ? I rejoice that I have lived to see the day when this responsibility is more deeply felt. I take the part in the present ceremony with which the Corporation have honoured me, sincerely thankful for the great privilege I enjoy. I rejoice to be surrounded by those who have worked, and will, I am sure, continue to work, faithfully for the public good ; and I trust that through many far distant years the building we now begin will conduce largely to the welfare of our beautiful city.

"Mr. Folkard, the Recorder of Bath, said he was very pleased to have the opportunity of being the first to congratulate the Mayor on the successful manner in which he had performed the task of laying the foundation stone of the new Municipal Buildings and he was glad to see so representative and distinguished a company to give countenance to this ceremony. It was an event that would mark a new epoch in the history of the city. He had no doubt that when the Guildhall was first erected it was found to be sufficient for the requirements of the Corporation in those days. But times had changed. Having referred to the crowded state of the Sessions Court at present when any sensational case came on, the bad ventilation and the almost intolerable condition of the atmosphere, the learned Recorder said this new building would, he hoped, be one worthy of the city. A building, he trusted, that would be well-ventilated, and one that would not have the banqueting room at the top of the Sessions Court, for this was the chief error in the present one. He hoped, in this new building, all these evils and these difficulties would be removed, and that they would have a convenient and well ventilated building, suitable for all purposes of the administrative duties of the Corporation. The administration of justice was of the highest importance, and they ought to have a fitting court for the magistrates and those whose duties required them to attend the Quarter Sessions. He hoped, in conclusion, that this building would be worthy of the city, and that it might remain for ages to come a memorial of the wisdom and foresight of the Mayor and Corporation of this city.

"The Earl of Cork, Lord-Lieutenant of Somerset, hoped on the present occasion to have remained a silent witness to one of the most interesting ceremonies in which he had ever taken part. It was something like thirty years ago when he had the pleasure of sitting side by side with their worthy Mayor to welcome the British Association into this city. That was, he believed, the first occasion on which he (the Mayor) held that high position, which he had filled so worthily as to have been elected to the office no less than seven times. To Mr. Murch he thought they were very much indebted for the present prosperity of the city. He was the originator of those magnificent new baths, the leading spirit in bringing forward once again before the public those monuments of the skill of ancient Romans, and also, as his reference to the subject showed, the Mayor hoped to see a day when this city as a health resort would become more frequented than ever.

" His Honour, Judge Caillard, went straight to his own department of the new building, and tersely expressed the three desiderata
of the new court to be as follows—to be able to see clearly, to
breathe freely, and to hear easily.   But he did not linger over the
subject, and the rest of his remarks he devoted to a warm
commendation of the city :—

" I have seen three beautiful cities—Florence, Edinburgh, and
Bath—each differing from the other two, each with lovely beauties
of its own, and I think I am not saying too much if I say that even
against the other two Bath fully holds her own.   There is another
city which it has not been my good fortune to see—of which the
imaginative Italian had said—' See Naples and then die.'   I
should say the motto more applicable to Bath is ' See Bath, taste
its healing waters, and then live and do well.'   One word only
will I add.   Those engaged in the administration of justice are
anticipating that they will enjoy a better court, but I think I may
say, as one amongst others, that when the time comes for us to
remove into the new courts we will still have a good feeling for
our old friend the Sessions Court in which we have worked for
many years.   We will say, ' Good-by, we have done a good work
together ; now we go to a better place.'

" Mr. Wodehouse, M.P., said :—In the presence of so many
gentlemen whose time and thought and labour have been directly
and lavishly devoted to the subject which is the occasion of this
ceremony, I feel how slender are my own claims to speak a word.
But I may be allowed to congratulate the Mayor and Corporation
and the Citizens of Bath generally upon the interesting and, from
a civic point of view, upon the memorable and historic character
of the proceedings in which we are engaged.   *Finis coronat opus—*
' the end crowns the work,' and if in one sense the laying of this
stone is only the beginning rather than the end, yet in another
sense it is an end.   Because it is the practical end of the stage of
deliberation and discussion upon places and sites and schemes,
and it marks the transition from the province of thought and
speech to the province of art and execution.   There has been much
discussion in the past as to this particular scheme, and I would say

this to the citizens of Bath, who have shown how critical they may be—that when there is a question of adding an ornament, either of art or of architecture, to their city, they do well to be critical and fastidious. For this reason, that the beauty of their city, naturally and architecturally, is one of their most precious possessions, and they are bound, equally by gratitude to former generations who have made this city beautiful, and by regard for generations who will come after them, to take every precaution that the fair lineaments of the Queen City of the West are not disfigured or spoiled. Because after all a thing of beauty is a joy for ever only on condition that it be not spoiled, and I therefore congratulate you all upon the prospect of possessing a building which critical eyes may contemplate with pleasure while it will greatly facilitate the transaction of your public business and promote the comfort and convenience of all who may be engaged in the transaction of your common civic affairs. Your Municipal Buildings are the outward and visible sign of the continuity of your civic life, and I say that a city which has, I believe, been in possession of a Municipal Charter from the time of Richard I ought to mark its pride in the inheritance of ancient rights and liberties by the grace and dignity of the structure that is at once both the shrine and the emblem of its ancient privileges. One word more and only one. We all know the city of Bath has had many ups and downs since King Bladud's time, and all who have studied its records are familiar with the fact that after periods of decline and depression the revival of the city has been due to the energies and exertions of individual men, public-spirited citizens of Bath. For instance, I may mention the names of Ralph Allen, the great architect Wood, whose works of genius delight us every day when we walk through this city ; and to the name of a celebrity of a different kind, and that is the name of Beau Nash. And I say with regard to the race of public-spirited citizens who in their day have contributed largely to the prosperity of the city, that they are not extinct at this hour, and you can have no better or more striking illustration of that race of men than the present Mayor of Bath. On various grounds no man can have a better claim to lay the memorial stone of this building. He has that claim not only in virtue of the energy and zeal with which he has conducted this particular work—an energy and zeal never slackened by the weight of four score years, nor even by the heavier and more depressing burden of domestic sorrow—but over and above that the honour and privilege of laying this stone are due to him by the long and most honourable record of all his previous services to the city of Bath. Therefore, it is most fitting his name should be associated with this work which in a human sense is for all time. As a last word I would simply express the hope that all who have been connected in any way with this building, from the Mayor, the architect, and the contractors, down to the lowest and youngest workman or manual labourer will have the reward of feeling that they have contributed to a good and long enduring work which will entitle them to the respect and gratitude of future generations.

"Colonel Ford said, as senior magistrate, he was glad to have the opportunity of making a few remarks on that occasion. He referred to the inconvenience and discomfort of the present Sessions Court, spoke of the time when the magistrates brought the matter under the notice of the Mayor, and thanked his Worship for doing what he had for the magistrates.

"Canon Brooke then offered up a special prayer, asking for a blessing upon the work, and that the building now commenced might grow to a perfect completion, with safety to all who should labour in the work and for the lasting benefit of those for whom it was designed. He further prayed that a spirit of wisdom and a sound mind might be granted to all who should therein direct the municipal affairs of the city, and that the law of justice might ever be faithfully and rightly administered in the new buildings."

APPENDIX TO PAGE 43.

ADDITIONAL EARLY MAYORS.

In my sketch of the Early Mayors I was glad to express my obligations to Mr. Austin J. King and Mr. B. H. Watts for their valuable book, *The Municipal Records of Bath*. The debt has now been increased by the kindness of Mr. Watts in giving me the results of more recent researches in the Muniment Room at the Guildhall and the discovery of many Mayors not previously mentioned. It is remarkable that Mr. Warner who gave many proofs of painstaking in his history should have overlooked the documents containing the information. By him, however, the innumerable musty Leases and Conveyances would not be opened with such keen Interest as they were by Mr. Watts. There were some points of chronology on which even the Deputy Town Clerk could not satisfy himself without consulting authorities, and we are both indebted to the learning and courtesy of Mr. Martin of the Record Office for solving the difficulties.

Mr. Watts has also discovered additional early members of Parliament and corrected a few other mistakes in Warner's history. One of these was the insertion of Thomas Ash and John Court as Mayors in 1583 and 1587, they having filled the office of Recorder. It has been a question whether William Sherston served so often as his son-in-law, William Prynne, states eight times, the common idea being that it was only seven. The latter number accords with the discoveries of Mr. Watts, four years being accounted for in the subjoined list and three in the list at the end of my chapter on the Early Mayors. Prynne's calculation may have been based on the idea that the nomination in the Charter of Elizabeth, 1590, and the subsequent election by the burgesses involved two distinct services, which was not the case. May I

add, however, that sensible as I am of the honour of frequent
re-election I could have gladly yielded the palm to so patriotic
and persevering a citizen as William Sherston.

It may be remembered that Warner's list of Mayors begins
with the year 1412, and ends with 1799, two years before the
publication of his book.   But between 1412 and 1615 there are
frequent omissions; Mr. Watts, while supplying not a few of
these, gives many names with dates so far back as 1280, and
seven without dates from deeds of about the same period.   His
additions are 92; at the head of the dated names I have
placed John Duport, discovered by Mr. Riley and referred to in
my sketch in Mr. Riley's words as " the very earliest mention of
a Mayor of Bath," though it does not appear in Mr. Warner's list.
These additions make the total number of years accounted for
382; the former time of municipal government in Bath, of
which there are no definite records, having been traced back to
the Saxon period.

MAYORS OF BATH.

Dates not known but supposed to be late in the thirteenth or
early in the fourteenth century.

Stephen de Devyses	Nicholas the Clerk
Thomas Sweyn	Gilbert the Tailor
William Sleh	Roger de Dichegate
William Serrel	

NAMES WITH ASCERTAINED DATES.

John Duport	1230	Roger Cole ... 1336
Henry the Tailor	1280	Roger Oft ... 1339
William the Cook	1293	Roger Oft ... 1340
William Serrel	1305	Roger Oft ... 1341
Adam Wytsone	1310	William Cubbel ... 1342
William the Cook	1310	John de Wyk ... 1343
John the Fisher	1316	William Cubbel ... 1344
Richard Wytesone	1317	Alexander le Deyghar ... 1345
John Cole	1326	Alexander le Deyghar ... 1346
John de Wyke	1327	Thomas Scote ... 1351
Roger Cole	1330	Walter le Carpenter ... 1353
Roger Cole	1331	John Gregory ... 1354
William Swayn	1332	Robert le Deyhar ... 1359
Roger Cole	1333	Walter le Carpenter ... 1360
Roger Cole	1335	John Gregory ... 1361

John Gregory	...	...	1362	John Sachfild ...	...	1587
Robert Wattes	...	...	1371	John Walley, jun.	...	1588
John Natton	...	...	1379	William Sherston	...	1589
William Rous	...	...	1392	William Sherston	...	1590
Robert Westpray	...	...	1393	Thomas Fytche	...	1591
Thomas Plomer ...	...	...	1398	John Sachefild ...	...	1592
Roger Testwode	...	...	1406	William Chapman	...	1593
Ralph Hunt	...	...	1408	William Heathe	...	1594
Richard Wydcombe	...	...	1418	William Moreford	...	1595
William Hogekyn	...	...	1435	John Sachfilde ...	...	1596
Robert Rogers	...	...	1474	William Heath ...	...	1597
John Davys	...	...	1553	William Sherston	...	1598
Mr. Trauncys	...	...	1568	John Chapman ...	...	1599
George Pearman	...	...	1571	John Sachfeild ...	...	1600
John Wyatt	...	...	1572	Thomas Power ...	...	1601
William Cavell ...	...	...	1574	William Heath ...	...	1602
Thomas Turner ...	...	...	1575	William Sherston	...	1603
George Pearman	...	...	1576	Christofer Stone	...	1604
George Pearman	...	...	1577	Walter Chapman	...	1605
John Wyatt	...	...	1578	John Parker	...	1606
Thomas Bushe	...	...	1579	Thomas Wiatt ...	...	1607
William Shareston	...	...	1580	William Clifte ...	...	1608
William Waley ...	...	...	1581	John Sherston ...	...	1609
George Perman	...	...	1582	John Sachefield ...	...	1610
John Chapman ...	...	...	1583	Christopher Stone	...	1611
William Shareston	...	...	1584	John Wood	...	1612
John Walley, senr.	...	...	1585	Richard Gay	...	1613
Thomas Fitche ...	...	...	1586	John Cutt	...	1614

From such Council minutes as are extant it appears that the Mayor, who was, under the Charter of Elizabeth, elected in September, was considered to remain in office until his successor had been sworn in.

The year in the above list, so far as regards the Mayors from 1553 downwards, is the year in which they were elected. It would seem from the Chamberlain's accounts that the Charter of Elizabeth, which is dated 4th September, 1590, changed the date for the election of Mayor. Down to 1592 the Chamberlain's accounts appear to have been made up to Lady-day and were presented in May or June. In 1593 a year and a quarter's accounts to Midsummer were passed on 10th September. In subsequent years the accounts were presented in October, apparently on the day when the newly-elected Mayor was sworn in. If the practice which was followed from 1594 obtained before that date it would seem that the Mayor was elected in May, all the Chamberlains accounts except one—that for 1572-3, which

C *

was passed on 20th May, 1573—having been presented in June.
The list of Mayors before 1553 has been compiled from deeds in
the possession of the Corporation, and all that can be said is that
the Mayors were in office the years stated, but whether elected or
retiring in such years cannot be determined   It will be noticed that
there are two Mayors entered for the year 1310—Adam Wytstone
was in office in February of that year and William the Cook in
December of the same year.

MEMBERS OF PARLIAMENT

Mentioned in early Corporation Deeds and Minutes.

1573. George Pearman.
       Edward Babor.
1583. George Pearman.
1590. John Walley, Senior.
1593. William Sherston.
       Mr. Price.
1598. William Sherston.
       Mr. Heath.
1602. Ditto.

APPENDIX TO PAGE 384.

MR. WILLIAM LONSDALE,

The First Curator of the Bath Museum.

While this last sheet is passing through the Press, a relative of
Mr. Lonsdale inquires whether that gentleman will be included
in my " Sketches." Unfortunately the plan of the book was not
sufficient for the purpose, but on referring to what was said in my
account of the Literary and Scientific Institution I feel that in
aiming at brevity I failed to do justice. For certainly such
valuable services as the first Curator of the Institution rendered to
the city demanded more than the mere passing mention which
they received in that chapter.

It is some satisfaction that more was said in a chapter on " Science in Bath," which I contributed in 1888 to the *Handbook* published for the use of the British Association on their visit here. The following is an extract : " In connection with the department of Natural Science at the Institution, the name of William Lonsdale ought always to be honoured. He worked unceasingly several years, first in founding the collection by large gifts of his own specimens and then in accurately arranging them. In 1825 he presented to the Institution 1159 specimens, including 290 fossils and 69 land and fresh-water shells. While the neat labels are interesting souvenirs of Lonsdale's personality, the names on them indicate an important stage in Geological science."

I am now enabled, by the kindness of Major Lonsdale, a great nephew, to add a few particulars of personal history. William Lonsdale was born in Bath, September 9th, 1794, baptised in St. James's Church, and probably educated in the city. At the age of fifteen he received a commission in the Army, and subsequently fought in two memorable battles, Salamanca in 1812 and Waterloo in 1815. Returning home in 1816, he was placed on half-pay, and devoted himself, at his mother's house at Batheaston, to the study of Geology. There is a family tradition that the impulse was given by a conversation which he heard in a public library in Bath between two ladies on the discovery of a remarkable stone. From that time until 1826, when he became honorary curator of the Bath Museum, he was engaged in studying the science and in forming the collection which he presented to the Institution.

His energetic and self-sacrificing work soon interested the most eminent Geological leaders ; especially were Professor Sedgwick and Sir Roderick Murchison desirous of obtaining for the nation the benefit of his services. By their influence he was invited to transfer them to the rooms of the Geological Society in London, which induced him to break away from the ties he had formed at Bath. In his new sphere he continued many years till his death, collecting, studying, arranging, writing ; and every year he gained fresh accessions to his list of distinguished friends. Still his habits were so retiring and his health, in later years, so precarious that he was little known either in social circles or at public gatherings. Not even when the British Association came to Bath in 1864 could he be persuaded to visit the scene of his early labours and mingle with his friends.

The regard which was widely cherished for him is happily shewn by some interesting letters preserved by his family, which I have been kindly allowed to read. Those of Sedgwick, Murchison and Charles Darwin reveal not only their high opinion of Lonsdale's scientific acquirements but their sincere friendship and personal sympathy. For Murchison he would have the charm of being to the last greatly interested in military matters, delighting to " fight his battles o'er again," and show the medals he had won at Salamanca and Waterloo. How Darwin valued him may be seen in two characteristic notes which I am allowed to introduce. Unfortunately the years are not given ; they were probably in the seventh decade of the century.

" DOWN, BROMLEY,

" KENT ; May 6th.

" MY DEAR LONSDALE,

" I received your letter with as much surprise as from one dead; for it so happened that 3 or 4 nights ago I was thinking about you and I saw you as plainly as in the old days in your little room at the Geolog. Soc. I was thinking how I could learn any news of you. I am sorry at the poor account that you give, and I know how long and how much you have suffered. I had quite forgotten about the coral, but I now remember its appearance. Your MS. is arrived and I am fairly astounded at the labour you have bestowed on the subject. It seems a very great pity that such labour should be wasted. Had I not better send the specimen and MS. to the Geolog. Soc. to be printed or kept in the archives ? It might be of extreme use to any one working on the subject.

"I have myself been ill for the last 9 months, but am slowly recovering and hope still to do a little work in Nat. History.

"Believe me, my dear Lonsdale, I shall ever remember your uniform kindness to me in old long past days, and our many pleasant conversations.

"I remain yours

"Very sincerely,

"CHARLES DARWIN."

"DOWN, BROMLEY,

"KENT, S.E. ; Feb. 1st.

"MY DEAR LONSDALE,

"It was very kind of you to send me such hearty congratulations and the newspaper. Our son's success, as you may believe, has delighted us. It was a pleasure to me to see your handwriting again and it is very little altered from old times. I am very sorry to hear so poor an account of your health. What a life of suffering you have led! You speak of Sedgwick in your letter; I hear from my son that though he looks extremely old, he seems cheerful, and talks to a wonderful degree. He has at last given up lecturing, and it is a pity, from all I hear, that he did not take this step earlier.

"My own health is considerably better, and though not free from discomfort I am able to do a fair share of work in Natural History. I have just published a rather large book on the variation of domesticated animals and plants; but I do not think it would interest you, even if you had strength to read it.

"I shall always retain very pleasant recollections of our former intercourse, and I earnestly hope that your health may cause you less suffering.

"Believe me, my dear Lonsdale,

"Yours very sincerely,

"CHARLES DARWIN."

INDEX.

	PAGE.
Aberdare, Lord	255, 258, 262, 263
Ablett ...	280, 281, 286
Albany, Duchess of ...	408
Accoucheurs ...	131
Adrian, Cardinal ...	50
Adelard ...	31
Agricola ...	10, 28
Akemannesceastre ...	6
Allen, Ralph ...	89, 178
Ælphege ...	18, 21, 23
Ælsig ...	28
Alwood ...	417
Amelia, Princess ...	84
Ancaster, Duke of ...	313
Anstey, C. ...	242
Antoninus ...	6
Armstrong, Archy ...	64
Arthur (King) ...	17
Athelstane ...	20—25, 34
Athenæum ...	227
Atterbury, Bishop ...	207
Auckland, Lord ...	32
Augusta, Princess ...	411
Austen, Jane ...	243
Baines, Bishop ...	215
Baines of Liverpool ...	112
Baldwin ...	418
Barbauld, Mrs. ...	286
Barham, F. ...	205
Barker, Benjamin ...	199
Barker, Thomas ...	192
Barker, T. Jones ...	201
Barlow, Dr. ...	140, 369, 379
Barrett, Dr. ...	238
Bartolozzi ...	194
Barton House ...	39
Bath Abbey Church ...	44, 49
Bath Abbey Library ...	67
Bath and W. of E. Society	133, 138
Bath Artists ...	202
Bath, a Saxon Burg ...	35
Bath Concerts ...	149, 159
Bath Corporation ...	111
Bath, Marquis of ...	52
Bath Mint ...	20, 25
Bath Monastery ...	20
Bathurst, Lord ...	291
Baue, Dr. ...	72, 151
Bear Inn ...	464
Beauclerk, Lady ...	284
Beaufort, Duke of ...	310
Beau Nash ...	21, 80—88, 354
Beckford ...	288, 322
Bellott ...	50, 51
Birch, Walter ...	270
Birde, Prior ...	49
Bishops of Bath and Wells ...	33
Bladud, Prince ...	2
Blessington, Lady ...	286
Blomefield, Rev. L. (see Jenyns)	
Boccaccio ...	279
Bonner ...	112
Bonnet ...	290
Boroughs, Origin of ...	35
Bowles, W. L. ...	380
Boyce, Dr. ...	312
Bradshaw ...	65
Brewster, Sir D. ...	160
Brinkworth ...	373
Britten ...	46
Broadhurst, Rev. T. ...	151
Brooke, Canon ...	430
Browne, R. Wilson ...	369
Bruce, John	55, 58, 61
Bruce, Knight ...	346
Brydon, J. M. ...	421
Brymer, Archdeacon ...	356
Brymer, James ...	356
Buller, Charles ...	262
Burgess and Oliver ...	421
Burke, Edmund ...	10
Burleigh, Lord ...	50, 51
Burnet, Bishop ...	121
Burney, Dr. ...	312
Burney, Frances ...	243
Busby, Dr. ...	312
Byron, Lord ...	276, 292, 296
Caillard, Judge ...	428
Calphurnia ...	15
Campbell, Lord ...	112
Campbell, Sir W. ...	265
Campbell, Thomas ...	335
Canute ..	26, 27
Carlyle, Thomas ...	284
Carlton, Sir D. ...	204
Carte, Rev. T.	206, 215
Cæsar ...	8
Carpenter, Dr. W. B. ...	385
Carteret, Sir P. ...	61, 62
Chaucer ...	39
Chandler, Mary ...	124
Chandos, Duke of ...	180
Charles II ...	56, 344
Charlotte, Princess ...	266, 413

	PAGE.
Chatham, Lord	259
Chandler, Rev. H.	207
Chapman family	345
Chesterfield, Lord	88
Cheyne, Dr.	121
Chilcot, T.	310
Chillingworth	204
Claudius	8
Clarendon, Lord	75
Clarke, Sir Andrew	237
Cleveland, Duke of	390
Clifford, Bishop	223
Cogan, Dr.	130—134
Cogan, Rev. E.	134
Coke, T. W.	166
Coleridge	271, 276
Colvin, Sidney	268, 271, 274, 284
Collingridge, Bishop	220
Conybeare, Professor	25
Cossham, Handel	385
Cork, Earl of	390, 424, 427
Cowper	194
Courtenay, Lord	291
Crabb, George	380
Cromwell, Oliver	65
Cruttwell, R....	126, 249
Cunningham, Allan	182, 186
Cunliffe, Sir F.	197
Danish Invasions	24
Darwin, Charles	436
Davis, Major	5, 389, 395, 407
Davy, Sir Humphry	382
De Ros, Lady	265
Dickens, Charles	243, 284
Disraeli, B.	135, 201, 233, 235
Dispensaries, Bath	375
Divines, Four	203, 286
Dixon, Captain	373
Dixon, Rev. J. M.	374
Donaldson, Walter	332
Donors to Bath Abbey	50
Donne, Dr.	57, 58
Domesday Book	27
Duncan, P. B.	10, 388
Duncan, J. S.	12, 388
Dunstan	18, 21, 23
Dunster Castle	65
Dyrham	17
Earle, Professor	3, 10, 18, 35, 247, 417
Eastlake	194
Edward I	38
Edward III	300
Edwards, R. P.	240
Eleanor of Provence	38
Elliott, Mrs.	52, 213
Elwin, Hastings	368
Elyot, Sir T.	77

	PAGE.
Empson	284
Errington, Archbishop	224
Essex, Earl of	47
Ethelreda	44
Ethelred	26
Falconer, Dr. R. W.	128, 356
Falconer, Dr. T.	127
Falconer, Dr. W.	125
Falkland, Lord	72
Fielding	89, 221, 243
Fitzgerald, Lord E.	255
Flaxman	194, 281
Fleming, Canon	239
Folkard, Mr. (Recorder)	426
Fonthill	292, 294, 296, 307
Ford, Col.	430
Forster, John	268, 269, 272, 284
Fox, C. J.	255, 274
Fox, Hon. H.	257
Fraser, Mrs.	12, 386
Freeman, Mr. (Bath)	407
Freeman, Professor	22
Gainsborough	182
Garrick	312
Gay, Mr. (Gay Street)	353
Geoffery of Monmouth	2
George III	156, 266, 331
George IV	136
Gibbes, Sir G.	135, 340
Gibbon	302
Gibson, Milner	135
Gilbert, Sir Davies	384
Gilpin, W.	248
Gladstone, Mr.	228
Glastonbury	22, 29
Glory of Regality	21
Godfrey, Bishop	29
Gore, R. T.	142, 369
Gough, J. B....	239
Goulburn, Dr.	230
Graves, Rev. R.	194
Gray	245
Greaves, Sir E.	70, 71
Green, Emanuel	348
Griffin, Gerald	332
Grimthorpe, Lord	177
Guidott, Dr.	68—78
Guilds, Ancient	35
Gurney, Russell	135
Hadrian	13, 28
Hales, John	203
Hamilton, Duke of	288
Hamilton, Duchess of...	308
Hamilton, Col.	290, 291, 293
Hamilton, Lady	297
Handley, Rev. E.	373, 374

		PAGE.
Hare, Francis	...	278, 286
Hare, Julius ...	...	... 281
Harington, Sir J.	...	40, 53
Harington, Dr. H.	...	143, 249
Harington, Sir E.	...	... 193
Hartley, Dr.	...	... 119
Hastings, Lady E.	...	... 353
Hawkins, Sir Cæsar	...	... 145
Hawarden, Viscount	...	97, 222
Hawley, Lady	...	... 410
Hayward, Dr.	...	... 254
Hayward & Wooster	...	... 421
Hazlitt, W.	...	... 279
Hedley, Dr. ...	...	225, 226
Henry VIII	...	41, 146, 221
Henrietta, Queen	...	... 59
Herschel, Caroline	...	... 158
Herschel, Sir W.	...	152—157
Herschel, Sir J.	...	... 161
Hervey, Lord A.	...	... 33
Hill, Commissioner	...	... 168
Hill, Rowland	...	... 116
Hippisley, Mr. (London)	...	... 410
Hoare, H. ...	...	... 353
Hoare, W. ...	...	... 188
Hoare, Prince	...	... 190
Hoare, Sir R. C.	...	... 254
Hogarth ...	...	... 183
Horner, Sir J.	...	... 145
Hospital, St. John's ...	...	38, 339
,, St. Catherine's	...	... 351
,, Mineral Water	...	... 350
,, Bellott's ...	...	353, 363
,, Royal United	...	... 365
,, Homœopathic	...	... 375
,, Casualty	...	367, 370
Houghton, Lord	...	... 279
Howard, Cardinal	...	... 226
Hugelinus ...	...	... 31
Humane Societies	...	... 132
Hunter, Rev. J.		
14, 228, 252, 340, 341, 378		
Hunter, Dr. Julian	...	... 254
Hunt, Leigh	...	... 279
Hyde Serjeant	...	... 66
Institution, Bath	...	11, 377
Irving, J. T. ...	...	... 416
Irvine	...	... 417
James I ...	...	51, 52
Jardine, Rev. D.	...	... 252
Jay, Rev. W.	...	... 208
Jekyll, Sir Joseph	...	... 353
Jenyns, Rev. L.	...	... 381
Jernegan ...	...	... 208
John de Villula	26—32, 33, 34, 40	
Johnson, Dr. ...	...	... 75
Jolly	...	40, 358

		PAGE.
Jomini ...	...	... 259
Jones, Dr. J.	...	... 69
Jorden, Dr. E.	...	71, 72
Kelston ..	...	... 145
Kemble Family	...	327—336
Kemble, Rev. C.	...	210, 216, 370
Kenrick, Rev. J.	...	... 252
Kilvert, Rev. F.	...	... 98
King, Austin J.	...	37, 178, 431
King, Bishop Oliver	...	49, 50
King Edward's School		... 352
Kingsley, Rev. C.	...	... 232
Kirkup ...	...	... 279
Lamb, Charles	...	... 281
Landor, Charles	...	... 286
Landor, W. S.	...	177, 267
Lanfranc ...	...	... 27
Langdale, Lord	...	... 259
Langley, Dr.	...	... 269
Lansdowne, Lord	...	196—380
Lanthony ...	...	... 273
Laud ...	33, 56—64, 206	
Lawrence, Sir T.	...	191, 201, 353
Lear, King ...	...	... 4
Leckie ...	...	... 279
Lefanu, Mrs. ...	...	318, 320, 329
Leicester, Earl of	...	... 47
Leighton, Sir F.	...	... 202
Leinster, Duke of	...	... 255
Leland ...	...	2, 21, 30
Lennox, Lady Sarah	...	255, 266
Leofric ...	...	... 18
Leo XII ...	...	217, 219
Leo XIII ...	...	... 236
Lewis, William	...	... 415
Linacre, Dr. ...	...	... 76
Linley Family	...	... 310
Linley, Miss ...	...	... 309
Lockart ...	...	... 284
Long (R.A.) ...	...	... 202
Long, Walter	...	... 315
Long, W. ...	...	253, 356, 358
Lonsdale, W. (Bath)	...	384, 431
Louis Philippe	...	... 201
Louis XVIII	...	... 258
Macaulay, Lord 62, 177, 215, 219, 243		
Macready ...	...	... 332
Magee, Archbishop	...	... 229
Mail Coaches ...	...	... 101
Mainwaring, Capt. R.	...	... 366
Malins, Vice-Chancellor	...	... 347
Malone ...	...	... 4
Manvers, Earl	...	378, 379, 386
Maplet, Dr. ...	...	... 70
Marshall Alderman ...	...	... 424
Martin (Record Office)	...	... 431

	PAGE.
Maskelyne, Prof.	356
Masters of St. John's	346
Mathews, Capt.	314
Mayhow, Dr.	74, 401
Mayors of Bath	32—43, 431
Medici, Marquis de	279
Melbourne, Lord	283
Members for Bath	38
Memorial Stone	422
Mendip Mines	52
Miller, Lady	245
Mitchell (C.E.)	356
Moore, Charles	160, 385
Moore, Gen. Sir J.	255, 257
Moore, Thomas	316, 318, 380
Monkland	136, 148, 243
Montague, Bishop	44—52, 213
Montague, Sir H.	50
Montaigne	240
More, Hannah	335
Municipal Records	37, 431
Munk, Dr.	137
Murch, Arthur	5
Murray, Col.	425
Murray, John	274
Murray, Sir G.	260
Napier, G., C. and H.	265
Napier, Lady	260, 263, 265
Napier, Sir C.	264
Napier, Sir W.	255, 284
Nash, Beau	21, 80, 178, 180
Nelson, Lord	297
Newman, Cardinal	226
New Municipal Buildings	417
Nicolai, Monsignor	219
Normanby, Lord	280, 287
Norman, George	142, 367—369
Norman, James	367
Norman Period	26
Nugæ Antiquæ	45, 47, 48, 51, 145, 151
Offa	18, 20, 340
Olaf	24
Oliphant, Mrs.	314
Oliver, Dr. W.	123, 224, 227
Orators, Noble	240
Oriel College	55, 56, 57, 67
Orlando Furioso	46
Osric	18, 19, 340
Ostorius	15
Overstone, Lord	135, 354
Palmer, John	101, 327—330
Parr, Dr. S.	251, 324
Parry, Dr.	137
Parry, Dr. C. H.	139
Parry, Sir E.	139
Peach	34, 55, 75, 179, 185, 209, 230, 246

	PAGE.
Pelham Family	189
Penley, Belville	105, 313, 327, 412
Pepys	73
Phipps, C. J.	415
Pierce, Dr.	74, 401
Pierrepont	114
Pilling	73
Pitcairn, Dr.	121
Pitt, Elder and Younger	91, 95, 96, 107, 188, 271, 289
Pius IX	226
Plautius	15
Pompeia	8
Pope Alexander	97, 121
Powlett, Lord	193
Poynton, Rev. J. J.	48, 49, 145
Priestley, Dr.	126
Prior Park	219, 221
Princess of Wales	4
Pring, Dr.	143
Prynne, W.	39, 40, 54
Pulteney, Hon. W.	354
Puritan Divines	57
Queen Elizabeth	37, 46—48, 102
Queensbury, Duchess of	84, 290
Queen Charlotte	200, 331
Queen of George II	207
Radcliffe, Dr.	83
Radway, Mr.	406
Redding, Cyrus	288
Reginald Fitz-Jocelin	341—344
Rembrandt	197
Reynell, Sir R.	73
Richmond, Duke of	255, 257
Riley, H.	36, 37
Robert, Bishop	29, 341
Roberts, Dr.	244
Robinson, Crabb	279, 281, 334
Roebuck, J. A.	261
Rogers (Cannington)	146
Rogers, Lady	46, 49
Rogers, Rev. S.	148
Rosebery, Earl of	103
Royal Visits to Bath	76
Rufus	34
Sackville, Lord	313
Salisbury, Marquis of	236
Saunders, E.	239
Savage, Sir Arnold	267, 276
Sayce, Professor	396
Sawle, Lady	284
Saxon Chronicle	37
Scarth, Rev. H. M.	16, 25, 52
Schliemann, Dr.	396
Scott, Sir Walter	25, 48, 271, 276, 284, 335

D*

	PAGE.
Scribonius	9
Scudamore, Lady	364
Sedgwick, Professor	167
Shaw, Col.	264
Sharpe, Samuel	135
Sheridan Family	114, 188, 243, 312, 325, 326, 412
Sherston, W.	39, 55, 56, 431
Shockerwick	185
Shum, F.	78, 155, 188, 193, 199, 284
Sibthorpe, Dr.	129
Sidney, Lady	45
Siddons, Mrs.	324, 327—336
Silcock, T. B.	421
Skrine, H. D.	98
Smith, Dr. W.	163
Smith, Rev. Stafford	97
Smollett	243
Soden, J.	141, 369
Solsbury	2
Somerset, Lord Fitzroy	258
Somerschall, Dr.	74
Southey	197, 198, 270, 274, 276, 281
South, Sir James	161
Soult, Marshal	257, 259
Spackman	192
Sparke, Michael	59
Stafford, Lord	63
Stanley, Dean	162
Stanhope, Earl	271
Star Chamber	49, 59—63
Stoker, Miss	318, 322
Stone, John	52, 422
Swainswick	6, 55, 65, 67
Sweyne	26
Tacitus	10, 19, 80
Tavistock, Lord	245
Taylor, Jeremy	206
Taylor, W. (Norwich)	271
Temple, Lord	189
Tennyson, Alfred	284
Thackeray	247
Theatre Royal	104, 105, 410
Thicknesse, Philip	183, 187
Thierry	28
Thomas á Becket	342
Thomas (Prior Park)	222
Thompson (Prior Park)	222
Thompson, Archbishop	231
Thuillier. Miss	273
Tickell, Mrs.	313—317
Times	229, 230, 233
Tottenham, Rev. E.	232
Trevelyan, Sir J.	96
Trevor, Sir J.	345

	PAGE.
Truro, Lord	347
Tunbridge Wells	84, 87
Tun Moot	87
Turner, Dr. W.	68, 78
Turner, J. S.	424
Turner, Sir G.	346
Vathek	305
Vaughan, Rev. R. A.	211
Vespasian	10
Victoria, Princess	5, 399
Vivian (Claverton)	98
Wade, General	90, 91, 92
Waller. Prior	342
Waller, Sir W.	73
Walker, Dr.	237
Walmesley, Dr.	228
Walpole, Horace	245, 311
Warburton, Bishop	89, 91, 97, 99, 222
Warner	9, 14, 35, 36, 247, 366
Watson, Dr. J.	112
Watts, B. H.	87, 178, 425, 431
Webb, Mr.	161
Webster, Capt.	82
Wells	28, 29, 30
Wellbeloved, Rev. C.	252
Wellington, Duke of	257, 260, 263, 264, 265, 304
White Hart	400
Widcombe Bridge	372
Wilberforce	210
Wild, Cardinal	224
William III	81, 82
William of Malmesbury	30
Willis, Dr.	83
Wiltshire (Shockerwick)	185
Winwood, Rev. H. H.	169, 171, 172
Wiseman, Cardinal	217, 219, 302
Wodehouse, E. R.	423
Wolsey, Cardinal	32, 77
Wollaston, Dr.	382
Wood, The Elder	2, 177, 223
Wood, The Younger	177
Wordsworth, W.	276, 281
Wren, Sir C.	181
Wyf of Bath	39
Xenoclochium	340
Xenophon	265
Yates, Rev. J.	52
York. Duke and Duchess of	413
Young, Mr. (Architect)	420
Zangemeister, Professor	396